Microsoft

FrontPage 2002

Complete Concepts
and Techniques

Microsoft FrontPage 2002

Complete Concepts and Techniques

Gary B. Shelly
Thomas J. Cashman
Michael L. Mick

COURSE TECHNOLOGY
25 THOMSON PLACE
BOSTON MA 02210

SHELLY
CASHMAN
SERIES®

Australia • Canada • Denmark • Japan • Mexico • New Zealand • Philippines • Puerto Rico • Singapore
South Africa • Spain • United Kingdom • United States

THOMSON
COURSE TECHNOLOGY

APPROVED COURSEWARE

PHOTO CREDITS: Microsoft FrontPage 2002 *Project 1, pages FP 1.04-05* Alex Haley, Allen Ginsberg, Ernest Hemingway, Courtesy of Corbis Corporation; handwriting, man at computer, typewriter, Courtesy of PhotoDisc, Inc.; *Project 2, pages FP 2.02-03* Bach, Beethoven, orchestra, violin, rose, saxophone, cherubs, keys, computer monitor, Courtesy of ArtToday; *Project 3, pages FP 3.02-03* Maps, man, woman, background image, computer chip, thinker, Courtesy of PhotoDisc, Inc.; globe, Courtesy of ArtToday. *Project 4, pages FP 4.02-03* Band photo, classroom, photo album, stairs, newspaper, Courtesy of PhotoDisc, Inc.; *Project 5, pages FP 5.02-03* Map background, Courtesy of PhotoDisc, Inc.; Cellular phones, Courtesy of Ericsson.

ISBN 0-7895-6334-7

2 3 4 5 6 7 8 9 10   BC   06 05 04 03 02

Microsoft
FrontPage 2002
Complete Concepts and Techniques

Contents

Preface

The Shelly Cashman Series® offers the finest textbooks in computer education. We are proud of the fact that our series of Microsoft Office 4.3, Microsoft Office 95, Microsoft Office 97, and Microsoft Office 2000 textbooks have been the most widely used books in education. With each new edition of our Office books, we have made improvements based on the software and comments made by the instructors and students who use our textbooks. The Microsoft Office XP books continue with the innovation, quality, and reliability that you have come to expect from the Shelly Cashman Series.

Office XP is the most significant upgrade ever to the Office suite. It provides a much smarter work experience for users. Microsoft has enhanced Office XP in the following areas: (1) streamlined user interface; (2) smart tags and task panes to help simplify the way people work; (3) speech and handwriting recognition; (4) an improved Help system; (5) enhanced Web capabilities; and (6) application-specific features. Each one of these enhancements is part of Microsoft FrontPage 2002 and is discussed in detail.

In this *Microsoft FrontPage 2002* book, you will find an educationally sound and easy-to-follow pedagogy that combines a step-by-step approach with corresponding screens. All projects and exercises in this book are designed to take full advantage of the FrontPage 2002 enhancements. The popular Other Ways and More About features offer in-depth knowledge of FrontPage 2002. The new Learn It Online page presents a wealth of additional exercises to ensure your students have all the reinforcement they need. The project openers provide a fascinating perspective of the subject covered in the project. The project material is developed carefully to ensure that students will see the importance of learning FrontPage for future coursework.

Objectives of This Textbook

Microsoft FrontPage 2002: Complete Concepts and Techniques is intended for a two-unit course that presents Microsoft FrontPage 2002. No experience with a computer is assumed, and no mathematics beyond the high school freshman level is required. The objectives of this book are:

- To teach students how to use FrontPage 2002
- To expose students to proper Web page design techniques
- To provide an introduction to managing collections of related Web pages
- To acquaint students with the proper procedures to create Web pages suitable for course work, professional purposes, and personal use
- To develop an exercise-oriented approach that allows learning by doing
- To introduce students to new input technologies
- To encourage independent study, and help those who are working alone
- To assist students preparing to take the Microsoft Office User Specialist examination for Microsoft FrontPage Core level

Approved by Microsoft as Courseware for the Microsoft Office User Specialist Program — Core Level

Microsoft FrontPage 2002: Complete Concepts and Techniques has been approved by Microsoft as courseware for the Microsoft Office User Specialist (MOUS) program. After completing the projects and exercises in this book, students will be prepared to take the Core level Microsoft Office User Specialist Exam for Microsoft FrontPage 2002. By passing the certification exam for a Microsoft software program, students demonstrate their proficiency in that program to employers. This exam is offered at participating centers, participating corporations, and participating employment agencies. See Appendix E for additional information on the MOUS program and for a table that includes the FrontPage 2002 MOUS skill set and corresponding page numbers on which a skill is discussed in the book or visit the Web site mous.net. To purchase a Microsoft Office User Specialist certification exam, visit desktopiq.com.

The Shelly Cashman Series Microsoft Office User Specialist Center Web page (Figure 1) has more than fifteen Web pages you can visit to obtain additional information on the MOUS Certification program. The Web page scsite.com.offxp/cert.htm includes links to general information on certification, choosing an application for certification, preparing for the certification exam, and taking and passing the certification exam.

FIGURE 1 The Shelly Cashman Series Microsoft Office User Specialist Center Web Page

The Shelly Cashman Approach

Features of the Shelly Cashman Series *Microsoft FrontPage 2002* books include:

- **Project Orientation:** Each project in the book presents a practical problem and complete solution in an easy-to-understand approach.
- **Step-by-Step, Screen-by-Screen Instructions:** Each of the tasks required to complete a project is identified throughout the project. Full-color screens accompany the steps.
- **Thoroughly Tested Projects:** Every screen in the book is correct because it is produced by the author only after performing a step, resulting in unprecedented quality.
- **Other Ways Boxes and Quick Reference Summary:** The Other Ways boxes displayed at the end of most of the step-by-step sequences specify the other ways to do the task completed in the steps. Thus, the steps and the Other Ways box make a comprehensive reference unit.
- **More About Feature:** These marginal annotations provide background information and tips that complement the topics covered, adding depth and perspective.
- **Integration of the World Wide Web:** The World Wide Web is integrated into the FrontPage 2002 learning experience by (1) More About annotations that send students to Web sites for up-to-date information and alternative approaches to tasks; (2) a MOUS information Web page so students can prepare for the MOUS Certification examinations; (3) an FrontPage 2002 Quick Reference Summary Web page that summarizes the ways to complete tasks (mouse, menu, shortcut menu, and keyboard); and (4) the Learn It Online page at the end of each project, which has project reinforcement exercises, learning games, and other types of student activities.

Organization of This Textbook

Microsoft FrontPage 2002: Complete Concepts and Techniques provides detailed instruction on how to use FrontPage 2002. The material is divided into five projects, five appendices, and a Quick Reference Summary.

Project 1 – Creating a FrontPage Web Using a Template In Project 1, students are introduced to the basic components of the World Wide Web and of HTML, the FrontPage environment, and they learn how to use FrontPage templates. Students create a simple three-page web consisting of a Home page, an Interests page, and a Favorites page. Topics include basic Web page editing and customization techniques; applying a theme using FrontPage commands and features; and saving, printing, and publishing the three pages to an available Web server. Students then can use a browser to view their own personal Web pages.

Project 2 – Adding a New Web Page to a Web In Project 2, students learn how to add a new page to an existing Web and then how to customize that page. Topics include basic Web page design criteria; setting up the page background; inserting tables, images, and a Photo Gallery component; adding, replacing, and applying special formatting features to text; and adding linked targets to the page. Students also learn how to preview the printout of a page.

Project 3 – Customizing and Managing Web Pages and Images In Project 3, students are introduced to techniques for using graphics and images in Web pages. Topics include opening an existing FrontPage web; displaying and using the Pictures toolbar to apply formatting to images; creating and applying a customized theme to a page; assigning a hyperlink to an image; creating an image map and assigning a URL to the image map hotspot; highlighting hotspots on an image map; copying and pasting from a Word document; inserting a hit counter, a shared border, and an AutoShapes drawing; using FrontPage reporting features, displaying and verifying the hyperlinks in a FrontPage web; inserting bookmarks and using bookmarks as targets of a link; previewing a FrontPage web in a browser; and modifying the navigation structure of a web.

Project 4 – Creating and Using Interactive Forms on the Web In Project 4, students are introduced to interactive forms. After learning the basics of forms, form handlers, and form data formats, students create a Web page with a form consisting of the most-used form fields. Topics include inserting a form in a Web page; inserting a table in a form; inserting a form in a table; creating a nested table; inserting radio buttons, drop-down menus, text boxes and check boxes in a form; inserting a line drawing AutoShape; adjusting form field properties; assigning text as a form field label; and choosing a form handler to save results to a database. Students also will learn to manage files in Folders view and modify HTML code directly within FrontPage.

Project 5 – Using Database Results and Frames in Web Pages In Project 5, students are introduced to frames Web pages and the Database Results Wizard. Topics include how frames work; using a frames template; saving frames Web pages; creating an initial Web page for a frame; adjusting the size of frames; modifying properties of a frame and of a frames page; creating hyperlinks to pages in frames; using an existing Web page as the initial page in a frame; opening the target of a hyperlink in a different frame; printing Web pages in frames; and displaying the No Frames view. Students learn how to use the Database Results Wizard and create a custom SQL query. During the course of creating the frames Web page, students import Web resources into an existing FrontPage Web, demonstrating how to use FrontPage to manage pre-existing related Web pages.

FIGURE 4-1

Appendices The book includes five appendices. Appendix A presents an introduction to the Microsoft FrontPage Help system. Appendix B describes how to use the speech and handwriting recognition capabilities of FrontPage 2002. Appendix C explains how to publish Web pages to a Web server. Appendix D shows how to reset the menus and toolbars. Appendix E introduces students to the Microsoft Office User Specialist (MOUS) Certification program.

Quick Reference Summary In Microsoft FrontPage 2002, you can accomplish a task in a number of ways, such as using the mouse, menu, shortcut menu, and keyboard. The Quick Reference Summary at the back of the book provides a quick reference to each task presented.

End-of-Project Student Activities

A notable strength of the Shelly Cashman Series *Microsoft FrontPage 2002* books is the extensive student activities at the end of each project. Well-structured student activities can make the difference between students merely participating in a class and students retaining the information they learn. The activities in the Shelly Cashman Series *Microsoft FrontPage 2002* books include the following.

- **What You Should Know** A listing of the tasks completed within a project together with the pages on which the step-by-step, screen-by-screen explanations appear.
- **Learn It Online** Every project features a Learn It Online page comprised of ten exercises. These exercises include True/False, Multiple Choice, Short Answer, Flash Cards, Practice Test, Learning Games, Tips and Tricks, Newsgroup usage, Expanding Your Horizons, and Search Sleuth.
- **Apply Your Knowledge** This exercise usually requires students to open and manipulate a file on the Data Disk. To obtain a copy of the Data Disk, follow the instructions on the inside back cover of this textbook.
- **In the Lab** Three in-depth assignments per project require students to apply the knowledge gained in the project to solve problems on a computer.
- **Cases and Places** Up to seven unique real-world case-study situations.

Shelly Cashman Series Teaching Tools

The ancillaries that accompany this textbook are Teaching Tools (ISBN 0-7895-6357-6) and MyCourse.com. These ancillaries are available to adopters through your Course Technology representative or by calling one of the following telephone numbers: Colleges and Universities, 1-800-648-7450; High Schools, 1-800-824-5179; Private Career Colleges, 1-800-477-3692; Canada, 1-800-268-2222; and Corporations and Government Agencies, 1-800-340-7450.

Teaching Tools

The contents of the Teaching Tools CD-ROM are listed below.

- **Instructor's Manual** The Instructor's Manual includes the following for each project: project objectives; project overview; detailed lesson plans with page number references; teacher notes and activities; answers to the end-of-project exercises; a test bank of 110 questions for every project (25 multiple-choice, 50 true/false, and 35 fill-in-the-blank) with page number references; and transparency references. The transparencies are available through the Figures in the Book. The test bank questions are the same as in ExamView and Course Test Manager.
- **Figures in the Book** Illustrations for every screen and table in the textbook are available in electronic form. Use this ancillary to present a slide show in lecture or to print transparencies for use in lecture with an overhead projector.
- **ExamView** ExamView is a state-of-the-art test builder that is easy to use. With ExamView, you quickly can create printed tests, Internet tests, and computer (LAN-based) tests. You can enter your own test questions or use the test bank that accompanies ExamView. The test bank is the same as the one described in the Instructor's Manual section.
- **Course Syllabus** Any instructor who has been assigned a course at the last minute knows how difficult it is to come up with a course syllabus. For this reason, sample syllabi are included that can be customized easily to a course.
- **Lecture Success System** Lecture Success System files are used to explain and illustrate the step-by-step, screen-by-screen development of a project in the textbook without entering large amounts of data.
- **Instructor's Lab Solutions** Solutions and required files for all the In the Lab assignments at the end of each project are available. Solutions also are available for any Cases and Places assignment that supplies data.
- **Project Reinforcement** True/false, multiple choice, and short answer questions.
- **Student Files** All the files that are required by students to complete the Apply Your Knowledge exercises are included.

- **Interactive Labs** Eighteen completely updated, hands-on Interactive Labs that take students from ten to fifteen minutes each to step through, help solidify, and reinforce mouse and keyboard usage and computer concepts. Student assessment is available.

MyCourse 2.0

MyCourse 2.0 offers instructors and students an opportunity to supplement classroom learning with additional course content. You can use Mycourse 2.0 to expand on traditional learning by completing readings, tests, and other assignments through the customized, comprehensive Web site. For additional information, visit mycourse.com and click the Help button.

Shelly Cashman Online

Shelly Cashman Online is a World Wide Web service available to instructors and students of computer education. Visit Shelly Cashman Online at scseries.com. Shelly Cashman Online is divided into four areas:

- **Series Information** Information on the Shelly Cashman Series products.
- **Teaching Resources** This area includes password-protected data, Series information, teaching tools, and certification and electronic aids.
- **Community** Opportunities to discuss your course and your ideas with instructors in your field and with the Shelly Cashman Series team.
- **Student Center** Dedicated to students learning about computers with Shelly Cashman Series textbooks and software. This area includes cool links and much more.

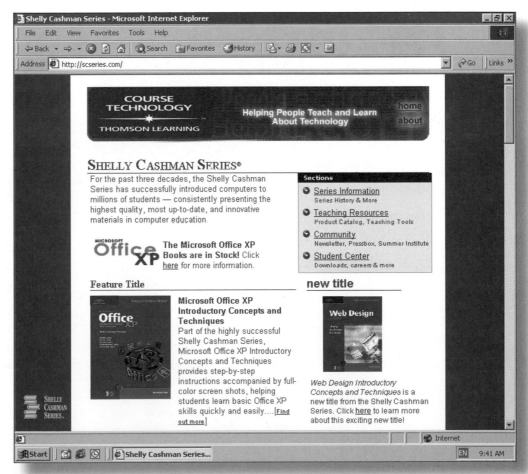

Acknowledgments

The Shelly Cashman Series would not be the leading computer education series without the contributions of outstanding publishing professionals. First, and foremost, among them is Becky Herrington, director of production and designer. She is the heart and soul of the Shelly Cashman Series, and it is only through her leadership, dedication, and tireless efforts that superior products are made possible.

Under Becky's direction, the following individuals made significant contributions to these books: Doug Cowley, production manager; Ginny Harvey, series specialist and developmental editor; Ken Russo, senior Web and graphic designer; Mike Bodnar, associate production manager; Mark Norton, technical analyst; Betty Hopkins and Richard Herrera, interior design; Christy Otten, Kellee LaVars, Stephanie Nance, Chris Schneider, Sharon Lee Nelson, Sarah Boger, Amanda Lotter, Michael Greco, and Ryan Ung, graphic artists; Jeanne Black and Betty Hopkins, QuarkXPress compositors; Lyn Markowicz, Nancy Lamm, Kim Kosmatka, Pam Baxter, Eva Kandarpa, Ellana Russo, and Marilyn Martin, copy editors/proofreaders; Cristina Haley, proofreader/indexer; Sarah Evertson of Image Quest, photo researcher; Ginny Harvey, Rich Hansberger, Kim Clark, and Nancy Smith, contributing writers; and Michelle French, graphic artist and cover art.

Finally, we would like to thank Richard Keaveny, associate publisher; Cheryl Ouellette, managing editor; Jim Quasney, series consulting editor; Alexandra Arnold, product manager; Erin Runyon, associate product manager; Francis Schurgot and Marc Ouellette, Web product managers; Rachel VanKirk, marketing manager; and Reed Cotter, editorial assistant.

Gary B. Shelly
Thomas J. Cashman
Michael L. Mick

Shelly Cashman Series – Traditionally Bound Textbooks

The Shelly Cashman Series presents the following computer subjects in a variety of traditionally bound textbooks. For more information, see your Course Technology representative or call 1-800-648-7450. For Shelly Cashman Series information, visit Shelly Cashman Online at **scseries.com**

COMPUTERS	
Computers	Discovering Computers 2002: Concepts for a Digital World, Web Enhanced, Complete Edition
	Discovering Computers 2002: Concepts for a Digital World, Web Enhanced, Introductory Edition
	Discovering Computers 2002: Concepts for a Digital World, Web Enhanced, Brief Edition
	Teachers Discovering Computers: Integrating Technology in the Classroom 2e
	Exploring Computers: A Record of Discovery 4e
	Study Guide for Discovering Computers 2002: Concepts for a Digital World, Web Enhanced
	Essential Introduction to Computers 4e (32-page)

WINDOWS APPLICATIONS	
Microsoft Office	Microsoft Office XP: Essential Concepts and Techniques (5 projects)
	Microsoft Office XP: Brief Concepts and Techniques (9 projects)
	Microsoft Office XP: Introductory Concepts and Techniques (15 projects)
	Microsoft Office XP: Advanced Concepts and Techniques (11 projects)
	Microsoft Office XP: Post Advanced Concepts and Techniques (11 projects)
	Microsoft Office 2000: Essential Concepts and Techniques (5 projects)
	Microsoft Office 2000: Brief Concepts and Techniques (9 projects)
	Microsoft Office 2000: Introductory Concepts and Techniques, Enhanced Edition (15 projects)
	Microsoft Office 2000: Advanced Concepts and Techniques (11 projects)
	Microsoft Office 2000: Post Advanced Concepts and Techniques (11 projects)
Integration	Integrating Microsoft Office XP Applications and the World Wide Web: Essential Concepts and Techniques
PIM	Microsoft Outlook 2002: Essential Concepts and Techniques
Microsoft Works	Microsoft Works 6: Complete Concepts and Techniques[1] • Microsoft Works 2000: Complete Concepts and Techniques[1] • Microsoft Works 4.5[1]
Microsoft Windows	Microsoft Windows 2000: Complete Concepts and Techniques (6 projects)[2]
	Microsoft Windows 2000: Brief Concepts and Techniques (2 projects)
	Microsoft Windows 98: Essential Concepts and Techniques (2 projects)
	Microsoft Windows 98: Complete Concepts and Techniques (6 projects)[2]
	Introduction to Microsoft Windows NT Workstation 4
	Microsoft Windows 95: Complete Concepts and Techniques[1]
Word Processing	Microsoft Word 2002[2] • Microsoft Word 2000[2] • Microsoft Word 97[1] • Microsoft Word 7[1]
Spreadsheets	Microsoft Excel 2002[2] • Microsoft Excel 2000[2] • Microsoft Excel 97[1] • Microsoft Excel 7[1] • Microsoft Excel 5[1]
Database	Microsoft Access 2002[2] • Microsoft Access 2000[2] • Microsoft Access 97[1] • Microsoft Access 7[1]
Presentation Graphics	Microsoft PowerPoint 2002[2] • Microsoft PowerPoint 2000[2] • Microsoft PowerPoint 97[1] • Microsoft PowerPoint 7[1]
Desktop Publishing	Microsoft Publisher 2002[1] • Microsoft Publisher 2000[1]

PROGRAMMING	
Programming	Microsoft Visual Basic 6: Complete Concepts and Techniques[1] • Programming in QBasic
	Java Programming: Complete Concepts and Techniques[1] • Structured COBOL Programming 2e

INTERNET	
Browser	Microsoft Internet Explorer 5: An Introduction • Microsoft Internet Explorer 4: An Introduction
	Netscape Navigator 6: An Introduction • Netscape Navigator 4: An Introduction
Web Page Creation and Design	Web Design: Introductory Concepts and Techniques • HTML: Complete Concepts and Techniques[1]
	Microsoft FrontPage 2002: Essential Concepts and Techniques • Microsoft FrontPage 2002[2]
	Microsoft FrontPage 2000[1] • JavaScript: Complete Concepts and Techniques[1]

SYSTEMS ANALYSIS	
Systems Analysis	Systems Analysis and Design 4e

DATA COMMUNICATIONS	
Data Communications	Business Data Communications: Introductory Concepts and Techniques 3e

[1]Also available as an Introductory Edition, which is a shortened version of the complete book
[2]Also available as an Introductory Edition, which is a shortened version of the complete book and also as a Comprehensive Edition, which is an extended version of the complete book

Microsoft FrontPage 2002

Creating a FrontPage Web Using a Template

You will have mastered the material in this project when you can:

O B J E C T I V E S

- Describe FrontPage and explain its key features
- Discuss the basic components of the World Wide Web
- Identify common elements of a Web page
- Define and describe a FrontPage web
- Start FrontPage
- Describe FrontPage window elements
- Create a FrontPage web using a template
- Apply a theme to a FrontPage web
- Add and modify text elements on a Web page
- Save and preview a Web page
- Delete a Web page from a FrontPage web
- Add and modify hyperlinks on a Web page
- Print a Web page
- Publish and test a FrontPage web
- Use FrontPage Help
- Quit FrontPage

Author, Designer, Editor, Publisher

Create Your Own Web Page

At first glance, these three famous authors, Ernest Hemingway, American novelist and short-story writer whose fiction often parallels his volatile life; Allen Ginsberg, American poet and high-profile spokesman for the Beat Generation; and Alex Haley, American author whose writing influenced the study of African-American history and genealogy, appear to have little in common with each other. The target audiences were unique to each author as these gifted artists provided enlightened perspective to historical literary moments. Regardless of the varying flavor and tone of these best-selling writers, each was highly respected for his literary genius. Hemingway, Ginsberg, and Haley shared a common thread: editors had the last word in the design of their works.

As an author of Web pages, you have the opportunity to make your contribution in Web publishing circles. As well as providing appeal and interest for Web page visitors, you can offer functionality and purpose for Web sites you develop. You are an author of a unique work in the online age of Web publishing. In your case, you are the writer and the editor of your own work.

In traditional publishing, an author writes a manuscript and an editor suggests content changes and marks up the pages with instructions for layout. The designer, in conjunction with the markups, lays out the pages and revises the layout until it is complete.

In Web page publishing, the author writes a text file and marks up the words with special HTML (hypertext markup language) character sequences, called tags, to indicate the various formatting features such as headings, bulleted lists, placement of inline images, hyperlinks to other pages, and more. HTML is a coding scheme that can be interpreted by a Web browser, such as Internet Explorer. Creating Web pages by writing HTML can be tedious and confusing, but a basic understanding of the process is valuable.

As an HTML document stored on an Internet server, a Web page can be retrieved and displayed on a computer with a Web browser. The HTML tags specify how the Web page displays and indicates links to other documents. These links to other documents, called hyperlinks, can be text, graphics, sound, or other media. Text links are known as hypertext.

The Web page creation capabilities of Microsoft FrontPage 2002 are designed for both experienced and beginning Web site developers with a simple yet powerful tool for designing and building great-looking, easy-to-navigate World Wide Web sites.

With FrontPage, you will create Web pages in this project constructing them almost as if you were creating them in a word processing environment, with no programming knowledge required. For example, formatting attributes such as fonts, borders, and bulleted lists look very close to the way they display in your browser, and many features and options are available using familiar elements such as toolbars, dialog boxes, and templates.

This project illustrates using a template to create a FrontPage Web page. Templates help organize and format the pages in a Web site using a consistent framework.

Just as authors interact with their audiences through their characters and stories, as a Web page designer, you can present an award-winning Web site to your visitors by blending all the features of the FrontPage Web site creation and management tool.

Microsoft FrontPage 2002

Creating a FrontPage Web Using a Template

C A S E   P E R S P E C T I V E

After you developed the Hilltop Community College Computer Club Web site, the club president, Jennifer Stuart, was very impressed. She wanted to know if she might pass along your name to others who had an interest in Web site development. You wholeheartedly agreed for her to do so, and she indicated that she already had a potential client for you. Nikki Patrio, a close friend of hers, was looking for help in developing a personal Web site. You indicated that Nikki should contact you, so you could set up a meeting to discuss her needs for the site.

At your first meeting, you explained to Nikki that making a simple Web site was very easy to do with Microsoft FrontPage. Because she indicated a desire both to learn about Web page creation and eventually to maintain her own Web site, you thought it appropriate that she learn some basics about Web page construction and maintenance in an incremental fashion. By learning about the components of a Web page, then building an initial Web site, and later making modifications to the Web site, she would accomplish her goal of learning how to create and how to maintain her Web site.

What Is Microsoft FrontPage?

Microsoft FrontPage is a Web page authoring and site management program that allows you to create and manage professional quality Web sites without programming. Microsoft FrontPage offers two key types of functionality, including:

- **Web page creation** Microsoft FrontPage allows you to create and edit Web pages without needing to know HTML or other programming languages. FrontPage includes many features that make Web page creation easy, such as templates, graphics, and more.
- **Web site management** Microsoft FrontPage allows you to view Web pages, publish them to the World Wide Web, and to manage existing Web sites. Using FrontPage, you can test and repair hyperlinks on a Web page, view all of the files and folders on a site, import image files, and more.

Project One — Personal Web Pages

To create the personal Web pages for this project, you determined the following needs, formatting requirements, and content requirements. The easiest way to develop a personal Web site would be to use the Personal Web template, and then make appropriate modifications to the generated pages.

Needs: A group of related Web pages is referred to as a **web** in Microsoft FrontPage. For this site, the web will include three Web pages: a Home page, an Interests page, and a Favorites page. The Home page introduces Nikki to site visitors (Figure 1-1a); the Interests page outlines her hobbies and interests (Figure 1-1b); and the Favorites page includes links to three Web sites, including her favorite site about science (Figure 1-1c). The Home page includes links to the other two pages in the

(a) Home Page

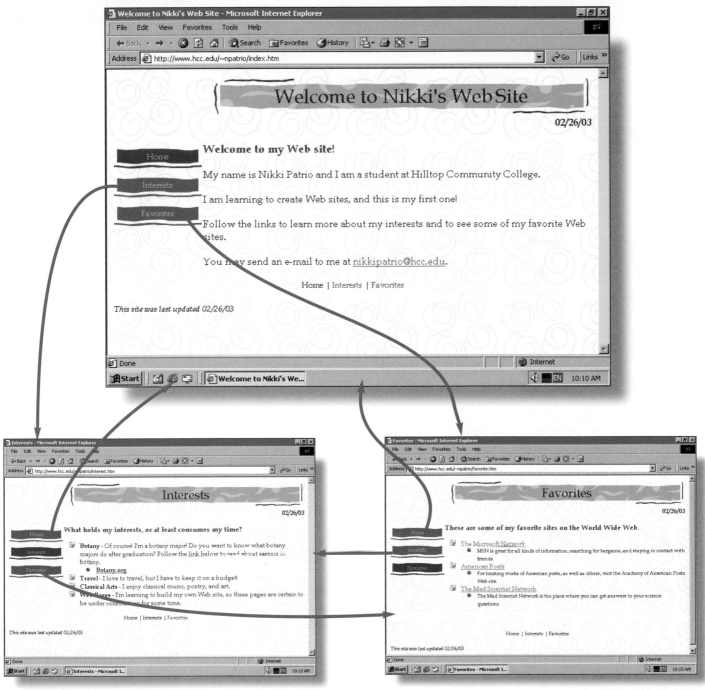

(b) Interests Page

(c) Favorites Page

FIGURE 1-1

FrontPage web. Once complete, you will publish the web to make it available for viewing on the World Wide Web.

Formatting Requirements: To create the Web pages, you will use the Personal Web template included in Microsoft FrontPage. The Web pages then should be formatted using the Poetic theme included in Microsoft FrontPage. The Home page should include graphical hyperlinks to the other pages in this web.

Content Requirements: The Home page lists Nikki's name, her position as a student at Hilltop Community College, and provides an e-mail address so visitors can contact her. The Interests page includes a minimum of four activities that she pursues due to personal interest, not necessarily vocation. The Favorites page includes links to at least three Web sites, one of which is a science-related site.

World Wide Web Basics

The **World Wide Web** (**WWW**), often referred to simply as the **Web**, consists of a worldwide collection of electronic documents that have built-in links to other related documents. Each of these electronic documents on the Web is called a **Web page**; a Web page can contain text, graphics, sound, and video, as well as connections to other documents. These connections to other documents, called **hyperlinks** or **links**, allow you to move quickly from one document to another, regardless of whether the documents are located on the same computer or on different computers in different countries.

A collection of related Web pages that you can access electronically is called a **Web site**. Most Web sites have a starting point, called a **home page**, which is similar to a book cover or table of contents for the site and provides information about the site's purpose and content. In a personal web, for example, the home page probably will list your name, your e-mail address, some personal information, and links to other information on your Web site.

Hypertext Markup Language (HTML)

A Web page is a file that contains both text and hypertext markup language (HTML). **Hypertext markup language** (**HTML**) is a formatting language that tells the browser how to display text and images; how to set up list boxes, hyperlinks, and other elements; and how to include graphics, sound, video, and other multimedia on a Web page.

HTML uses a set of special instructions called **tags** to define the characteristics of items such as formatted text, images, hyperlinks, lists, and forms. HTML tags are used throughout the text document to indicate (or mark) how these

Table 1-1 Common HTML Tags	
HTML TAG	*FUNCTION*
<HTML> </HTML>	Indicates the beginning and end of a Web document.
<HEAD> </HEAD>	Indicates the beginning and end of the header section of a Web document (used for the title and other document header information).
<TITLE> </TITLE>	Indicates the beginning and end of the Web page title. The title displays in the title bar of the browser, not in the body of the Web page itself.
<BODY> </BODY>	Indicates the beginning and end of the main section (body) of the Web page.
<Hn> </Hn>	Indicates the beginning and end of a section of text called a heading, which uses a larger font than normal text. In the tag, <Hn>, n indicates the size of the heading font; sizes range from <H1> through <H6>.
<P> </P>	Indicates the beginning of a new paragraph; inserts a blank line above the new paragraph. The end tag of </P> is optional. It will insert a blank line below the new paragraph, unless followed by a new paragraph.
<B> </B>	Indicates the beginning and end of a section of bold text.
<I> </I>	Indicates the beginning and end of a section of italic text.
<U> </U>	Indicates the beginning and end of a section of underlined text.
<UL> </UL>	Indicates the beginning and end of an unordered (bulleted) list.
<OL> </OL>	Indicates the beginning and end of an ordered (numbered) list.
<LI> </LI>	Indicates that the item in the tag is an item within a list.
<HR>	Inserts a horizontal rule.
<A> </A>	Indicates the beginning and end of a hyperlink.
HREF="URL"	Indicates a hyperlink to a file in the location specified by the URL in quotation marks.
<IMG SRC="URL">	Inserts an inline image in the page. The URL in quotation marks specifies the location of the image.
<CENTER> </CENTER>	Indicates that the text, graphic, or other elements between the tags should display centered on the Web page.
<LEFT> </LEFT>	Indicates that the text, graphic, or other elements between the tags should display left-aligned on the Web page.
<RIGHT> </RIGHT>	Indicates that the text, graphic, or other elements between the tags should display right-aligned on the Web page.

items should display and function when viewed as a Web page in a **browser**, which is a software program used to access and view Web pages. HTML thus is considered a **markup language**, because the HTML tags mark elements in the text file.

Although HTML includes hundreds of tags, most Web developers use only a small subset of these tags when building a Web page. Table 1-1 lists some of the more commonly used HTML tags and an explanation of their functions.

Defining the type and layout of an element on a Web page requires one or more HTML tags. As shown in Table 1-1, HTML tags begin with the less than sign (<) and end with the greater than sign (>). Tags may be entered as either uppercase or lowercase. Tags often are used in pairs to indicate the beginning and end of an element or format. The end tag contains a forward slash (/). The tag, <B>, for example, indicates the beginning of a section of bold text, and </B> indicates the end of a section of bold text. To display the text, World Wide Web, as bold text, you would type the tags as follows:

```
<B>World Wide Web</B>
```

You also can use tags in combination to apply multiple formatting features to text or other Web page elements. The tag

```
<CENTER><B>World Wide Web</B></CENTER>
```

for example, would center the words on the page. If you use HTML tags in combination, as in the example above, be sure to place the end tags in an order opposite that of the beginning tags.

HTML tags can contain keywords that further define the appearance of the element created by the tag. Keywords take the form

```
keyword=value
```

where keyword is an HTML tag describing a characteristic of a Web page element and value is one of a range of numbers or words describing that characteristic. Instead of using the CENTER tag to center text on the page, for instance, you can use the keyword, ALIGN, and the value, CENTER. The tag, which you can use within another tag, might display as

```
<B ALIGN=CENTER>My Favorite Web Sites</B>
```

The tag tells the browser to display the text in bold and center the text on the page.

All of these elements are defined using HTML tags. The HTML used to create a Web page is called the **HTML source**, or **source code**. Figure 1-2 shows the HTML source for the Web page displayed in Figure 1-1c on the next page.

More About

HTML

The World Wide Web Consortium (W3C) develops and updates common Web protocols. To learn more about the latest changes to HTML, visit the FrontPage 2002 More About Web page (scsite.com/fp2002/more.htm) and then click W3C.

FIGURE 1-2

Viewing HTML Source Code

To see the HTML tags that FrontPage creates as you build a Web page, you can use the HTML tab. The HTML tab allows you to display HTML tags and then edit them just as you would edit text using a word processing program, utilizing standard editing commands such as cut, paste, find, and replace.

Most Web browsers allow you to view the HTML source for the Web page currently displayed in the browser window. If you are using Internet Explorer, for example, you can click the Source command on the View menu to display the HTML source.

Many HTML tags exist to help you design a Web page exactly as you want. Although a more detailed discussion of HTML is beyond the scope of this book, when using FrontPage to develop Web pages, you do not need to know every HTML tag. Instead, you simply determine the best way to convey the information and then make those changes on the Web page using FrontPage commands. FrontPage inserts the appropriate HTML code for you.

Web Browsers

You access and view Web pages using a software program called a Web browser. A **Web browser**, also called simply a **browser**, is a software program that requests a Web page, interprets the HTML codes and text used to create the page, and then displays the Web page on your computer screen. Today, the two more popular browsers are **Microsoft Internet Explorer** and **Netscape Navigator** (Figure 1-3a and 1-3b). Browsers have special buttons and other features to help you navigate through Web sites.

Different browsers will display the same Web page with slight variations. Netscape Navigator, for example, may display fonts, hyperlinks, tables, and other Web page elements in a manner different from Microsoft Internet Explorer. Some special features in a Web page may be available when using one browser, but may not work at all with a different browser. When developing a Web site, you should test the Web pages using Netscape Navigator, Microsoft Internet Explorer, and any other browsers your audience might use to ensure that the Web pages display correctly in the various browsers.

(a) Microsoft Internet Explorer

(b) Netscape Navigator

FIGURE 1-3

The Web pages that comprise a Web site are stored on a server, called a Web server. A **Web server**, or **host**, is a computer that delivers (serves) requested Web pages. Every Web site is stored on and run from one or more Web servers; a Web server can have thousands of Web pages available for viewing. Multiple Web sites also can be stored on the same Web server. For example, many Internet service providers grant their subscribers storage space on a Web server for their personal or company Web sites. Each Web page on the Web site is comprised of one or more files that are stored on the hard disk of the Web server or other computer.

A Web server runs **Web server software** that allows it to receive the requests for Web pages and sends the pages over the Internet to your browser, so you can view them on your computer. For example, when you enter a Web page address in your browser, your browser sends a request to the server; the server then uses the Web server software to fetch the Web page and send it to your browser.

Testing Web Pages in Browsers

When testing Web pages in various browsers, you may want to test the pages in several versions of the same browser (usually the two most recent versions). Consider whether you need to test the pages on both PC and Macintosh platforms.

Uniform Resource Locators (URLs)

Each Web page on a Web site has a unique address called a **Uniform Resource Locator (URL)**. As shown in Figure 1-4, a URL consists of a protocol, a domain name, the path to a specific document, and the file name of the document. Most Web page URLs begin with http://. The **http** stands for **Hypertext Transfer Protocol**, the communications protocol used to transfer pages on the Web. The **domain name** identifies the Web server or computer on the Internet where the Web document is located. The **path** and **file name** indicate where the Web document is stored on the computer. In the URL shown in Figure 1-4, for example, the domain name is www.nationalgeographic.com, the path to the file is /ngm/, and the file name is index.htm.

```
http://www.nationalgeographic.com/ngm/index.htm
```

FIGURE 1-4

Each hyperlink on a Web page is associated with a URL, thus making it possible for you to navigate the Web using hyperlinks. When you click a hyperlink on a Web page, you are issuing a request to display the Web document specified by the URL. If, for example, you click a hyperlink associated with the URL, http://www.scsite.com/index.htm, your browser sends a request to the server whose domain name is www.scsite.com. The server then fetches the page named index.htm and sends it to your computer, where the browser displays it on your screen.

Elements of a Web Page

Although Web pages can be as distinctive and unique as the individuals who create them, almost every Web page has several basic features, or **elements**. Web page elements include basic features such as the background, text, hyperlinks, and images; and more advanced features such as forms and frames. As you begin to view Web pages through the eyes of a Web page developer, you will notice that most Web pages use variations on one or more of the elements identified in Figure 1-5.

Window Elements

The **title** of a Web page is the text that displays on the title bar of the browser window when the Web page displays. The **background** of a Web page is either a solid color or a small graphic image that provides a backdrop against which the other elements display. Like the wallpaper in Windows, a background color or graphic can be **tiled**, or repeated, across the entire page.

Text Elements

On a Web page, the **body** is the text that makes up the main content of a Web page, as opposed to the **header** where the page title and other information about the page is contained. The body of the Web page usually uses the default font format, known as **Normal text**. You also can format Normal text to display in color or in bold, italic, or underlined styles. **Headings** are used to separate different paragraphs

FIGURE 1-5

of text or different sections of a Web page. Headings generally are a larger font size than normal text and usually are bold or italic.

Many Web pages present a series of text items as a **list**. Typically, lists are numbered or bulleted. A **numbered list** (also called an **ordered list**) presents an ordered list of items, such as the steps in this project. Numbers precede the items in a numbered list. A **bulleted list** (also called an **unordered list**) presents an unordered (unnumbered) list of items. Bulleted lists often use a small image called a **bullet** to mark each item in the list.

Hyperlink Elements

A **hyperlink**, or **link**, is an area of the page that you click to instruct the browser to go to a location in a file or to request a file from a Web server. On the World Wide Web, hyperlinks are the primary way to navigate between pages and among Web sites. Links not only point to Web pages, but also to graphics, sound, multimedia, e-mail addresses, program files, and even other parts of the same Web page. Text hyperlinks are the most commonly used hyperlinks. When text is used to identify a hyperlink, it usually displays as underlined text, in a color different than the regular text.

Image Elements

Web pages typically use several different types of graphics, or images. An **image** is a graphic file that can be inserted on a Web page and displayed in a Web browser. An **inline image** is an image or graphic file that is not part of the page's HTML file itself. Rather, an inline image is a separate graphic file that is merged into the page as it displays. The HTML file contains an <IMG SRC> tag that tells the browser which graphic file to request from the server, where to insert it on the page, and how to display it. Some inline images are animated, meaning they include motion and change in appearance. Inline images often are used to identify hyperlinks.

An **image map** is a special type of inline image that is divided into sections, with a hyperlink associated with each section. Clicking one of the sections, called a **hotspot**, instructs the browser to link to a Web page, graphic, sound, e-mail address, or other file.

As just described, the background of a Web page is the solid color, image, or pattern that serves as the backdrop on which text, images, hyperlinks, and other elements display on the Web page. If you use an image for the background, the image is repeated across and down the page.

Horizontal rules are lines that display across the page to separate different sections of the page. Although the appearance of a horizontal rule varies, many Web pages use an inline image as a horizontal rule.

Form, Table, and Frame Elements

A **form** is an area of a Web page that allows the viewer to enter data and information to be sent back to the Web server. Input elements within the form, such as **option buttons,** which allow for a single choice among several choices, or **text boxes,** which provide an area for the user to enter text, instruct the individual what items to enter and how to send them to the server.

A **table** is used to present text and graphics in rows or columns. The intersection of a row and a column is called a **cell.** The text or graphic within a cell often is used as a hyperlink. The border width of the table determines the width of the grid lines surrounding the cells. When the border width is greater than zero, grid lines surround the cells. When the border width is set to zero, grid lines do not display.

A **frame** allows you to divide the display area of the browser into sections, so the browser can display a different Web page in each frame. Web pages with frames have many possible applications. You can display a table of contents for your Web site in a smaller frame, for example, while displaying different content pages in a separate main frame. Users can click hyperlinks in the smaller table of contents frame and display the linked page in the main frame.

FrontPage Webs

As previously defined, a collection of related Web pages that you can access electronically is called a Web site. A typical Web site contains one to several thousand Web pages, often with links to other pages in the same Web site and pages on separate Web sites.

In FrontPage, a group of related pages is called a **web.** A **FrontPage web** consists of the Web pages, images, and other files, folders, and programs that make up the related content that will comprise the Web site. The Web pages in a FrontPage web usually are related by topic or purpose; most webs use a series of hyperlinks to connect the related pages. A Web site may consist of one or more FrontPage webs.

When working with a web in FrontPage, the web that currently is open is called the **current web**. Once created, a FrontPage web can be stored on the computer on which FrontPage is installed or on a Web server anywhere on the World Wide Web. Using FrontPage, you can upload and download a complete web to and from your computer and a Web server. **Publishing** involves sending, or uploading, copies of Web pages, image files, and other files, folders, and programs to a server where they then are made available on the World Wide Web. To publish a FrontPage web, you must have access to a Web server to which you are allowed to upload files. As you complete this project, you will use FrontPage to develop and publish your own web to the World Wide Web.

Starting and Customizing FrontPage

To learn how to develop a Web site, you will start FrontPage and then use a template to create a Personal web that introduces an individual, describes the person's hobbies and interests, and lists several favorite Web sites. To start FrontPage, Windows must be running. Perform the following steps to start FrontPage.

Steps **To Start and Customize FrontPage**

1 **Click the Start button on the Windows taskbar and then point to Programs on the Start menu. Point to Microsoft FrontPage on the Programs submenu.**

The Start menu and Programs submenu display (Figure 1-6).

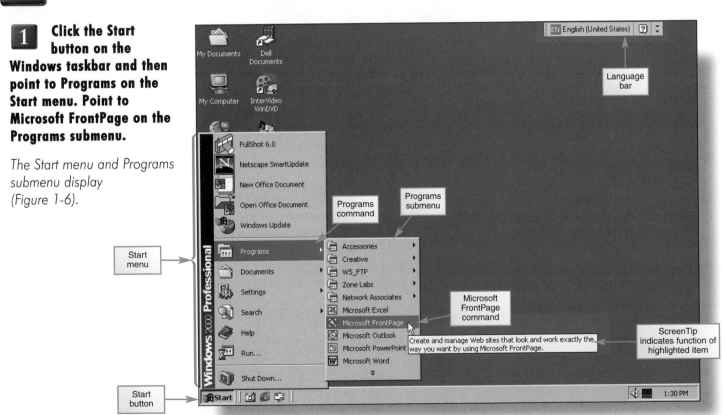

FIGURE 1-6

2 **Click Microsoft FrontPage. If necessary, click the Page icon on the Views bar. If the New Page or Web task pane displays, click Show at startup at the bottom of the task pane to remove the check mark. Point to the Close button in the upper-right corner of the task pane title bar.**

The Microsoft FrontPage window opens in Page view (Figure 1-7). When you first create a new web, an empty page is displayed.

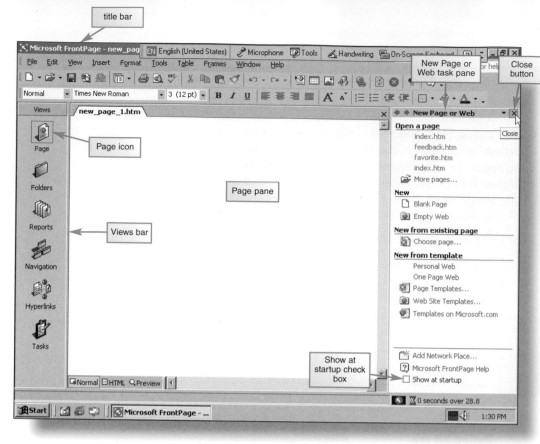

FIGURE 1-7

3 **Click the Close button. If the Language bar displays, click the Minimize button (see Figure 1-11a on page FP 1.18).**

The New Page or Web task pane closes, resulting in the maximum width for the new page. The Language Indicator button in the tray status area means the Language bar is minimized (Figure 1-8).

Other Ways

1. Double-click FrontPage icon on desktop

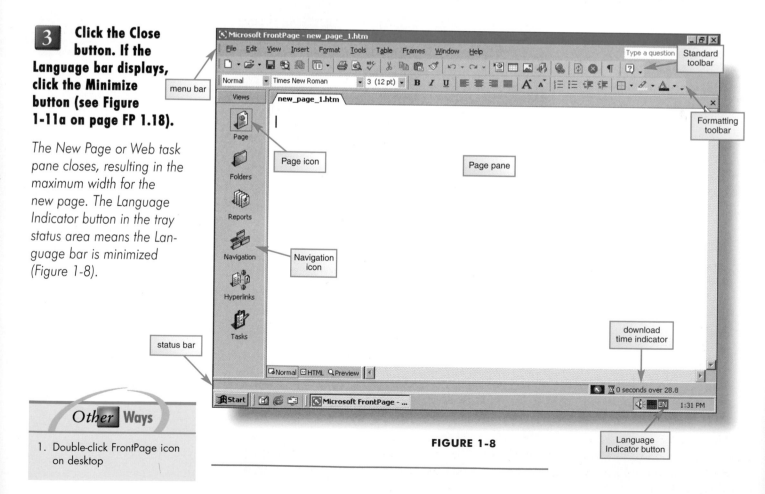

FIGURE 1-8

When you start FrontPage, the FrontPage window displays the same way it displayed the last time you quit FrontPage. Thus, if the New Page or Web task pane previously displayed on the right side of the window and the Show at startup check box was selected, then the task pane will display when you start FrontPage.

A **task pane**, such as the one shown in Figure 1-7, enables users to carry out some FrontPage tasks more quickly. As you work through creating a web, you will find that certain FrontPage operations result in displaying a task pane. Besides the New Page or Web task pane shown in Figure 1-7, FrontPage provides two additional task panes: the Clipboard task pane and the Search task pane. These task panes are discussed as they are used. You can display or hide a task pane by clicking the **Task Pane command** on the **View menu**. You can activate additional task panes by clicking the down arrow to the left of the Close button on the task pane title bar (Figure 1-7) and then selecting a task pane in the list. Using the Back and Forward buttons on the left side of the task pane title bar, you can switch between task panes.

In this book, to allow the maximum window space in the FrontPage window, the New Page or Web task pane that displays at startup is closed.

The FrontPage Window

The **FrontPage window** consists of a variety of features to help you work efficiently. It contains a title bar, status bar, menu bar, toolbars, Views bar, and a pane that displays different content, depending on the current view.

Title Bar

The **title bar** (Figure 1-8) displays the application name, Microsoft FrontPage, and the location of the current FrontPage web. If you open a web saved in the web-pages folder on drive C, for example, the title bar will display the title, Microsoft FrontPage – C:\npatrio, on the title bar.

Status Bar

The **status bar**, which is located at the bottom of the FrontPage window, consists of a message area and a download time indicator (Figure 1-8). As you are developing a page or web, the message area on the left side of the status bar displays information on file location, file name, hyperlinks, and more. The **download time indicator** displays the number of seconds it will take the page to download on the Web, based on a certain connection speed.

Menu Bar

The **menu bar** displays the FrontPage menu names (Figure 1-8). Each name represents a menu of commands that allows you to create, retrieve, edit, save, print, and publish a FrontPage web. To display a menu, such as the Format menu, click the Format menu name on the menu bar. If you point to a command with an arrow on the right, a submenu displays, from which you can choose a command.

When you click a menu name on the menu bar, a **short menu** displays listing only basic or the most recently used commands (Figure 1-9a on the next page). If you wait a few seconds or click the arrows at the bottom of the short menu, the full menu displays. The **full menu** lists all the commands associated with a menu (Figure 1-9b on the next page). You also can display a full menu immediately by double-clicking the menu name on the menu bar. In this book, when you display a menu, you should always display the full menu using one of the techniques shown on the next page.

1. Click the menu name on the menu bar and then wait a few seconds.
2. Click the menu name and then click the arrows at the bottom of the short menu.
3. Click the menu name and then point to the arrows at the bottom of the short menu.
4. Double-click the menu name on the menu bar.

Both short and full menus display some **dimmed commands** that appear gray, or dimmed, instead of black, which indicates they are not available for the current selection. A command with a dark gray shading in the rectangle to the left of it on a full menu is called a **hidden command** because it does not display on a short menu. As you use FrontPage, it automatically personalizes the short menus for you based on how often you use commands. That is, as you use hidden commands on the full menu, FrontPage *unhides* them and places them on the short menu.

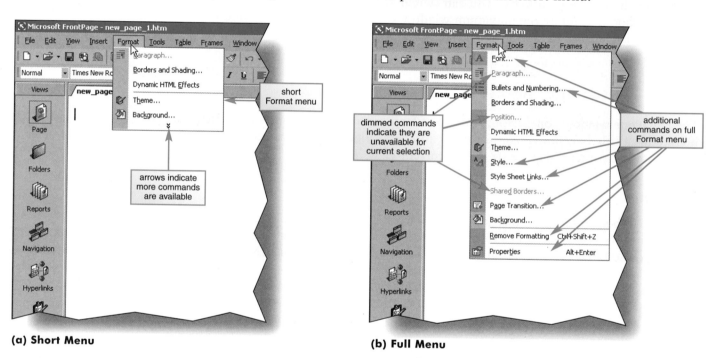

(a) **Short Menu**   (b) **Full Menu**

FIGURE 1-9

Toolbars

A **toolbar** consists of buttons that allow you to perform tasks more quickly than when using the menu bar. To save a Web page, for example, you can click the Save button on a toolbar, instead of clicking File on the menu bar and then clicking Save on the File menu. Each button uses a graphical representation to help identify the button's function.

When you first start FrontPage, some of the buttons on the toolbars are dimmed (or grayed) to indicate that the toolbar buttons are inactive. When a button or command is **inactive**, the function performed by that button or command is not available. Once you have opened a Web page or a web, the buttons on the FrontPage toolbars are **active**, meaning you can use them to perform tasks in FrontPage. Figure 1-10a and Figure 1-10b show the buttons on each of the two toolbars that display when you open a Web page or web using FrontPage: the Standard toolbar and the Formatting toolbar. The book explains each button in detail when it is used.

Sizing Toolbar Buttons

If you have difficulty seeing the small buttons on the toolbars, you can increase their size, click View on the menu bar, point to Toolbars, click Customize on the Toolbars submenu, click the Options tab, click the Large icons check box, and then click the Close button.

STANDARD TOOLBAR The Standard toolbar (Figure 1-10a) contains buttons that execute commonly used commands such as Open, Print, Save, Cut, Copy, Paste, and many more. The Standard toolbar also contains a Microsoft FrontPage Help button that you can click to start **FrontPage Help,** which is a collection of reference materials, tips, and other assistance you can access at any time while using FrontPage.

FORMATTING TOOLBAR The Formatting toolbar (Figure 1-10b) contains buttons used to execute commonly used formatting commands that allow you quickly to change font, font size, and alignment. It also contains buttons, such as Bold, Italic, and Underline, which allow you to change text formats and create lists.

FrontPage has several other toolbars to help you perform your work. You can display a toolbar by right-clicking any toolbar to display a shortcut menu that lists the available toolbars and then clicking the name of the toolbar you want to display. A **shortcut menu** contains a list of commands that are related to the items to which you are pointing when you right-click.

The FrontPage Help System

Need Help? It is no further than the Ask a Question box in the upper-right corner of the window. Click the box that contains the text, Type a question for help (Figure 1-12 on page FP 1.20), type help, and then press the ENTER key. FrontPage will respond with a list of items you can click to learn about obtaining help on any FrontPage-related topic. To find out what is new in FrontPage 2002, type what's new in FrontPage in the Ask a Question box.

FIGURE 1-10a

FIGURE 1-10b

Views Bar

The **Views bar,** which is located at the left of the FrontPage window, contains icons that allow you to switch to different views of your web (Figure 1-8 on page FP 1.14). The icon indicating the current view displays selected on the Views bar. When you first create a new web, FrontPage displays in Page view. A **view** provides a different way of looking at the information in your web, so you can effectively manage your Web site. The selected view determines how the FrontPage window displays. For example, **Navigation view** displays a graphical representation of the web's **structure,** which is the set of relationships among the pages in a FrontPage web.

Toolbars

You can move a toolbar to any location on the screen. Drag the move handle (Figure 1-10a) to the desired location. Once the toolbar is in the window area, drag the title bar to move it. Each side of the screen is called a dock. You can drag a toolbar to a dock so it does not clutter the window.

More About

Resetting Toolbars

If your toolbars have a different set of buttons than shown in Figures 1-10a and 10b on page FP 1.17, it probably means that a previous user added or deleted buttons. To reset a toolbar to its default, right-click the toolbar and then click Customize. When the Customize dialog box displays, click the Toolbars tab, click the toolbar name, and then click the Reset button. When the Reset Toolbar dialog box displays, click the OK button. Click the Close button in the Customize dialog box.

A web's structure defines the overall site organization and navigation, determining the pages that are linked, how many levels of pages exist, and so on. The structure of one Web site, for example, might be linear, with few levels; another site might use a hierarchical structure, with several levels of pages. Table 1-2 identifies the icons on the Views bar and provides a description of each view.

Table 1-2	Views Bar Icons	
ICON	VIEW	DESCRIPTION
	Page	Used for creating, editing, and previewing Web pages. Page view displays Web pages in a manner similar to how they will display in a Web browser.
	Folders	Displays a view of a web that shows how the content of the web is organized. Similar to Windows Explorer, you can create, delete, copy, and move folders in Folders view.
	Reports	Allows you to analyze a web's contents. You can calculate the total size of the files in your web, show which files are not linked to any other files, identify slow or outdated pages, group files by the task or person to whom the files are assigned, and so on.
	Navigation	Used to create, display, print, and change a web's structure and navigation. Navigation view also allows you to drag and drop pages into the web structure.
	Hyperlinks	Displays a list showing the status of the hyperlinks in the web. The list includes both internal and external hyperlinks, and graphically indicates whether the hyperlinks have been verified or whether they are broken.
	Tasks	Displays a list of the tasks required to complete or maintain a web.

Speech Recognition

With the **Office Speech Recognition software** installed and a microphone, you can speak the names of toolbar buttons, menus, menu commands, list items, alerts, and dialog box controls, such as OK and Cancel. You also can dictate entries, such as text and numbers. To indicate whether you want to speak commands or dictate entries, you use the **Language bar** (Figure 1-11a). You can display the Language bar in two ways: (1) click the Language Indicator button in the taskbar tray status area by the clock, and then click Show the Language bar on the menu (Figure 1-11b); or (2) click the **Speech command** on the **Tools menu**.

FIGURE 1-11a

FIGURE 1-11b

If the Language Indicator button does not display in the tray status area, and if the Speech command is unavailable (dimmed) on the Tools menu, the Office Speech Recognition software is not installed. To install the software, you first must start Word and then click Speech on the Tools menu.

Using a Template to Create a FrontPage Web

Designing a Web site is a complex process that requires you to make decisions concerning the structure of the Web site and the appearance and content of each Web page within the site. When developing a web composed of several pages, for example, you should use a consistent layout and design on each page. In addition, you should be sure to link appropriate pages using a navigation scheme that is easy to understand. To help simplify this process, FrontPage includes several wizards and preformatted webs that will help you create a set of pages for a Web site. These preformatted webs are called templates.

A FrontPage **template** is a series of Web pages that are organized and formatted with a basic framework of content upon which you can base new pages and new FrontPage webs. Each template consists of linked Web pages that already include basic elements such as headings, formatted text, images, and hyperlinks.

When you create a new web, you can choose to:

▶ Create an empty web or a web with one page
▶ Import a web from a Web server or your personal computer
▶ Create a web using a template or wizard

Table 1-3 on the next page outlines the options from which you can choose when creating a FrontPage web.

Table 1-3 on the next page outlines the options from which you can choose when creating a FrontPage web.

More About

Creating Templates

You can make a template from your own Web page. Click File on the menu bar and then click Save As. When the Save As dialog box displays, click FrontPage Template in the Save as type list. Click the Save button. When the Save As Template dialog box displays, if necessary, modify the Title, Name, and Description fields. Click the OK button.

Table 1-3   FrontPage Web Options

OPTION	TYPE	DESCRIPTION
One Page Web	Template	Creates a FrontPage web with a single page (a home page). Used to create a FrontPage web from scratch with no suggested content.
Corporate Presence Wizard	Wizard	Creates a FrontPage web with pages tailored to an organization's Web site.
Customer Support Web	Template	Creates a FrontPage web to help organizations improve a company's online customer support, particularly for software companies.
Share Point-based Team Web Site	Template	Creates a Web site for team collaboration with a team events calendar, library for shared documents, task list, and contact list. Must be created on a Web server.
Database Interface Wizard	Wizard	Creates a FrontPage Web site that allows you to connect to a database, and then view, update, delete, or add records.
Discussion Web Wizard	Wizard	Helps you create a discussion group with threads, a table of contents, and full-text searching.
Empty Web	Template	Creates a FrontPage web with nothing in it. Used to create a FrontPage web from scratch with no suggested content.
Import Web Wizard	Wizard	Imports an existing web into a new FrontPage web. Starts the Import Web Wizard, which guides you through the process of importing an existing Web site.
Personal Web	Template	Creates a FrontPage web with Web pages about individual's interests, photos, and favorite Web sites.
Project Web	Template	Creates a FrontPage web designed to support a project. The web includes pages for a list of members, a schedule, status, archive, and discussions.

After you create a page or web using a template, you can customize the page or web. To reduce the editing work required to finish your Web site, you should choose the template closest to your desired site design and structure. Because FrontPage creates many files for a web, it is advisable to create the project using the computer's hard drive (typically drive C:) rather than the floppy drive (A:). The following steps show how to use a template to create a FrontPage web.

Steps **To Use a Template to Create a FrontPage Web**

1 **Click the New Page button arrow on the Standard toolbar. Point to Web on the New Page menu.**

The New Page menu displays (Figure 1-12).

FIGURE 1-12

2 Click Web. When the Web Site Templates dialog box displays, click the Personal Web icon.

The Web Site Templates dialog box displays, prompting you for information needed to create a new FrontPage web. The Personal Web icon is selected; the Description area describes the web the Personal Web template creates. The Specify the location of the new web text box indicates the location where FrontPage will store the new web (Figure 1-13).

FIGURE 1-13

3 Click the Specify the location of the new web text box and select the default location text. Type C:\npatrio, or a location specified by your instructor, in the text box. Point to the OK button.

The new location displays in the text box. FrontPage will save the new web in the npatrio folder on drive C (Figure 1-14).

FIGURE 1-14

Click the OK button.

FrontPage begins creating a set of folders and making copies of the Web pages in the Personal Web template for you to customize. When finished, the FrontPage window displays in Page view (Figure 1-15).

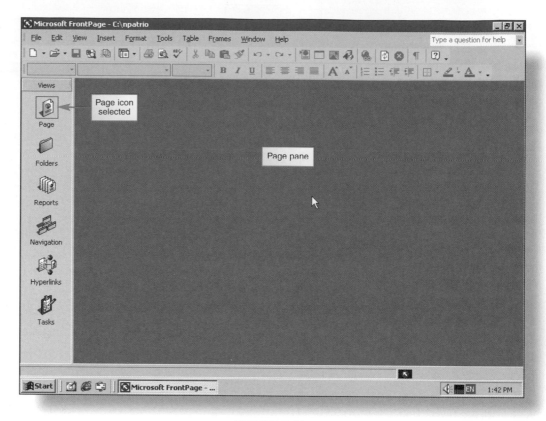

FIGURE 1-15

Other **Ways**

1. On File menu point to new, click Page or Web
2. In Voice Command mode, say "File, New, Page" or "File, New, Web"

While FrontPage is copying the Personal Web template pages, FrontPage briefly displays a Create New Web dialog box indicating that FrontPage is creating the new web in the folder, npatrio, on drive C and the status of the copying process.

Opening and Modifying a Web Page in Page View

After making a copy of the Personal Web template pages, the FrontPage window displays in **Page view**. The Page icon on the Views bar is inside a rectangle to indicate that Page view is selected. When a web is opened, the path and name of the web displays on the title bar. When you create a new web, FrontPage automatically creates certain files and folders, such as Web pages, images, and other files in the web. The **Page pane** displays the page currently being edited. If no page in the web is opened to edit, the Page pane is empty and appears dark gray. To list the file names of all of the files and folders in the current FrontPage web, you can display the Folder List pane, if it is not already displayed. You then can use the Folder List to select a page to edit. Perform the following steps to display the Folder List pane.

Steps **To Display the Folder List Pane**

1 **Click the Toggle Pane button arrow on the Standard toolbar. Point to Folder List on the Toggle Pane menu.**

The Toggle Pane menu displays (Figure 1-16).

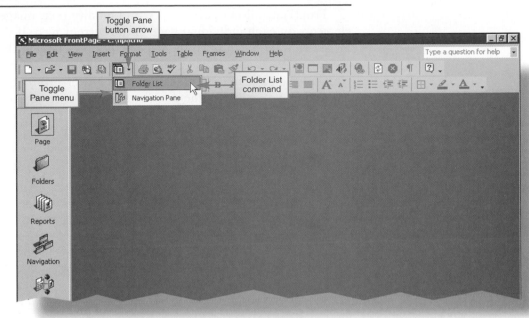

FIGURE 1-16

2 **Click Folder List.**

The Folder List pane displays (Figure 1-17). The Toggle Pane button can be used to hide or display the Folder List pane as needed.

FIGURE 1-17

Other **Ways**

1. Click the Toggle Pane button
2. Press ALT+V, press E
3. In Voice Command mode, say "View, Folder List"

Opening a Web Page in Page View

FrontPage allows you to open and modify text, images, tables, and other elements on each individual page in the current web. If the page is in the current web in any view, you can open the page by double-clicking the page's icon or file name. To open a Web page in Page view, for example, you simply double-click the file name of the page in the Folder List pane. After FrontPage displays the page in the Page pane, you can edit the page by selecting text, images, and other elements. The page being edited in Page view is referred to as the **active page** or **current page**. Once you open a page, the Page pane displays the active page as a tabbed page. The file name of the active page, such as index.htm, appears in the tab at the top of the Page pane. The following step shows how to open a Web page in Page view.

Steps **To Open a Web Page in Page View**

1 Double-click the file name, index.htm, in the Folder List pane.

The Home Page displays in the Page pane (Figure 1-18). The page contains place-holder text that you can edit to display your own message. A small pencil icon in the Folder List pane indicates that the Home Page file, named index.htm, is open. The flat **Normal tab** *at the bottom of the Page pane indicates that you can edit the page. The tab at the top of the Page pane shows the name of the file opened for edit.*

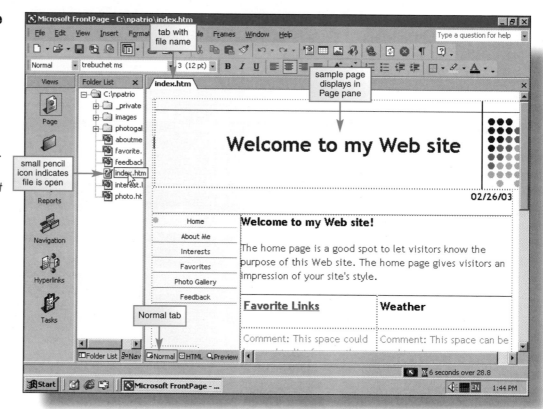

FIGURE 1-18

When you open a page in Page view, the page displays on the Normal tab in the Page pane. The Normal tab, which is the default tab in Page view, is a **WYSIWYG (What You See Is What You Get)** design tool that displays a page as it will appear in a Web browser. As you create or modify a Web page using the Normal tab, FrontPage displays the page as it will display on the Web, while generating the needed HTML code for you. If you insert an image on a page, for example, FrontPage automatically enters the proper HTML code (in this case, the <IMG> tag). Using FrontPage, you can insert text, images, hyperlinks, and other elements without having to type any HTML code.

As shown in Figure 1-18, the Folder List pane displays the pages and folders in the current web. When you first create a new Personal web, it contains three folders: images, _private, and photogallery — included in the Personal web. The **images folder** is a convenient place to store image files used in the FrontPage web. The **_private folder** holds files that you can use on the Web pages in the current web, but do not want people who are browsing your web to access individually. If you store a logo image in the _private folder, for example, you can use this on your Web pages, but others browsing your web cannot access the logo image. The **photogallery folder** is where FrontPage stores thumbnail images when a particular component, which is discussed later, is used. FrontPage also automatically creates a file named **index.htm** (or default.htm, depending on your server), which serves as the home page for your Web.

Applying a Theme to a FrontPage Web

When developing a web that consists of many pages, you should maintain a consistent, professional layout and design throughout all of the pages. The pages in a web, for example, should use similar features such as background color, margins, buttons, and headings. To help you create pages with a cohesive and professional appearance, FrontPage includes a gallery of more than 60 preset themes. A **theme** is a unified set of design elements and color schemes for bullets, fonts, graphics, navigation bars, and other page elements.

When applied to a web, a theme formats the Web page elements (images, backgrounds, text, and so on) so they share a consistent layout and design. You also have the option of applying themes to individual pages. The theme affects all aspects of a page's appearance, including text, color, and images, as follows:

▶ **Text:** A theme uses a unique set of fonts for the body text and headings.
▶ **Colors:** A theme uses a color scheme to set the color of body text, headings, hyperlinks, table borders, page background, and more.
▶ **Images:** A theme uses images (graphics) for several page elements, such as the background, bullets, horizontal rules, and more.

When you insert new elements on a page that uses a theme, FrontPage automatically formats those elements to match the theme. FrontPage also automatically applies the theme to any new pages you create in the web.

Each FrontPage template uses a default theme. When you selected the Personal Web template in the previous set of steps, FrontPage automatically applied a theme to the web. The steps on the next page show how to preview the default theme used for the web, apply a new theme to the web, and then preview the new theme applied to your web.

More *About*

Additional Themes

The list of available themes on your computer may be much shorter than the list illustrated in this project. If Install Additional Themes displays in the Themes list, it indicates that only the typical themes were installed initially. To install the remaining themes, click Install Additional Themes and then click the Yes button. FrontPage will prompt you to insert the FrontPage CD-ROM and will guide you through the installation of the remaining themes.

To Apply a Theme to a FrontPage Web

1 **Click Format on the menu bar and then point to Theme (Figure 1-19).**

FIGURE 1-19

2 **Click Theme. Scroll to and then point to Poetic in the Themes list.**

The Themes dialog box displays. The Sample of Theme area allows you to preview a sample page using the currently selected theme. The Themes list box lists all of the themes provided with FrontPage (Figure 1-20).

FIGURE 1-20

3 Click Poetic in the Themes list. If necessary, click All pages in the Apply Theme to area. Click Vivid colors. Point to the OK button.

The All pages option button and the Vivid colors check box are selected. FrontPage displays a sample page in the Sample of Theme area of the Themes dialog box to show how the Poetic theme will apply a color scheme, background image, and headings to a Web page (Figure 1-21).

FIGURE 1-21

4 Click the OK button. If a Microsoft FrontPage dialog box displays, click the Yes button.

FrontPage displays a message on the status bar, indicating that FrontPage is applying the new theme to all pages in the web. When finished, FrontPage displays in Page view. The active page, index.htm, displays in the Page pane with the Poetic theme background (Figure 1-22).

FIGURE 1-22

Other Ways

1. Press ALT+O, press H
2. In Voice Command mode, say "Format, Theme"

The **Themes dialog box** (Figure 1-20 on page FP 1.26) contains options you can select to control how the current web uses themes. As you saw in Step 3, clicking the **All pages** option button instructs FrontPage to apply the theme to every page in the current web. Selecting the **Vivid colors** check box changes the theme's normal set of colors to a brighter color scheme. Selecting the **Active graphics** check box animates certain graphic elements. Selecting the **Background picture** check box applies a textured background image to the pages in the current web. Clicking the **Modify button** allows you to modify the color, graphics, and text of the selected theme.

While applying a theme to a web, FrontPage displays information about the operation in progress on the status bar. Depending on the number of pages in the web, this process can take anywhere from a few seconds to a few minutes. When FrontPage has applied the theme to every page in the current web, FrontPage displays in Page view. Once the theme is applied, FrontPage changes the background, fonts, and graphics used in the web. Applying the Poetic theme, for example, adds a swirl pattern to the white background.

If you want to add your own graphics or color sets to a preset theme, you can change and customize the theme. You can change a theme's background picture or heading font, for example, to create a new theme that displays a company logo on every page.

Editing Text on a Web Page

As you have learned, a FrontPage template is a series of linked Web pages that are organized and formatted with a basic framework of content upon which you can base new pages and new FrontPage webs. To help you design your own Web page, the template Web pages include placeholders for basic page elements such as headings, formatted text, images, and hyperlinks.

Adding your own content to the page involves editing one or more placeholders to convey the desired information – or deleting them altogether. On the home page of your Personal web, for example, you will want to edit the text to introduce yourself, delete any unneeded text, and add new text to complete the page. Perform the following steps to edit text on a Web page.

Steps **To Edit Text on a Web Page**

1 Position the insertion point at the beginning of the second paragraph, which begins with the text, The home page is a good spot... (Figure 1-23).

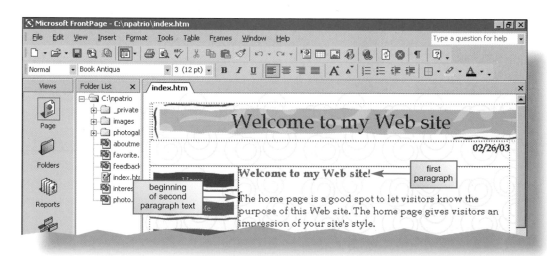

FIGURE 1-23

2 **Drag through the text to select it.**

The selected text is highlighted (Figure 1-24).

FIGURE 1-24

3 **Type** My name is Nikki Patrio and I am a student at Hilltop Community College. **as the second paragraph. (You may substitute your personal information here.)**

The replacement text replaces the selected text (Figure 1-25). The asterisk in the tab indicates changes made to the page are not yet saved.

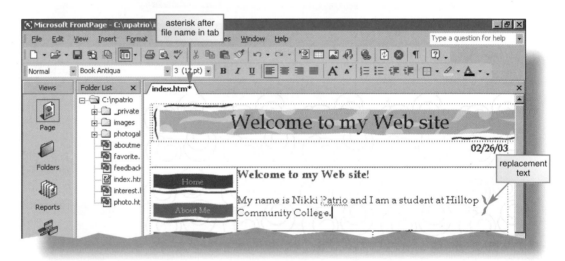

FIGURE 1-25

In the previous steps, you edited a section of the placeholder text on the template page, which now displays your desired information. The other text sections remain unchanged.

Using FrontPage, you can edit and add text just as you would with word processing software. To begin editing, you position the insertion point where you want to make a change and then perform the desired action. You even can move around the text using your mouse or the arrow keys. If you make a mistake typing, you can use the BACKSPACE key or the DELETE key to correct the mistake.

Adding New Text to a Web Page

If you want to include additional text beyond that contained in the template, you can add new text to the Web page. Just as you add new text to a word processing document, you add new text to a Web page by positioning the insertion point where you want the text to display and then typing the text. The steps on the next page show you how to add text to a Web page.

Steps **To Add New Text to a Web Page**

1 **Press the ENTER key to start a new paragraph below the second paragraph.**

The insertion point displays at the beginning of the new paragraph (Figure 1-26).

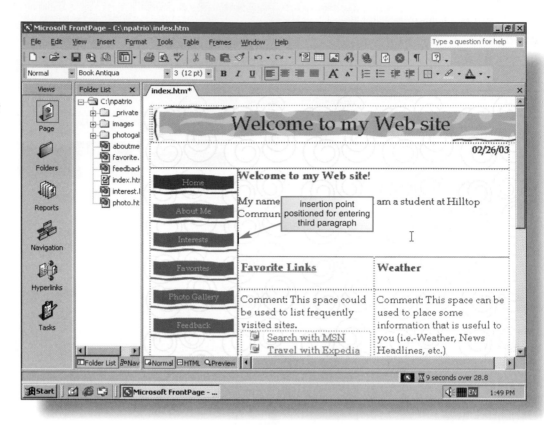

FIGURE 1-26

2 **Type** I am learning to create Web sites, and this is my first one! **as the third paragraph.**

The new text displays as the third paragraph on the Web page (Figure 1-27).

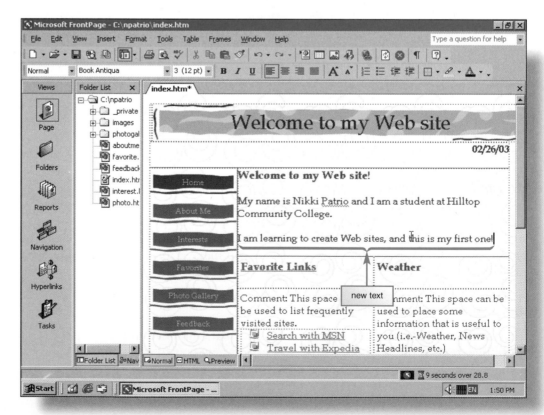

FIGURE 1-27

3 **Press the ENTER key to start a new paragraph. Type** Follow the links to learn more about my interests and to see some of my favorite Web sites. **as the fourth paragraph.**

The inserted text automatically wraps to the next line as you type (Figure 1-28).

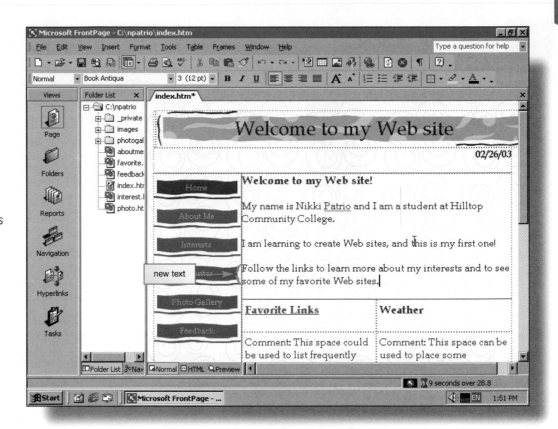

FIGURE 1-28

Editing and adding text on a Web page using FrontPage is similar to editing a word processing document. On the Normal tab of Page view, you can insert, delete, cut, copy, and paste text, just as you would with word processing software.

As with many word processing applications, FrontPage automatically checks your spelling as you type and underlines misspelled words with a red wavy line. In the Home Page, for example, the spell checker does not recognize the word, Patrio, and thus underlines it with a red wavy line. To add an unrecognized word to the spell checker dictionary, right-click the underlined word and then click Add to dictionary on the shortcut menu. To correct a misspelled word, right-click the underlined word and then click the correct spelling on the shortcut menu.

Deleting Text Positioned with Tables

Often, cells in a table are used in a Web page to position textual elements. A table may contain only a single cell with text, multiple cells containing text, or it may contain another nested table. A table contained within another table is called a **nested** table. Although tables are discussed in a later project, the template used for this page incorporates tables to position some sections of text and also contains some nested tables. Because some of these tables and cells are not used in the Web you are developing, they should be deleted. Use the steps on the next page to select the tables and cells to be deleted.

Steps **To Select Tables and Cells**

1 **Click in the cell that contains the text, Favorite Links.**

The insertion point displays at the end of the text (Figure 1-29).

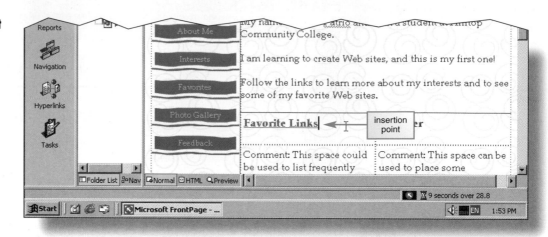

FIGURE 1-29

2 **Click Table on the menu bar and then point to Select. Point to Table on the Select submenu.**

The Table menu and the Select submenu display (Figure 1-30).

FIGURE 1-30

3 **Click Table.**

The selected cells are highlighted (Figure 1-31).

1. Click top-left cell in table, SHIFT+click bottom-right cell in table
2. Click cell in table, press ALT+A, press C, press T
3. Click cell in table, in Voice Command mode, say "Table, Select, Table"

FIGURE 1-31

You should exercise care in selecting the table cells you want to delete. Because tables often are nested, you inadvertently may select material that you want to keep. Verify that the selected cells and/or tables are correct and then perform the following steps to delete the selected tables and cells.

 To Delete Selected Tables and Cells

1 **Right-click one of the selected cells. Point to Delete Cells on the shortcut menu.**

The shortcut menu displays (Figure 1-32).

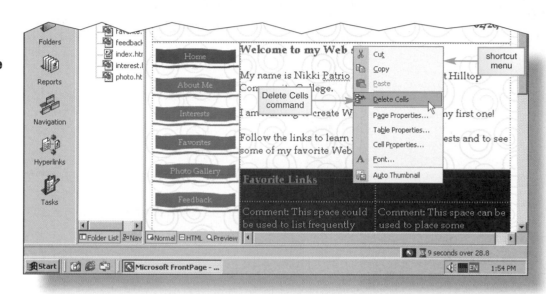

FIGURE 1-32

2 **Click Delete Cells.**

The selected cells are deleted (Figure 1-33).

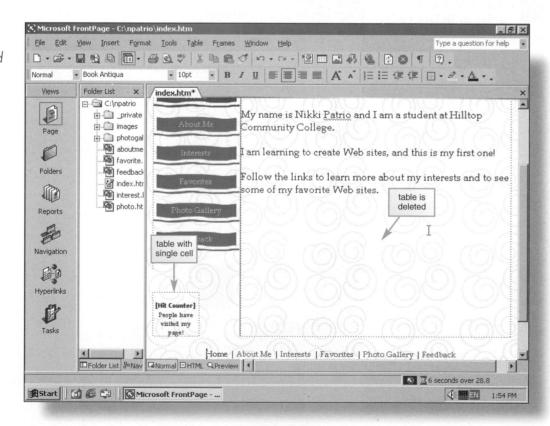

FIGURE 1-33

3 **Position the mouse pointer above the table with a single cell containing the text, People have visited my page!**

The mouse pointer becomes a down-pointing arrow (Figure 1-34).

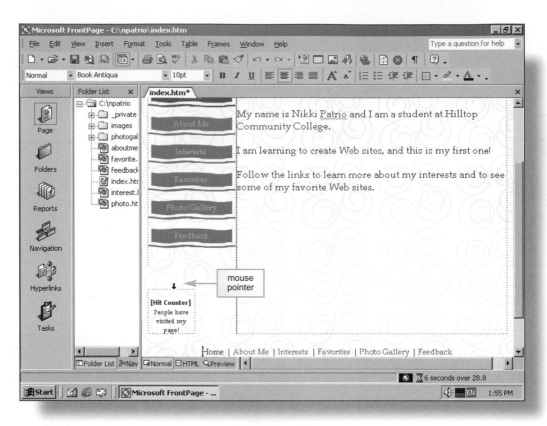

FIGURE 1-34

4 **Right-click and point to Delete Cells on the shortcut menu.**

The Table is selected and the shortcut menu displays (Figure 1-35).

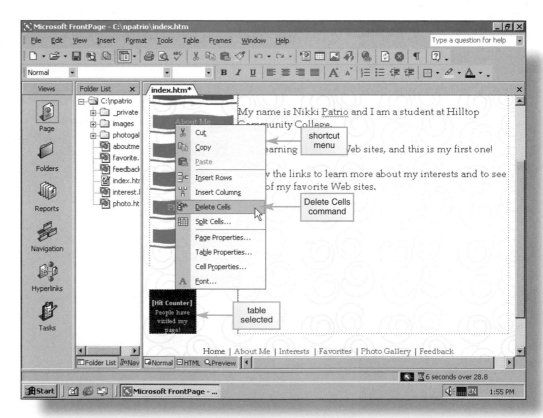

FIGURE 1-35

5 **Click Delete Cells.**

The selected table is deleted (Figure 1-36).

FIGURE 1-36

Other Ways

1. On Table menu click Delete Cells
2. Press ALT+A, press D
3. In Voice Command mode, say "Table, Delete Cells"

Editing a Bulleted List

In the previous steps, you edited the file, index.htm, which FrontPage created as the default home page. To complete the web, you need to edit the other pages in the web. The template for the Interest page, for example, includes a bulleted list of interests for customization.

Recall that a bulleted list is an unordered list of items, which usually uses small icons called bullets to indicate each item in the list. In Page view, you can edit the bulleted list on the Interests page, changing, adding, and deleting items as needed to customize it to your interests. Complete the following steps to edit the bulleted list.

Steps | To Edit a Bulleted List

1 **Double-click the file name, interest.htm, in the Folder List pane.**

The Interests page displays on the Normal tab in the Page pane (Figure 1-37). The template for the Interests page includes a bulleted list of items; a bullet image precedes each item in the list. In the Folder List, a small pencil displays on the icon next to the file name, interest.htm, to indicate that the file is open. Also, tabs at the top of the page indicate the pages currently opened for edit.

FIGURE 1-37

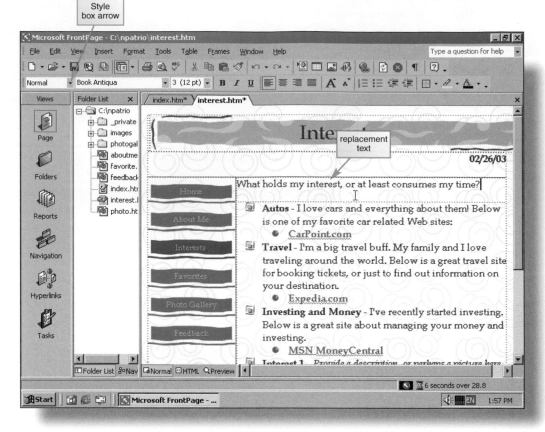

2 Drag through the first line of text that begins, Here is a good place, to select it. Type **What holds my interest, or at least consumes my time?** as the new text.

The replacement text replaces the selected text (Figure 1-38).

FIGURE 1-38

3 Drag through the text just entered to select it. Click the Style box arrow. If necessary, scroll down, and then point to Heading 3 in the Style list.

The Style list displays. It contains a list of styles for text, such as lists, headings, and normal text (Figure 1-39).

FIGURE 1-39

4 Click Heading 3 in the Style list.

The selected text displays with a style of Heading 3 (Figure 1-40).

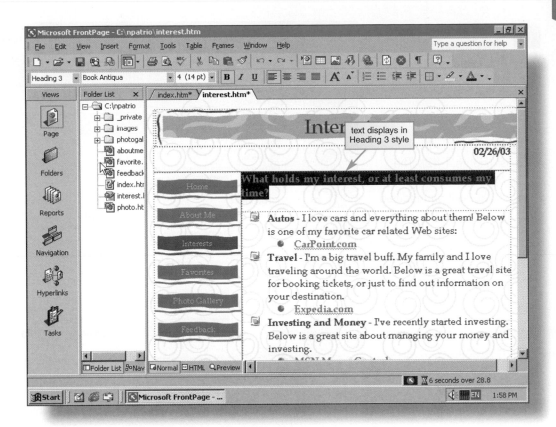

FIGURE 1-40

5 Drag through the text of the first line in the bulleted list to select it. Type Botany - Of course! I'm a botany major! Do you want to know what botany majors do after graduation? Follow the link below to read about careers in botany. **as the first item.**

The replacement text replaces the place holder text in the bulleted list (Figure 1-41).

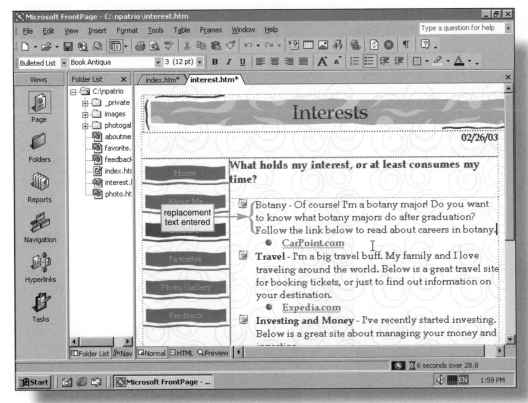

FIGURE 1-41

6 Drag through the first hyperlink to select it and then type `Botany.org` **as the new link.**

The replacement text replaces the hyperlink text in the bulleted list (Figure 1-42). The actual hyperlink has not changed, but will be modified later.

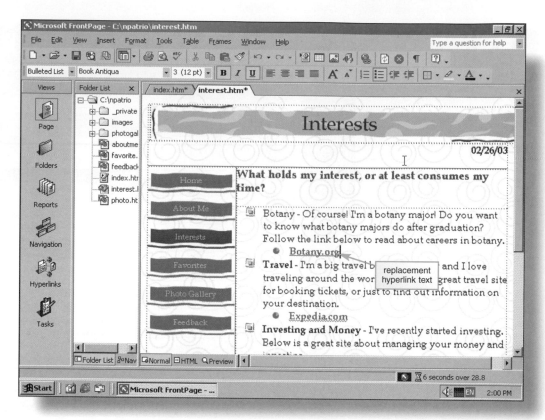

FIGURE 1-42

7 Drag through the remaining lines of text in the bulleted list and their respective hyperlinks, **then type** `Travel - I love to travel, but I have to keep it on a budget!` **as the second item. Press the ENTER key.**

The replacement text replaces the placeholder text in the bulleted list (Figure 1-43). A third bullet displays below the last item in the list.

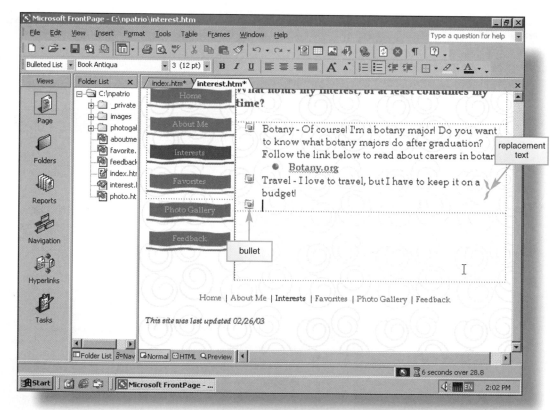

FIGURE 1-43

8 **Type** Classical Arts - I enjoy classical music, poetry, and art. **as the next item in the bulleted list. Press the ENTER key.**

The new text displays next to the bullet as the next item in the bulleted list (Figure 1-44).

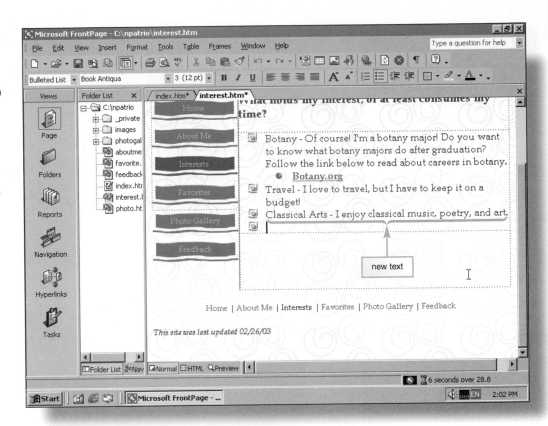

FIGURE 1-44

9 **Type** Web Pages - I'm learning to build my own Web site, so these pages are certain to be under construction for some time. **as the last item in the bulleted list.**

The new text displays next to the bullet as the last item in the bulleted list (Figure 1-45).

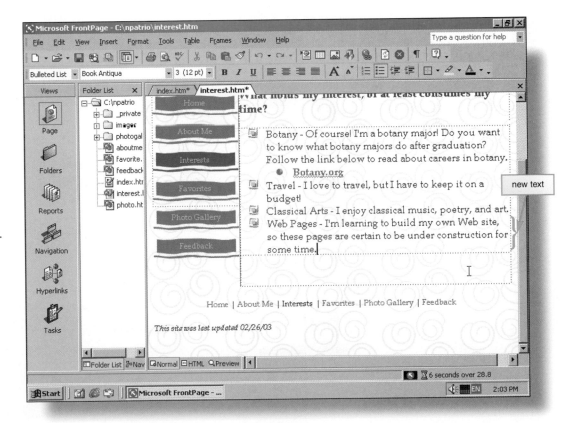

FIGURE 1-45

10 Select the word, Botany, just after the first bullet. Point to the Bold button on the Formatting toolbar (Figure 1-46).

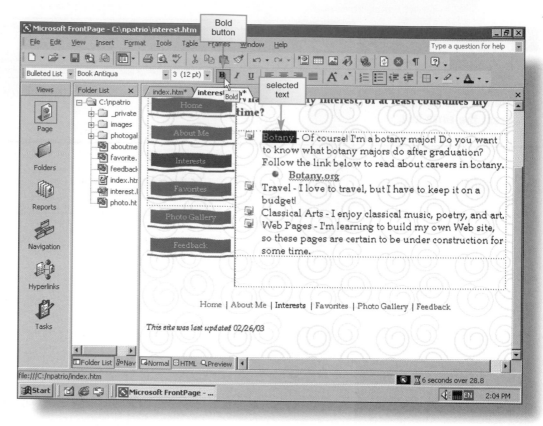

FIGURE 1-46

11 Click the Bold button. Select the word, Travel, just after the second bullet.

The word Botany displays in bold text in the bulleted list (Figure 1-47).

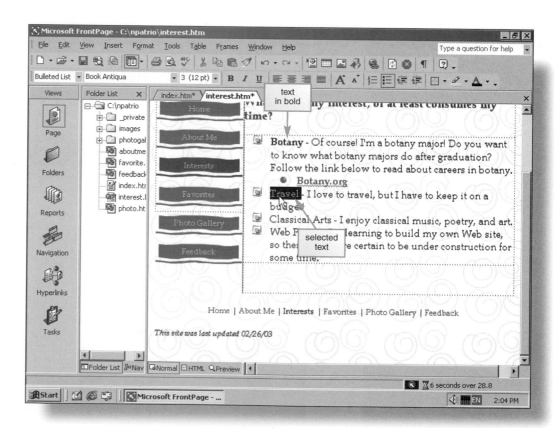

FIGURE 1-47

12 Repeat Step 11 to bold the word, Travel, just after the second bullet; the words, Classical Arts, just after the third bullet; and the words, Web Pages, just after the fourth bullet.

The modified words display in bold next to their respective bullets in the bulleted list (Figure 1-48).

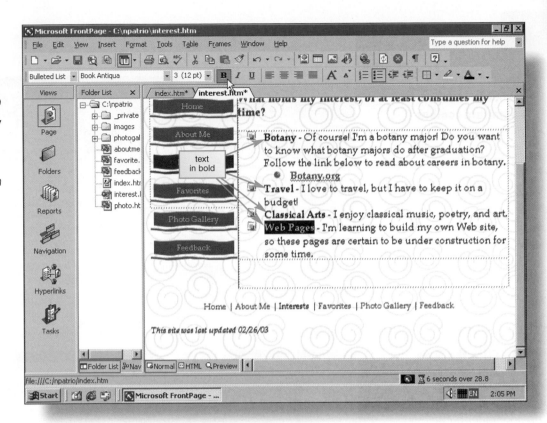

FIGURE 1-48

You have edited the items in a bulleted list successfully, deleted some items, added two items to the list, and modified some text properties. As you add text and make edits to a Web page, FrontPage automatically generates HTML source code that defines how the Web page will display on the Web. To see how your changes will display on the Web, you can click the Preview tab to preview the Web page. Before previewing the page, however, you should save your work to retain any changes.

Saving a Web Page

FrontPage allows you to save a Web page to many different locations, including the current web, a different Web, or a location on a network. To save a Web page to the current web, use the Save button on the Standard toolbar. Complete the steps on the next page to save the Web page to the current web.

Steps **To Save a Web Page**

1 **Point to the Save button on the Standard toolbar (Figure 1-49).**

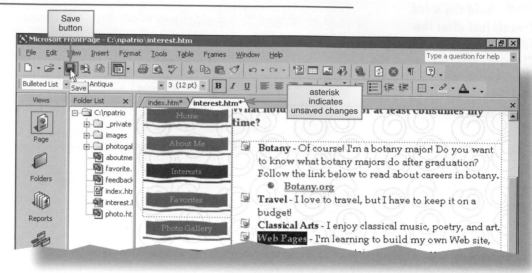

FIGURE 1-49

2 **Click the Save button.**

The Web page is saved in the npatrio folder on drive C. Note that the asterisk following the file name interest.htm in the tab has disappeared (Figure 1-50). The file name index.htm still has an asterisk, indicating that the page has changes that have not yet been saved.

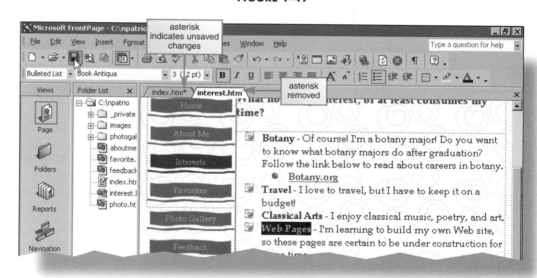

FIGURE 1-50

3 **Click the tab index.htm at the top of the Page pane. Click the Save button on the Standard toolbar.**

Changes to the Home Page are saved in the npatrio folder on drive C (Figure 1-51).

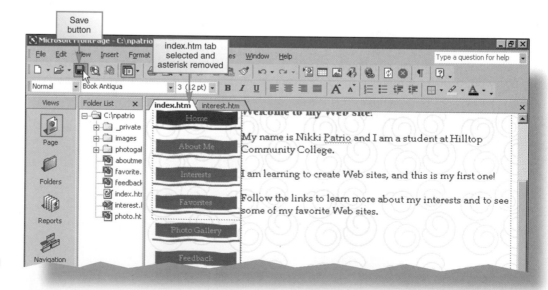

FIGURE 1-51

Clicking the **Save button** on the Standard toolbar saves the active page in HTML format, using the default file name, interest.htm. Because the Web page was opened from the current web, FrontPage saves the page without prompting you for a file name or file location. If you save a new Web page, clicking the Save button will cause FrontPage to display a Save As dialog box that prompts you to enter a file name. When you save a Web page, FrontPage also will prompt you to save any new images, sound files, or other objects to the same location as the page.

Once you have saved a Web page, you can preview how the page will display when viewed on the World Wide Web.

Other Ways

1. On File menu click Save
2. Press CTRL+S
3. In Voice Command mode, say "File, Save"

Previewing a Web Page Using the Preview Tab

Clicking the **Preview tab** allows you to preview your page as it will display when viewed by a site visitor. To preview the page, you may click the Preview tab in Page view. FrontPage will not display a Preview tab if you have not installed Microsoft Internet Explorer version 3.0 or later on your computer. In such a case, you can click **Preview in Browser** on the File menu. The following steps show how to preview the page using the Preview tab.

Steps **To Preview a Web Page Using the Preview Tab**

1 **In Page view, click the Preview tab at the bottom of the Page pane.**

FrontPage displays the Web page on the Preview tab in the Page pane (Figure 1-52). The Preview tab displays how the page will display on the Web when viewed with a Web browser.

2 **When you have finished viewing the Web page, click the Normal tab.**

The Web page displays in the Normal tab in the Page pane. With FrontPage, most Web page development and design takes place in the Normal tab in Page view.

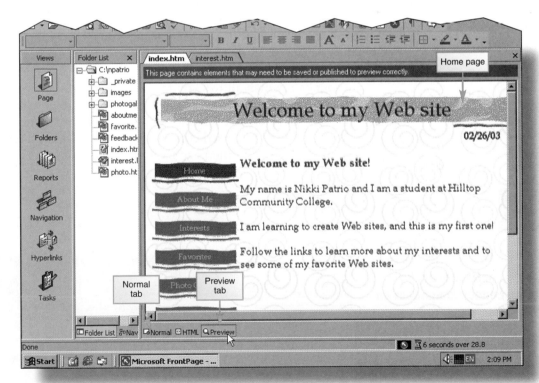

FIGURE 1-52

Other Ways

1. On Normal tab in Page view, press CTRL+PAGE UP
2. On HTML tab in Page view, press CTRL+PAGE DOWN

When you display a page on the Preview tab, a comment at the top of the Page pane may indicate that the page contains some elements that may need to be saved or published to preview correctly. Some elements, such as Link bars, may not display properly until viewed on the Web. While it does not offer perfect viewing, using the Preview tab does eliminate the need to save a partially completed Web page continuously, preview it in your Web browser to test it, return to FrontPage to make changes, and so on.

Before you publish your web, you may want to add other elements to the page, such as a Link bar or a graphical page banner. In FrontPage, you can add elements such as these using built-in FrontPage objects, called components.

Modifying Components

An active element, called a **component**, is a dynamic, built-in FrontPage object that is evaluated and executed when you save the page or, in some cases, when you display the page in a Web browser. Most components generate HTML automatically using the text, image files, and other items you supply. Examples of FrontPage Web components include a **Hit counter component** that keeps track of the number of visitors to a Web site and a **Photo Gallery component** that arranges a group of thumbnail images of photos on a page.

When working on a web, you easily can identify a component. Position the mouse pointer on the component and the shape of the pointer changes to look like a hand holding a written list.

A commonly used Web component is a Link bar. In FrontPage, a **Link bar** is a collection of graphical or textual buttons each containing a link to related Web pages in the current FrontPage web. The Poetic theme you applied to the web includes a Link bar on the left side of the page. The Link bar may be used for **parent-child navigation**, which allows you to move between the Home Page (the parent) and the Interests page or Favorites page (the children), or for **same-level navigation**, which allows you to move back and forth between the Interests and Favorites pages. Another commonly used component is a page banner. The following steps show you how to modify the page banner in the current web.

Steps **To Modify a Page Banner**

1 **Position the mouse pointer over the page banner component on the Home page.**

The mouse pointer changes shape to indicate that the designated item is a component (Figure 1-53).

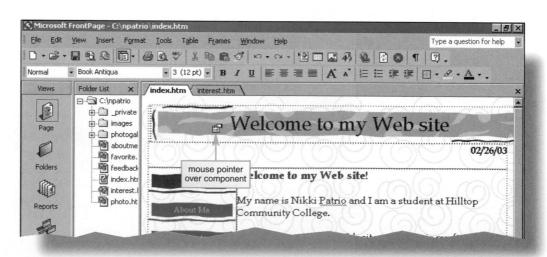

FIGURE 1-53

2   **Right-click the page banner and point to Page Banner Properties on the shortcut menu.**

The shortcut menu displays (Figure 1-54).

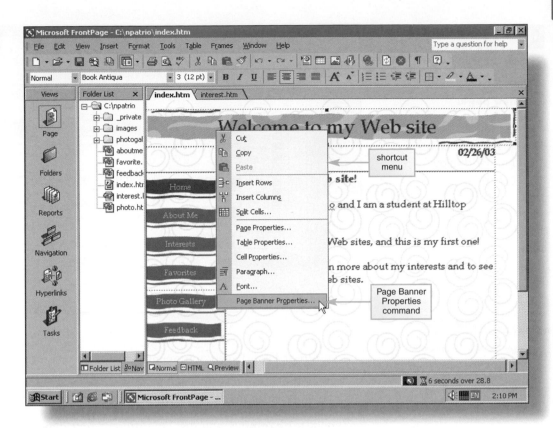

FIGURE 1-54

3   **Click Page Banner Properties. When the Page Banner Properties dialog box displays, select the text in the Page banner text box. Type** Welcome to Nikki's Web Site **as the replacement text. If necessary, click Picture in the Properties area. Point to the OK button.**

The new page banner text is entered (Figure 1-55).

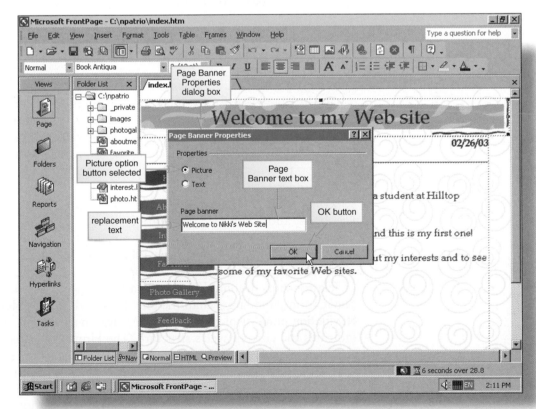

FIGURE 1-55

Microsoft **FrontPage 2002**

4 **Click the OK button. Click the Save button on the Standard toolbar to save the modified page.**

After the save process is complete, the modified page banner displays (Figure 1-56).

FIGURE 1-56

Other **Ways**

1. Double-click component

Different FrontPage components have different properties. The options that display in the component Properties dialog boxes vary, based on the properties of each specific component. Most FrontPage components change automatically in response to changes you make in the FrontPage web. The page banner you just changed, for example, will display different text depending on the page title, on all pages where a page banner has been inserted and which have been included in your Web site navigation structure.

Deleting a Web Page from a Web

FrontPage provides several ways to delete pages from a current web. You can delete a page in Page view, for example, by selecting in the Folder List pane the file name of the page to delete and pressing the DELETE key. By holding down the CTRL key, you can select multiple files to delete at the same time. You also can delete individual pages in Navigation view by clicking the appropriate page icon and then clicking Delete on the shortcut menu. Finally, by selecting the Navigation tab at the bottom of the Folder List pane, you can see a smaller Navigation Pane from where you can select and delete individual pages. In this project, you will delete the Photo Gallery, Feedback, and About Me pages in Navigation view to create a web with three pages: a Home page, an Interests page, and a Favorites page.

In FrontPage, **Navigation view** allows you to create, change, display, and print a web's structure and navigation. As previously discussed, a web's structure is the set of relationships among the pages in a FrontPage web; Navigation view includes a Navigation pane larger than the one displayed in the Folder List pane. This **Navigation pane** displays a graphical diagram similar to an organization chart that indicates the current web's structure. The Home page displays at the top (parent) level of the chart, and linked pages display at the lower (child) levels. You may choose to rotate the navigation structure to either a portrait or a landscape view by clicking the Portrait/Landscape button on the Navigation toolbar. You also may choose to view the Folder List pane while in Navigation view by clicking View on the menu bar and then clicking Folder List.

Making changes to the web's structure in Navigation view, such as deleting a page, allows you to see immediately how the change affects the structure. Complete the following steps to delete the Photo Gallery, Feedback, and About Me pages from the current web.

 To Delete a Web Page from a Web

1 **Click the Navigation icon on the Views bar. If necessary, click the Toggle Pane button on the Standard toolbar to display the Folder List pane.**

The current web displays in Navigation view, showing a graphical diagram of the web structure of the current web (Figure 1-57). A rectangular page icon represents each page in the web. The Folder List pane displays the file names for the pages in the Web. The Navigation toolbar displays under the Formatting toolbar. All buttons on the Formatting toolbar are dimmed, which indicates they currently are unavailable.

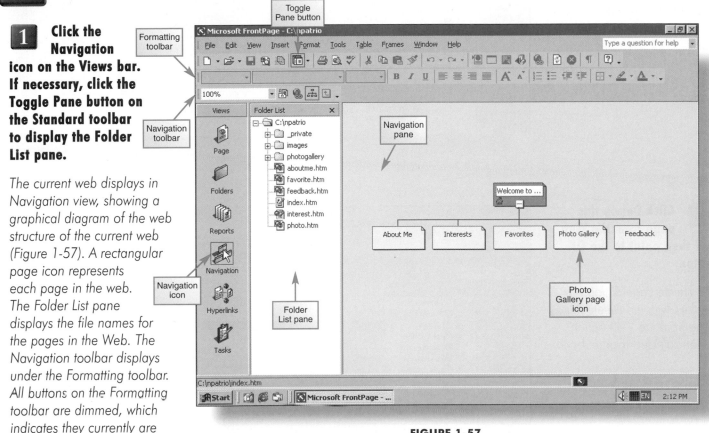

FIGURE 1-57

2 **Right-click the Photo Gallery page icon. Point to Delete on the shortcut menu.**

A shortcut menu displays (Figure 1-58). The shortcut menu contains commands to manage individual pages within a FrontPage web.

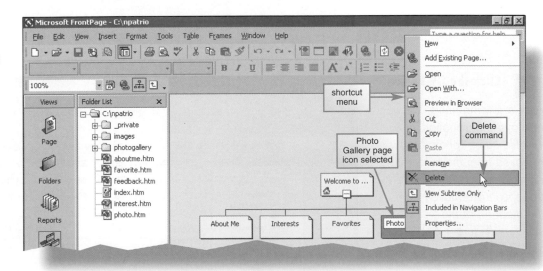

FIGURE 1-58

3 **Click Delete on the shortcut menu.**

The Delete Page dialog box displays, asking you what you want to do (Figure 1-59). The dialog box provides two options: you can remove this page from all navigation bars or delete the page from the web.

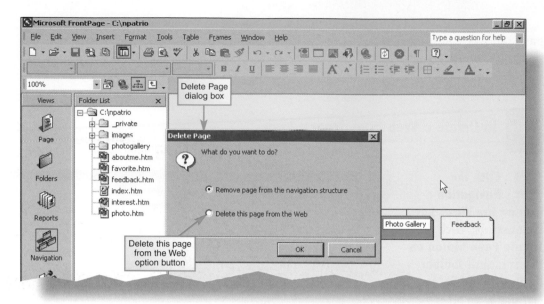

FIGURE 1-59

4 **Click Delete this page from the Web and then point to the OK button.**

The Delete Page dialog box displays with the Delete this page from the Web option button selected (Figure 1-60).

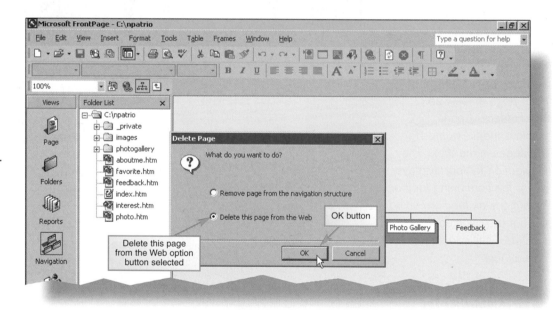

FIGURE 1-60

5 **Click the OK button.**

After a few moments, the web displays in Navigation view. The file name (photo.htm) is removed from the Folder List pane, and the Photo Gallery page icon is removed from the diagram of the web structure (Figure 1-61).

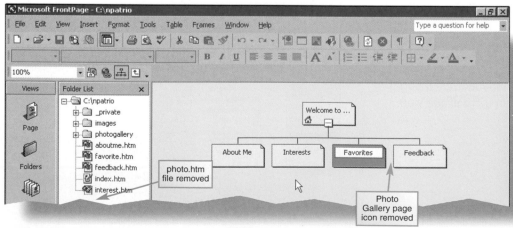

FIGURE 1-61

6 **Repeat steps 2 through 5 for the About Me page and the Feedback page.**

The web displays in Navigation view with the About Me and the Feedback page icons removed. The file names aboutme.htm and feedback.htm are removed from the Folder List pane (Figure 1-62).

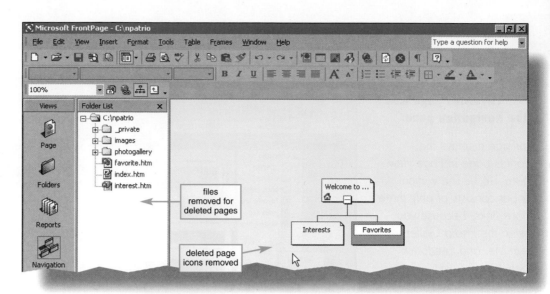

FIGURE 1-62

Other Ways

1. On Edit menu click Delete
2. Click file name in Folder List pane, press DELETE key
3. Right-click file name in Folder List pane, click Delete on shortcut menu
4. Click page icon in Navigation pane, press DELETE key
5. In Voice Command mode, say "Edit, Delete" or say "Delete"

If you choose to remove a Web page from the navigation structure, the Web page still exists on disk and can be linked to other pages. If you choose to delete a page from the web, as you did in the previous steps, the Web page is deleted from disk and removed from all Link bars.

When you make changes to your web's navigation structure in Navigation view — for example, adding or deleting a page from the structure, or creating a new page — those changes are saved automatically when you switch to another view, such as Page view. You also can open files from Navigation view by double-clicking the page icon. Double-clicking the Favorites page icon, for example, will open the Favorites page so you can edit the final page in the current web.

Managing Hyperlinks on a Web Page

The final page to edit is the Favorites page, which contains hyperlinks to some of Nikki's favorite Web sites. Because you are using a template, the page already includes some placeholder hyperlinks. You can edit the links much like you edited the bulleted list on the Interests page.

Recall that a hyperlink, or link, is an area of the page that you click to instruct the browser to go to a location in a file or to request a file from a server. Often, a hyperlink consists of text or a picture that is associated with a URL that points to a page on the World Wide Web. Using FrontPage, you can create text or image links on your Web page. Adding a hyperlink to a Web page involves inserting text or an image on a Web page and then associating the text or image with a URL.

FrontPage provides several ways to associate a URL with the text or image on a Web page. You can type the URL, select a file within the current web or on your computer, or specify an e-mail link. You also can browse the Web to display the page to which you want to hyperlink; FrontPage automatically displays the URL in the appropriate text box.

To learn how to manage hyperlinks on a Web page, you will edit the existing hyperlinks on the Favorites page and the Interests page, and then add a new hyperlink. Complete the steps on the next page to change an existing hyperlink on a Web page.

Microsoft FrontPage 2002

Steps | **To Change a Hyperlink on a Web Page**

1 **Double-click the Favorites page icon in the Navigation pane.**

FrontPage displays the Favorites page in Page view (Figure 1-63). The vertical Link bar consists of only three buttons links, because you deleted the Photo Gallery, About Me, and Feedback pages.

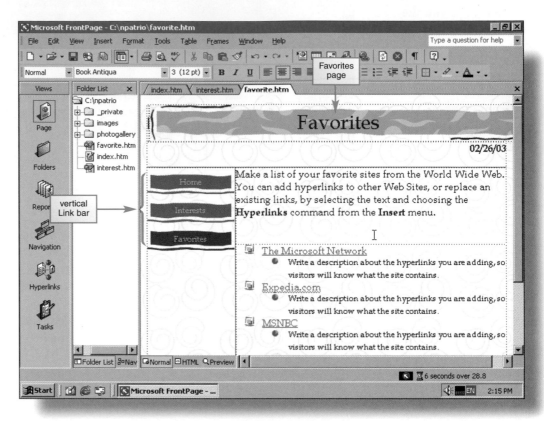

FIGURE 1-63

2 **Select the first paragraph of text, which begins with, Make a list of your favorite sites. Click the Style box arrow on the Formatting toolbar and then click Heading 3. Type** These are some of my favorite sites on the World Wide Web. **as the replacement text. Press the DELETE key twice.**

The replacement text replaces the placeholder text and extra blank lines are deleted (Figure 1-64). The list entries are underlined, which identifies them as hyperlinks.

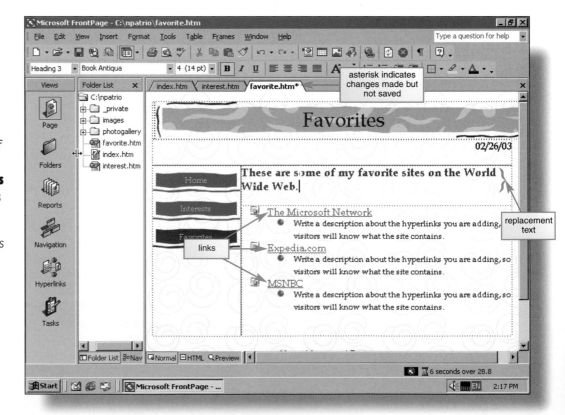

FIGURE 1-64

3 **Below the first hyperlink, select the text that begins with, Write a description.** Type MSN is great for all kinds of information, searching for bargains, and staying in contact with friends. **as the replacement text.**

The replacement text replaces the placeholder text (Figure 1-65).

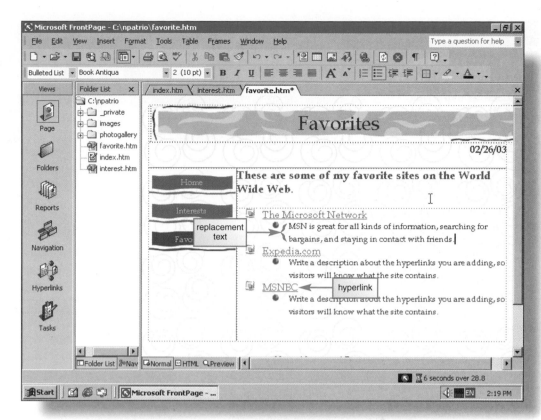

FIGURE 1-65

4 **Click the second hyperlink text, which reads, Expedia.com, to select it. Click the Insert Hyperlink button on the Standard toolbar.**

The Edit Hyperlink dialog box displays, with the current URL, http://www.expedia .com, in the Address box (Figure 1-66). The Edit Hyperlink dialog box contains options that allow you to change the current URL and specify the URL of the Web resource to which you want to link.

FIGURE 1-66

5 **Select Expedia.com in the Text to display text box. Type** American Poets **as the replacement hyperlink text. Select the text, http://www.expedia.com, in the Address box. Type** http://www.poets.org **as the new URL. Point to the OK button.**

The Edit Hyperlink dialog box displays with the replacement hyperlink text replacing the placeholder hyperlink text and the URL for The Academy of American Poets in the URL text box (Figure 1-67).

FIGURE 1-67

6 **Click the OK button. Position the mouse pointer on the American Poets hyperlink.**

American Poets displays as the hyperlink text for the second item in the Favorites list. The URL for the American Poets Web page displays on the status bar (Figure 1-68). A ScreenTip prompts you to press CTRL+click to follow a hyperlink.

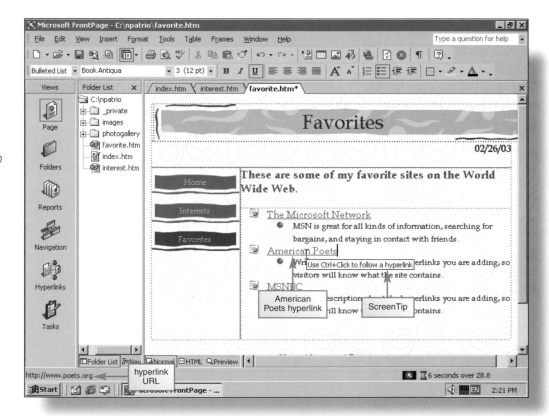

FIGURE 1-68

7 Repeat steps 3 through 6 to replace the text below the American Poets hyperlink with For locating works of American poets, as well as others, visit the Academy of American Poets Web site., the hyperlink text for MSNBC with The Mad Scientist Network, and http://www.madsci.org for the URL. Replace the text below The Mad Scientist Network hyperlink with The Mad Scientist Network is the place where you can get answers to your science questions.

The replacement text and hyperlinks replace the original placeholder text and hyperlinks (Figure 1-69).

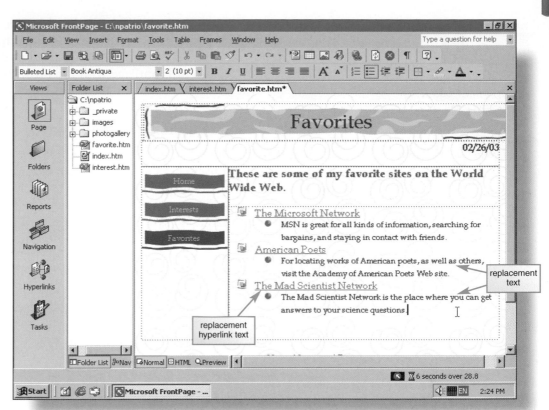

FIGURE 1-69

8 Save the changes to this page by clicking the Save button on the Standard toolbar. Click the interest.htm tab to view the Interests page. Replace the URL for the link Botany.org with http://www.botany.org and then click the Save button on the Standard toolbar to save the changes to the page. Position the mouse pointer on the Botany.org hyperlink.

The hyperlink URL displays on the status bar (Figure 1-70).

FIGURE 1-70

You also can edit a URL by clicking the World Wide Web button in the Edit Hyperlink dialog box and browsing the Web to locate the Web resource to which you want to link. Once the desired page is displayed in the browser (Internet Explorer) window, return to FrontPage with the browser still open and the browser automatically will return the URL of the current page to the Address list box.

Adding an E-Mail Hyperlink to a Web Page

Using the Edit Hyperlink dialog box, you also can create e-mail hyperlinks in a Web page. When a user clicks an **e-mail hyperlink** on your Web page, the Web browser will start the designated e-mail program, such as Microsoft Outlook Express, and prompt the user to enter a message. The message automatically is addressed to the e-mail address specified in the e-mail hyperlink. Many Web pages include e-mail hyperlinks to allow visitors to send questions, comments, or requests via e-mail, simply by clicking the e-mail hyperlink.

E-mail hyperlinks use the **mailto protocol**, which is an Internet protocol used to send electronic mail. Because not all Web browsers and e-mail programs support the mailto protocol, you should specify the e-mail address somewhere on the Web page. The easiest way to do this is to use the e-mail address as the hyperlink text for the e-mail hyperlink. Complete the following steps to add an e-mail hyperlink to a Web page.

Steps **To Add an E-Mail Hyperlink to a Web Page**

1 **Click the tab named index.htm at the top of the Page pane. Position the insertion point at the end of the fourth paragraph, which begins, Follow the links to learn more about. Press the ENTER key. Type** You may send an e-mail to me at nikkipatrio@hcc.edu. **as the new text.**

The Home Page displays in the Page pane (Figure 1-71). Using the e-mail address as the e-mail hyperlink text provides a quick way for users to identify your e-mail address.

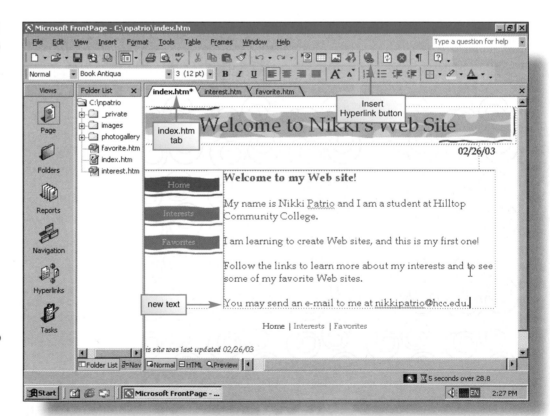

FIGURE 1-71

2 Drag through the text, nikkipatrio@hcc.edu, to select it. Click the Insert Hyperlink button on the Standard toolbar. When the Insert Hyperlink dialog box displays, point to the E-mail Address button on the Link to bar.

The Insert Hyperlink dialog box displays (Figure 1-72). The E-mail Address button is selected.

FIGURE 1-72

3 Click the E-mail Address button. Type nikkipatrio@hcc.edu in the E-mail address text box. Point to the OK button.

The complete e-mail hyperlink displays in the URL text box (Figure 1-73). FrontPage automatically adds the mailto protocol before the e-mail address. It instructs the Web browser to start the designated e-mail program and address the message to the indicated e-mail address.

FIGURE 1-73

4 | **Click the OK button. Position the mouse pointer on the e-mail hyperlink.**

The e-mail hyperlink displays on the Home page. The URL for the e-mail hyperlink displays on the status bar, using the mailto protocol before the e-mail address, nikkipatrio@hcc.edu (Figure 1-74).

5 | **Click the Save button on the Standard toolbar.**

The modified page is saved on disk as part of the current web. The asterisk in the tab of the modified page is removed.

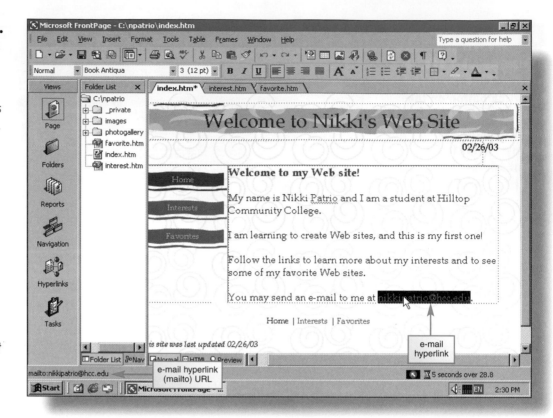

FIGURE 1-74

You now have included two new types of text hyperlinks — hyperlinks to other Web pages on the Favorites and Interests pages, and an e-mail hyperlink on the Home page.

Printing a Web Page Using FrontPage

Once you have created a Web page and saved it on disk, you may want to print the page. A printed version of a document — in this case, a Web page — is called a **hard copy** or **printout**.

To print a page in Page view, you open the Web page so it displays in the Page pane and then click the Print button on the Standard toolbar. After you print the first page, you can open additional pages to print the remaining pages in the web. To print the Home page of your Personal web, complete the following steps.

More About

Printing

When you print a Web page, a header and footer are included by default on each page. To change the header or the footer, or to change the print margins, click File on the menu bar and click Page Setup before printing. When the Print Page Setup dialog box displays, you may enter new values for these items.

Steps **To Print a Web Page**

1 **Ready the printer. If necessary, double-click the file name, index.htm, in the Folder List pane or click the tab index.htm at the top of the Page pane to display the Home page in the Page pane. Click File on the menu bar and then point to Print.**

The File menu displays (Figure 1-75).

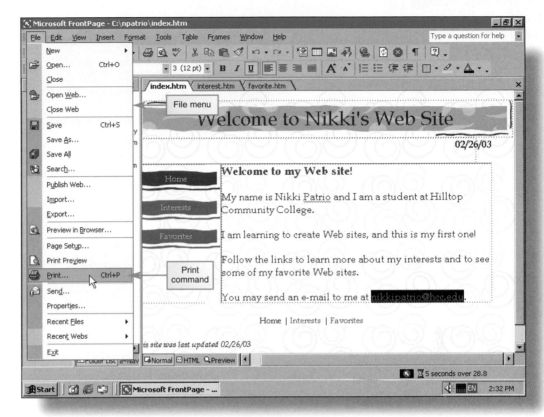

FIGURE 1-75

2 **Click Print. When the Print dialog box displays, point to the OK button.**

The Print dialog box displays (Figure 1-76). The All option button in the Print range area is selected, indicating that the entire document will print, regardless of its length.

FIGURE 1-76

3 **Click the OK button.**

The FrontPage message box displays, showing the status of the print process. The Home page prints (Figure 1-77). FrontPage prints hyperlinks and images on the Web page as they display on the Normal tab in Page view.

FIGURE 1-77

1. Click Print button on Standard toolbar
2. Press CTRL+P, click OK button
3. Press ALT+F, press P
4. In Voice Command mode, say "File, Print"

The **Print dialog box** in Figure 1-76 on the previous page provides many printing options. In the **Print range area**, the **All option button** instructs FrontPage to print the entire document. The **Pages option button** lets you print selected pages of a multiple-page document. The **Number of Copies box** allows you to specify the number of copies you wish to print.

To print the Web page as shown in Figure 1-77, the Web page must display on the Normal tab in Page view. FrontPage also allows you to print the HTML source for a home page. To print the HTML source for a home page, click the HTML tab to display the Web page on the HTML tab and then print the page. You cannot, however, print a Web page on the Preview tab in Page view. When the page displays on the Preview tab, FrontPage disables the printing function.

Publishing a FrontPage Web

If you have access to a Web server, FrontPage provides an easy way to publish your Web pages to the World Wide Web. As previously mentioned, **publishing a Web page** is the process of sending copies of Web pages, image files, multimedia files, and any folders to a Web server. Once saved on the Web server, the Web pages and files are available on the World Wide Web. With FrontPage, you can publish your Web using a series of dialog boxes that step you through the process.

Many schools and companies provide a small amount of space on their Web servers for students and employees to publish personal Web pages and related files. For a modest fee, most Internet service providers (ISPs) also will provide space for publishing personal Web pages. An **Internet service provider (ISP)** is an organization that has a permanent connection to the Internet and provides temporary connections to individuals and companies for a fee. Some other Web-based services, such as Tripod, provide space on their Web servers for individuals to publish personal Web pages. To pay for the cost of maintaining these servers, these companies place advertisements at the top or bottom of your personal Web pages.

To publish your web to the World Wide Web, you will need access to an ISP, preferably one with Microsoft FrontPage Server Extensions installed. Without FrontPage Server Extensions, some functionality in your web may not be available, such as most form handlers, hit counters, and other component features. With the server extensions, FrontPage will maintain your files and hyperlinks, comparing your local files to those on the server and updating any changes the next time you publish the web. Also, with the server extensions installed, FrontPage can publish your web using **HTTP (Hypertext Transfer Protocol)**. Without the server extensions, your web will be published using **FTP (File Transfer Protocol)**. Both HTTP and FTP are methods of transferring files over the Internet.

The following steps show how to publish your FrontPage web to a Web server. These steps work only if you have an account that grants you publishing rights on a Web server. To ensure that you publish your Personal web successfully, be sure to substitute the URL of your own Web server when you see the URL, http://www .hcc.edu/npatrio/, in the following steps. If you do not know which URL to use, see your instructor for more information.

More About

Publishing a Web Page

FrontPage allows you to choose from options that allow you to publish only changed Web pages or publish all Web pages, which overwrites all previously published Web pages with the most recent versions. Click Tools on the menu bar and then click Options. When the Options dialog box displays, click the Publish tab, and then select the desired options.

More About

Quick Reference

For a table that lists how to complete tasks covered in this book using the mouse, menu, shortcut menu, and keyboard, visit the Shelly Cashman Series Office XP Web page (scsite.com/offxp/qr.htm) and then click Microsoft FrontPage 2002.

Steps To Publish the FrontPage Web

1 If necessary, save any unsaved pages. Point to the Publish Web button on the Standard toolbar (Figure 1-78).

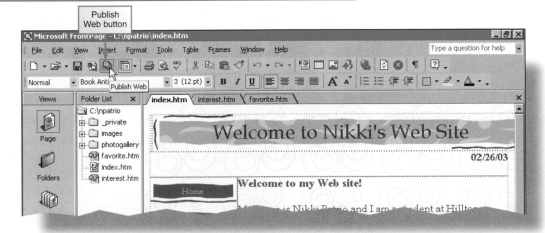

FIGURE 1-78

2 **Click the Publish Web button.**

The Publish Web dialog box displays, overlaid by the Publish Destination dialog box (Figure 1-79). The Enter publish destination box displays the URL of the location where FrontPage will publish the Home page of the current web. FrontPage will publish all other files in the same directory or folders within that directory.

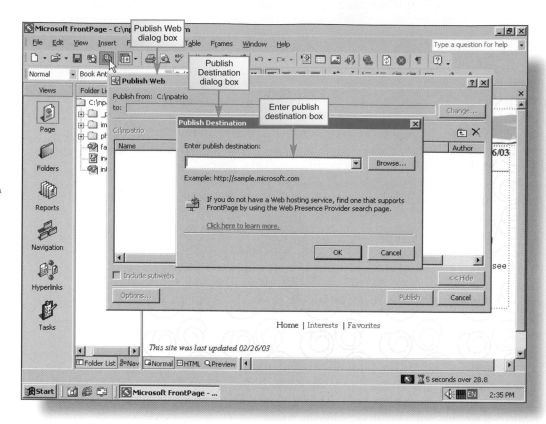

FIGURE 1-79

3 **Type** http:// www.hcc.edu/ ~npatrio/ **in the Enter publish destination box. Be sure to substitute your own URL when you see the URL, http://www.hcc.edu/ ~npatrio/. Point to the OK button.**

The destination URL displays in the Enter publish destination box (Figure 1-80). If your Web server does not have the FrontPage Server Extensions installed, you will need to begin the URL with ftp rather than http.

FIGURE 1-80

4 **Click the OK button. If a Microsoft dialog box displays indicating that a web does not exist at your location, click the OK button.**

The Enter Network Password dialog box displays, requesting authorization information to allow you to publish your web to the server entered in the Enter publish destination box (Figure 1-81).

FIGURE 1-81

5 **Type your name in the User Name text box, and then type your password in the Password text box. Point to the OK button.**

The password entered displays as asterisks for security purposes (Figure 1-82).

FIGURE 1-82

6 **Click the OK button. When the Publish Web dialog box is visible, point to the Publish button.**

The Publish Web dialog box displays a list of files and folders that are to be published (Figure 1-83).

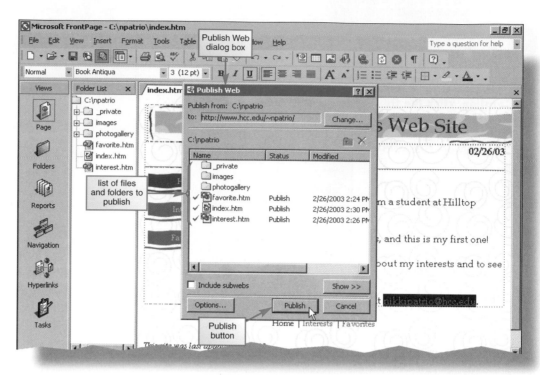

FIGURE 1-83

7 **Click the Publish button. When publishing the web is complete, do not click the Done button.**

The Microsoft FrontPage dialog box displays a status bar indicating the progress of the file transfer. When FrontPage has finished publishing the web, the Microsoft FrontPage dialog box displays the message, Web site published successfully! and provides links you can click to view your published web site and a log of files published (Figure 1-84).

FIGURE 1-84

Other **Ways**

1. On File menu click Publish Web
2. Press ALT+F, press U

Of the many files FrontPage will transfer, most of them contain elements in the Poetic theme selected for the web. The publishing process may take a few minutes, depending on the number of files in the web.

FrontPage remembers the location to which you published the current web, so the next time you click the Publish Web button on the Standard toolbar, FrontPage will automatically publish to the previous location. To publish to a new location, you can change the URL listed in the Enter publish destination text box.

Testing the FrontPage Web

Now that you have published the web, it is available to anyone on the World Wide Web. You should take the time to test the newly published web to ensure the pages look as you expected and the hyperlinks work. Complete the following steps to test your Personal web.

Steps To Test the FrontPage Web

1 **Click the Click here to view your published web site link (see Figure 1-84 on the previous page).**

The Internet Explorer window opens and displays the Home page of your web in the browser window (Figure 1-85).

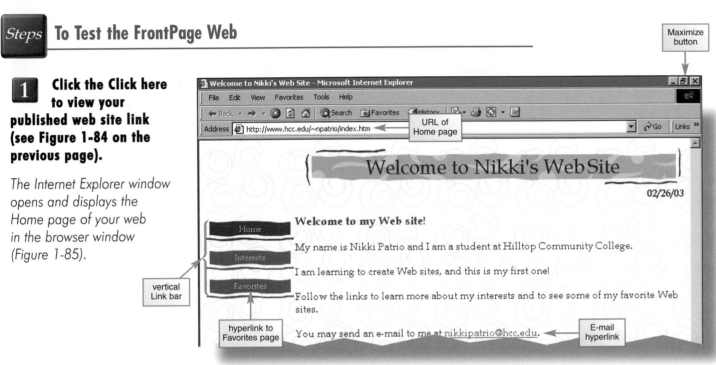

FIGURE 1-85

2 **If necessary, click the Maximize button on the Internet Explorer title bar. Click the Favorites hyperlink on the Link bar.**

The Favorites page displays (Figure 1-86). The Link bar displays the button hyperlink to the Favorites page in a different color than that of the button hyperlinks to the Home page and to the Interests page. This is done to indicate that it links to the currently displayed page.

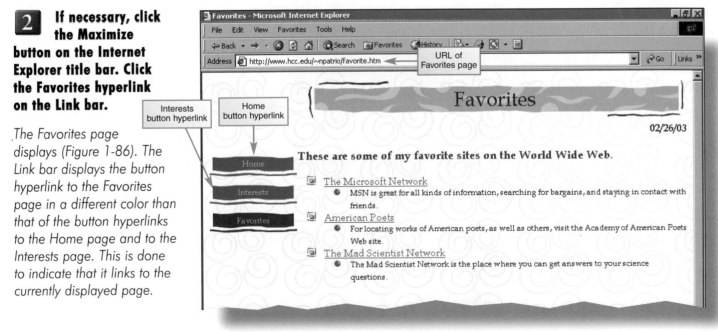

FIGURE 1-86

3 **Click the Interests button on the Link bar. When the Interests page displays, point to the Botany.org hyperlink.**

The Interests page displays (Figure 1-87). The Link bar displays a button hyperlink to the Favorites page, which is located at the same level as the Interests page. The Link bar also includes a button hyperlink to the Home page, which is located at the parent level.

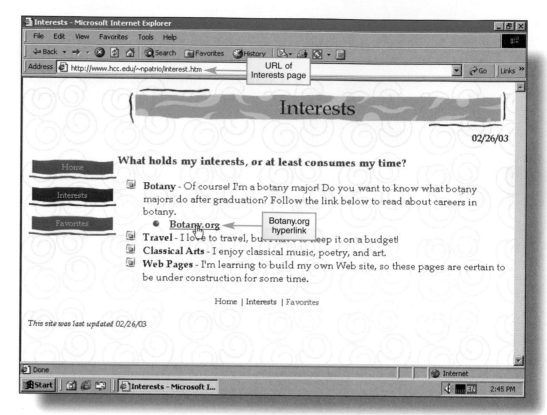

FIGURE 1-87

4 **Click the Botany.org hyperlink.**

The Botanical Society of America home page displays in the Internet Explorer window (Figure 1-88).

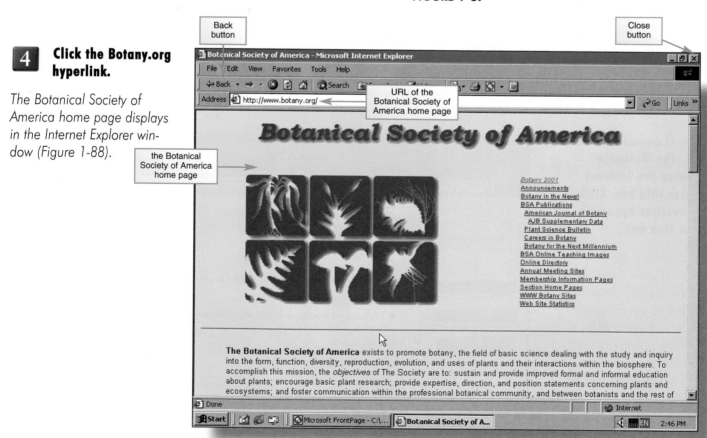

FIGURE 1-88

5 **Click the Back button to return to the Interests page. After viewing all Web pages for accuracy and ensuring the hyperlinks function properly, click the Close button on the Internet Explorer title bar to close the browser.**

The Internet Explorer window closes. The FrontPage window displays with the Home page in Page view and the Microsoft FrontPage dialog box still displayed (Figure 1-89).

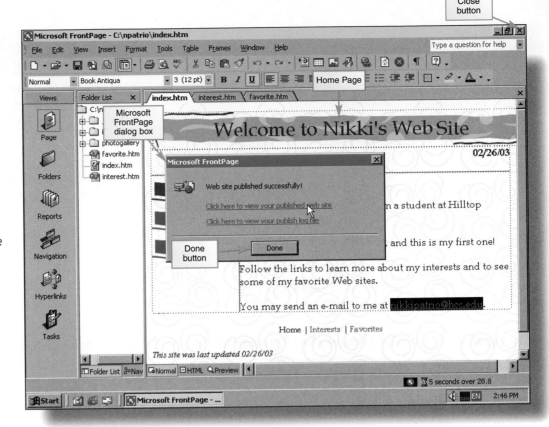

FIGURE 1-89

When you first link to your published site, the Web server displays a default Web page, called index.htm, in the URL in the Address bar. In your Personal web, the Home page uses the file name, index.htm, and thus displays as the default page.

FrontPage Help System

Reference materials and other forms of assistance are available using the **FrontPage Help system.** You can display these materials, print them, or copy them to other Windows applications. Table 1-4 on the next page summarizes the categories of online Help available.

The FrontPage Help System

The best way to become familiar with the FrontPage Help system is to use it. The FrontPage Help System can provide technical information about your system and network, in addition to help with FrontPage.

Table 1-4 FrontPage Help System

TYPE	DESCRIPTION	HOW TO ACTIVATE
Answer Wizard	Answers questions or searches for terms that you type in your own words.	Click the Microsoft FrontPage Help button on the Standard toolbar. If necessary, maximize the Help window by double-clicking its title bar. Click the Answer Wizard tab.
Ask A Question box	Answers questions or searches for terms that you type in your own words.	Type a question or term in the Ask a Question box on the menu bar and then press the enter key.
Contents sheet	Groups Help topics by general categories. Use when you know only the general category of the topic in question.	Click the Microsoft FrontPage Help button on the Standard toolbar. If necessary, maximize the Help window by double-clicking its title bar. Click the Contents tab.
Detect and Repair command	Automatically finds and fixes errors in the application.	Click Detect and Repair on the Help menu.
Hardware and Software Information	Shows Product ID and allows access to system information and technical support information.	Click About Microsoft FrontPage on the Help menu and then click the appropriate button.
Index sheet	Similar to an index in a book. Use when you know exactly what you want.	Click the Microsoft FrontPage Help button on the Standard toolbar. If necessary, maximize the Help window by double-clicking its title bar. Click the Index tab.
Office Assistant	Similar to the Ask a Question box in that the Office Assistant answers questions that you type in your own words, offers tips, and provides help for a variety of FrontPage features.	Click the Office Assistant icon. If the Office Assistant does not display, click Show the Office Assistant on the Help menu.
Office on the Web command	Use to access technical resources and download free product enhancements on the Web.	Click Office on the Web on the Help menu.
Question Mark button	Identify unfamiliar items in a dialog box.	In a dialog box, click the Question Mark button and then click an element in the dialog box.
What's This? command	Used to identify unfamiliar items on the screen.	Click What's This? on the Help menu, and then click an item on the screen.

Quitting FrontPage

Once you have finished the steps in the project and developed and published your Personal web, you can quit FrontPage. Complete the following steps to quit FrontPage.

Other Ways

1. On File menu click Exit
2. Press ALT+F, X
3. Press ALT+F4
4. In Voice Command mode, say "File, Exit"

TO QUIT FRONTPAGE

1 If necessary, click the Done button. Click the Close button on the right side of the FrontPage title bar (see Figure 1-89 on page FP 1.65).

2 If necessary, click the Close button on the Internet Explorer title bar to quit Internet Explorer.

The Windows desktop displays.

CASE PERSPECTIVE SUMMARY

Nikki was very pleased, not only with the resulting Web pages, but also with the ease with which they could be created using FrontPage. She expressed great enthusiasm about learning of additional capabilities in FrontPage and in making future enhancements to her web. You assured her that upgrading her web would be comparatively easy using FrontPage, and that improvements could be implemented in several stages. She is anxious to get started on the next project.

Project Summary

Having completed Project 1, you developed a Personal web and posted the pages to a personal Web site. In this project, you learned the basic World Wide Web concepts, including HTML and the elements of a Web page. You learned how to create a FrontPage web using a template, to apply a theme, and to edit the placeholder text on a template page. You also learned how to modify a bulleted list, modify a FrontPage component, and edit and add hyperlinks on a Web page, including an e-mail hyperlink. You gained an understanding of how to use the tabs in Page view to edit page layout and to preview a Web page. Finally, you learned how to print Web pages and publish a web to the World Wide Web.

What You Should Know

Having completed this project, you now should be able to perform the following tasks:

▶ Add an E-Mail Hyperlink to a Web Page *(FP 1.54)*
▶ Add New Text to a Web Page *(FP 1.29)*
▶ Apply a Theme to a FrontPage Web *(FP 1.25)*
▶ Change a Hyperlink on a Web Page *(FP 1.50)*
▶ Delete a Web Page from a Web *(FP 1.46)*
▶ Delete Selected Tables and Cells *(FP 1.33)*
▶ Display the Folder List Pane *(FP 1.23)*
▶ Edit a Bulleted List *(FP 1.35)*
▶ Edit Text on a Web Page *(FP 1.28)*
▶ Modify a Page Banner *(FP 1.44)*
▶ Open a Web Page in Page View *(FP 1.22)*

▶ Preview a Web Page Using the Preview Tab *(FP 1.43)*
▶ Print a Web Page *(FP 1.56)*
▶ Publish the FrontPage Web *(FP 1.59)*
▶ Quit FrontPage *(FP 1.66)*
▶ Save a Web Page *(FP 1.41)*
▶ Select Tables and Cells *(FP 1.32)*
▶ Start FrontPage *(FP 1.13)*
▶ Test the FrontPage Web *(FP 1.63)*
▶ Use a Template to Create a FrontPage Web *(FP 1.19)*

More About

Microsoft Certification

The Microsoft Office User Specialist (MOUS) Certification program provides an opportunity for you to obtain a valuable industry credential — proof that you have the FrontPage 2002 skills required by employers. For more information, visit the Shelly Cashman Series MOUS Web page at scsite.com/offxp/cert.htm.

Learn It Online

Instructions: To complete the Learn It Online exercises, start your browser, click the Address bar, and then enter scsite.com/offxp/exs.htm. When the Office XP Learn It Online page displays, follow the instructions in the exercises below.

1 Project Reinforcement TF, MC, and SA

Below FrontPage Project 1, click the Project Reinforcement link. Print the quiz by clicking Print on the File menu. Answer each question. Write your first and last name at the top of each page, and then hand in the printout to your instructor.

2 Flash Cards

Below FrontPage Project 1, click the Flash Cards link. When Flash Cards displays, read the instructions. Type 20 (or a number specified by your instructor) in the Number of Playing Cards text box, type your name in the Name text box, and then click the Flip Card button. When the flash card displays, read the question and then click the Answer box arrow to select an answer. Flip through Flash Cards. Click Print on the File menu to print the last flash card if your score is 15 (75%) correct or greater and then hand it in to your instructor. If your score is less than 15 (75%) correct, then redo this exercise by clicking the Replay button.

3 Practice Test

Below FrontPage Project 1, click the Practice Test link. Answer each question, enter your first and last name at the bottom of the page, and then click the Grade Test button. When the graded practice test displays on your screen, click Print on the File menu to print a hard copy. Continue to take practice tests until you score 80% or better. Hand in a printout of the final practice test to your instructor.

4 Who Wants to Be a Computer Genius?

Below FrontPage Project 1, click the Computer Genius link. Read the instructions, enter your first and last name at the bottom of the page, and then click the Play button. Hand in your score to your instructor.

5 Wheel of Terms

Below FrontPage Project 1, click the Wheel of Terms link. Read the instructions, and then enter your first and last name and your school name. Click the Play button. Hand in your score to your instructor.

6 Crossword Puzzle Challenge

Below FrontPage Project 1, click the Crossword Puzzle Challenge link. Read the instructions, and then enter your first and last name. Click the Play button. Work the crossword puzzle. When you are finished, click the Submit button. When the crossword puzzle redisplays, click the Print button. Hand in the printout.

7 Tips and Tricks

Below FrontPage Project 1, click the Tips and Tricks link. Click a topic that pertains to Project 1. Right-click the information and then click Print on the shortcut menu. Construct a brief example of what the information relates to in FrontPage to confirm you understand how to use the tip or trick. Hand in the example and printed information.

o n l i n e

8 Newsgroups

Below FrontPage Project 1, click the Newsgroups link. Click a topic that pertains to Project 1. Print three comments. Hand in the comments to your instructor.

9 Expanding Your Horizons

Below FrontPage Project 1, click the Articles for Microsoft FrontPage link. Click a topic that pertains to Project 1. Print the information. Construct a brief example of what the information relates to in FrontPage to confirm you understand the contents of the article. Hand in the example and printed information to your instructor.

10 Search Sleuth

Below FrontPage Project 1, click the Search Sleuth link. To search for a term that pertains to this project, select a term below the Project 1 title and then use the Google search engine at google.com (or any major search engine) to display and print two Web pages that present information on the term. Hand in the printouts to your instructor.

Apply Your Knowledge

1 Modifying a Corporate Presence Web

Instructions: Start FrontPage. Open the file, index.htm, from the Project 1/Starting folder on the Data Disk. See the inside back cover of this book for instructions for downloading the Data Disk or see your instructor for information on accessing the files required in this book.

1. If necessary, double-click the file index.htm in the Folder List pane to display The Starting Block home page in Page view.
2. Click the Link bar component in the top-left of the page to select it. Press the DELETE key three times to delete the Link bar component and to move the graphic to the top of the page.
3. Click the third item in the bulleted list to select it and then type the best value on all of our products as the new text.
4. Add a fourth item in the bulleted list by pressing the ENTER key and then type expert advice on equipment, training, and supplies as the new text.
5. Select the heading, Contact Information, and then type Team Meeting as the new text.
6. Position the insertion point after the word, Sales:, and then type sales@startingblock.com as the e-mail hyperlink text. Create an e-mail hyperlink that sends e-mail to sales@startingblock.com (Figure 1-90 on the next page).
7. Click the Preview tab to preview the Web page. When you have finished, click the Normal tab.
8. Print and then save the Web page.
9. Click the Navigation icon on the Views bar. Delete the Contents Web page.
10. Double-click the Products page icon to open the Products Web page.
11. Double-click the Link bar component. If necessary, edit the properties to include hyperlinks at the child level. Select the Home Page check box and the Parent Page check box.
12. Double-click the Products Page Banner component. Edit the page banner text by typing Gear and Supplies as the new text.
13. Print and save the Web page and then close FrontPage. Hand in the printouts to your instructor.

(continued)

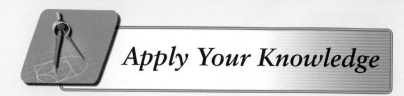

Apply Your Knowledge

Modifying a Corporate Presence Web *(continued)*

FIGURE 1-90

In the Lab

1 Creating and Modifying a One-Page Web

Problem: After a wonderful but too brief vacation, you decide to develop a one-page web with information about your trip. The page should include a description of your vacation, one or more links to Web sites related to your destination, and your contact information.

Instructions: Perform the following tasks.

1. Create a new web using the One Page Web template. In the New dialog box, click One Page Web and then type C:\Project1\vacation, or a location specified by your instructor, in the Specify the location of the new web text box. Click the OK button.
2. Double-click the file name, index.htm, in the Folder List pane to open the Home Page.
3. Apply the Travel theme to the web. Be sure to select Background picture.
4. When FrontPage has finished applying the theme, insert a Page Banner with the word Hawaii, or the name of your vacation location. Type the text in Table 1-5 on the next page, or text of your own choosing, to describe your vacation. Set the title to a style of Heading 1. When you have finished typing the text, press the ENTER key.
5. Type The State of Hawaii and press the ENTER key. Type Islands: followed by three spaces. Type each island name separated by three spaces. Press the ENTER key. Use the information in Table 1-6 to create hyperlinks for the State of Hawaii and for each of the islands.
6. Type Ed Wiens, University of Waterloo as the author name (you can substitute your name and school for the text shown here). Press the ENTER key.
7. Type Please e-mail comments and questions to ewiens@uwaterloo.edu. as the last line of text (you can substitute your e-mail address for the address shown here).
8. Drag through the e-mail address text to select it. Create an E-mail hyperlink to the e-mail address, ewiens@uwaterloo.edu (you can substitute your e-mail address for the address shown here).
9. Save the Web page (Figure 91 on the next page). Print the Web page, write your name on the page, and hand it in to your instructor.
10. Quit Internet Explorer and FrontPage.

Table 1-5   Vacation Description
PARADISE IN THE PACIFIC
I recently had the extreme pleasure of traveling with my family to visit the island paradise of Hawaii. Actually, I should say islands, because there are several islands in the state of Hawaii, each with its own features. On this trip, we spent most of our time on Maui, leaving us a good excuse for a return visit to explore the other islands! Diving in Molokini crater was a breathtaking experience — especially when the shark swam beneath us! Another meaningful meaningful experience, but in a very different vein, took place when we visited Oahu to tour Pearl Harbor. Although a somber excursion, it is not to be missed. If you are wondering if Hawaii should be your next vacation spot, visit the links below for a preview of what this Paradise in the Pacific has to offer!

(continued)

In the Lab

Creating and Modifying a One-Page Web *(continued)*

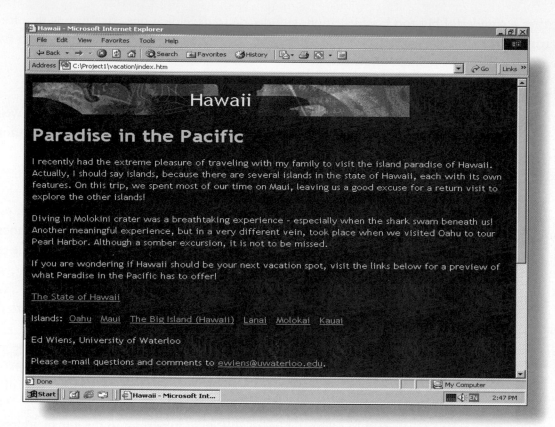

FIGURE 1-91

Table 1-6 Island Hyperlinks*	
TEXT FOR HYPERLINK	*URL FOR HYPERLINK*
The State of Hawaii	http://www.hawaii.worldweb.com
Oahu	http://www.oahu.worldweb.com
Maui	http://www.maui.worldweb.com
The Big Island (Hawaii)	http://www.bigisland.worldweb.com
Lanai	http://www.lanai.worldweb.com
Molokai	http://www.molokai.worldweb.com
Kauai	http://www.kauai.worldweb.com

* If you encounter an inoperative URL, use the Google search engine, google.com, to find a similar Web page.

In the Lab

2 Creating and Modifying a Personal Web

Problem: You have decided to develop a Personal web with information about your favorite Web sites. In addition to an introductory Home page, you plan to include a page of links to sites on Web security, clip art, entertainment, and other Web sites of interest.

Instructions: Perform the following tasks.

1. Create a new web using the Personal Web template. In the New dialog box, click Personal Web and then type C:\Project1\funsites, or a location specified by your instructor, in the Specify the location of the new web text box. Click the OK button.
2. Click the Navigation icon on the Views bar. Delete the Interests, Feedback, and Photo Gallery pages from the web.
3. Double-click the Home Page page icon in the Navigation pane to open the Home Page.
4. If necessary, apply the Bubbles theme, or another of your choosing, to the web. Be sure to apply the theme to all pages in the Web and to check Vivid colors, Active graphics, and Background picture.
5. Select and delete all table cells under Favorite Links and under Weather. Select and delete the table containing the hit counter component.
6. Double-click the Page Banner component. In the Page Banner Properties dialog box, select the text in the Page banner text box and type Fun and Favorites.
7. Select the Link bar and then edit the properties to include hyperlinks to child pages below Home. Remove the check mark from the Home Page check box.
8. Delete the first paragraph of placeholder text.
9. Select the placeholder text in the second paragraph and then type Looking for links to fun sites, resources for building Web pages, or for securing your computer? Browse through my collection of favorite Web links to get information on each of these subjects. as the replacement text.
10. Save the Web page. Open the About Me page. Replace all placeholder text with information about yourself and the course for which you are doing this assignment. See your instructor for relevant course information.
11. Save the Web page. Open the Favorites page.
12. Select the first paragraph of placeholder text and then type A topical listing of some of my favorite Web sites. as the replacement text.
13. Edit the bulleted list of hyperlinks to include the sites and URLs listed in Table 1-7 on page FP 1.75. Use the underlined text as the hyperlink text and type the descriptions in the placeholder text for each hyperlink. Include any other sites of interest to you.
14. Save the Web page (Figure 1-92 on the next page).
15. Print the Home page, About Me page, and the Favorites page, write your name on the pages, and hand them in to your instructor.
16. If you have access to a Web server, publish the web. Once you have tested the Web pages in your browser, close your browser and then quit FrontPage.

(continued)

In the Lab

Creating and Modifying a One-Page Web *(continued)*

(a)

(b)

FIGURE 1-92

In the Lab

Table 1-7 Bulleted List Hyperlinks *	
HYPERLINK TEXT AND DESCRIPTION	**URL**
<u>ZoneAlarm</u> Free personal firewall software to protect your computer when online.	http://www.zonelabs.com
<u>Shields Up!</u> A tutorial and testing software for understanding Internet connection security.	http://grc.com
<u>FrontPage Updates</u> Microsoft Office FrontPage Update site.	http://officeupdate.microsoft.com
<u>Clip Art</u> The Whole Internet Guide to Clip Art Web site contains more clip art than you may ever need!	http://best-of-web.com/computer/clipart_index.shtml
<u>Abbott and Costello</u> The Official Bud Abbott and Lou Costello Web site highlights the antics of these classic comedians.	www.abbottandcostello.net
<u>Games Online</u> Visit FreeArcade.com when you are tired of just playing solitaire!	http://www.freearcade.com/

* If you encounter an inoperative URL, use the Google search engine, google.com, to find a similar Web page.

3 Creating and Modifying a Corporate Presence Web

Problem: As the owner of The Sweet Tooth, you want to develop a Web site that will provide customers with information about your line of confections for all occasions, as well as bakery goods.

Instructions: Perform the following tasks.

1. Create a new web using the Corporate Presence template. In the New dialog box, click Corporate Presence and then type C:\Project1\sweets, or a location specified by your instructor, in the Specify the location of the new web text box. Click the OK button.
2. When the Corporate Web Wizard displays, click the Next button. When prompted for information about the company, use the information in Table 1-8 on the next page to fill in the fields and choose which pages to include in your web. Choose Sweets as the web theme. If necessary, click the Vivid colors, Active graphics, and Background picture check boxes. When you have finished, click the Finish button.
3. When FrontPage is finished copying the template pages, if necessary, click the Toggle Pane button arrow on the Standard toolbar and then click Folder List on the Toggle Pane button menu to display the Folder List pane. Open the Home page.
4. Select the Link bar component at the top of the page and press the DELETE key three times to delete it and to move the Page banner to the top of the page. Select the horizontal Link bar component below the Page banner. Delete it and the blank line that follows.
5. Select the vertical Link bar and, if necessary, edit the properties to include hyperlinks at the child level. Select the Home Page check box and the Parent Page check box.

(continued)

In the Lab

Creating and Modifying a One-Page Web *(continued)*

Table 1-8 Corporate Presence Web Field Information	
FIELD	**INFORMATION**
Main pages to include in Web	Products/Services
Home page information	Mission statement Contact information
Products/Services information	2 Products 0 Services
Additional information	Pricing information
What should appear at the top of each page	Page title Links to your main Web pages
What should appear at the bottom of each page	E-mail address of your webmaster Date page was last modified
Under Construction icon	No
Full name of company	The Sweet Tooth
One-word version of name	Sweets
Company's street address	421 Wilmore Drive Los Angeles, CA 90621
Telephone and fax numbers	641-555-2639 641-555-2329
E-mail address of your webmaster	webmaster@sweettooth.com
E-mail address for general information	info@sweettooth.com
Choose Web theme	Sweets, with Active graphics
Show Tasks view after Web is uploaded	No

6. Click the first paragraph to select it, click the Style box arrow and then click Heading 3. Type Welcome to The Sweet Tooth! as the new text.

7. Delete the header, Our Mission. Select the second paragraph. Type Our goal is to be the single source for all of your confectionary needs. For satisfying your own sweet tooth, or that of a friend, we're sure to have what you crave! If you desire to produce your own sweet designs, we can provide the raw materials for your creations. Check with us often as we continually update our products with delightful new creations that are certain to tickle your taste buds! as the new text (Figure 1-93).

8. Scroll down and select the third paragraph under the header, Contact Information. Press the DELETE key three times to delete the text from the page.

9. Click the HTML tab. View and then print the HTML source code for the Home Page. Click the Normal tab. Save and then print the Web page.

10. Open the Product 1 page by double-clicking the prod01.htm file in the Folder List pane. Double-click the Page banner and replace the text in the Page banner text box with Prepackaged.

11. Open the Product 2 page by double-clicking the prod02.htm file in the Folder List pane. Replace the text in the Page banner text box with Make-My-Own.

12. Open the Products page by double-clicking the products.htm file in the Folder List pane.

13. Select all of the text on the page. Type Select from our holiday specialties, all-occasion, or novelty-packaged line of products to enjoy our scrumptious selections, or choose from components in Make-My-Own to express your personal designs in confectionary creativity! as the new text.

14. Print and save the Web page, and then close FrontPage. Hand in the printouts to your instructor.

In the Lab

(a)

(b)

FIGURE 1-93

Cases and Places

The difficulty of these case studies varies:
▶ are the least difficult; ▶▶ are more difficult; and ▶▶▶ are the most difficult.

1 ▶   Your course in Classical Literature requires you to produce a one-page review of a book assigned for reading every two weeks. Your instructor wants you to create the review as a Web page. Using the One Page Web template, develop a Web page that includes the following information about a book of your choice: title, author, copyright year, publisher, and a brief review. Use a bulleted list for these items. Include a hyperlink to your e-mail address at the bottom of the page.

2 ▶   You want to make your resume available on the Web. Using the One Page Web template, create a text-only home page that includes information about your educational history and work experience. Apply the theme of your choice to the web. Include a hyperlink to your e-mail address at an appropriate location in the resume.

3 ▶▶   In preparation for an upcoming 50th wedding anniversary for your grandparents, you were asked to develop a Web site for them. Using the Personal Web template, develop a Web site that includes a Home Page, an Interests page, and a History page (modify the Favorites page, including the Page Banner). Edit the Link bar properties to include child level pages, and select the Home Page check box and the Parent Page check box. Edit the placeholder text to include your own replacement text. The Home page should include an e-mail hyperlink to your Web address as the creator of the site (webmaster). You also should include a link to the e-mail address of your grandparents.

4 ▶▶   As coordinator of intramural basketball at your school, you have decided to develop a Web page that lists upcoming games, scores of recent games, and current league standings. Using the One Page Web template, develop a Web page that lists the information shown in Table 1-9 and Table 1-10. The Web page should include an e-mail hyperlink to your Web address and a hyperlink to the intramural sports Web page at http://www.hcc.edu/intramurals/ (you may substitute your own Web address).

Table 1-9 Games and Scores	
GAME/SCORE	*DATES/TIMES/RESULTS*
Upcoming Games	Shaw Hall vs. Baker Hall, Tuesday, 7:00 p.m. Wright Hall vs. Meadows Hall, Thursday, 6:00 p.m. Winners (above) playoff, Saturday, 2:00 p.m.
Recent Scores	Shaw Hall vs. Bradford House, 66-48 Janssen Hall vs. Wright Hall, 56-62 Tenney Hall vs. Burritt Annex, 82-72

Table 1-10 Current League Standings		
TEAM	*WON*	*LOST*
Shaw Hall	6	1
Baker Hall	6	1
Wright Hall	5	2
Meadows Hall	5	2
Bradford House	4	4
Janssen Hall	4	4
Tenney Hall	3	5
Burritt Annex	1	7

Cases and Places

5 ▶▶▶ As a budding Web developer, you have offered to build a Web site for a local hardware store. Using the Corporate Web Presence template, develop a Web site that includes at least a Home page and two pages for product lines (use categories you would expect to find in a hardware store, such as Electrical and Plumbing). Edit the placeholder text on each page to include information about their return policy and store hours.

Microsoft FrontPage 2002

PROJECT

Adding a New Web Page to a Web

You will have mastered the material in this project when you can:

OBJECTIVES

- List Web page design criteria
- Add a new Web page to an existing FrontPage web
- Rename a Web page
- Change the title of a Web page
- Change the label of a Web page
- Change the theme for a single Web page
- Set the Web page background color
- Insert a table on a Web page
- Merge cells in a table
- Undo and redo actions in FrontPage
- Insert a clip art image in a Web page
- Replace an image on a Web page
- Copy and paste items on a Web page
- Use a table to control alignment on a Web page
- Change table properties
- Add a heading to a Web page
- Insert a horizontal rule
- Add normal text
- Add a Photo Gallery component
- Insert Link bars on a Web page
- Print preview a Web page
- Save a Web page with embedded images
- Publish changes to an existing FrontPage web

Web Designers
Composers in a New Era

The most notable Web designer of the modern era, Tim Berners-Lee, created the global Internet-based hypertext system known as the World Wide Web. The limitations faced by Berners-Lee and other early Web developers and designers are virtually obsolete due largely to increased Internet access speed, browser plug-ins that enhance Web site content, and an upsurge in the capabilities of many Web browsers. Web design software products offer interactivity, animation, and sound, taking Web designs to the next level.

The objective of an accomplished Web page designer is to create high-quality, noteworthy Web pages that are admired by colleagues, win awards, and are models of exceptional style.

This appreciation does not come from verbose, complex, overanimated designs, but from thoughtful planning, sensitivity to viewers, and focus on detail. Among the skills required are a thorough understanding of the diverse community of potential viewers and the goal to be achieved by the Web page.

The Internet is rich with examples of exemplary Web sites utilizing content and graphics that draw thousands of visitors and keep their attention as they offer their wares and services, provide information, educate, and entertain.

Literature abounds with examples of authors who pursue very similar objectives as they prepare a first draft and continue to rewrite as they struggle to get the words right. In his book, *On Writing Well*, respected Yale University English professor William Zinsser states, "Writing improves in direct ratio to the things we can keep out of it that shouldn't be there."

In the world of musical arrangements, celebrated composers exhibit the struggles they experience as they toil to score their greatest pieces in scrupulous detail and thought. Some are eccentric; others are driven to seclusion to write the ultimate concerto or symphony. Two such great virtuosos are composers of the nineteenth century. Schumann and Smetana composed masterpieces in unusual circumstances. Each experienced comparable fame and both suffered progressive deafness.

Robert Schumann, whose beautiful musical compositions still grace the world, had to spend the final years of his life in a mental institution, where many of the hundreds of his compositions were composed. In his diary, Schumann wrote that his hallucinations drove him to write, "glorious music with instruments sounding more wonderful than one ever hears on earth." Some of his best works, such as *Kreisleriana*, the *Spring* symphony, and the *Manfred Overture*, were written at the urging of inner voices coming from "angels who hovered over me." As his deafness progressed, he would hear complete original scores in his mind, with the final chord ringing continuously until he forced himself either to write out the entire piece or go on to another composition.

One of Schumann's many famous musical contemporaries, Czechoslovakian composer Bedrich Smetana, also began to lose his hearing at the height of his fame. A continuous high-pitched E note from a violin — a condition now known as tinnitus — sounded inside his ear, driving him to madness. Yet, he continued to compose some of his more beautiful pieces. Today, Czechs consider this gifted composer of hundreds of works, including *The Bartered Bride*, *Ma Vlast* (My Country), and the lovely *Die Moldau*, to be their supreme national composer.

To join the company of eminent composers, your finished product must leave a unique and lasting impression on those who will visit your Web page. With the perpetual growth of the World Wide Web and an international audience, using FrontPage 2002 can provide you with the tools you need to produce superior Web sites. In this project, you will learn proper design techniques to ensure an attractive and tasteful work as you create a new personal Web page for Nikki Patrio that includes photos from the Photo Gallery.

Always consider the purpose of your page and intended audience to help you shape information and content and select consistent components. Structure your information so the casual reader can grasp your concept. Group topics onto a single page. Decide on and test the hyperlinks so browsers can navigate with ease. Animation and graphics can contribute to the purpose of your page, but remember that the more complex your page, the more time required to create it and download it.

As you create your new Web page, in time, you may find yourself among this era's eminent Web designers.

Microsoft FrontPage 2002

Adding a New Web Page to a Web

PROJECT
2

C A S E   P E R S P E C T I V E

After creating her initial personal Web site, Nikki Patrio has some ideas about what she wants to see next. The Web site currently consists primarily of text and hyperlinks. Because Nikki describes herself as a visual person by nature, she wants to use the Internet's rich sources of unique images to enhance her Web pages. She plans to display photos of friends and family members, as well. Nikki has some concerns, however, about adding photos to her Web site. First, it takes a great deal of time for large pictures to download and display. She realizes that this could discourage visitors from viewing her Web site. Second, she wants to associate a brief, explanatory caption with each photo, but does not want to clutter the photo collection with too much text. Finally, she is concerned that the theme she selected for her Web pages might detract from the appeal of her photos.

You assure her that the photos can be added to her Web pages effortlessly, and all of her valid concerns can be addressed easily by using features provided in FrontPage.

Introduction

Every Web page designer wants to build a high-quality Web page that is attractive, gets the attention of new visitors, is admired by colleagues, and even may be imitated. This appreciation does not come from complicated or over-animated designs, but from thoughtful planning, sensitivity to viewers, and careful attention to detail. You must have a thorough understanding of the diverse community of potential viewers and the goal to be accomplished by the Web page.

Web page development consists of two phases: design and implementation. **Design** consists of understanding the audience, determining the purpose of the Web page, then selecting and organizing the individual elements that, together, will achieve that purpose. **Implementation** consists of creating the HTML statements and organizing files and folders to give substance to the design. Sometimes the design and implementation tasks are separated, with a design group rendering the design and another group responsible for the implementation.

Designing a Web page is an iterative process. Typically, you would perform some analysis concerning the requirements of the Web page, then call upon your creativity to arrive at a design that satisfies those requirements in its functionality, and is also attractive.

Once a page is designed, it is a simple matter to create it using an HTML editor, such as Microsoft FrontPage. Microsoft FrontPage has many rich features that will assist you in implementing Web page designs, from the simple to the complex. In this project, you will learn some of the criteria used to arrive at well-designed Web pages and then implement the design for the Photos page shown in Figure 2-1 on the next page.

(a) Home Page

FIGURE 2-1

(b) Photos Page

Web Page Design Criteria

If you ask several experienced Web page designers what the criteria are for a good Web page design, you will get as many different answers. Each designer will emphasize different elements that he or she thinks are important. A basic set of common criteria exists, however, on which all developers can agree.

When a Web page is well designed, the mechanics of the page almost disappear, enabling the users to concentrate on their research, exploration, or pleasure. Table 2-1 on the next page lists several important criteria with their associated guidelines for designing and developing Web pages. The list is by no means exhaustive.

Table 2-1	Criteria and Guidelines for Designing Web Pages
CRITERIA	*GUIDELINES*
Authentication	• Announce who is responsible for the existence of the Web page. • Name the sponsoring organization and author of the Web page. • Use clear, concise titles that identify or announce the purpose of the page. • List appropriate dates, such as the date written or the date the page was last changed. • List the sources for information or other data used on the Web page.
Aesthetics	• Ensure the Web page looks good and is easy to navigate. • Provide functionality and clear organization. • Select good metaphors to represent your concepts and ideas. • Use complementary color schemes. • Eliminate the use of too many animated graphics on a single page. • Avoid long paragraphs of plain text.
Performance	• Keep the pages relatively short. Long pages take time to display. • Web page design should be a compromise between many graphics vs. speed of display. • Use the 10 second response rule when possible: A user will wonder if something is wrong after waiting about 10 seconds without a response.
Consistency	• Use the same colors, locations, and navigation techniques for all related pages. • Maintain a uniform look and feel for all related pages. • Utilize themes and templates to ensure consistency.
Validity	• As with any paper, story, or other literary piece, proofread the text for accuracy. • Verify all the hyperlinks to ensure they are valid. • Check the image, sound, or movie files used in the Web pages. • View the Web page using different browsers. Not every HTML trick or every file format is supported in all browsers.
Images	• Use alternate text in your Web page to provide support for text-only browsers. • Note the size of a large image next to a hyperlink so viewers can decide whether or not to download it. • Use thumbnail images to provide a preview of larger images. • Use universally recognized images for items such as Forward and Back buttons. Remember that you have a global audience.
Hyperlinks	• Ensure that each Web page stands on its own; users can enter from any page of the web. • Provide hyperlinks to resources mentioned in the page. • Use clear navigation hyperlinks such as Next, Back, and Home. • At a minimum, always have a hyperlink to the site's Home page. • Limit the number of hyperlinks. • Avoid click here hyperlinks.
External Files	• Note the type of file, such as .avi for compressed video files, or .jpg for image files. • Include a notation of the size of the file next to the hyperlink.

Viewing HTML Code

In addition to using the HTML tab, you can click Reveal Tags on the View menu. This will display (or hide) HTML tags in Page view when the Normal tab is selected. Place your mouse cursor on any tag and the details of the tag will appear in a ScreenTip.

Each individual Web page should have one purpose or present one concept. Avoid splitting one concept into two parts simply to reduce the size of a page. Likewise, refrain from combining two unrelated ideas just to make a Web page larger.

To help you learn new tips and techniques, examine a number of well-designed pages. View the HTML source to see how other developers created the effects that interest you.

Many HTML style guides are accessible on the Web. Style guides can contain rules, guidelines, tips, and templates that assist you in creating Web pages. Use any Web search engine and search for the keywords, html style guide. Your school or local library also may have an HTML style guide available.

Web Page Composition

Although not true of all Web pages, a typical Web page is composed of three common sections: the header, the body, and the footer (Figure 2-2). The **header** can contain text or images that identify the sponsoring site, the author, or the purpose of the page. Many business Web sites place an advertisement in the header area, because this is the first part of the Web page that shows in the browser's display area. The header also can contain hyperlinks to related pages at the Web site. The header is an important part of the Web page. Viewers evaluate your site from their first impression of the header information. An appealing header will pique their interest, so they will want to see what else is on the page.

The **body** of the Web page contains information and other materials that initially bring visitors to the Web page. The information will be conveyed with combinations of text, images, animation, and hyperlinks.

The **footer** of the Web page provides contact information and sometimes navigation controls. You would expect to find the name and perhaps the e-mail address of the author of the Web page or other official contact person responsible for the Web site. Hyperlinks to other resources at the Web site, such as the Home page or Help information, also may be included in this section.

When designing a Web page, it is useful to divide the page into these three logical sections to ease the design process. You can focus your attention on completing one of the three sections, test it, and then proceed to the next one.

Web Page Composition

Do not confuse the header, body, and footer sections of a Web page with the <HEAD> and <BODY> tags in HTML, which are code segments. Information placed within a <HEAD> tag pair typically does not display on the Web page.

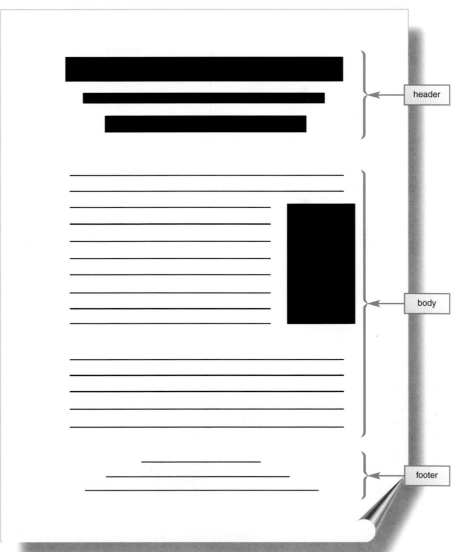

FIGURE 2-2

Designing the Web Page

Ideally, you would create several Web page design alternatives and then discuss with other designers the merits and shortcomings of each. The leading contenders then are refined, until a final design is agreed upon. In practice, usually you will work alone and thus be responsible for these tasks yourself.

Several techniques, including brainstorming and word association, are available for use during the creative process. As with any artistic endeavor, form follows function. If something appears on the Web page, then it serves some purpose. If something serves no purpose, then it should not be on the Web page.

After discussion with Nikki, you design a Photos page, as illustrated in Figure 2-3. Although the pages previously created followed the typical page design, this one varies somewhat because it is composed primarily of pictures. Even so, you can easily identify the header and body sections and that no footer section is used.

More About

Web Page Design

Discover tips, tricks, and techniques for designing Web pages by perusing the numerous formal and informal Best of the Web sites. These sites contain links to outstanding Web pages. Use a search engine to find Best of the Web sites or visit the FrontPage 2002 More About page (scsite.com/fp2002/more .htm) and then click Web Page Design.

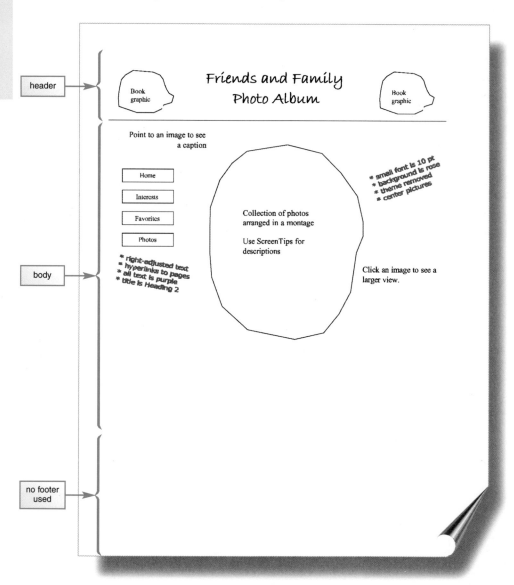

FIGURE 2-3

The header contains two images and a heading that identifies the page. The body of the page contains the desired photos arranged in a montage, each with descriptive information in the form of a ScreenTip. The navigation hyperlinks are on the left, consistent with the previous pages.

Notice the **notations** on the design document indicating special formatting requirements such as color, text size, and alignment. With the design of the page completed, you now can implement the design using FrontPage.

Adding a New Web Page to an Existing FrontPage Web

In Project 1 you learned that you can create a new FrontPage web in several ways. You can import an existing Web from a Web server. You can use a template or wizard. Templates and wizards, such as the one used in Project 1, are great work-saving devices. As you develop customized webs, you will want to add new Web pages to the web when the need arises. To add a new Web page to an existing web, you start FrontPage and then open the original FrontPage web. Start FrontPage using the steps summarized below.

TO START FRONTPAGE

1 Click the Start button on the taskbar. Point to Programs on the Start menu.

2 Click Microsoft FrontPage on the Programs submenu.

The FrontPage window opens and an empty page displays.

Opening an Existing FrontPage Web

Perform the following steps to open the FrontPage web created in Project 1. If you did not complete Project 1, see your instructor for a copy.

Steps **To Open an Existing FrontPage Web**

1 **Click the Open button arrow on the Standard toolbar. Point to Open Web on the Open menu.**

The Open menu displays (Figure 2-4).

FIGURE 2-4

More *About*

The FrontPage Help System

Need Help? It is no further than the Ask a Question box in the upper-right corner of the window. Click the box that contains the text, Type a question for help (Figure 2-4), type help, and then press the ENTER key. FrontPage will respond with a list of items you can click to learn about obtaining help on any FrontPage-related topic. To find out what is new in FrontPage 2002, type what's new in FrontPage in the Ask a Question box.

2 Click Open Web. When the Open Web dialog box displays, if necessary, click the Look in box arrow and select the folder location where you stored the web for Project 1 (e.g., C:\npatrio). Point to the Open button in the Open Web dialog box.

The Open Web dialog box displays with the folder selected (Figure 2-5). The new location displays in the text box. Use the drive and location that are appropriate for your environment.

FIGURE 2-5

3 Click the Open button. Double-click index.htm in the Folder List pane.

The previous web is loaded, and the file, index.htm, displays in Page view (Figure 2-6). Note that the date components indicate the current date.

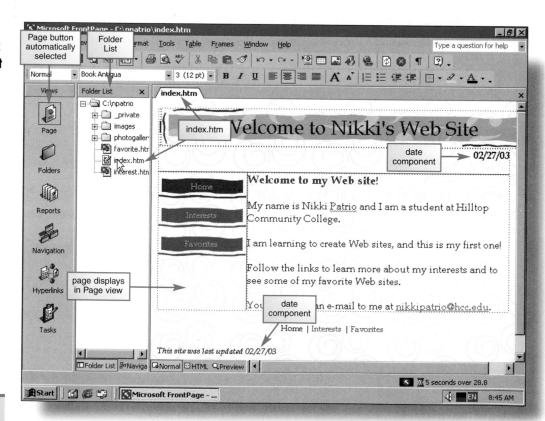

FIGURE 2-6

Adding a New Web Page

The FrontPage toolbar contains the **New Page button** that you can use to add a new Web page to the current web. A new page can be added in Page, Folders, or Navigation view. If you are using Link bars or banners in your web, as was done in Project 1, then you should add new pages after changing to Navigation view and then indicating the location of the new page by selecting a page icon in the Navigation pane. The new page icon will be inserted as a child below the selected page icon. This allows the Link bars to be updated correctly by FrontPage and preserves the visual relationship in the graphical tree diagram in the Navigation pane.

When a new page is added in Page view, FrontPage displays the new page just as it does when an existing web is first opened. Such a new page does not show in the Folder List pane until it has been saved. Adding a new page in Navigation view, however, causes that page to be saved and added to the Folder List as soon as the view is refreshed.

Because you are going to use Link bars on this page, you should add the page in Navigation view. Perform the following steps to insert a new page in Navigation view in the current FrontPage web.

Steps **To Add a New Web Page to an Existing Web**

1 **Click the Navigation button on the Views bar. If necessary, click the Home Page icon to select it. Point to the Create a new normal page button on the Standard toolbar.**

FrontPage displays in Navigation view (Figure 2-7). The Home Page icon is identified by a small house figure in the lower-left corner of the icon.

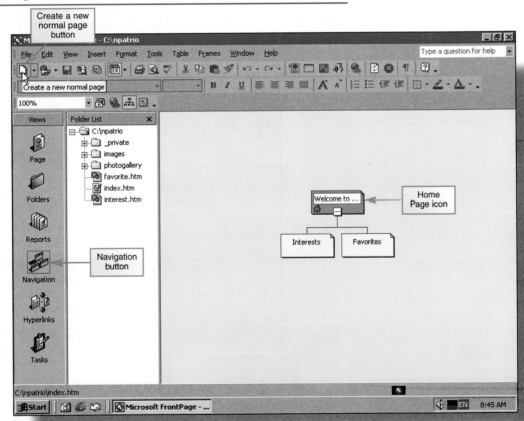

FIGURE 2-7

Microsoft **FrontPage 2002**

2 Click the New Page button.

A new page icon labelled, New Page 1, displays in the Navigation pane (Figure 2-8).

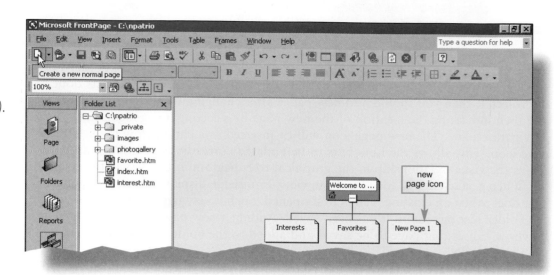

FIGURE 2-8

3 Click View on the menu bar and then point to Refresh.

The View menu displays (Figure 2-9).

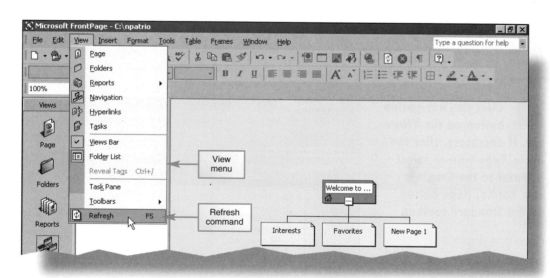

FIGURE 2-9

4 Click Refresh.

The new page displays in the Folder List pane as new_page_1.htm (Figure 2-10).

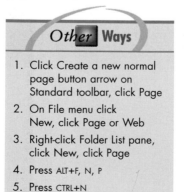

Other **Ways**

1. Click Create a new normal page button arrow on Standard toolbar, click Page
2. On File menu click New, click Page or Web
3. Right-click Folder List pane, click New, click Page
4. Press ALT+F, N, P
5. Press CTRL+N

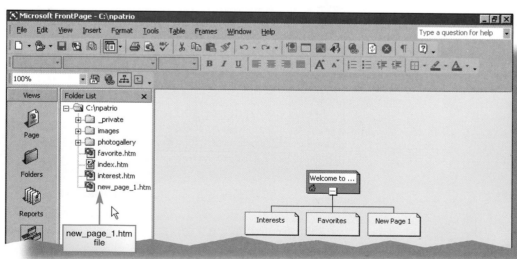

FIGURE 2-10

To control the location of the new Web page in the graphical tree diagram, you selected a Web page icon before clicking the New Page button. Because you clicked the top-level page, New Page 1 was added just below it, as shown in Figure 2-10. If you were to insert another page with the Home page selected, New Page 2 would be added on the same level as New Page 1. If you were to click New Page 1 and then click New Page, New Page 2 would be added below New Page 1, creating a three-level graphical tree diagram.

Renaming a Web Page

Because a file name like new_page_1.htm is not very descriptive, you should rename the file with a more meaningful name. Because the new page is included in the navigation structure for the web, it was added to the Home page Link bars automatically. Link bars use references to file names to locate the corresponding Web pages. Renaming files within FrontPage assures that such references will be maintained, as FrontPage modifies references to the files automatically.

Perform the following steps to change the name of the newly created page.

 Steps **To Rename a Web Page**

1 **Right-click the file name new_page_1.htm. Point to Rename on the shortcut menu.**

The shortcut menu displays (Figure 2-11).

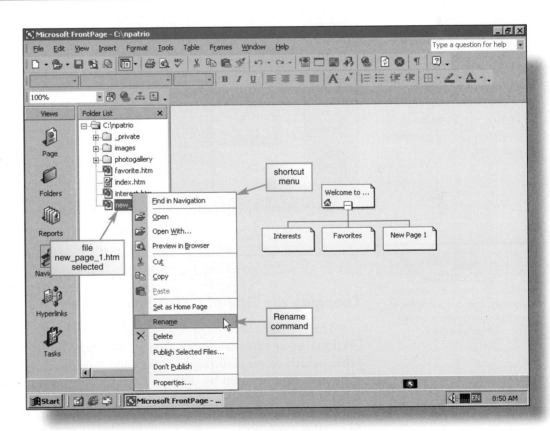

FIGURE 2-11

2 **Click Rename on the shortcut menu.**

The new_page_1.htm file name is selected, and an edit text box displays around the file name (Figure 2-12).

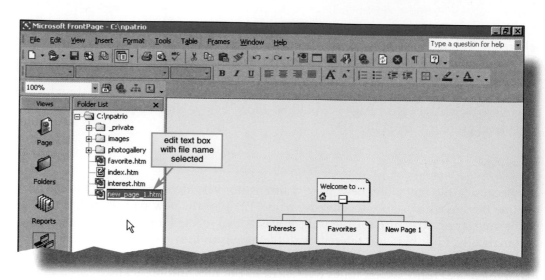

FIGURE 2-12

3 **Type** photos.htm **as the new file name and then press the ENTER key.**

A Rename dialog box displays during the renaming process and then closes automatically. The Folder List pane reflects the renamed file, photos.htm (Figure 2-13).

FIGURE 2-13

Other Ways

1. Click file name in Folder List pane to select it, click file name again, type new file name in edit text box

Changing the Title of a Web Page

The title of a Web page displays in the title bar of most browsers and in any bookmarks or favorites for that page. Although this is not the same as the page label, which displays in page banners and navigation bars created by FrontPage, the same text often is used by default. Each file, or page, in a web has its own title. The default title for a new page is New Page 1, corresponding to the default label of New Page 1 and the default file name of new_page_1.htm. You may change the title of a file without modifying its file name or label. Titles should reflect the name of the organization or purpose of the Web page.

The following steps change the title of the newly created page to a name reflecting its purpose. This title will be placed on the title bar of browsers and in favorites or bookmark lists.

Steps **To Change the Title of a Web Page**

1 **Right-click the New Page 1 page icon. Point to Properties on the shortcut menu.**

The shortcut menu displays (Figure 2-14).

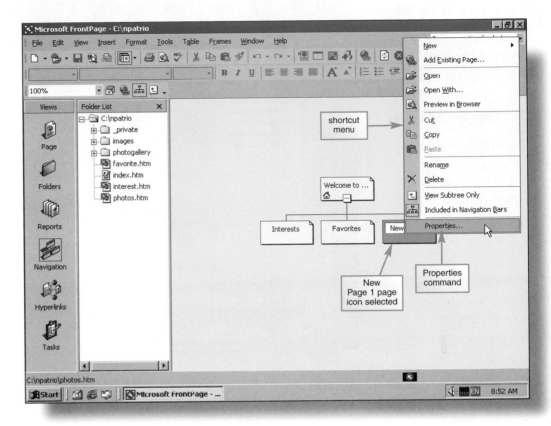

FIGURE 2-14

2 **Click Properties. If necessary, click the General tab.**

The photos.htm Properties dialog box displays, and the default title is selected (Figure 2-15).

FIGURE 2-15

3 **Type** Friends and Family **in the Title text box. Point to the OK button.**

The new title replaces the old (Figure 2-16).

4 **Click the OK button.**

The Page Properties dialog box closes. Although not visible at this point, the title has been changed.

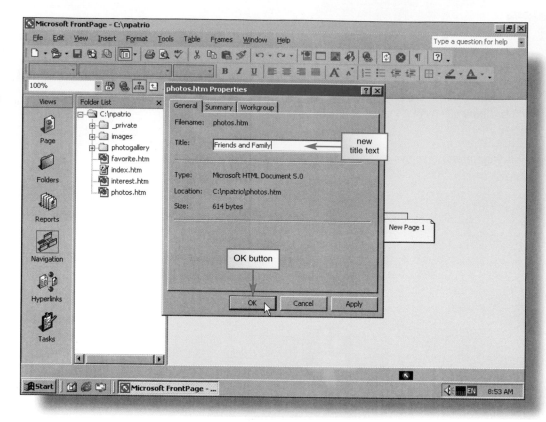

FIGURE 2-16

Other Ways

1. Right-click file name in Folder List pane, click Properties on shortcut menu, type new title in Title text box in General sheet in Properties dialog box
2. Right-click Page pane, click Properties on shortcut menu, type new title in Title text box in General sheet in Properties dialog box

Although FrontPage allows you to enter very long titles, browser title bars display approximately 80 to 90 characters, so keep this limitation in mind when entering the title.

Changing the Page Label of a Web Page

As you have seen, changing the title of a Web page did not affect the page label. FrontPage uses the page labels displayed in Navigation view as the labels for Link bars. If you change a page title, you also may want the labels on corresponding Link bars to match. You can change the text that is displayed on a Link bar by changing the page labels in Navigation view.

Perform the steps on the next page to change the page label of the Photos page to indicate the content of the page in the labels of Link bars.

To Change the Page Label of a Web Page

1 Right-click the New Page 1 page icon. Point to Rename.

The shortcut menu displays (Figure 2-17).

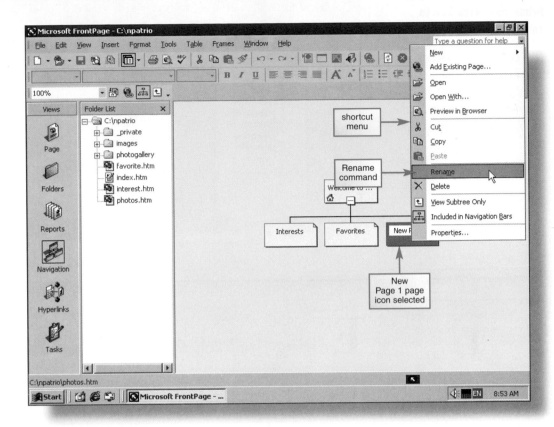

FIGURE 2-17

2 Click Rename.

An edit text box displays around the default label, and the label is selected (Figure 2-18).

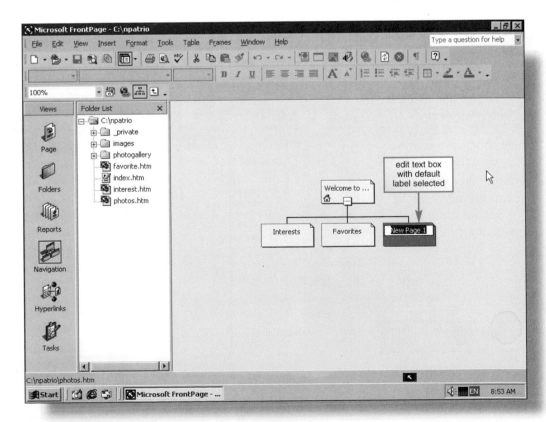

FIGURE 2-18

3 Type Photos in the edit text box. Press the ENTER key to save the new label.

The edit text box closes, and the new label displays in the page icon (Figure 2-19). If a new label is longer than the room available in the page icon, it still exists.

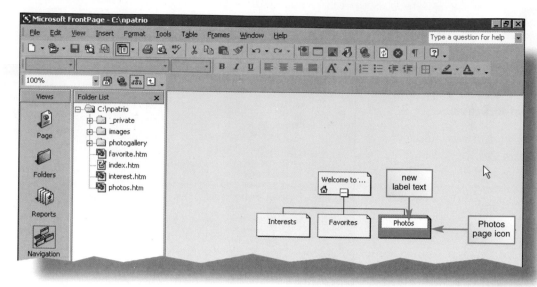

FIGURE 2-19

Editing the Web Page

The tasks required to create the Photos Web page consist of selecting the page background; inserting headings, images, and text; inserting a Photo Gallery component; and testing the page. In FrontPage, Web pages are edited in Page view. Perform the following steps to edit the Photos page.

Steps **To Edit a Web Page in Page View**

1 Double-click the Photos page icon in the Navigation pane.

The file photos.htm opens in Page view (Figure 2-20). The display area is empty, however, the theme for the web is applied to the page automatically.

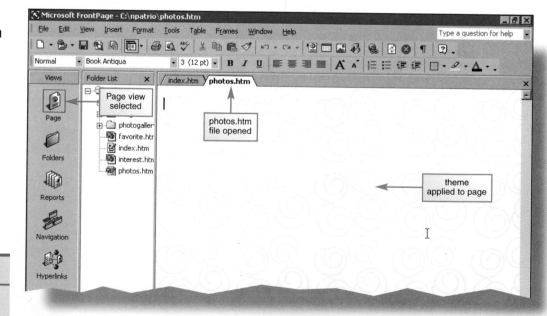

FIGURE 2-20

With the page open in Page view, you can start customizing the Web page to implement the design shown in Figure 2-3 on page FP 2.08. Because this web had a theme applied before adding the new page, the theme was applied to the new page automatically. In this case, a background color with no theme applied is desired. The first step is to remove the current theme from only this page, but not from the rest of the web. After the theme has been removed, the default background color will be changed.

Changing the Theme for a Single Web Page

Themes typically are applied to an entire web, as was done in Project 1. In some cases, a particular page in a web might not present well with the current theme, yet the theme is attractive for the remainder of the web. With FrontPage, it is easy to apply a different theme, or no theme at all, to an individual page in a web.

Perform the following steps to remove the current theme from the Photos page.

Steps **To Change the Theme for a Web Page**

1 **Click Format on the menu bar and then click Theme. When the Themes dialog box displays, point to (No Theme) in the Themes list.**

The Themes dialog box displays. The Sample of Theme area displays a sample page using the currently selected theme (Figure 2-21).

FIGURE 2-21

2 **Click (No Theme). If necessary, click Selected page(s). Point to the OK button.**

The Sample of Theme area displays a sample page using no theme (Figure 2-22).

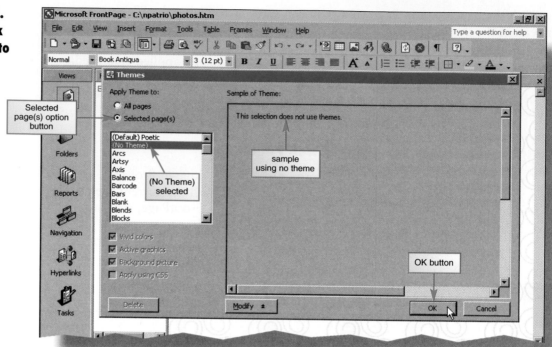

FIGURE 2-22

3 **Click the OK button.**

The Photos page displays with no theme applied (Figure 2-23).

FIGURE 2-23

1. Press ALT+O, H

Now that the Photos page no longer has the theme applied, you can change the default background and text colors.

Changing the Background Color of a Web Page

The **background** of a Web page can be a solid color, an image, or a pattern that is repeated across and down the page. You can select a color from within FrontPage, select an image or pattern stored on your local computer, or copy an image or pattern from any Web page on the World Wide Web.

Because the current theme was removed, the Photos page displays in the default background color white. According to the design, you are to use a solid color for the background. Perform the steps on the next page to change the background color of the Web page to a solid color.

To Change the Background Color

1 **Click Format on the menu bar and them point to Background.**

The Format menu displays (Figure 2-24). The **Format menu** contains commands to manage Web page formatting items such as themes, style sheets, and backgrounds.

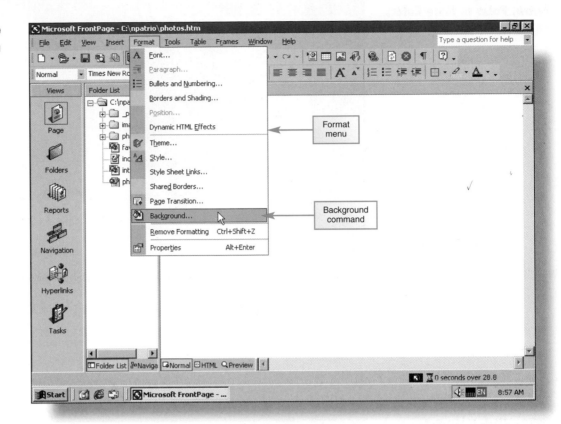

FIGURE 2-24

2 **Click Background. If necessary, click the Background tab. In the Colors area, point to the Background box arrow.**

The Page Properties dialog box displays (Figure 2-25). The **Background sheet** contains settings to control the background image or color.

FIGURE 2-25

3 **Click the Background box arrow. Point to More Colors on the color palette.**

A palette of available background colors displays (Figure 2-26).

FIGURE 2-26

4 **Click More Colors. Click the indicated color. Point to the OK button.**

The More Colors dialog box displays (Figure 2-27). The selected color will display Hex={FF,CC,FF} in the Value text box.

FIGURE 2-27

5 Click the OK button. Point to the OK button in the Page Properties dialog box.

The More Colors dialog box closes (Figure 2-28). The Page Properties dialog box is visible with the selected color displaying in the Background box.

FIGURE 2-28

6 Click the OK button.

The Page Properties dialog box closes (Figure 2-29). The page displays with the selected color as the background color.

FIGURE 2-29

1. Right-click Web page, click Page Properties on shortcut menu, click Background tab

2. Press ALT+O, K, click Background tab

When you click the Background box arrow, the color palette displays and allows you to select the color of your choice.

Selecting **More Colors** on the color palette displays a More Colors dialog box (Figure 2-27 on page FP 2.22) with additional predefined colors available. For even more colors, click the Custom button in the More Colors dialog box to display a Color dialog box (Figure 2-30) in which you can mix your own color, save it as a custom color, and then use it as the background color.

Web Page Colors

FrontPage uses hue, saturation, and luminosity to specify colors. Hue represents a gradation of color, such as red or blue. Saturation is the amount of color in a hue. Luminosity is the brightness of a hue. Many sites offer help on selecting appropriate colors for Web pages. For more information about selecting colors for Web pages, visit the FrontPage 2002 More About page (scsite.com/fp2002/more .htm) and then click Web Page Colors.

FIGURE 2-30

Inserting a Table on a Web Page

Tables are used frequently in applications to present information in a clear, concise format. Disciplines such as mathematics, engineering, and chemistry all take advantage of tables. A computer spreadsheet is laid out in the form of a table with rows and columns. Many different applications exist for which tables are an ideal solution.

Tables

A table can have a different background color or image than the rest of the Web page. The Table Properties dialog box contains options that allow you to choose a different background color or an image file to display as a table background.

An HTML table consists of one or more rows containing one or more columns. The intersection of a row and column is called a **cell.** Any Web page component, such as text or an image, can be placed in a cell.

Normally, you would use tables on a Web page to display any type of information that looks best in rows and columns, such as a list of products and their corresponding prices. In Web pages, tables also can be used to accomplish special design effects, such as positioning of elements on a Web page.

You can create a table and insert your entire Web page in the cells. Using tables, you can define headings, sidebars, and captions and use other creative design techniques.

In the Photos Web page, you will use a table with three rows and three columns to control the positioning of images, text, and the photo gallery (Figure 2-3 on page FP 2.08). Perform the following steps to insert a table in a Web page.

Steps To Insert a Table in a Web Page

1 Click the Insert
Table button on
the Standard toolbar.

*The Insert Table grid
displays (Figure 2-31). A
grid is a graphical means
of displaying the number of
rows and columns used in a
table. You can indicate how
many rows and columns the
table will have by dragging
through the grid.*

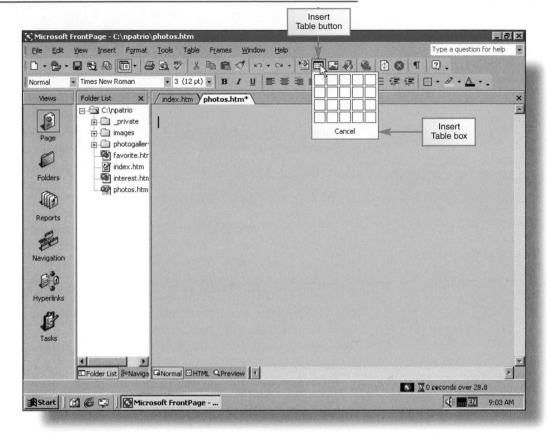

FIGURE 2-31

2 Point to the cell
in the third row
and third column to select
nine squares in the grid.

*The nine squares are selected
(Figure 2-32). This indicates
a three-row table with three
columns, for a total of nine
cells.*

FIGURE 2-32

3 Click the mouse button.

A table displays in the Web page with three rows and three columns (Figure 2-33). The table extends across the width of the Web page. Each cell is the same size.

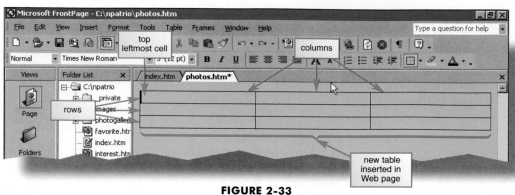

FIGURE 2-33

Other Ways

1. On Table menu click Insert, click Table
2. Press ALT+A, I, T

The Insert Table grid opens with only four rows and five columns. You can add more rows or columns simply by continuing to drag through the grid. FrontPage will add more rows and columns automatically.

Extra rows can be added to the bottom of the table on the Web page by positioning the insertion point in the last column of the last row and then pressing the TAB key. You also can insert rows or columns anywhere in the table by positioning the insertion point and then clicking Insert on the Table menu and then clicking Rows or Columns. A dialog box will display, allowing you to choose whether to insert rows or columns, the number to insert, and whether they should display above or below the current insertion point.

Merging Cells in a Table

When using a table to position items on a Web page, it is not unusual that some items span multiple cells in the table. By merging two or more cells in a table, you can set alignments more complex than straight rows and columns.

Perform the following steps to merge cells in the table that you just inserted.

Steps **To Merge Cells in a Table**

1 Click the leftmost cell in the middle row of the table. Hold down the SHIFT key and click the rightmost cell in the middle row. Right-click one of the selected cells. Point to Merge Cells on the shortcut menu.

The selected middle cells are highlighted, and a shortcut menu displays (Figure 2-34).

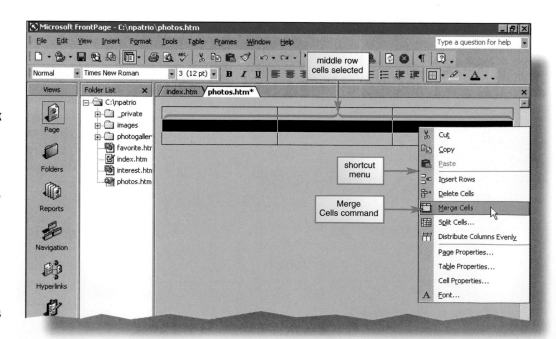

FIGURE 2-34

2 **Click Merge Cells. Click the top leftmost cell to remove the highlighting.**

The selected middle cells are merged into a single cell spanning three columns (Figure 2-35).

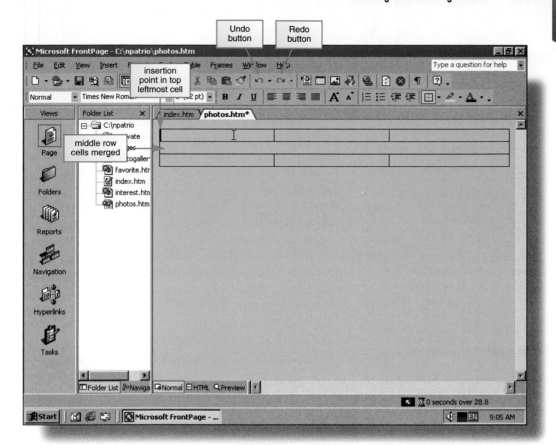

FIGURE 2-35

Other Ways

1. On Table menu click Merge Cells
2. Press ALT+A, M
3. Select cells, in Voice Command mode, say "Table, Merge Cells"

Undoing and Redoing Actions

Even if you take great care when creating your Web pages, you may make mistakes or you may want to make an immediate change. FrontPage provides facilities to help you undo errors with the **Undo button** on the Standard toolbar (Figure 2-35) or the **Undo command** on the Edit menu. Thus, if you make a change or a mistake, undo it using either the Undo button or the Undo command. FrontPage will reverse your action up to 30 consecutive actions.

Also available for quick reversal of errors and changes are the **Redo button** on the Standard toolbar and the **Redo command** on the Edit menu. Redo reverses the effect of the last Undo command. If you decide the undo is incorrect, you can click the Redo button or Redo command to restore the last change you made. Redo is available for 30 consecutive actions.

Both the Undo button and the Redo button have arrows that allow you to see the most recent undo or redo commands, respectively. This allows you to see what actions you would be undoing or redoing before actually selecting them, and to select more than one consecutive action to undo or redo.

As you work with FrontPage, you will find that using the Undo and Redo buttons facilitates the creative process. You can add and rearrange items to see if they work, knowing you can return to a previous starting point with little effort.

Other Ways

1. Press ALT+E, U to undo
2. Press ALT+E, R to redo
3. Press CTRL+Z to undo
4. Press CTRL+Y to redo

Inserting an Image in a Web Page

Regardless of how impressive your written message, people always will respond to images. The viewer's eye is drawn naturally to a picture before reading any text. The choice and quality of images you use largely will determine whether someone will take the time to read your Web page or pass it by.

Much of the Web's success is due to its capability of presenting images. Because of the impact of images on the Web, it is important to master the image options necessary to include pictures on your Web pages.

Along with the text heading, the Photos page has two images in the header. The table you inserted in earlier steps will be used to control the amount of horizontal spacing between the images and the text. The image on the left will be right-aligned in the left cell of the table. The image on the right will be left-aligned in the right cell of the table. The text, which is inserted later in the project, will be centered in the middle cell.

The goal of the images at the top of the page is to reflect the concept that the Photos page is a like a computer-based photo album. Therefore, an image with an inviting cartoon caricature of a book is appropriate. Refer to Table 2-1 on page FP 2.06 for criteria on the appropriate use of metaphors in your Web designs.

FrontPage includes a library of ready-to-use images and photographs, called **clip art**, you can insert into your Web pages. Some images are probably available on your local machine, but many more are accessible online. You also can use images from many different sources outside of FrontPage. You may use clip art from the FrontPage library or from the Data Disk to select an image for the Photos Web page.

To insert an image, you first position the insertion point at the desired location, and then select the image. Perform the following steps to insert an image in the Web page.

Clip Art

One way to organize your clip art is to create a personal collection list using the Clip Organizer. On the Insert menu, point to Picture and then click Clip Art. When the Insert Clip Art task pane displays, click Clip Organizer. You can create you own collections and even drag clips from one collection and drop them into the collections where you want them.

Steps To Insert a Clip Art Image in a Web Page

1 If necessary, click the top leftmost cell of the table to position the insertion point. Click Insert on the menu bar and then point to Picture. When the Picture submenu displays, point to Clip Art.

The Insert menu and the Picture submenu display (Figure 2-36).

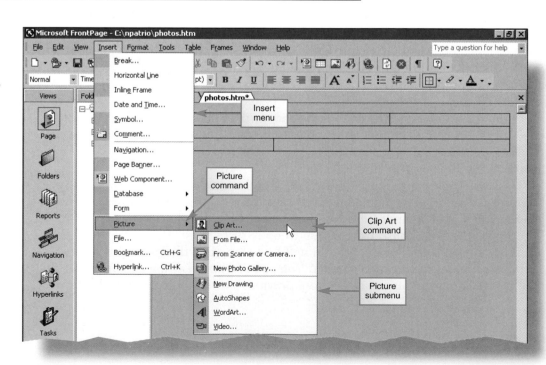

FIGURE 2-36

2 Click Clip Art. If the Add Clips to Organizer dialog box displays, click Later. When the Insert Clip Art task pane displays, type books in the Search text text box. Point to the Search button.

The Insert Clip Art task pane displays (Figure 2-37). You can search for an image file or clip art file from your personal collections or collections from Office on your local computer, or from Microsoft collections on the World Wide Web.

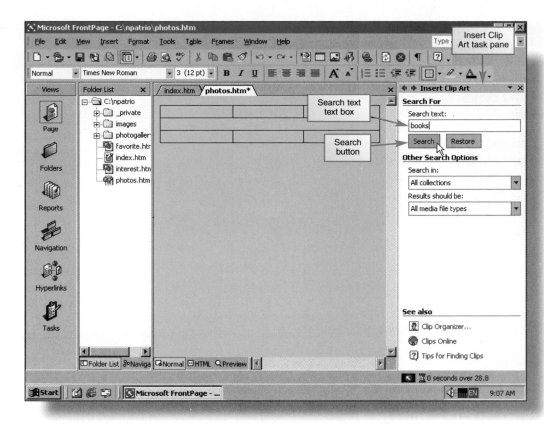

FIGURE 2-37

3 Click the Search button.

The results of your search display as small sample preview images (Figure 2-38). Your sample images may be different.

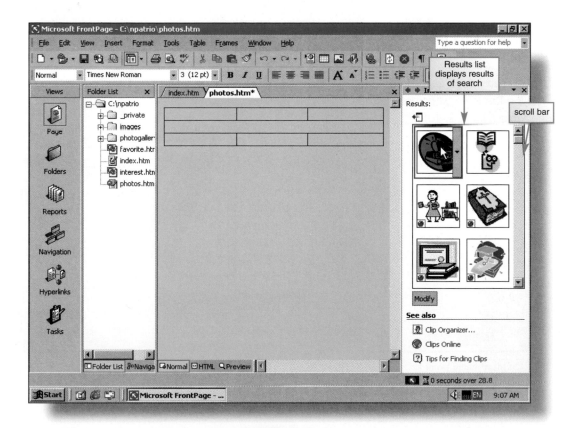

FIGURE 2-38

4 **If necessary, scroll down the Results list until an image of a book displays, or another image of your choice. Point to the image.**

When you point to the image, a box arrow displays on its right (Figure 2-39). A ScreenTip displays category, size, and file type information about the selected clip.

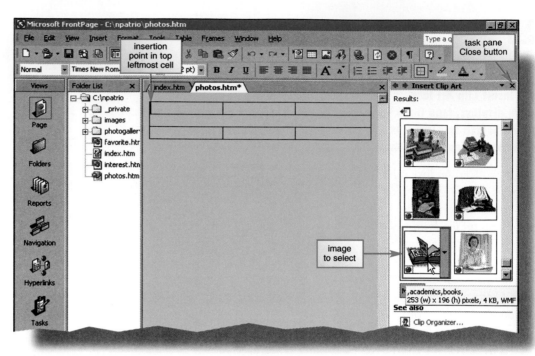

FIGURE 2-39

5 **Click the box arrow and then click Insert on the shortcut menu to insert the clip art on your Web page. Click the Close button on the task pane.**

The clip art image is inserted into the top leftmost cell of the table (Figure 2-40).

FIGURE 2-40

Other Ways

1. On Insert menu point to Picture, click Clip Art
2. On Insert menu point to Picture, click From File
3. Press ALT+I, P, C
4. Press ALT+I, P, F
5. Click Insert Picture From File button on Standard toolbar

As you can see in Figure 2-39, many samples of clip art may be available. Typically, the number of images on your local machine is limited. To obtain a large number of images, you can connect to the World Wide Web.

Replacing an Image in a Web Page

Once an image has been inserted into the Web page, you may decide that it is not as appealing as you originally thought. While there may be many reasons to change an image, replacing an image in a Web page is as easy as inserting the original image. You may replace the image simply by selecting a different image from the results of a search, or by using an image available on your local machine.

Many images used on a Web page may appear to be irregular in shape, when in fact they are rectangular. When the background color of the image is not the same as that of the Web page, the rectangular shape of the image becomes very obvious. To hide this rectangular shape, you can use images that have the same background color as your Web page, or you can use images that have a **transparent** background. Using images with a transparent background allows the color or image used in a Web page background to show through the background of the inserted image, thus hiding the rectangular shape of the image.

Perform the following steps to replace the image just inserted with a similar one from the local machine that has a transparent background.

More About

Images

The more images your Web site contains, the longer it takes to download your Web pages. To count the total number of images in your Web site, on the View menu, point to Reports, and then click Site Summary. In the Pictures row, the Count column lists the number of pictures in your web. Pictures located in hidden folders normally are not included in this report.

 To Replace a Clip Art Image in a Web Page

1 **Right-click the image to be replaced. Point to Picture Properties on the shortcut menu.**

A shortcut menu displays, and eight small boxes, called ***sizing handles****, display around the selected image (Figure 2-41).*

FIGURE 2-41

2 Click Picture Properties. When the Picture Properties dialog box displays, if necessary, click the General tab. Point to the Browse button in the Picture source area.

The Picture Properties dialog box displays. The name and location of the current image file is selected in the Picture source text box (Figure 2-42).

FIGURE 2-42

3 Click the Browse button. Insert the Data Disk in drive A. When the Picture dialog box displays, if necessary, click the Look in box arrow and select the book02.gif file in the Project2 folder. Point to the Open button in the Picture dialog box.

The Picture dialog box displays with the book02.gif file in the A:\Project2 folder selected (Figure 2-43). Use the drive and location that are appropriate for your environment.

FIGURE 2-43

4 **Click the Open button. Point to the OK button.**

The Picture dialog box closes. The replacement image file name and location display in the Picture source text box (Figure 2-44).

FIGURE 2-44

5 **Click the OK button. If necessary, resize the replacement image by dragging the sizing handles.**

The selected image replaces the previous image (Figure 2-45). Sizing handles display around the selected image. The mouse pointer changes to a double-headed arrow when positioned on a sizing handle.

FIGURE 2-45

Other Ways

1. Click image, click Insert Picture From File button on Pictures toolbar

Copying and Pasting an Image on a Web Page

One of the features of Windows applications is the capability of copying information from one Windows application and inserting it in another Windows application. You can cut or copy portions of a Web page to a temporary storage area in computer memory, called the **Clipboard**, and then paste the contents of the Clipboard to other areas of the Web page. **Copy, Cut,** and **Paste** are useful when you want to move an item to another location or have the same item appearing several times in various places throughout the Web page. The computer clip art image you just inserted is to be inserted again, this time in the rightmost cell of the table.

You can, of course, insert the clip art image using the steps you performed previously for inserting an image. You also can copy the image to the Clipboard and then paste the image from the Clipboard to the Web page at the location of the insertion point. In this instance, the copy and paste operation would be more efficient, because you would have to maneuver through several windows to get the image from the Microsoft Clip Gallery or from an image on disk. Perform the following steps to copy and then paste the book image to another location on the Web page.

More *About*

Copying and Pasting

You can copy images to a Web page by dragging the image from another Windows application to FrontPage. In addition to the Copy and Paste commands on the Edit menu, you also may use the shortcut keys, CTRL+C and CTRL+V.

 Steps **To Copy and Paste an Image on a Web Page**

---

1 If necessary, click the clip art image to select it. Click Edit on the menu bar and then point to Copy.

The image is selected and the Edit menu displays (Figure 2-46). The **Copy command** *copies a selected item to the Clipboard.*

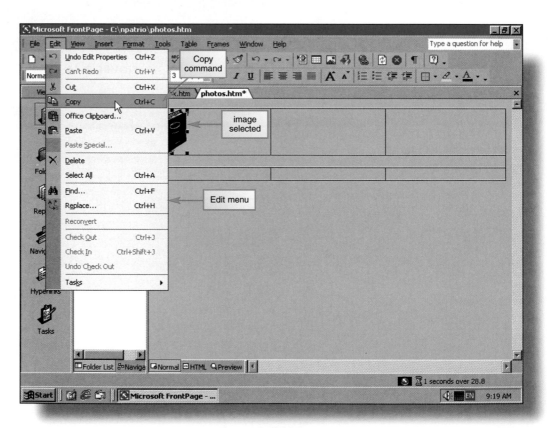

FIGURE 2-46

2 Click Copy and then click the top rightmost cell of the table to position the insertion point. Click Edit on the menu bar and then point to Paste.

*The Edit menu displays (Figure 2-47). The image is copied to the Clipboard. The **Paste command** inserts the contents of the Clipboard at the location of the insertion point.*

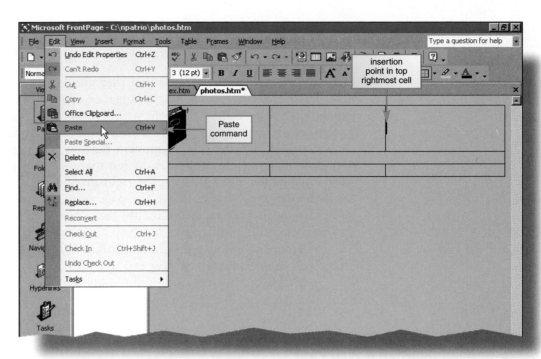

FIGURE 2-47

3 Click Paste.

The image on the Clipboard is copied to the rightmost table cell (Figure 2-48).

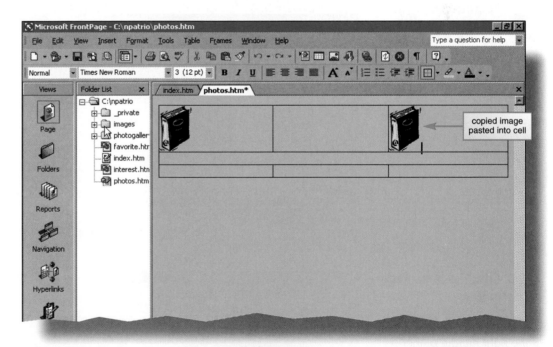

FIGURE 2-48

You can copy text or an entire table and then paste it in a similar fashion. Although the contents of the Clipboard can be inserted into other Windows applications, some objects will not display as you would expect. Because other Windows applications do not understand HTML, they will not make an accurate copy of the three row, three column table if you were to try pasting it. You can, however, copy or cut and paste the clip art images and any text into other Windows applications. You will lose any special formatting applied to the text, however. This, again, is because of the problem with translating HTML.

Other Ways

1. Press ALT+E, C to copy
2. Press ALT+E, P to paste
3. Press CTRL+C to copy
4. Press CTRL+V to paste

Using Tables to Control Alignment on a Web Page

One advantage of using tables is that they allow you to control the arrangement of items on the Web page. You can arrange, or **align**, the current text or image to the left within a table cell, to the right within a table cell, or centered in the table cell. The default alignment for newly inserted items is left-aligned.

FrontPage provides three alignment buttons on the Formatting toolbar. The **Align Left button** aligns an item at the left margin of the page or table cell. The **Align Right button** aligns items at the right margin of the page or table cell. The **Center button** centers items across the page or in a table cell. You simply select the paragraph or image by clicking it, and then click the appropriate alignment button on the Formatting toolbar.

To demonstrate how to align items on a Web page, you will select the clip art image you inserted in the leftmost cell and right-align it in the cell, which results in the clip art image aligning at the right along with text that will follow later. Perform the following steps to align an item on a Web page.

Steps **To Align Items on a Web Page**

1 **If necessary, click the clip art image in the leftmost cell to select it. Point to the Align Right button on the Formatting toolbar.**

The clip art image is selected (Figure 2-49)

FIGURE 2-49

2 **Click the Align Right button.**

The clip art image is aligned at the right margin of the table cell (Figure 2-50). The Align Right button on the Formatting toolbar is selected to denote that the image has been right-aligned.

FIGURE 2-50

The image is right-aligned in the leftmost table cell on the Web page. In later steps you use the Center button to center text and other items on the Web page.

Adjusting Table Borders

Another useful feature of tables is the capability of moving the outside borders of a table and the borders between individual cells, thus providing added flexibility in controlling spacing on the Web page.

You can adjust the borders of the table to control vertical and horizontal spacing. The bottom border can be dragged up or down to control vertical spacing. The right border can be dragged right or left to control horizontal spacing. The borders between cells also can be moved to control spacing within the table.

As shown in Figure 2-50 on the previous page, the clip art images do not consume all the space in their respective cells. You can adjust the borders between the cells to reduce the space in the two outside cells and increase the space in the center cell, thus providing more room for the heading. Perform the following steps to adjust the borders of table cells.

Steps **To Adjust Table Cell Borders**

1 **Point to the cell border between the first and second cell.**

The mouse pointer changes to a double-headed arrow (Figure 2-51).

FIGURE 2-51

2 **Drag the cell border left, to the right edge of the clip art image and release the mouse button.**

The cell border moves to the left (Figure 2-52).

FIGURE 2-52

3 Point to the cell border between the second and third cell. Drag the cell border right, to the left edge of the clip art image, so that the rightmost cell is approximately the same size as the leftmost cell.

The cell border moves to the right (Figure 2-53).

FIGURE 2-53

1. On Table menu point to Table Properties, click Cell
2. Right-click cell, click Cell Properties on shortcut menu
3. Press ALT+A, R, E

Moving the cell to occupy the minimum width for the images allows more space in the center cell for the Photos page heading text. You should insert the images in the table cells before adjusting the cell borders so that you can see how much space is available. Adjusting table and cell borders is a powerful way of controlling spacing on a Web page.

Modifying Table Properties

A number of table properties can be adjusted to control how the table will display on your Web page. You can adjust the horizontal alignment of the table with respect to the Web page. You may adjust the width of the table as a percentage of the entire page, or as some number of pixels. A **pixel**, short for **picture element**, is the smallest addressable element on your computer screen. Instead of dragging cell borders, you also may set the cell width directly by specifying the width as a percentage of the table, or as some number of pixels.

Tables and the individual cells are surrounded by a default table border. You can adjust the properties of the border, such as the width, color, and use of a 3-D shadow. When using a table for spacing purposes, you most likely will not want the table borders to be seen. You can turn off the border display and adjust other table properties by using the **Table Properties command** on the Table menu. Perform the steps on the next page to modify table properties.

To Modify the Properties of a Table

1 If necessary, click in one of the cells of the table. Click Table on the menu bar. Point to Table Properties and then point to Table.

*The Table menu and Table Properties submenu display (Figure 2-54). The **Table menu** contains commands to manage tables. The **Table Properties submenu** contains commands to access properties of tables or individual cells.*

FIGURE 2-54

2 Click Table on the Table Properties submenu. When the Table Properties dialog box displays, click the Alignment box down arrow in the Layout area and point to Center.

*The Table Properties dialog box displays (Figure 2-55). Options in this dialog box allow you to control various aspects of the table border and table background. The **Alignment box** in the **Layout area** allows you to control the horizontal alignment of the table on the Web page.*

FIGURE 2-55

3 **Click Center. If necessary, in the Layout area click Specify width and click In pixels. Type 688 in the Specify width text box. Point to the Size box down arrow in the Borders area.**

The alignment for the table is set to Center and the width is set to 688 pixels (Figure 2-56).

FIGURE 2-56

4 **Click the Size box down arrow until zero (0) displays in the Size box. Point to the OK button.**

Zero (0) displays in the Size box indicating that no visible border will display around the table cells (Figure 2-57).

FIGURE 2-57

5 **Click the OK button.**

The table width is set and the table border is replaced with dashed lines (Figure 2-58). These lines show you where the cell borders are and also indicate that no visible border will display when the Web page displays in a browser.

FIGURE 2-58

You have adjusted the borders around table cells and turned off the display of the table border. Now that the size of the center cell has been adjusted, you can insert the heading for the Web page.

Inserting a Heading in a Web Page

Text on a Web page can take many forms, such as a heading, ordered and unordered lists, menus, and normal text. To this text, you can apply special formatting such as different fonts, colors, and sizes. You use the Formatting toolbar for the more frequently used formatting options.

The process of entering text using FrontPage has several steps. You might skip one or more of the steps, depending on the current settings. The first step is to select a text style. The **Style box** on the Formatting toolbar contains styles such as lists, menu items, headings, and normal text.

After selecting a style, you may change the font type for the text or use the font type associated with the chosen style. A **font** is another name for character set. Some commonly used fonts are Courier, Helvetica, and Arial. You change the font using the **Font box** on the Formatting toolbar.

Next, you select a color for the text. The default color is black. A text color that complements the background color or image you have chosen is preferred so your text does not fade in and out as it moves across a background image or pattern. You do not want your page to be difficult to read because of poor color selection. To change the color of text, use the **Font Color button arrow** on the Formatting toolbar. You can choose from a set of standard colors, from a set that matches a theme if a theme is applied, or mix your own custom colors.

The Formatting toolbar contains many text formatting options. The **Font Size box** allows you to increase or decrease the size of the characters in your text. Using the **Bold, Italic,** and **Underline** buttons, you can format certain text in bold, italic, or underline.

The Photos page heading, which will be placed in the center table cell, consists of Heading 2 as its style, and maroon for the font color. The font and font size used are the default for the style of Heading 2. The heading also is centered in the cell. The text on either side of the photo gallery will use the same font color, but will have a style of Normal and a font size of 2 (10 pt). Perform the steps on the next page to set the style and color, and then insert the heading in the center cell.

Steps To Add a Heading to a Web Page

1 If necessary, click the top center table cell to position the insertion point. Click the Style box arrow. If necessary, scroll down and then point to Heading 2 in the Style list.

The insertion point displays in the top center table cell, and the Style list displays (Figure 2-59). It contains a list of styles available for use when developing Web pages.

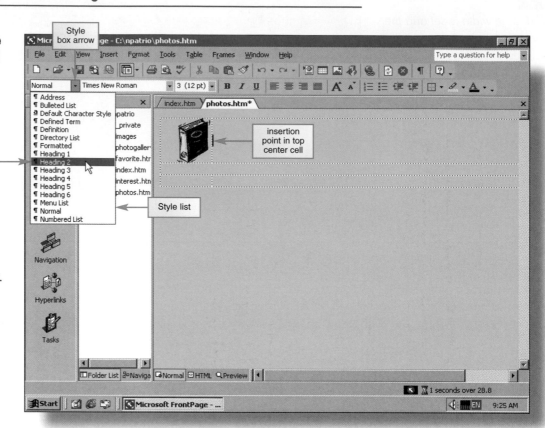

FIGURE 2-59

2 Click Heading 2. Click the Center button on the Formatting toolbar. Type Friends and Family **in the top center cell. Press** SHIFT + ENTER. **Type** Photo Album **to enter the remainder of the text.**

The text displays centered in the top middle table cell with a style of Heading 2 (Figure 2-60). The font and the font size associated with the style Heading 2 are displayed in the Font box and the Font Size box, respectively. The Bold button on the Formatting toolbar is selected automatically. Your font and font size may be different.

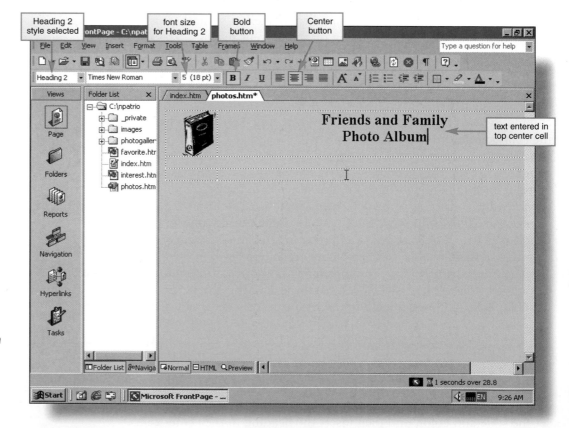

FIGURE 2-60

3 Drag through the text to select it. Click the Font Color button arrow. When the color palette displays, point to the Maroon button in the Standard Colors area.

The color palette displays (Figure 2-61).

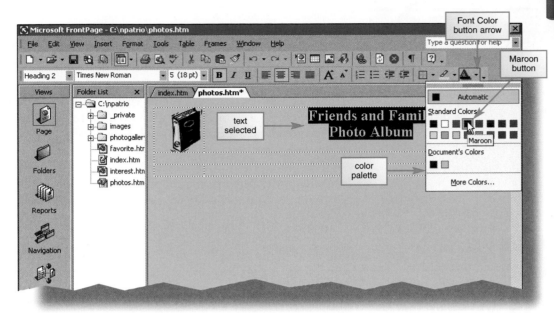

FIGURE 2-61

4 Click the Maroon button. Click the second row of the table to deselect the text.

The text displays centered in the center topmost cell with a color of maroon (Figure 2-62).

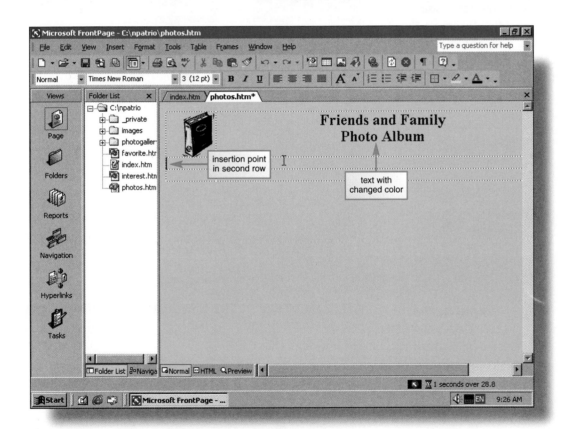

FIGURE 2-62

Other Ways

1. On Format menu, click Font, click Font tab
2. Right-click, click Font, click Font tab
3. Press ALT+ENTER

Because it is the part of the page that first-time viewers initially see in their browsers, it is important to format the header of the Web page so it is appealing and draws further interest. The body of the Web page keeps the viewer's attention when it is verbalized and formatted appropriately. It is customary to separate logical sections of Web pages, such as the header and body, using dividing elements called horizontal lines, or horizontal rules.

More About

Horizontal Rules

After adding a horizontal line, or rule, you can modify its appearance. Double-click the line, and in the Horizontal Line Properties dialog box, change the alignment, width, height, and color properties. If your page uses a theme, you can change only the alignment of the line.

Inserting a Horizontal Rule

The use of elements such as a horizontal rule can add a special look to your pages, as well as provide the viewer with visual clues concerning the location of information on the Web page. Horizontal rules are used to break up the page into sections, and to separate elements on the page. A **horizontal rule** is a small, thin line that spans the entire Web page.

You will use a horizontal rule to separate the header section of the Web page from the body. Perform the following steps to insert a horizontal rule below the table cells containing the clip art images and heading.

Steps **To Add a Horizontal Rule to a Web Page**

1 If necessary, click the second table row to position the insertion point. Click Insert on the menu bar, and then point to Horizontal Line.

*The Insert menu displays (Figure 2-63). The **Insert menu** contains commands to insert various elements in the current Web page.*

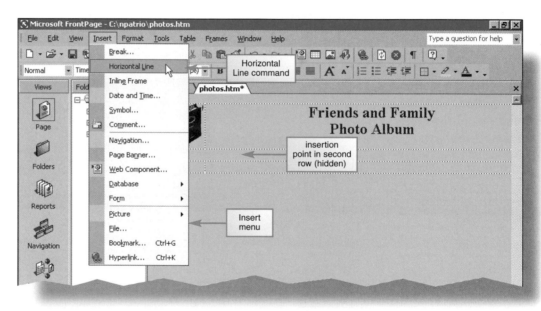

FIGURE 2-63

2 Click Horizontal Line. Press the DELETE key to remove the trailing blank line.

The horizontal rule displays in the middle row (Figure 2-64).

FIGURE 2-64

Other Ways

1. Press ALT+I, L

You can adjust the properties of the horizontal rule, such as the thickness and length, by right-clicking the horizontal rule and then clicking Horizontal Line Properties on the shortcut menu. The alignment of the horizontal rule also can be controlled using the Align Left, Center, and Align Right buttons on the Formatting toolbar.

Adding Normal Text to a Web Page

Notice in Figure 2-62 on page FP 2.43 that the style and font reverted to the default values. This occurs whenever you move the insertion point with the mouse or arrow keys. You need to set the style, font, and color again in preparation for entering more text.

The steps for adding normal text are similar to the steps you used previously to add the heading: set the style, and either use the associated font, font size, and color, or manually set these properties. According to the design, the text in the leftmost bottom cell is to be aligned along the top edge of the cell, while the text in the right-most cell is to retain a default alignment. Follow these steps to add the normal text that will display on the Web page.

 To Add Normal Text to a Web Page

1 **Right-click the bottom leftmost cell. Point to Cell Properties on the shortcut menu.**

The shortcut menu displays (Figure 2-65).

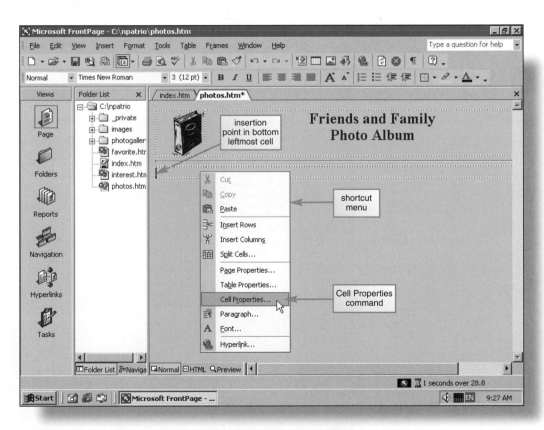

FIGURE 2-65

2 **Click Cell Properties. When the Cell Properties dialog box displays, in the Layout area, click the Vertical alignment box arrow and point to Top.**

The Vertical alignment list displays the choices for vertical alignment in the cell (Figure 2-66).

FIGURE 2-66

3 **Click Top. Click the OK button.**

The Cell Properties dialog box closes (Figure 2-67). Although no change is visible, when an item is displayed in this cell, it will be aligned along the top cell edge.

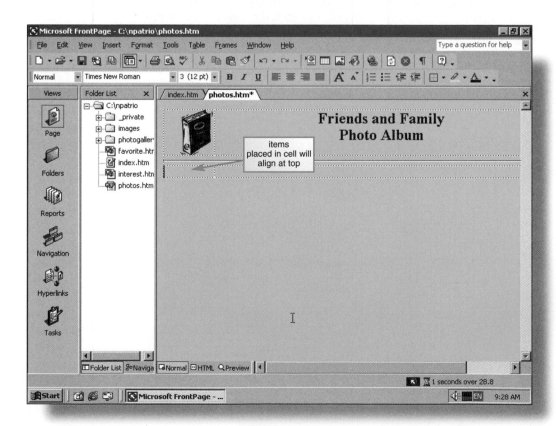

FIGURE 2-67

4 If necessary, click Normal in the Style list. If necessary, click the Font box arrow on the Formatting toolbar and then click Times New Roman. Click the Align Right button on the Formatting toolbar. Click the Font Size box arrow on the Formatting toolbar and then point to 2 (10 pt).

The Style box indicates Normal style, the Font box indicates Times New Roman, and 2 (10 pt) is selected in the Font Size list (Figure 2-68).

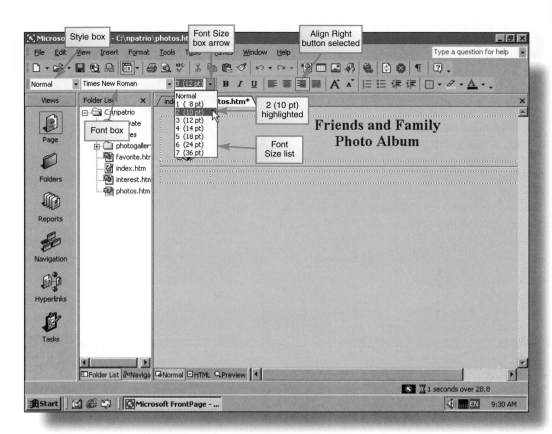

FIGURE 2-68

5 Click 2 (10 pt). **Type** Point to an image to see a caption **in the bottom leftmost cell.**

The text entered displays right-aligned on the Web page (Figure 2-69).

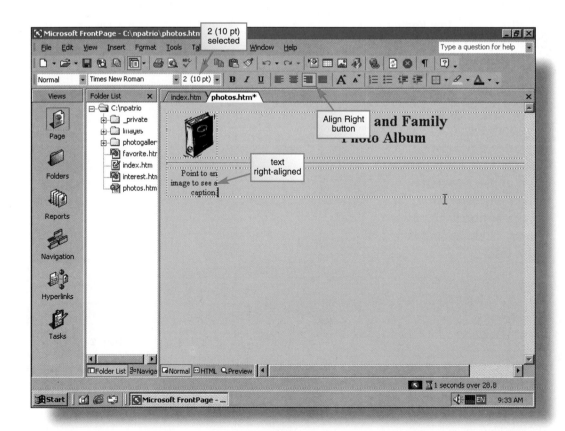

FIGURE 2-69

6 Drag through the entered text to select it. Click the Font Color button arrow on the Formatting toolbar and then click the Maroon button in the color palette. Click the bottom center cell to deselect the text.

The newly entered text displays with maroon as the font color (Figure 2-70).

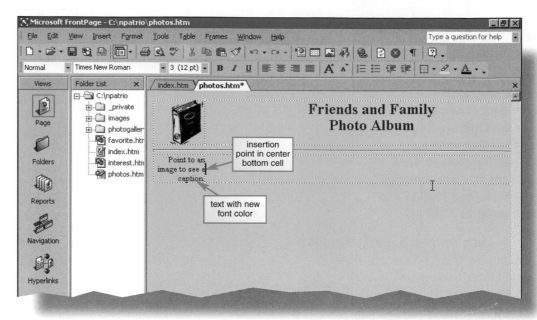

FIGURE 2-70

7 Click the rightmost bottom cell to position the insertion point. If necessary, click Normal in the Style list and click Times New Roman in the Font list. Click the Font Size box arrow and then click 2 (10 pt). Type Click an image to see a larger view in the cell. Drag through the entered text to select it. Click the Font Color button arrow on the Formatting toolbar and then click the Maroon button in the color palette. Click the bottom center cell.

The newly text entered displays in Normal style, Times New Roman font, with a font size of 10 pt and a font color of maroon (Figure 2-71).

FIGURE 2-71

Other Ways

1. Select text, right-click text, click Font on shortcut menu
2. Select text, press ALT+ENTER

You can see from the previous steps that the Formatting toolbar is very useful when entering text. You can change styles, fonts, size, and other properties very quickly as you move through the body of the Web page.

Adding a Photo Gallery Component

One strength of Web pages is the capability to display images as well as text. Some information is better communicated in a textual form, while much fits the old adage of a picture being "worth a thousand words." This is especially true when dealing with photographic clip art, because photos are meant to be seen, not just described. There are issues, however, with using photos in a Web page. First of all, the data files for photos tend to be large. Visitors to a Web page may not wait for the page to download when large pictures slow down the process. Also, when positioning text with photographs, it can be tedious and difficult to get an arrangement that is pleasing, especially when dealing with a large number of pictures.

FrontPage has a component called a Photo Gallery that presents solutions to many of these problems. A **Photo Gallery component** offers several customizable layouts for photos and provides for captions. The montage layout displays captions as ScreenTips when the mouse pointer rests on them. The pictures used in the layouts are actually thumbnail images of the original pictures, created automatically by using the Photo Gallery component. A **thumbnail image** is a small image that is a hyperlink to a larger version of the same picture. Using a thumbnail version of an image can speed up the time it takes to load a Web page, because only a smaller version is used. When you click the thumbnail image, the full-sized version of the file is loaded in your browser.

Perform the following steps to insert a Photo Gallery component.

More About

Photo Gallery Components

The Photo Gallery component offers four layouts: Horizontal, Vertical, Montage, and Slideshow. You should examine each to determine which option is most appropriate for the photos you want to display.

Steps | **To Add a Photo Gallery Component**

---

1 If necessary, click the middle cell in the bottom row of the table to position the insertion point. Click the Center button on the Formatting toolbar.

The insertion point displays centered in the middle cell of the bottom table row (Figure 2-72).

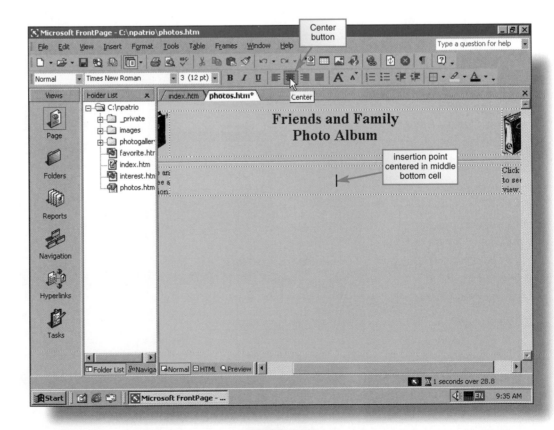

FIGURE 2-72

2 **Click Insert on the menu bar and then point to Web Component.**

The Insert menu displays (Figure 2-73).

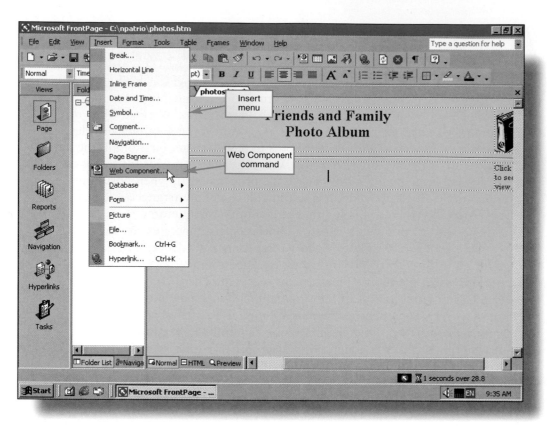

FIGURE 2-73

3 **Click Web Component. When the Insert Web Component dialog box displays, click Photo Gallery in the Component type list. Click the montage arrangement icon in the Choose a Photo Gallery Option list. Point to the Finish button.**

The Insert Web Component dialog box displays with the Photo Gallery component type and the montage option selected (Figure 2-74). A brief description of the selected layout displays.

FIGURE 2-74

4 Click the Finish button. If necessary, when the Photo Gallery Properties dialog box displays, click the Pictures tab. Point to the Add button.

The Photo Gallery Properties dialog box displays (Figure 2-75). The **Pictures sheet** contains settings to control the content, format, and text for a Photo Gallery.

FIGURE 2-75

5 Click the Add button. When the Add menu displays, point to Pictures from Files.

The Add menu displays (Figure 2-76). The commands on the Add menu enable you to obtain pictures from files, a scanner, or a camera.

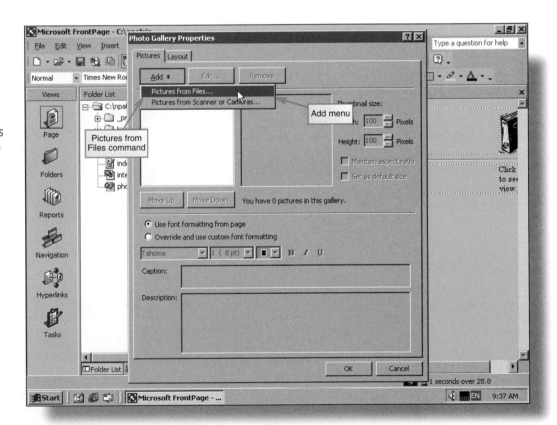

FIGURE 2-76

6 Click Pictures from Files. Insert the Data Disk in drive A. When the File Open dialog box displays, if necessary, click the Look in box arrow and select the Jennifer on phone.jpg file in the Project2 folder. Point to the Open button in the File Open dialog box.

The File Open dialog box displays (Figure 2-77). Use the drive and location that are appropriate for your environment.

FIGURE 2-77

7 Click the Open button. When the File Open dialog box closes and the Photo Gallery Properties dialog box again is visible, click the Caption text box and type Jennifer, on the phone! in the text box. Verify that a check mark displays in the Maintain aspect ratio check box. Point to the Add button.

The selected options for the Photo Gallery Properties dialog box are shown in Figure 2-78.

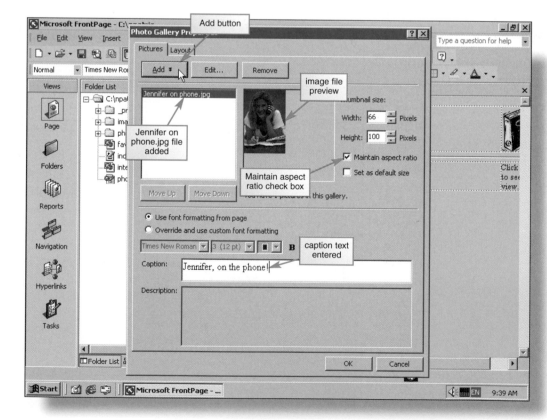

FIGURE 2-78

8 **Repeat Step 5 through Step 7 for the photos listed in Table 2-2, typing the associated text for each photo caption. After adding the last photo, point to the OK button.**

The remaining photos are added to the Photo Gallery list of photos (Figure 2-79). The Photo Gallery Properties dialog box indicates the number of pictures added.

FIGURE 2-79

9 **Click the OK button. Drag the table borders, if necessary, to adjust positioning of the text and images.**

The Photo Gallery Properties dialog box closes, and the Photo Gallery component generates and displays thumbnail images for the inserted photos on the Photos page (Figure 2-80).

Other Ways

1. On Insert menu point to Picture, click New Photo Gallery
2. Press ALT+I, P, P

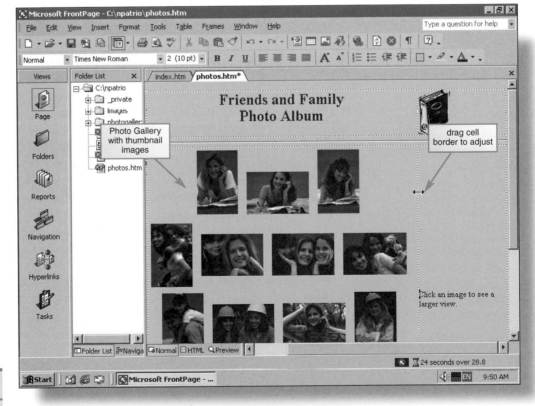

FIGURE 2-80

The thumbnail images are hyperlinks to their corresponding full-sized images. When a viewer clicks the thumbnail, the full-size image displays, much like a Web page would do. The browser, however, is displaying an image file not a Web page, so hyperlinks are not available to navigate back to the previous page. The viewer must click the browser's Back button to display another page.

Table 2-2	
PHOTO FILE NAME	*CAPTION*
Jennifer on phone.jpg	Jennifer, on the phone!
Danielle on phone.jpg	Danielle, on the phone!
Nikki on phone.jpg	Me, on the phone!
Nikki and sister.jpg	Big sister gives little sister a ride!
Jennifer with brother.jpg	Jennifer, with brother, Matt.
Jennifer and brother and sister.jpg	Jennifer, with brother, Matt, and sister, Diane.
Nikki and sister2.jpg	Nikki and Adrianne
Nikki and Dad.jpg	Me, with my Dad, when I was a bit younger.
Camille and Nikki in hard hats.jpg	Is Camille wearing my hat?
Jennifer on phone at car.jpg	Jennifer, still on the phone!
Jennifer in hard hat.jpg	Jennifer, at her Dad's new building site.
Jennifer with phone and credit card.jpg	Hmmm, she must be shopping - see the smile?
Nikki in hard hat.jpg	Should I become an architect?
Jennifer on car phone.jpg	Jennifer always finds a phone, wherever she is!

Inserting Link Bars on a Web Page

As previously discussed, Link bars are a commonly used component. The Poetic theme you applied to the web includes two Link bars — a **vertical Link bar** on the left-hand side of the page and a **horizontal Link bar** on the bottom. Link bars typically are used for either child-level navigation, which allows you to move between the Home Page (the parent) and the Interests page or Favorites page (the children) or same-level navigation, which allows you to move back and forth between pages at the same level, such as the Interests and Favorites pages. In the Personal Web template, both Link bars on a given page have the same navigation properties: links on the Home page are used for child-level navigation, and links on the child pages are set for same-level navigation. Each Link bar also has an additional link to the Home page.

Perform the steps on the next page to insert a Link bar component for the Photos page.

Steps **To Add a Link Bar Component**

1 **Position the insertion point at the end of the text in the bottom leftmost cell. Press the ENTER key. Click Insert on the menu bar and then point to the Navigation command.**

The insertion point displays in the leftmost cell of the bottom table row (Figure 2-81).

FIGURE 2-81

2 **Click Navigation. When the Insert Web Component dialog box displays, click Bar based on navigation structure in the Choose a bar type list. Point to the Next button.**

The Insert Web Component dialog box displays with the Link Bars component type already selected (Figure 2-82). A brief comment displays about the type of Link bar to be added.

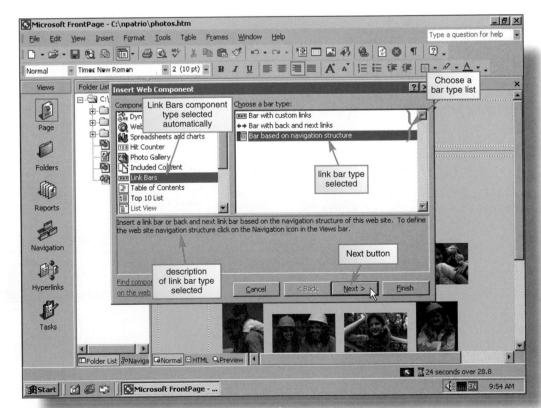

FIGURE 2-82

3 **Click the Next button. When the Choose a bar style list displays in the Insert Web Component dialog box, scroll down, if necessary, and click the icon for a graphical style based on the 'Poetic' theme. Point to the Next button.**

The Insert Web Component dialog box displays with a bar style selected based on the Poetic theme (Figure 2-83). A brief description of the selected style displays.

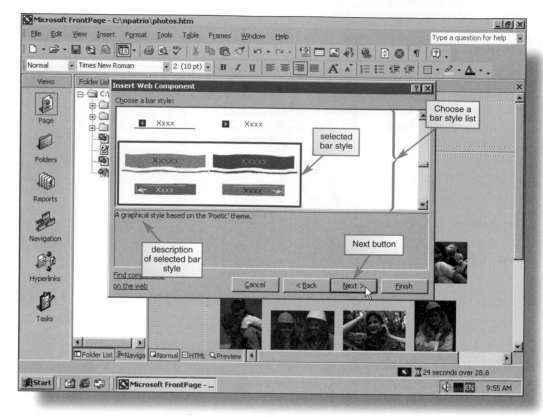

FIGURE 2-83

4 **Click the Next button. When the Choose an orientation list displays in the Insert Web Component dialog box, click the icon to insert the Link bar with the links arranged vertically. Point to the Finish button.**

The Insert Web Component dialog box displays with a vertical Link bar orientation selected (Figure 2-84). Some descriptive text indicates the arrangement to be used for the links.

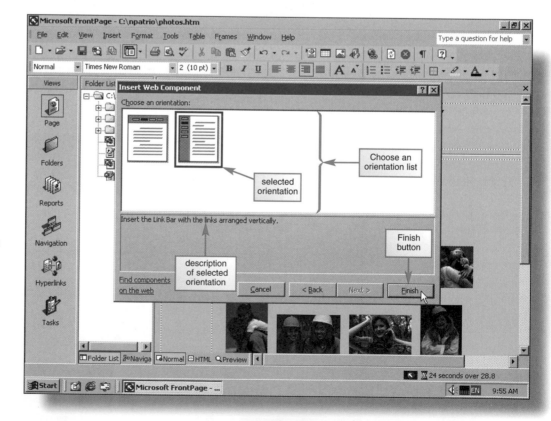

FIGURE 2-84

5 **Click the Finish button. When the Link Bar Properties dialog box displays, if necessary, click the General tab. Click Child pages under Home in the Hyperlinks to add to page area. Click Home page in the Additional pages area. Point to the OK button.**

The Link Bar Properties dialog box displays with child pages under Home and Home page selected (Figure 2-85). A diagram displays to indicate hierarchial relationships between the page on which the Link bar will display and the pages to which the Link bar will link.

FIGURE 2-85

6 **Click the OK button. Drag the cell borders to adjust positioning of the text, if necessary. Click the Preview tab and position the mouse pointer over a picture in the Photo Gallery.**

The Photos page displays with a Link bar based on the Poetic theme (Figure 2-86). The caption text for the indicated photo displays as a ScreenTip.

7 **Click the Normal tab.**

1. On Insert menu click Web Component, click Link Bars
2. Press ALT+I, V
3. Press ALT+I, W

FIGURE 2-86

Because the Photos page was added to the Web in Navigation view — thereby establishing a navigation structure with the Photo page as a child to the Home page — FrontPage was able to create the proper links for the Link bar automatically.

In addition to the Home page, the Link bar you just added also links to the other child pages in the web – the Interests page and the Favorites page. If you delete one of these pages from the current web, the Link bar component automatically removes links to the deleted page from the Link bars on all pages in the current web.

Previewing and Printing a Web Page

In Project 1, you printed the Web page without previewing it on the screen. By previewing the Web page, you can see how it will look when printed without generating a printout, or hard copy. Previewing a Web page using the Print Preview command on the File menu can save time, paper, and the frustration of waiting for a printout only to discover it is not what you want. You must be using the Normal tab in Page view to use print preview, as this command is not accessible when using the Preview tab.

You also can print the Web page while in print preview. Perform the following steps to preview and then print the Photos Web page.

Steps **To Preview and Print a Web Page**

1 **Ready the printer according to the printer instructions. Verify that the Normal tab is selected. Click File on the menu bar and then point to Print Preview (Figure 2-87).**

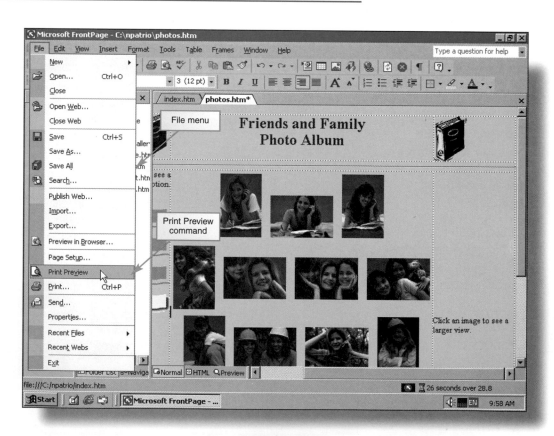

FIGURE 2-87

2 **Click Print Preview.**

FrontPage displays a preview of the Web page in the preview pane and the mouse pointer changes to a magnifying glass when positioned over the image of the page (Figure 2-88). You may click on the image to zoom in for a closer view.

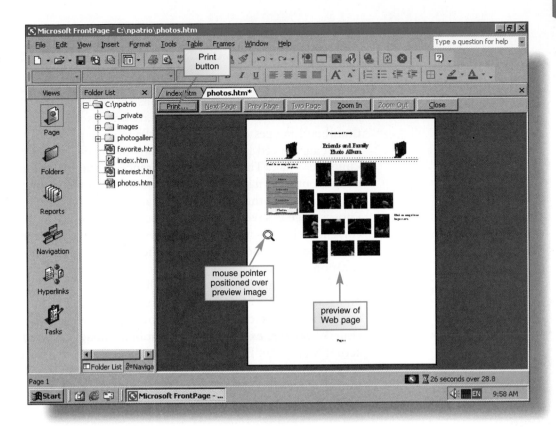

FIGURE 2-88

3 **Click the Print button on the Print Preview toolbar. Click the OK button in the Print dialog box.**

The preview pane closes and the Web page prints. When the printing operation is complete, retrieve the printout (Figure 2-89).

FIGURE 2-89

Other Ways

1. Press ALT+F, V

The Print Preview toolbar contains buttons to scroll through a multi-page printout, to zoom in and out of the Web page, and to close the preview pane. You can use print preview to determine the page number of a particular page in a multi-page printout, and then print only that page. This allows you to print only that section of a long Web page you are working on, thus saving time and paper.

Saving the Web Page and Embedded Images

Once you have finished editing the Web page you should save it on disk. With the Photos page, the save operation consists of saving the HTML and the clip art images for the Web page. Neither the clip art images you inserted in earlier steps nor the thumbnail images created by FrontPage were physically inserted in the Photos page. FrontPage placed HTML instructions to include the clip art image files using an <img src=> tag. This tag has a reference to the file name containing the clip art image, but the image still must be saved with the Web page.

Because the thumbnail images are part of a Photo Gallery component, when the Photos page is saved, they are saved automatically in the photogallery folder in the current web. When the Photos Web page is saved, it contains only the HTML tags referencing the book clip art file and special commands referencing the Photo Gallery component. The original photo images are referenced by pages created by the Photo Gallery component in the photogallery folder. FrontPage will save the clip art and photo image files in the web folders as well. As a default, FrontPage will save the image files to the current folder. You may, however, want to have all images used in your Web page, except for the thumbnail images, stored in a folder separate from the actual Web page. Because FrontPage created an images folder when this new web was created, it makes sense to place the images in that folder. Perform the following steps to save the Photos page, along with the embedded image files.

Steps **To Save a Web Page and Embedded Images**

1 **Click the Save button on the Standard toolbar. When the Save Embedded Files dialog box displays, point to the Change Folder button.**

The Save Embedded Files dialog box displays (Figure 2-90). This dialog box shows the file names of the clip art images you inserted in the Web page.

FIGURE 2-90

2 Click the Change Folder button. When the Change Folder dialog box displays, click the images folder and then point to the OK button.

The Change Folder dialog box displays (Figure 2-91). The images folder is selected.

FIGURE 2-91

3 Click the OK button in the Change Folders dialog box. Point to the OK button in the Save Embedded Files dialog box.

The Save Embedded Files dialog box indicates that the images folder will be used to store the images selected (Figure 2-92).

FIGURE 2-92

4 **Click the OK button. When the Save Embedded Files dialog box closes, point to the tab, index.htm.**

The Save Embedded Files dialog box is closed and the Photos page and the clip art image files are saved (Figure 2-93).

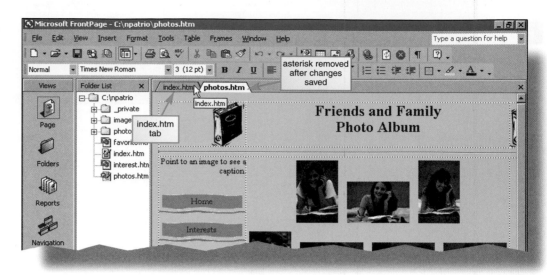

FIGURE 2-93

5 **Click the index.htm tab to view the Home page.**

The Home page displays with the Link bar updated to include the Photos page (Figure 2-94).

FIGURE 2-94

Other **Ways**

1. On File menu click Save
2. Press ALT+F, S
3. Press CTRL+S

It is important that all clip art images are saved as part of the FrontPage web. These image files must be available when publishing the FrontPage web to a Web server. If you do not save them and then publish the FrontPage web, those <img src=> tags will be broken, because the files referenced by the tags will not be on the Web server. Thus, the Web page will not display properly.

Publishing Changes to an Existing FrontPage Web

In Project 1, Nikki's Personal web was published on the World Wide Web. You since have added a new Web page and the accompanying image files to the FrontPage web. For these new items to be available on the World Wide Web, you must publish the Personal web again.

When you publish a FrontPage web that has been published before, FrontPage will install only those parts of the web that are new or that have changed since the last time the web was published. This reduces the amount of data transfer that takes place, which is good for webs with many folders, Web pages, and files.

The following steps summarize how to publish changes to a FrontPage web. Be sure to substitute your own URL or an error will occur. If you do not know what URL to use, ask your instructor.

TO PUBLISH CHANGES TO AN EXISTING FRONTPAGE WEB

1 Click the Publish Web button on the Standard toolbar. Because this web was published previously, FrontPage does not display the Publish Destination dialog box, but assumes that you will publish to the same location.

2 Type your user name and password. Click the OK button.

3 Click the Done button.

You now can view the Photos page by entering http://www.hcc.edu/~npatrio/ photos.htm (use your own URL) in any browser and pressing the ENTER key. Be sure to test the hyperlink to the Home page and from the Home page to the Photos page.

Quitting Microsoft FrontPage

When you have published Nikki's web, you can quit Microsoft FrontPage. Perform the following step to quit FrontPage.

TO QUIT MICROSOFT FRONTPAGE

1 If necessary, click the Done button. Click the Close button on the FrontPage title bar.

The FrontPage window closes and the Windows desktop displays.

CASE PERSPECTIVE SUMMARY

Nikki was surprised at how easy it was to create a photo album page using FrontPage. She showed great interest in adding graphics to the page and in understanding how the Link bars worked for navigation between pages. She has begun to ask questions about other components in FrontPage and about the possibility of customizing some features. You explained that FrontPage has many useful components, and that much more can be done to customize pages in her web. She is making a list of ideas for future projects and will present them to you at a later time.

Project Summary

In creating the Personal web, you gained knowledge of HTML basics and Microsoft FrontPage. Project 2 introduced you to essential Web page development. You learned about good design criteria. Using FrontPage, you created a new Web page providing your own original content. You removed an applied theme and changed the background color of the Web page. You inserted a table and adjusted the table properties. Using appropriate images, you inserted clip art to enhance the appearance of the Web page and later replaced the clip art with a more suitable image. Then, you added text and learned how to change formats such as style, font, font size, and alignment. Next, you inserted horizontal rules. You inserted photographs in a Photo Gallery, including captions for each picture. You learned how to insert Link bars for navigation, and then you previewed your Web page before printing. Finally, you saved a Web page along with the embedded image files and published the changes to your existing page.

What You Should Know

Having completed this project, you now should be able to perform the following tasks:

▶ Add a Heading to a Web Page *(FP 2.41)*

▶ Add a Horizontal Rule to a Web Page *(FP 2.44)*

▶ Add a Link Bar Component *(FP 2.54)*

▶ Add a New Web Page to an Existing Web *(FP 2.09)*

▶ Add Normal Text to a Web Page *(FP 2.45)*

▶ Add a Photo Gallery Component *(FP 2.49)*

▶ Adjust Table Cell Borders *(FP 2.27)*

▶ Align Items on a Web Page *(FP 2.36)*

▶ Change Table Cell Properties *(FP 2.38)*

▶ Change the Background Color of a Web Page *(FP 2.20)*

▶ Change the Page Label of a Web Page *(FP 2.16)*

▶ Change the Theme for a Web Page *(FP 2.19)*

▶ Change the Title of a Web Page *(FP 2.14)*

▶ Copy and Paste an Image on a Web Page *(FP 2.34)*

▶ Edit a Web Page in Page View *(FP 2.18)*

▶ Insert a Clip Art Image in a Web Page *(FP 2.28)*

▶ Insert a Table in a Web Page *(FP 2.24)*

▶ Merge Cells in a Table *(FP 2.26)*

▶ Modify Table Properties *(FP 2.38)*

▶ Open an Existing FrontPage Web *(FP 2.09)*

▶ Preview and Print a Web Page *(FP 2.58)*

▶ Publish Changes to an Existing FrontPage Web *(FP 2.63)*

▶ Quit Microsoft FrontPage *(FP 2.63)*

▶ Rename a Web Page *(FP 2.13)*

▶ Replace a Clip Art Image in a Web Page *(FP 2.31)*

▶ Save a Web Page and Embedded Images *(FP 2.60)*

▶ Start FrontPage *(FP 2.09)*

Learn It Online

Instructions: To complete the Learn It Online exercises, start your browser, click the Address bar, and then enter scsite.com/offxp/exs.htm. When the Office XP Learn It Online page displays, follow the instructions in the exercises below.

1 Project Reinforcement TF, MC, and SA

Below FrontPage Project 2, click the Project Reinforcement link. Print the quiz by clicking Print on the File menu. Answer each question. Write your first and last name at the top of each page, and then hand in the printout to your instructor.

2 Flash Cards

Below FrontPage Project 2, click the Flash Cards link. When Flash Cards displays, read the instructions. Type 20 (or a number specified by your instructor) in the Number of Playing Cards text box, type your name in the Name text box, and then click the Flip Card button. When the flash card displays, read the question and then click the Answer box arrow to select an answer. Flip through Flash Cards. Click Print on the File menu to print the last flash card if your score is 15 (75%) correct or greater and then hand it in to your instructor. If your score is less than 15 (75%) correct, then redo this exercise by clicking the Replay button.

3 Practice Test

Below FrontPage Project 2, click the Practice Test link. Answer each question, enter your first and last name at the bottom of the page, and then click the Grade Test button. When the graded practice test displays on your screen, click Print on the File menu to print a hard copy. Continue to take practice tests until you score 80% or better. Hand in a printout of the final practice test to your instructor.

4 Who Wants to Be a Computer Genius?

Below FrontPage Project 2, click the Computer Genius link. Read the instructions, enter your first and last name at the bottom of the page, and then click the Play button. Hand in your score to your instructor.

5 Wheel of Terms

Below FrontPage Project 2, click the Wheel of Terms link. Read the instructions, and then enter your first and last name and your school name. Click the Play button. Hand in your score to your instructor.

6 Crossword Puzzle Challenge

Below FrontPage Project 2, click the Crossword Puzzle Challenge link. Read the instructions, and then enter your first and last name. Click the Play button. Work the crossword puzzle. When you are finished, click the Submit button. When the crossword puzzle redisplays, click the Print button. Hand in the printout.

7 Tips and Tricks

Below FrontPage Project 2, click the Tips and Tricks link. Click a topic that pertains to Project 2. Right-click the information and then click Print on the shortcut menu. Construct a brief example of what the information relates to in FrontPage to confirm you understand how to use the tip or trick. Hand in the example and printed information.

8 Newsgroups

Below FrontPage Project 2, click the Newsgroups link. Click a topic that pertains to Project 2. Print three comments. Hand in the comments to your instructor.

9 Expanding Your Horizons

Below FrontPage Project 2, click the Articles for Microsoft FrontPage link. Click a topic that pertains to Project 2. Print the information. Construct a brief example of what the information relates to in FrontPage to confirm you understand the contents of the article. Hand in the example and printed information to your instructor.

10 Search Sleuth

Below FrontPage Project 2, click the Search Sleuth link. To search for a term that pertains to this project, select a term below the Project 2 title and then use the Google search engine at google.com (or any major search engine) to display and print two Web pages that present information on the term. Hand in the printouts to your instructor

online

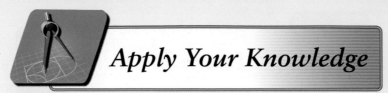
Apply Your Knowledge

1 Modifying a Corporate Presence Web

Instructions: Start FrontPage. Open the web, Starting, that you modified in Project 1. If you did not complete this exercise for Project 1, see your instructor for a copy of the required files.

1. If necessary, double-click the file, index.htm, in the Folder List pane to display The Starting Block home page in Page view.

2. On the Format menu, click Themes. Scroll down until you see the theme In Motion and select it, or another theme as directed by your instructor. Select Vivid colors, Active graphics, and Background picture. Apply the theme to all pages in the web.

3. Click the graphic in the upper-left corner of the page. On the Insert menu, point to Picture and then click Clip Art. Search on the Web for a sports graphic of your choice that fits the selected theme. Replace the current image with a image of your choice. Alternatively, you may use the image, runner01.gif, in the Project2 folder on your Data Disk. See the inside back cover of this book for instructions for downloading the Data Disk or see your instructor for information on accessing the files required in this book. Drag the sizing handles to size the image appropriately.

4. Select the text under the Home page banner that reads, for all of your sporting needs. Click the Italic button on the Formatting toolbar. Click the Font Color button arrow and change the text color to green, or a color of your choice, from the current theme.

5. Select the first paragraph that begins, As the largest sporting, and change the color to purple to match text in the vertical Link bar, or a color of your choice, from the theme colors.

6. Select the text after each bullet and all remaining text that is the default color (black). Change the color of the selected text to purple, or a color of your choice.

7. Click the Preview tab to preview the Web page. When you have finished, click the Normal tab.

8. Print and save the Web page and then close FrontPage. Hand in the printouts to your instructor.

FIGURE 2-95

In the Lab

1 Modifying a Navigation Component on a Corporate Presence Web

Problem: The Sweet Tooth Web site that you began developing has an interesting and appropriate theme. Some of the pages, however, have no navigation bars — users can use only the Back button on their browsers to return to a previous Web page. You want to modify the web to include appropriate Link bars for all pages.

Instructions: Perform the following tasks.

1. Open the Sweet Tooth web that you began in Project 1. If you did not complete that exercise for Project 1, see your instructor for a copy of the required files.
2. In the Folder list pane, double-click the file prod01.htm to open the Prepackaged page in Page view.
3. Click the Navigation button in the Views bar to view the navigation structure of this web. Note that the Prepackaged and Make-My-Own pages are shown on the same level, with the Products page as a parent to both. Double-click the Prepackaged page to display it in Page view.
4. Double-click the Link bar text in the left border to open the Link Bar Properties dialog box. Note that the hyperlinks currently selected are for the child level, of which there currently are none. Furthermore, because this is a shared border, making changes here would affect all other pages in the web. Click the Cancel button to close the Link Bar Properties dialog box.
5. Position the insertion point just before the paragraph that begins, This paragraph contains. On the Insert menu, click Navigation. Select a bar type based on the navigation structure. Click the Next button. Select a bar style using the page's theme. Click the Next button. Select a horizontal orientation for the Link bar. Click the Finish button.

FIGURE 2-96

(continued)

In the Lab

Modifying a Navigation Component on a Corporate Presence Web *(continued)*

6. In the Link Bar Properties dialog box, select Back and Next for hyperlinks. Select Home page and Parent page as additional pages. Click the OK button.

7. Press the right-arrow key to deselect the Link bar. Press the ENTER key. Save the changes to this page.

8. In the Folder list pane, double-click the file, prod02.htm, to open the Make-My-Own page in Page view.

9. Position the insertion point just before the paragraph that begins, This paragraph contains. On the Insert menu, click Navigation. Select a bar type based on the navigation structure. Click the Next button. Select a bar style using the page's theme. Click the Next button. Select a horizontal orientation for the Link bar. Click the Finish button. In the Link Bar Properties dialog box, select Back and Next for hyperlinks. Select Home page and Parent page as additional pages. Click the OK button. Press the right-arrow key to deselect the Link bar. Press the ENTER key. Save the changes to this page.

10. Click the Preview tab to preview the changes made to this page. Note that the Make-My-Own page has links for Back, Home, and Up. These link to the Prepackaged, Home, and Products pages, respectively. Click the Back button. The Prepackaged page displays. Note that the links here are almost the same, except for order and a Next button instead of a Back button. The Next button links to the Make-My-Own page. The order and links on each page are due to the position of the page in the web's navigation structure.

11. Print and save the each changed Web page, and then close FrontPage. Hand in the printouts to your instructor.

2 Modifying a Personal Web

Problem: Earlier, you created a Personal web about your favorite Web sites. You have decided to add a page with links to some of your favorite summer activities.

Instructions: Perform the following tasks.

1. Open the web, funsites, that you began in Project 1. If you did not complete that exercise for Project 1, see your instructor for a copy of the required files.

2. In Navigation view, select the Home page. Click the New Page button on the Standard toolbar to create a new page as a child to the Home page, with the current theme applied.

3. Save the new page as summer.htm, change the page label to Summer Fun, and change the page title to Sumertime Favorites. Open this page in Page view.

4. On the Insert menu, click Page Banner. When the Page Banner Properties dialog box opens, verify that Picture is selected and that the text in the Page banner text box is Summer Fun. Click the OK button.

5. Position the insertion point below the newly added page banner. Click the Insert Table button on the Standard toolbar and drag through the cells to insert a 4x4 table.

6. Type Some things I like in the in the top row, first column of the table. Select the text and click the Bold button on the Formatting toolbar. Click the Align Right button. Change the font color to a color from the current theme. In the next cell to the right, insert the clip art image, summerWithSun.gif, from the Data Disk. Type are: in the top row, third column. Select the text, click the Bold button, and change the font color to match the first text. In the top row, fourth column, insert a clip art image of your choice representing summer, or you may use the file, sunInShades.gif, from the Data Disk.

In the Lab

7. Type Cookouts: in the leftmost cell of the second row. Change the text color to a color from the theme, make it bold and right-aligned. In the next cell to the right, insert a clip art image of your choice representing cookouts, or you may use the file, grill01.gif, from the Data Disk.

8. Type Going to the beach: in the leftmost cell of the third row. Change the text color to a color from the theme, make it bold and right-aligned. In the next cell to the right, insert a clip art image of your choice representing a beach, or you may use the file, beachToys.gif, from the Data Disk. In the third column, insert another beach image of your choice, or you may use the file, beachVolley.gif, from the Data Disk.

9. Type Rides at the amusement park: in the leftmost cell of the bottom row. Change the text color to a color from the theme, make it bold and right-aligned. In the next cell to the right, insert a clip art image of your choice representing amusement park rides, or you may use the file, coaster.gif, from the Data Disk. In the third column, insert another amusement park image of your choice, or you may use the file, funCar.gif, from the Data Disk.

10. Merge the second and third cells of the second row into a single cell. Do the same for each following row.

11. Center the table alignment and specify the width as 80 percent. Drag the cell borders to align the text and images. Preview the Web page and adjust the alignment as needed to obtain a page similar to that shown in Figure 2-97.

12. Save the Web page. Save the embedded images to the images folder for the web. Print the changed Web pages and submit them to your instructor.

FIGURE 2-97

In the Lab

3 Adding a New Page and a Photo Gallery to a One-Page Web

Problem: Your one-page vacation web includes a description of your recent vacation, but no images of the activities you enjoyed or of the views afforded on your trip. You decide to enhance the description by adding a page that will contain some pictures in an attractive layout.

Instructions: Using the vacation web you created in Project 1, perform the following tasks. If you did not complete this exercise in Project 1, see your instructor for a copy of the required files.

1. Add a new page to the current web navigation structure, with the current theme applied. Rename the page file name as pictures.htm.
2. On the Insert menu, click Page Banner. Add a Picture Page Banner with Page banner text of Vacation Pictures. Click the OK button. Press the ENTER key.
3. Type, go back to. Add a Link bar with a single hyperlink to the parent level.
4. Insert a Photo gallery component. Choose the Slide Show layout. Insert the picture files, captions, and descriptions listed in Table 2-3, or Hawaii images and text of your own choosing, to illustrate your vacation (Figure 2-98).
5. Open the file, index.htm. At the end of the paragraph that begins, If you are wondering, type, Take a look at our and then after the text, insert a Link bar with a hyperlink to the child level.
6. Save the Web pages and preview them by viewing them in your browser.
7. Print the Web pages, write your name on the pages, and give them to your instructor.
8. Close your browser and quit FrontPage.

Table 2-3 Hawaii Image Files, Captions, and Descriptions		
FILE NAME	*CAPTION*	*DESCRIPTION*
Hawaii map.jpg	Map of Hawaiian Islands	Most of the time, we were on Maui. On the last day, we took a trip to Oahu.
view from the air01.jpg	View from the plane	Flying over the islands provides a wonderful view.
waterfall01.jpg	Waterfall on the road to Hauna	The road to Hauna provided many opportunities to see picturesque scenery.
bird of paradise.jpg	Bird of Paradise	The flora was very colorful. This picture was taken just outside our hotel room!
coastline01.jpg	Rugged coastline	While many areas had great beaches, at some places the drop to the ocean was steep and rough.
memorial01.jpg	USS Arizona Memorial	Visiting Hawaii would have been incomplete without a trip to Pearl Harbor. The memorial provides a dignified remembrance of the price of peace.
ship at Pearl Harbor.jpg	Ship at Pearl Harbor	Touring the USS Missouri was a popular option.
hammocks on beach.jpg	Home, away from home!	Looks like the perfect retirement spot - complete with furniture!

In the Lab

FIGURE 2-98

Cases and Places

The difficulty of these case studies varies:
▶ are the least difficult; ▶▶ are more difficult; and ▶▶▶ are the most difficult.

1 ▶ In preparation for graduation, you created a text-only Web page in Project 1 to post your resume on the Web. Using that web, modify the text to use different font sizes for different sections, such as the title and section headings. Use bold and italics where appropriate. To position the various elements of your resume, cut and paste them into a table with no visible borders.

2 ▶ You want to improve the appearance of the web you created for your course in Classical Literature from Project 1. Insert a two-column table with four rows per book review. For each review, use one cell each in the left column for book title, author, copyright year, and publisher. In the right column, merge the corresponding four cells into one and place the review text for the book in this merged cell. Do the same for all reviews completed.

3 ▶▶ In preparation for an upcoming 50th wedding anniversary for your grandparents, you were asked to develop a Web site for them. You created a Personal web that includes a Home page, an Interests page, and a History page. Edit the History page to include a Photo Gallery of pictures in the lives of your grandparents. Edit the caption text to provide brief descriptions of each photo. Use the exercise in Project 1 to develop the initial web.

4 ▶▶ Using Clip Art from the Web, enhance with appropriate images the intramural basketball Web page that you created in Project 1. Include hyperlinks to several of your favorite sports-oriented Web sites. Use a table to position text, images, and hyperlinks. Cut and paste the existing text to insert it into the table. Apply an appropriate theme to the web.

5 ▶▶▶ You have decided to develop a web to promote your favorite sport, and you want to illustrate it with appropriate images. Create a new web with at least a parent and two child pages. Apply an appropriate theme. On one child page, add links to various sites on the Web for this sport. On another child page, place at least five clip art images from the Web along with text describing each image, using appropriate fonts, font sizes, and colors. Insert these within a table to arrange a pleasing presentation. Modify each page's title and label to reflect their purpose. Add a navigation bar to each page. Let child pages link to each other, as well as to the parent page.

Microsoft FrontPage 2002

Customizing and Managing Web Pages and Images

You will have mastered the material in this project when you can:

- ■ Discuss the types of images used on the Web
- ■ Create and apply a custom theme
- ■ Expand an existing table
- ■ Add a hit counter
- ■ Add a shared border
- ■ Change the navigation structure of a Web
- ■ Copy and paste from a Word document
- ■ Insert bookmarks into a Web page
- ■ Display the Pictures toolbar
- ■ Modify image properties
- ■ Insert an AutoShapes drawing object in FrontPage
- ■ Create an image map hotspot
- ■ Use a graphic image as a hyperlink
- ■ Use FrontPage to manage tasks
- ■ Use reporting features of FrontPage
- ■ Verify the hyperlinks in a FrontPage web

Gain Riches of Knowledge and Information

Traveling the Online Silk Road

World Wide Web trade routes link a global marketplace filled with riches and resources; a modern-day Silk Road laden with wares and amenities that offer quality and convenience. Each Web site leads to a labyrinth of new ones, brimming with information, ideas, and entertainment. As a merchant-explorer in an electronic world, you can journey from exciting page to page, traveling from a university, to a food company, or an art museum, all with a few clicks of the mouse.

Connecting a global population, the World Wide Web has made it possible for organizations, corporations, educational institutions, individuals, and special interest groups to travel a worldwide route of communication, commerce, and learning.

Long before the birth of the Web, the Silk Road connected the world. For 2,000 years, this road — a tenuous thread of communication and commerce that stretched from China to Europe — was a highway for caravans of merchants laden with silk, gold, and glass, trading goods and sharing culture along the way. Like the Web, the Silk Road was not merely a single route. It had many different branches that connected different towns.

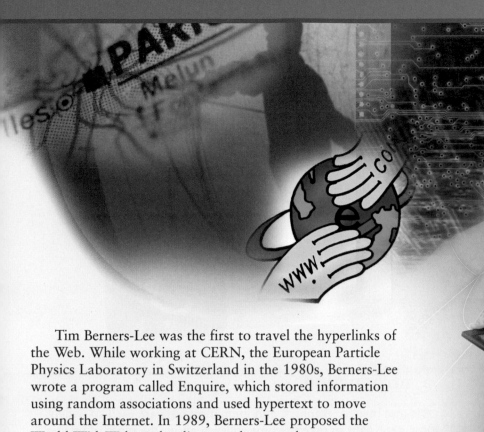

Tim Berners-Lee was the first to travel the hyperlinks of the Web. While working at CERN, the European Particle Physics Laboratory in Switzerland in the 1980s, Berners-Lee wrote a program called Enquire, which stored information using random associations and used hypertext to move around the Internet. In 1989, Berners-Lee proposed the World Wide Web, and online travel was underway.

Today, all you need is Internet access, and a Web browser, and you are ready to explore this electronic Silk Road. Your Web browser is your golden tablet, providing passage between linked Web sites all over the world.

Browsing the World Wide Web is the Silk Road to learning essential Web site design. Looking at other's work, you quickly can recognize good and bad practices. The successful Web site must be innovative and effective to stand out. One way to achieve this effect is to use images and graphics in your Web page design. In good Web pages, images are not simply shown, they are integrated to furnish information, display pictures of goods and services, and permit navigation.

In this project, you will learn about using the Internet's rich sources to find interesting text and unique graphics to enhance the Web pages you have created. Using the Photo Gallery, you will display images, select from layouts that you can customize, add captions and descriptions, and change the sizes of photos. Artfully combined, these elements ensure your success in developing an attractive and efficient Web site.

As ancient travelers discovered and traded treasures on the Silk Road, you can garner rich ideas, inspiration, and design by browsing the World Wide Web, thus experiencing the wonder and wealth of the Web.

Microsoft FrontPage 2002

Customizing and Managing Web Pages and Images

PROJECT

3

CASE PERSPECTIVE

With your help, Nikki Patrio has created an attractive photo collage that enhances the layout of her Photos Web page. Now, she decides to make the page more appealing by using a lighter background, similar to the Network theme, but with colors she likes. She wants the Photos page to reflect the last date it was changed and have a counter for the number of visitors. Nikki wants visitors to be able to link to the Photos page using a graphical hyperlink from the Home page. She has created her résumé in a Word document and plans to publish it to her Web site using hyperlinks to its various sections.

To manage her Web site properly, Nikki requires a place to record ideas for new pages, and, because she has visited Web sites with broken links, she needs the capability of determining whether any of the hyperlinks on her Web pages are broken. You know that FrontPage includes tools and features to help her easily change the hyperlinks, modify the theme of her choice, and incorporate data from other Office applications, such as her résumé in Word. FrontPage has additional features that can help her plan and manage Web pages as well.

Introduction

Because images, graphics, and animation now are used so widely, it is important to take the time to learn about the types of images used on the Web and to master the graphics editing options necessary to customize Web pages. You should know the characteristics, advantages, and disadvantages of each type of image file so that you can ascertain the best type of image to use for a particular situation.

Project 3 introduces you to customizing a Web page. You will create a transparent GIF image, an image map, and bookmarks. You also will see how easy it is in FrontPage to make significant changes to an existing theme. You will create hotspots for an image map and copy text from a Word document directly into FrontPage.

Most of the pages that you develop in this project are customizations of previous work. The Home page will have three new links added (Figure 3-1a). A clip art image and an AutoShapes drawing object will be added close together. Both the image and the object will link to the Photos page, which will be modified to use a customized theme (Figure 3-1b). A new link will be added to the Link bar automatically, and this link will take visitors to a new Resume page (Figure 3-1c). The Resume page will consist of several long sections of text, which will be copied from Word. You will insert bookmarks, which will allow a user to click a hyperlink at the top of the Resume page and immediately go to the corresponding section. A shared border will be added to all pages to consistently display the last date the pages were updated.

To help you in this process, some important concepts and definitions are presented.

(a) Home Page

(b) Photo Page

(c) Resume Page

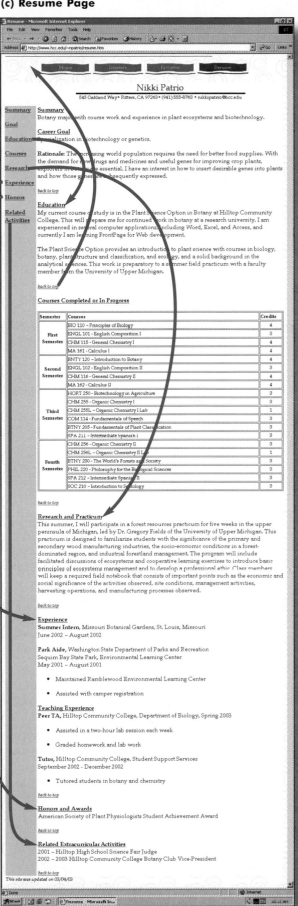

FIGURE 3-1

FP 3.05

Image File Formats

Many different formats are used to represent images on computers. Table 3-1 shows some of the various image file formats. Numerous graphics editors and tools are available that allow you to create and edit images. For example, you can create your own custom buttons, bullets, dividers, and background images. Most browsers display only two types of image file formats: GIF and JPEG. FrontPage can import images in several other formats, including BMP, TIF, WMF, RAS, ESP, PCX, PCD, PNG and TGA, and then convert them to GIF or JPEG images.

More About

Image File Formats

FrontPage allows you to import many different image file formats, including the Portable Network Graphics (PNG) format. Although FrontPage does support the PNG file format, many Web browsers cannot display PNG pictures without a special plug-in. In general, it is better to use only GIF or JPEG images in your Web pages.

More About

Obtaining Images

You can browse the World Wide Web and select any image to insert on your Web page. Be sure that you have permission to use the image before placing it on your FrontPage web as some images on the Web are copyrighted.

Table 3-1 Image File Formats	
IMAGE FILE TYPE	**DESCRIPTION**
BMP	Windows bitmap file format – device-independent format, introduced with Windows 3.0 and increasingly supported by Windows applications.
EPS	Encapsulated postscript file format – an extension of the Postscript file graphics format developed by Adobe systems.
GIF	Graphic Interchange Format file format – a popular graphics exchange format used by the CompuServe Information Service and other online graphics sources. GIF is a licensed product for developers of commercial, for-profit software; however, for the nonprofit personal home page, a license agreement is not required.
JPEG	Joint Photographic Expert Group file format – used for true color 24-bit photographic images scanned or digitized from films.
PCX	Paintbrush file format – used in Windows Paintbrush and other paint programs and supported by many desktop publishing and graphics programs.
PNG	Portable Network Graphics file format – a file format for the lossless, portable, well-compressed storage of raster images.
RAS	Sun Raster file format – the raster image file format developed by Sun Microsystems, Inc.
TGA	Targa file format – a photo-realistic image format designed for systems with a Truevision display adapter.
TIF (or TIFF)	Tagged Image File format – supported by many desktop publishing programs.
WMF	Windows Metafile format – a vector graphics format used mostly for word processing clip art.

Regardless of the file type, an image is displayed on a computer screen using small points of color called pixels. As you may recall, a **pixel**, or **picture element**, is the smallest addressable point on the screen. An image is formed on the screen by displaying pixels of different color. The combined group of different-colored pixels makes up the image. The **image file** contains the information needed to determine the color for each pixel used to display the image.

The **bit resolution** of an image refers to the number of bits of stored information per pixel. With an **8-bit image**, eight bits of information are stored for each pixel. Using the binary numbering system, you can represent up to 256 numbers using 8 bits. Thus, an 8-bit image can have a maximum of 256 colors, with each number representing a different color.

A **24-bit image** can have up to 16.7 million colors. These types of images have near-photographic quality. Each pixel, however, consumes three times the storage of a pixel in an 8-bit image, which results in a larger file size for an image with the same number of pixels.

GIF Image Files

GIF stands for **Graphic Interchange Format**. GIF files use 8-bit resolution and support up to 256 colors. GIF files support indexed color image types, line art, and grayscale images.

Special types of GIF files, called **animated GIFs**, contain a series of images that are displayed in rapid succession, giving the appearance of movement. Special animated GIF editors are available to combine the series of images and set the display timing.

The GIF89a format contains a **transparency index**. This index allows you to specify a transparent color, which causes the background of the Web page to display through the color that has been set as transparent. If you are using line art, icons, or images such as company logos, make sure they are in the GIF89a format. You then will be able to take advantage of the transparency index.

JPEG Image Files

JPEG stands for **Joint Photographic Expert Group**. The advantage to using JPEG files is the high-color resolution. JPEG supports 24-bit resolution, providing up to 16.7 million possible colors. If you are including photographic images in your Web page, they must use JPEG format because of the support for full color.

When you insert an image that is not in GIF or JPEG format, FrontPage automatically converts it to the GIF format if the image has eight or fewer bits of color. The image is converted automatically to JPEG format if the image has more than eight bits of color.

With FrontPage, you can import image files into the current FrontPage web, insert images in Web pages, align images with text, and create and edit image maps. The editing commands in FrontPage, such as crop, rotate, and resize, allow you to change the appearance of the image. In addition, you can change its brightness and contrast, make it black and white, or give the image beveled edges.

FrontPage can work with graphics editing programs such as the **Clip Art Gallery**, which is a tool for previewing and managing clip art, pictures, sounds, video clips, and animation. The Clip Art Gallery contains a collection of clip art and pictures you can insert into your Web pages. You used the Clip Art Gallery to create the Photos page in Project 2.

More About

Photographic Images

Be careful when using photographic images with 24-bit color. Many computers do not have a monitor and display adapter that supports 24-bit color. If you change your Windows color setting to a lower bit resolution, you can preview a Web page to see how the images look before you publish the Web page.

Modifying an Existing Web Page

Because Nikki wanted to change her original design for the Photos page once she saw it on the computer, you decide to use the theme currently used with the other pages, and then modify elements of the theme for this page only. Applying these modifications is a simple task with FrontPage.

To modify the Photos Web page, you need to start FrontPage and then open the original FrontPage web. Perform the following steps to open the Photos page in the Personal web created in Project 2. If you did not complete Project 2, see your instructor for a copy.

TO OPEN AN EXISTING PAGE IN A FRONTPAGE WEB

1 Click the Start button on the taskbar. Point to Programs on the Start menu.

2 Click Microsoft FrontPage on the Programs submenu.

3 Click the Open button arrow on the Standard toolbar. Point to Open Web on the Open menu.

Microsoft FrontPage 2002

4 Click Open Web. If necessary, when the Open Web dialog box displays, click the Look in box arrow and select the folder location where you stored the web for project 2 (e.g., C:\npatrio). Point to the Open button in the Open Web dialog box.

5 Click the Open button. Double-click photos.htm in the Folder List pane.

The previous web is loaded, and the file, photos.htm, displays in Page view (Figure 3-2).

FIGURE 3-2

Creating and Applying a Customized Theme to a Web Page

Applying a theme to an existing Web page is essentially the same procedure used to apply a theme to a new web. When modifying a page that already contains certain graphic elements, such as a background color or image, be aware that applying a theme will permanently alter such existing properties. In fact, once a theme has been applied, you cannot access the background properties of the page to apply an image or a color — they are under the control of the theme. You would need to remove or modify the theme to make such changes. You can effectively remove the theme by applying a theme selection of No Theme to the Web page, as was done in Project 2. If you are not certain that you will want to use a theme, you might want to make a backup copy of your FrontPage web by saving it in an alternate location before applying the theme.

A customized theme can be created easily by using an existing theme as a starting point, making changes to that theme, and then saving the modified theme with a new name. To create and apply a customized theme to an existing Web page, perform the following steps.

Steps **To Create and Apply a Customized Theme**

1 **Click Format on the menu bar and then click Theme. If necessary, when the Themes dialog box displays, scroll down and click Poetic in the Themes list. Click the Modify button. When the What would you like to modify? area displays, point to the Graphics button.**

The Themes dialog box displays. The Sample of Theme area displays a sample page using the currently selected theme (Figure 3-3). Additional buttons display that allow you to modify aspects of the theme and to save the modifications.

FIGURE 3-3

2 **Click Graphics. If necessary, when the Modify Theme dialog box displays, click the Item box arrow and select Background Picture from the drop-down list. If necessary, click the Picture tab. Point to the Browse button.**

The Modify Theme dialog box displays (Figure 3-4). The item to modify displays in the Item list box. The current file used as the background picture for the theme displays in the Background Picture text box.

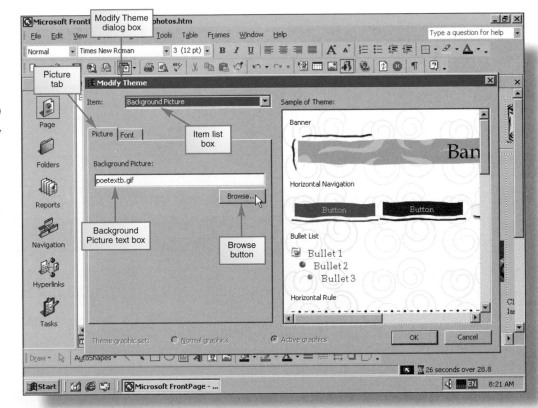

FIGURE 3-4

3 **Click Browse. When the Open File dialog box displays, select the netbkgnd3.gif file from the Project3 folder on the Data Disk. Point to the Open button.**

The Open File dialog box displays (Figure 3-5).

FIGURE 3-5

4 **Click Open. Click the Item box arrow and point to Horizontal Rule in the drop-down list.**

A list of items that can be customized for a theme displays along with a sample of the theme using the file netbkgnd3.gif as the background picture (Figure 3-6).

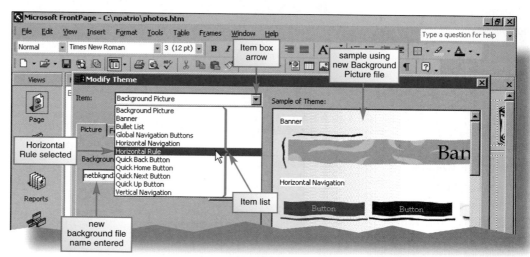

FIGURE 3-6

5 **Click Horizontal Rule. Point to the Browse button.**

The current horizontal rule file name, poehorsa.gif, and a sample of the theme using this horizontal rule displays (Figure 3-7).

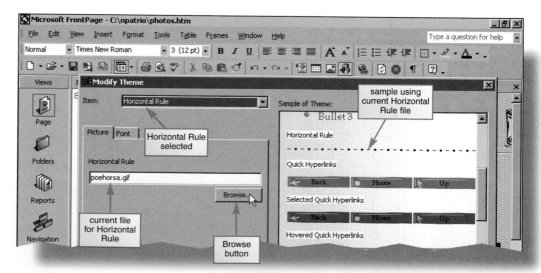

FIGURE 3-7

6 Click Browse. When the Open File dialog box displays, select the anetrule3.gif file from the Project3 folder on the Data Disk. Click the Open button. Point to the OK button.

A sample of the theme using the file anetrule3.gif as the horizontal rule displays (Figure 3-8).

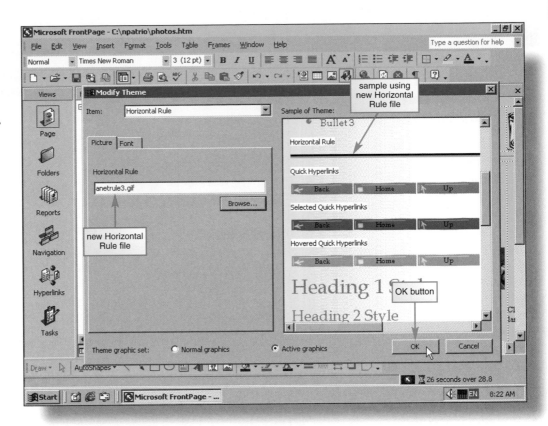

FIGURE 3-8

7 Click the OK button. Click the Save As button in the Themes dialog box. When the Save Theme dialog box displays, type Poetic Network in the Enter new theme title text box. Point to the OK button in the Save Theme dialog box.

The Save Theme dialog box displays with the new name for the modified theme (Figure 3-9). By saving the modified theme with a new name, a new theme is created.

FIGURE 3-9

8 **Click the OK button. Verify that Selected page(s) and Vivid colors are selected. Point to the OK button in the Themes dialog box.**

The Save Theme dialog box closes and the newly created theme is saved. The name of the new theme displays in the themes list and a sample of the new theme displays (Figure 3-10).

FIGURE 3-10

9 **Click the OK button.**

The new theme is applied to the current page (Figure 3-11). The background picture and horizontal rule reflect the modified theme.

FIGURE 3-11

By saving changes to a theme as a new theme, the original theme remains unchanged. If you do not want a new theme, you simply may save the changes to the original theme.

Expanding a Table

You may recall that tables often are used to position elements in a Web page. Items in the Photos page were placed within a table for this very reason. You already have learned how to merge table cells, and how to delete cells and even entire tables. As you make changes to the Web page, however, you may need additional rows, columns, or both, in your table. Rather than creating a new table with the required rows and columns, you can expand an existing table to accommodate new elements.

Perform the following steps to add a row to an existing table.

Steps **To Add a Row to a Table**

1 **Position the insertion point in the last row of the table. Click Table on the menu bar. Point to Insert and then point to Rows or Columns.**

The Insert submenu displays (Figure 3-12).

FIGURE 3-12

2 **Click Rows or Columns. If necessary, when the Insert Rows or Columns dialog box displays, select Rows. Verify that the Number of rows text box is set to 1 and that the location selected is Below selection. Point to the OK button.**

The Insert Rows or Columns dialog box displays (Figure 3-13).

FIGURE 3-13

3 **Click OK. Position the insertion point in the middle cell of the inserted row.**

The insertion point is positioned in the new row at the bottom of the table (Figure 3-14).

FIGURE 3-14

Other Ways

1. Right-click table, click Insert Rows
2. Press ALT+A, I, N
3. Click cell in table, in Voice Command mode, say "Table, Insert, Rows or Columns, OK"

Additional columns may be added to an existing table as easily as rows. Because FrontPage makes it easy to add or delete table rows and columns, you do not have to know the final dimensions of the table before you create it. You simply may modify the table size as needed.

Adding a Hit Counter Component

FrontPage provides a number of components that allow you easily to add common functionality to your pages. One feature often seen on Web pages is a hit counter. A **hit counter** is a component that displays a counter to indicate the number of times a Web page is accessed.

Perform the following steps to add a hit counter component to the Photos page.

Steps **To Add a Hit Counter**

1 **If necessary, position the insertion point in the middle cell of the last row inserted. Right-click the cell and then click Cell Properties on the shortcut menu. When the Cell Properties dialog box displays, in the Layout area, select Center for Horizontal alignment and Middle for Vertical alignment. Point to the OK button.**

The Cell Properties dialog box displays with Center selected for the Horizontal alignment and Middle for the Vertical alignment for the cell (Figure 3-15).

FIGURE 3-15

2 **Click the OK button. If necessary, click the Font Color box arrow and select the Automatic font color for this theme. Type** You are visitor **and then click Insert on the menu bar. Point to Web Component. Be sure to include a space after the word, visitor.**

The text is inserted in the middle cell and the Insert menu displays (Figure 3-16).

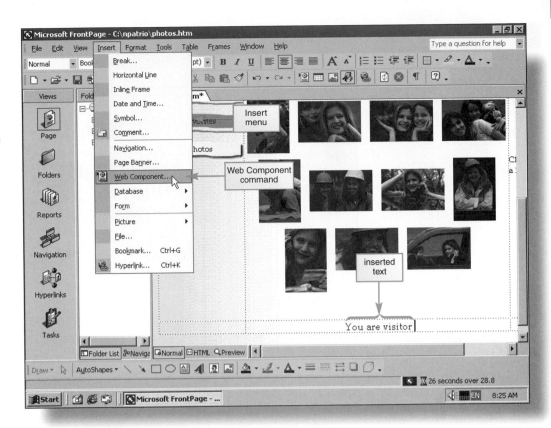

FIGURE 3-16

3 **Click Web Component. When the Insert Web Component dialog box displays, click Hit Counter in the Component type list. Click the second graphic in the Choose a counter style list. Point to the Finish button.**

The Insert Web Component dialog box displays with the Hit Counter component type and the counter style selected (Figure 3-17). A brief description of a hit counter component displays.

FIGURE 3-17

4 Click the Finish button. When the Hit Counter Properties dialog box displays, verify that the second Counter Style is selected. Point to the OK button.

The Hit Counter Properties dialog box displays with the second Counter Style selected (Figure 3-18).

FIGURE 3-18

5 Click the OK button.

A hit counter component is inserted (Figure 3-19). Placeholder text within square brackets indicates where the hit counter will display when viewed on a Web server with the FrontPage Server Extensions installed.

FIGURE 3-19

Other Ways

1. Press ALT+I, W
2. In Voice Command mode, say "Insert, Web Component"

When the page is viewed, either in a browser or on the Preview tab, the hit counter displays as a missing graphic with a textual description. To view the hit counter, the page must be published and viewed on a Web server containing the FrontPage Server Extensions. The program that actually increments and displays the graphic counter is a part of the FrontPage Server Extensions. The count itself is stored on the server in a file in the _private folder of the Web site.

Adding a Shared Border

Earlier, you learned that Web pages often have common sections that display similar, or sometimes identical, information on each page. An example of similar, but not identical, information might be Link bars or page banners. In these cases, the same format and location is used on multiple pages, although the content may change from page to page. Identical information that might appear on multiple pages in a Web could be such items as a copyright notice, an e-mail address for the page author, or a date indicating when the page was last updated. Rather than duplicating this identical information for each page, it would be much easier to enter or change it in one location and then have the information propagated to all pages automatically. Placing the information within a shared border does this. A **shared border** provides a means for including standard content at the top, bottom, left, or right edges of a page, or for all pages, in a Web.

The Home, Interests, and Favorites pages each contain a line at the bottom indicating when the page was last changed. This line was inserted automatically as a result of using the Personal Web template. Although each line displays the same information, the information is not in a shared border and could be changed on one of the pages without affecting the others, leaving the pages inconsistent. Additionally, when new pages are added to the Web, such as the Photos page, they do not contain this line automatically. By removing this information from each individual page and inserting it into a shared border for all pages, the same information will appear on all pages currently in the Web and also for any new pages added subsequently.

Perform the following steps to place the date last updated into a shared border for all pages.

More About

Shared Borders

Shared borders do not have to be plain text. You can assign a color or even an image to the background of any shared border. Right-click the shared border and then click Border Properties.

 To Add a Shared Border

1 Position the insertion point below the table. Click Format on the menu bar and then point to Shared Borders.

The Format menu displays with the Shared Borders command selected (Figure 3-20).

FIGURE 3-20

2 **Click Shared Borders. When the Shared Borders dialog box displays, verify that All pages is selected in the Apply to area. Click Bottom. Point to the OK button.**

A dotted line displays across the bottom of the page preview graphic in the Shared Borders dialog box (Figure 3-21).

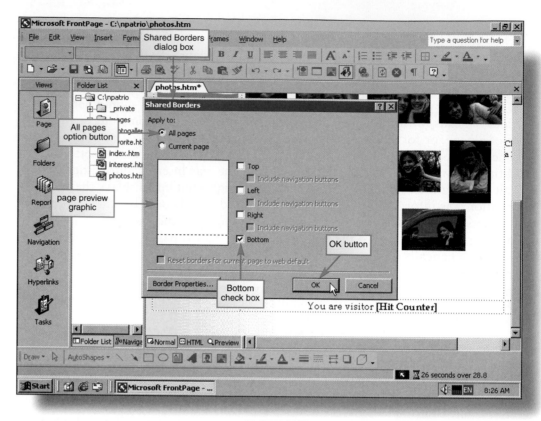

FIGURE 3-21

3 **Click the OK button.**

A bottom shared border is inserted with a comment component as placeholder text (Figure 3-22).

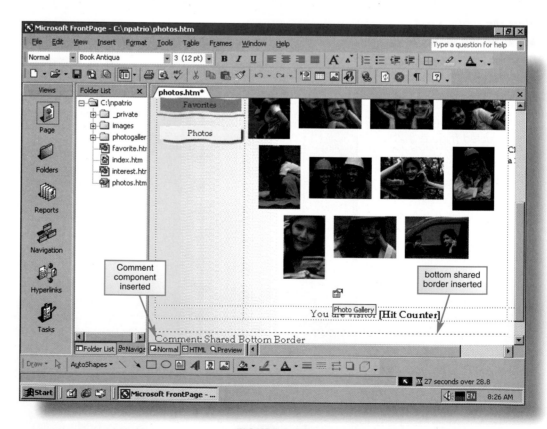

FIGURE 3-22

4 If necessary, scroll down to display the comment component. Click the comment component in the shared border to select it. On the Formatting toolbar, click the Font Size box arrow and select 2 (10 pt). Click the Italic button. **Type** This site was updated on **and then click Insert on the menu bar. Point to Date and Time. Be sure to include a space after the word, on.**

The replacement text replaces the comment component in the shared border and the Insert menu displays with Date and Time selected (Figure 3-23). Note that when the insertion point is placed within a shared border, the shared border displays as a rectangular area.

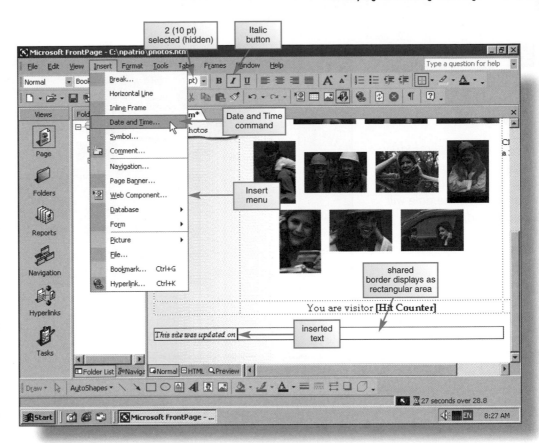

FIGURE 3-23

5 Click Date and Time. If necessary, when the Date and Time dialog box displays, click Date this page was last automatically updated. Click the Date format box arrow. If necessary, scroll to the format representing a two-digit month, a two-digit day, and a two-digit year (mm/dd/yy).

The Date and Time dialog box displays with a list of date formats (Figure 3-24).

FIGURE 3-24

6 **Click the selected date format. Verify that the Time format selected is (none). Point to the OK button.**

A Date format of mm/dd/yy is selected (Figure 3-25). A time format of (none) indicates that only the date will be displayed, not a time.

FIGURE 3-25

7 **Click the OK button. Click the Save button on the Standard toolbar to save the changes to the page. Point to the Close button.**

A Date and Time component displaying the date that the page was last updated is inserted (Figure 3-26).

FIGURE 3-26

8 Click the Close button. Double-click the file name, index.htm, in the Folders list to open the Home page. If necessary, scroll down to the bottom of the page. Drag through the line above the shared border to select it.

The line inserted by the Personal Web template, indicating the date that the page was last updated, is highlighted (Figure 3-27).

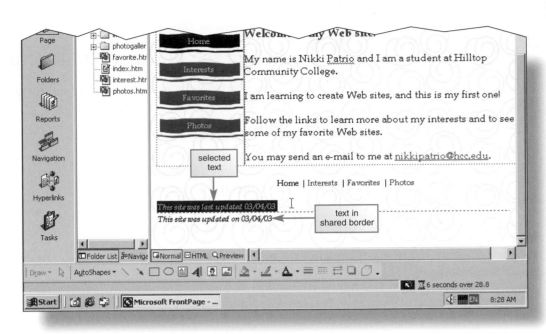

FIGURE 3-27

9 Press the DELETE key.

The duplicate line is removed and only the shared border indicates the date that the page was last updated (Figure 3-28).

10 Save and close the Home page. Repeat Steps 8 and 9 for the Favorites and Interests pages, saving the changes and then closing each page.

FIGURE 3-28

Other Ways

1. Press ALT+O, D
2. In Voice Command mode, say "Format, Shared Borders"

When a shared border is inserted, FrontPage automatically includes a comment component to identify the shared border while editing in FrontPage. A **comment component** is a component that displays text visible only in FrontPage, but not when the page is viewed in a browser or on the Preview tab. Because the date last updated must be visible in a browser, the comment component is replaced with normal text.

When adding a date and time component, you have a choice of two dates to use. The Date this page was last automatically updated choice reflects the date the page was last changed, either from manual editing or from a change elsewhere in the Web that caused automatic updating. The Date this page was last edited choice yields the date that the page was last saved with FrontPage.

Modifying the Navigation Structure of a Web Site

Previously, when you added a new Web page, you did so in Navigation view, so that the page was automatically added to the navigation structure of the web. Recall that the navigation structure affects the links that display on Link bars when the Link bar type is Bar based on navigation structure. Therefore, if the position of a page in the navigation structure is changed, the Link bars may change as well. A new page added in Page view will not display added Link bars of this type until it is saved and added to the navigation structure of the web.

Creating a New Page in Page View

Recall that when a web has a theme applied, any new page will display with the theme applied automatically. Because the shared border just added was applied to all pages, it also will be applied automatically to any new page.

Perform the following step to create a new page in Page view.

 To Add a New Page in Page View

1 **Click the Create a new normal page button on the Standard toolbar.**

A new page is created with the current theme applied and the shared border inserted (Figure 3-29).

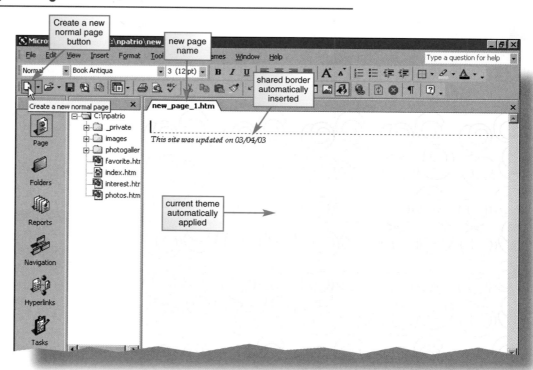

FIGURE 3-29

Although the new page has the theme of the current web applied, it has no hyperlinks to navigate to other pages in the web. A simple way to add such links is to add a Link bar component with hyperlinks based on the navigation structure, as was done in Project 2.

Perform the following steps to add a Link bar component.

TO ADD A LINK BAR COMPONENT

1 Click Insert on the menu bar and then click Navigation.

2 Click Bar based on navigation structure in the Choose a bar type area. Click the Next button.

3 Verify that Use Page's Theme is selected and then click the Next button.

4 Verify that the horizontal arrangement is selected and then click the Finish button.

5 Click Child pages under Home. Click Home page in the Additional pages area. Click the OK button.

6 Click the Center button on the Formatting toolbar.

The Link bar component is added, centered on the page (Figure 3-30). A message displays indicating that the page must be added to the Navigation view for the hyperlinks to display.

FIGURE 3-30

Modifying the Navigation Structure

When a new page was created in Page view, you saw the theme and shared border applied automatically. In order for a Link bar based on the navigation structure to display hyperlinks, the page must be added to the navigation structure. Because visitors will access the Photos page only from the Home page, its position in the navigation structure needs to be changed as well.

Perform the steps on the next page to modify the navigation structure of the web.

Steps **To Modify the Navigation Structure**

1 Click the Save button on the Standard toolbar. When the Save As dialog box displays, point to the Change title button.

The Save As dialog box displays with a default name and title for the new Web page (Figure 3-31).

FIGURE 3-31

2 Click the Change title button. When the Set Page Title dialog box displays, type Resume and then point to the OK button.

The Set Page Title dialog box displays with the new page title (Figure 3-32).

FIGURE 3-32

3 **Click the OK button. Drag through the default file name and then type resume.htm as the new file name. Point to the Save button.**

The Set Page Title dialog box closes and the Save As dialog box displays with the new page title and new file name (Figure 3-33).

FIGURE 3-33

4 **Click the Save button. Point to the Navigation button on the Views bar.**

The new page is saved with a file name of resume.htm (Figure 3-34). The file, resume.htm, appears in the Folder List pane.

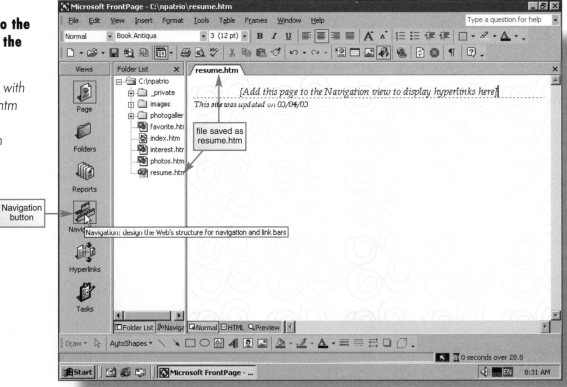

FIGURE 3-34

5 **Click the Navigation button. Drag the file, resume.htm, from the Folder List pane and drop it under the Home page icon in the Navigation pane. Point to the Photos page icon.**

The Resume page is added to the navigation structure of the web (Figure 3-35).

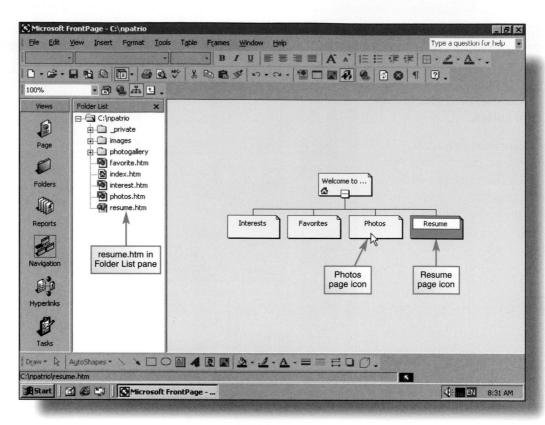

FIGURE 3-35

6 **Drag the Photos page icon and drop it under the Interests page icon in the Navigation pane.**

The Photos page no longer displays as a child page under the Home page and now displays as a child page under the Interests page (Figure 3-36).

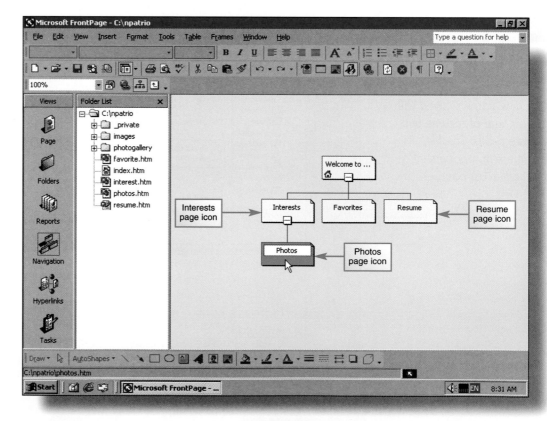

FIGURE 3-36

7 **Double-click the Resume page icon in the Navigation pane.**

The Resume page displays in Page view with the Link bar displaying hyperlinks to the Home page and to the child pages under the Home page (Figure 3-37).

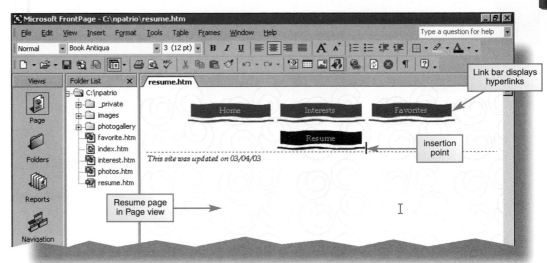

FIGURE 3-37

The Photos page also could be removed from the Link bars by deleting it from the navigation structure. This would remove it from the navigation structure diagram displayed in Navigation view. By placing it under a page that does not link to child pages, the Photos page remains visible in the diagram but does not appear on any Link bars. By placing the Resume page under the Home page, it appears on the Link bars of other pages that link to the child pages under Home. These hyperlinks, as well as a link to the Home page, also display on the Resume page.

Other Ways

1. On View menu click Navigation
2. Press ALT+V, N
3. In Voice Command mode, say "Navigation"
4. In Voice Command mode, say "View, Navigation"

Copy and Paste from a Word Document

You have learned that typing text in FrontPage is like typing text in a word processor. You also have learned that you can copy and paste items, such as images and text, in FrontPage. Images, text, or even tables can be copied and pasted from other Office applications into your Web pages just as easily.

The World Wide Web is often used for electronic publishing today. This means that sometimes people will create Web pages to reflect what previously was produced only in a printed form. This might be a résumé, scholarly paper, or even an entire book. Such a document already may exist in an electronic form, such as a Word document, but not in a form suitable for publication on the Web. Although a given word processor may allow you to save a document as a Web page, the result may not appear exactly as you want. Rather than retyping a large amount of text, you can copy the text from the document and use FrontPage to paste it where you want it to appear in the Web page.

Although the text from the résumé could be copied and pasted directly into a Web page, some thought should be given to the resulting presentation in a Web browser. Because the document will result in a long page, text hyperlinks will be used as an index to allow the user to navigate directly to sections of interest. A table will be used to control the positioning of both the document and the hyperlinks on the Web page. Because the current background pattern may distract the user from the text of the résumé, the table background color and other properties will be modified to present the résumé as a document overlaying the Web page.

Use the following steps on the next page to create a table and modify it prior to incorporating the résumé text.

Steps To Use a Custom Background Color for a Table

1 If necessary, position the insertion point after the horizontal Link bar on the Resume page. Click the Insert Table button on the Standard toolbar and drag through a 3 by 3 table.

The insertion point displays after the Link bar (Figure 3-38).

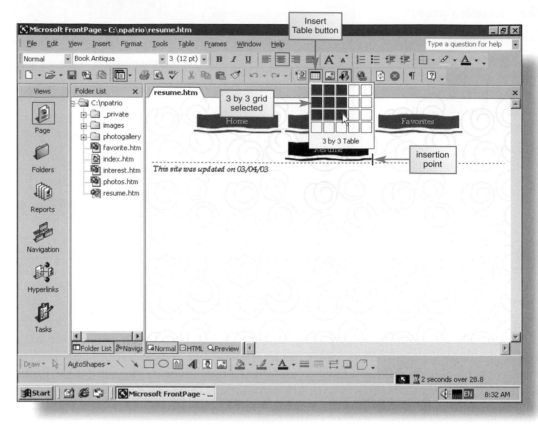

FIGURE 3-38

2 Click the mouse button. When the new table displays, right-click the left cell of the bottom row. Click Table Properties on the shortcut menu. When the Table Properties dialog box displays, select Center in the Alignment box in the Layout area and set Size to 0 in the Borders area. Point to the Color box arrow in the Background area.

The Table Properties dialog box displays with the alignment set to Center and the border size set to 0 (Figure 3-39).

FIGURE 3-39

3 Click the Color box arrow. Click More Colors. When the More Colors dialog box displays, click the white hexagon to display a hex value in the Value text box. Drag through FF,FF,FF in the Value text box to select it. Type FC,FC,FC as the new hex value. Point to the OK button in the More Colors dialog box.

The new custom color hex value of FC,FC,FC displays (Figure 3-40).

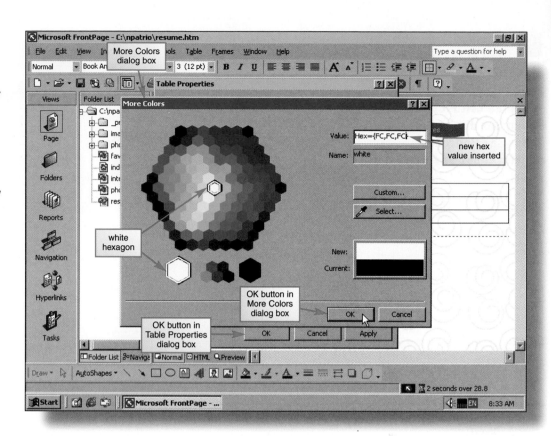

FIGURE 3-40

4 Click the OK button in the More Colors dialog box. Click the OK button in the Table Properties dialog box.

The table displays with a new background color and with dotted lines for cell borders, indicating that the borders will not display (Figure 3-41).

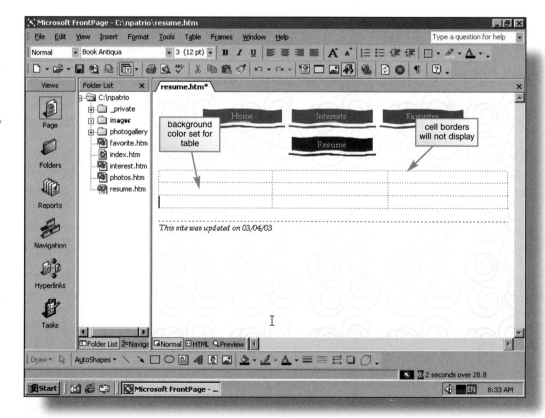

FIGURE 3-41

5 Right-click the left cell of the bottom row. Click Cell Properties on the shortcut menu. When the Cell Properties dialog box displays, select Left in the Horizontal alignment box and then select Top in the Vertical alignment box in the Layout area. Point to the Color box arrow in the Background area.

The Cell Properties dialog box displays with the Horizontal alignment set to Left and the Vertical alignment set to Top (Figure 3-42).

FIGURE 3-42

6 Click the Color box arrow. Click More Colors. When the More Colors dialog box displays, click the white hexagon to display a hex value in the Value text box. Drag through FF,FF,FF in the Value text box to select it. Type DF,DF,DF as the new hex value. Click the OK button in the More Colors dialog box. Click the OK button in the Cell Properties dialog box. Point to the Bold button on the Formatting toolbar.

The cell displays with a background color different from that of the table (Figure 3-43).

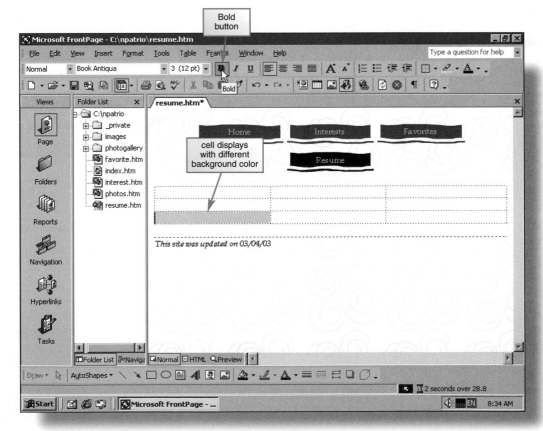

FIGURE 3-43

7 Click the Bold button. If necessary, click the Font Color arrow and select the Automatic font color for this theme. Type Summary and then press the ENTER key. Type each of the remaining text items listed in Table 3-2, following each, except the last, with the ENTER key.

The entered text displays in bold in the leftmost bottom cell (Figure 3-44). The cell expands as text is entered.

FIGURE 3-44

8 Drag the right borders of the left and middle columns to the left until they approximate that shown in Figure 3-45. Position the insertion point in the rightmost cell in the top row.

Text longer than the column width automatically wraps (Figure 3-45).

FIGURE 3-45

9 Hold down the SHIFT key and click the rightmost cell in the second row to select both cells. Right-click the selected cells and then click Cell Properties on the shortcut menu. When the Cell Properties dialog box displays, select Center in the Horizontal alignment box and then select Top in the Vertical alignment box in the Layout area. Point to the OK button.

The Cell Properties dialog box displays with the Horizontal alignment set to Center and the Vertical alignment set to Top (Figure 3-46).

FIGURE 3-46

10 Click the OK button. Click the middle rightmost cell to position the insertion point. Click Format on the menu bar and then point to Borders and Shading.

The insertion point is centered in the rightmost cell of the middle row (Figure 3-47).

FIGURE 3-47

11 **Click Borders and Shading. If necessary, when the Borders and Shading dialog box displays, click the Borders tab. Click the top edge border button in the Preview area. Point to the OK button.**

The Preview area displays a graphic indicating where the new border will be applied (Figure 3-48).

FIGURE 3-48

12 **Click the OK button. Click the rightmost cell in the top row to position the insertion point.**

A top border is applied to the rightmost cell of the middle row (Figure 3-49).

FIGURE 3-49

Although the résumé could be copied and pasted directly into a Web page, using the table just inserted will make viewing and navigating easier and more pleasant for the user. Now that the table is prepared, use the following steps on the next page to copy text from a résumé in Word and paste it into the Web page.

Other **Ways**

1. Press ALT+O, B
2. In Voice Command mode, say "Format, Borders and Shading"

Table 3-2 Text for Resume Index	
TEXT	*TEXT*
Summary	Research
Goal	Experience
Education	Honors
Courses	Related Activities

Steps | **To Copy and Paste from a Word Document**

1 Click the Start button on the taskbar. Point to Programs on the Start menu. Click Microsoft Word on the Programs submenu. If necessary, when Microsoft Word displays, close the New Document task pane. Click the Open button on the Standard toolbar. When the Open dialog box displays, select the file, Nikki Patrio resume.doc, from the Project3 folder on the Data Disk. Point to the Open button.

The Open dialog box displays in Microsoft Word, with the Word document file, Nikki Patrio resume.doc, selected (Figure 3-50).

FIGURE 3-50

2 Click the Open button. If necessary, click View on the menu bar and then click Normal. Drag through the first line of text to select it and then press CTRL+C to copy it to the Clipboard. Point to the Microsoft FrontPage button in the taskbar button area.

The Word document containing the resume is opened and displays in Normal view (Figure 3-51). The selected text is copied.

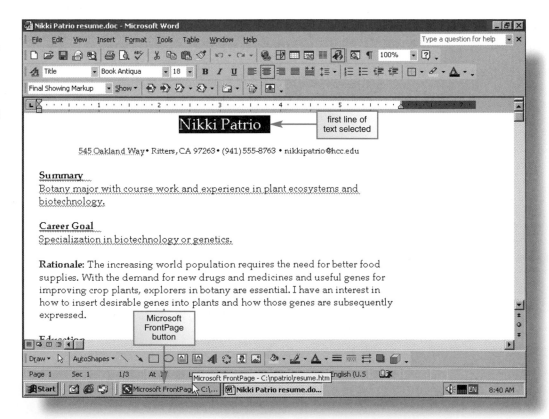

FIGURE 3-51

3 **Click the Microsoft FrontPage button to switch to FrontPage. If necessary, click the top rightmost cell to position the insertion point. Press CTRL+V to paste the copied text from Word into the Web page. Press the BACKSPACE key to delete the extra line. Select the text and change the font size to 5 (18 pt). Point to the Microsoft Word button in the taskbar button area.**

The pasted text displays in the Resume page in Page view (Figure 3-52).

4 **Click the Microsoft Word button to switch to Word and then drag through the second line of text to select it. Do not drag beyond the last letter in the line. Copy the text, switch to FrontPage, and then position the insertion point in the middle rightmost cell. Paste the copied text. If necessary, press the BACKSPACE key to delete any extra blank line that displays. If necessary, drag the lower right sizing handle to resize the cell so that the text aligns along the top of the cell and does not wrap.**

The pasted text displays in the Resume page (Figure 3-53). The text may wrap if the width of the cell is not large enough.

FIGURE 3-52

FIGURE 3-53

5 **Switch to Word and then drag through the remaining text in the résumé to select it, including the table. Copy the text and then switch to FrontPage. Click the bottom rightmost cell to position the insertion point. Paste the copied text. Press the BACKSPACE key to delete any extra lines and spaces, but leave one blank line at the end.**

The remaining text is pasted in the Resume page (Figure 3-54).

6 **Right-click the Microsoft Word button on the taskbar and then click Close on the shortcut menu. If a dialog box displays prompting you to save changes to the document, click No. If necessary, select all of the pasted text and then click the Font Color button on the Formatting toolbar to ensure that all pasted text has the same font color.**

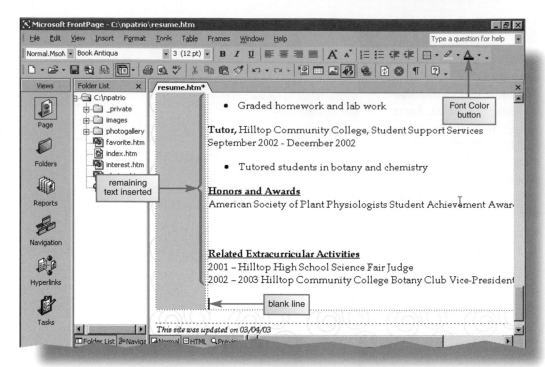

FIGURE 3-54

Using Bookmarks

When you create a Web page, it is natural to assume that you may have to create one or more hyperlinks from that page to another page. The ability to link from one Web page to other pages of interest is one of the most basic and powerful features of the World Wide Web. Not all links are created for the same purpose or in the same manner, however. In Project 1, you created two types of links. One type provided an e-mail link, so users could e-mail the owner of the page. Another type provided a hyperlink from one Web page to another. You also can create a hyperlink that has a bookmark as its destination. A **bookmark** is a location, or selected text, that you have marked on a page.

Adding a Bookmarked Location

When designing a Web page, it is good to keep in mind how the user will interact with that page. If there are a number of links to relatively short pieces of information, and the user is likely to go back and forth from one page to another visiting these links, it may be better to place all of the information on a single Web page. This avoids having to reload each page as it is visited, which increases the perceived speed at which the pages can be reached. This approach must be balanced against having an overly large Web page, particularly if the user will not care to visit most of it. You also may want to link the user to a place in the Web page other than the top. This is a particular advantage when publishing a document as a Web page, because you have the ability to create hyperlinks to various sections of the document. These allow the user to move quickly from an index or table of contents to view the section of interest in the document. In a long document, particularly one containing a large amount of text, this prevents requiring the user to scroll down through the document in order to find the desired section. In both of these cases, using a bookmark can help accomplish the task.

Perform the following steps to bookmark a location in the current Web page.

 To Bookmark a Location in a Web Page

1 **Position the insertion point to the left of the horizontal Link bar at the top of the page. Click Insert on the menu bar and then point to Bookmark.**

The insertion point is positioned where the bookmark for this location is to be added (Figure 3-55).

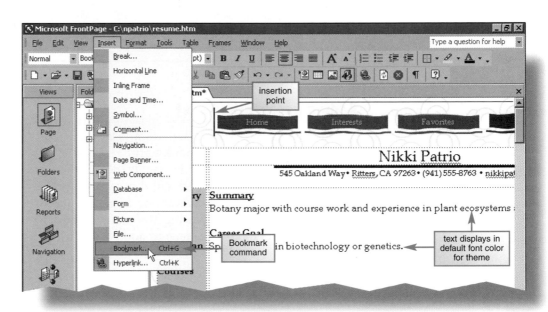

FIGURE 3-55

2 **Click Bookmark. When the Bookmark dialog box displays, type** Top **in the Bookmark name text box. Point to the OK button.**

The Bookmark dialog box displays (Figure 3-56). The name of this bookmark is entered in the Bookmark name text box.

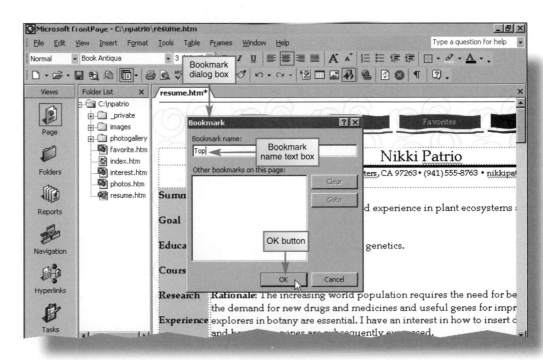

FIGURE 3-56

3 Click the OK button. Position the insertion point in the third row of the table, before the underlined word, Summary.

The Resume page displays with the bookmark flag icon, indicating the bookmarked location (Figure 3-57).

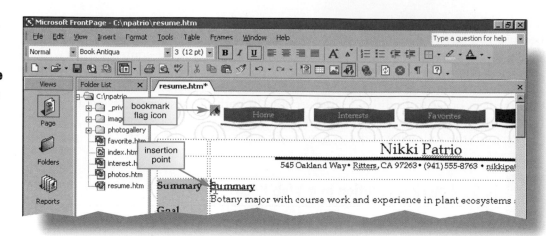

FIGURE 3-57

Adding Bookmarked Text

In FrontPage, if you bookmark a location or an image, a graphic flag icon indicates the presence of a bookmark. Text also can be bookmarked; however, it displays with a dashed underline. If the text was previously underlined, that underline is not removed and will display normally when the page is viewed. When editing the page, however, the original underline is not visible because the dashed underline, indicating a bookmark, obscures it.

Perform the following steps to add bookmarked text to the current Web page.

Steps **To Bookmark Text in a Web Page**

1 Drag through the underlined word, Summary, in the third row of the table to select it. Click Insert on the menu bar and then click Bookmark. When the Bookmark dialog box displays, point to the OK button.

The Bookmark dialog box displays (Figure 3-58). The highlighted word, Summary, is the location for the bookmark that will be added. The highlighted text is inserted automatically as the default name for this bookmark in the Bookmark name text box.

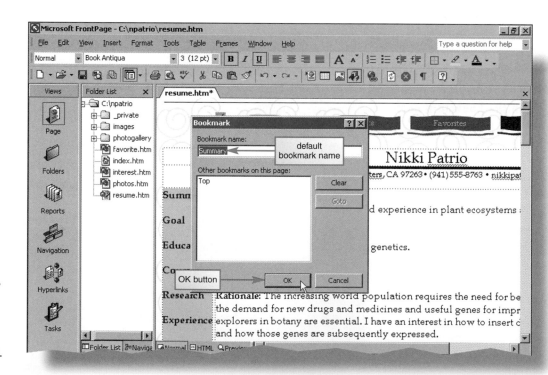

FIGURE 3-58

2 Click the OK button. Position the insertion point before the underlined words, Career Goal.

The Resume page displays, and the text, Summary, has a dashed underline, indicating that it is bookmarked (Figure 3-59).

3 Repeat Steps 1 through 3 to bookmark each of the remaining text items listed in Table 3-3, selecting only the words indicated in the table. Use the default name as the bookmark name in each case.

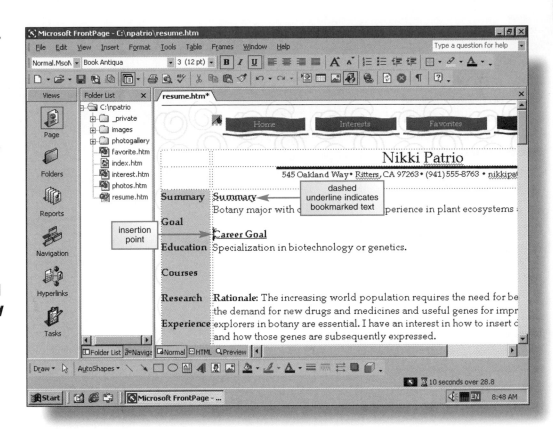

FIGURE 3-59

Adding Hyperlinks to Bookmarks

Once the bookmarks are identified, making hyperlinks to them is done in a similar fashion as the previous hyperlinks you have created. Hyperlink addresses that target a bookmark on a page, rather than just the page itself, have the same format as a URL addressing the page, with the addition of the bookmark. A pound sign (#) preceding the bookmark name identifies a bookmark in a URL, as shown in Figure 3-63 on page FP 3.41.

Perform the following steps on the next page to create text hyperlinks to bookmarks in the Web page.

Other Ways

1. Press ALT+I, K
2. Press CTRL+G
3. In Voice Command mode, say "Insert, Bookmark"

More About

Hyperlinks to Bookmarks

Hyperlinks to bookmarks do not have to be located on the same Web page as the bookmark. You can establish a hyperlink to a bookmark on another Web page by selecting the page name in the Create Hyperlink dialog box and then selecting the desired bookmark on that page.

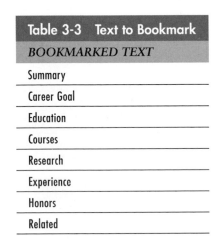

Table 3-3 Text to Bookmark
BOOKMARKED TEXT
Summary
Career Goal
Education
Courses
Research
Experience
Honors
Related

To Create a Hyperlink to a Bookmark

1 **Drag through the text, Summary, in the left column of the third row in the table. Right-click the selected text and then point to Hyperlink on the shortcut menu.**

The text, Summary, is selected and the shortcut menu displays (Figure 3-60).

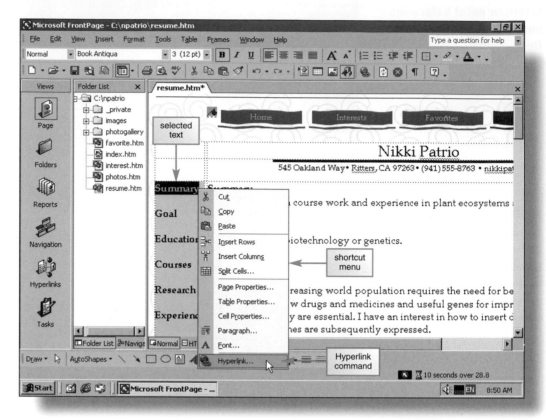

FIGURE 3-60

2 **Click Hyperlink. When the Insert Hyperlink dialog box displays, point to the Bookmark button.**

The Insert Hyperlink dialog box displays (Figure 3-61).

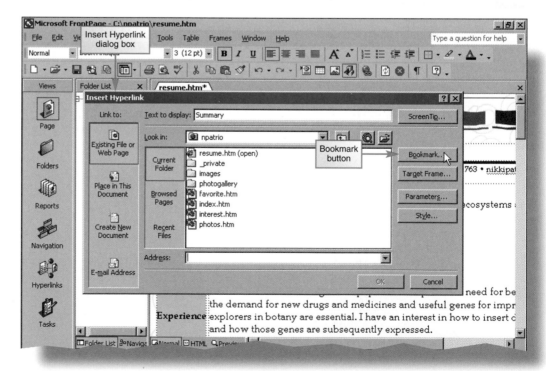

FIGURE 3-61

3 Click the Bookmark button. When the Select Place in Document dialog box displays, click Summary in the list of bookmarks. Point to the OK button.

The bookmark, Summary, is selected (Figure 3-62).

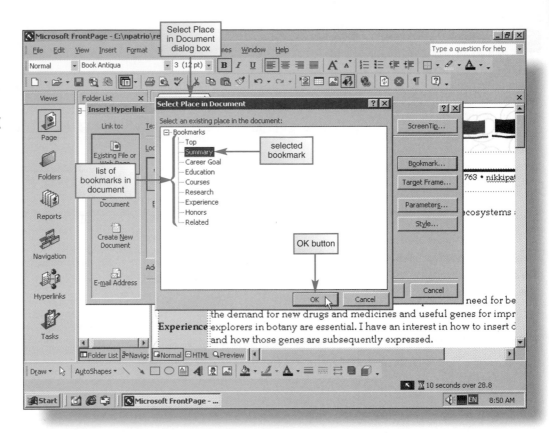

FIGURE 3-62

4 Click the OK button. Point to the OK button in the Insert Hyperlink dialog box.

The Select Place in Document dialog box is closed and the pound sign in the Address text box indicates that a bookmark will be used in the hyperlink (Figure 3-63).

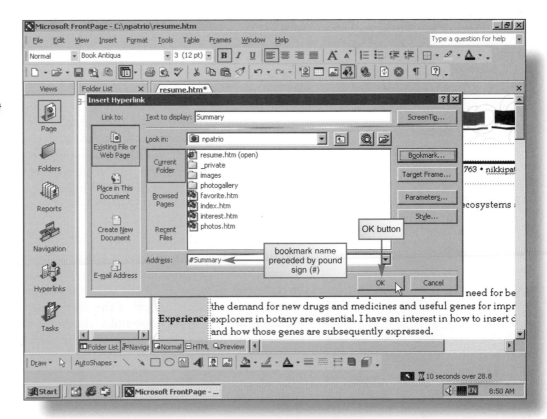

FIGURE 3-63

5 Click the OK button. Point to the hyperlink, Summary.

The bookmark URL displays on the status bar (Figure 3-64). Because it links to a location on the same page, the full hyperlink address is not displayed.

6 Repeat Steps 1 through 5 to create hyperlinks to each of the remaining bookmarks, as listed in Table 3-4.

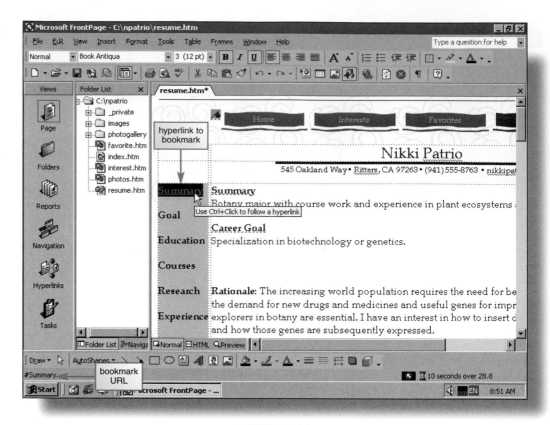

FIGURE 3-64

Once users have followed a hyperlink to a bookmark on the same Web page, they could simply scroll back to return to the previous location. If the page is very long or if the original hyperlink was not at the top of the page, however, it may be tedious, at best, for the users to find their way back. It is common to provide a "Back" link to take the user back to the location that linked to the bookmark. Although using the Back button in the Web browser could achieve the same visible effect, there is a subtle difference. Using the browser's Back button to return removes the current page from the browser's list of recently visited links. By using a Back link, the list of links the user has followed recently is preserved, even though a different page is not really loaded.

Use of a Back link will work if only one hyperlink targets a given bookmark. If multiple hyperlinks target the same bookmark, there is no way to determine the source of the hyperlink to which the user should be returned. Because all of the links that target your text bookmarks will come from text near the top of the Web page, they may all target the same location for their Back hyperlinks, the name at the top of the page. Use the following steps to create a Back link for each of the text bookmarks.

Table 3-4 Bookmark Hyperlinks	
HYPERLINKED TEXT	BOOKMARK
Summary	Summary
Goal	Career Goal
Education	Education
Courses	Courses
Research	Research
Experience	Experience
Honors	Honors
Related Activities	Related

Steps **To Create Back Hyperlinks**

1 Position the insertion point in the first empty line after the paragraph beginning with Rationale, after the the Career Goal bookmark. Click the Font Size box arrow and then click 2 (10 pt). Click the Italic button on the Standard toolbar. Type back to top as text for the back hyperlink.

The text, back to top, is inserted (Figure 3-65).

FIGURE 3-65

2 Drag through the text, back to top, to select it. Right-click the selected text and then click Hyperlink on the shortcut menu. When the Insert Hyperlink dialog box displays, click the Bookmark button. When the Select Place in Document dialog box displays, click Top in the list of bookmarks. Point to the OK button.

The bookmark for the hyper-link is selected (Figure 3-66).

FIGURE 3-66

3 Click the OK button. Click the OK button in the Insert Hyperlink dialog box. Point to the hyperlink, back to top.

The bookmark URL displays on the status bar (Figure 3-67).

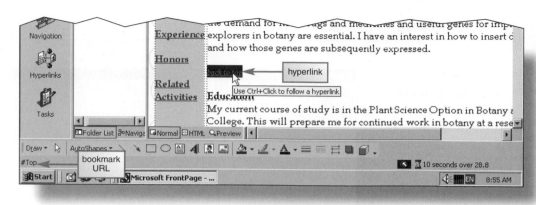

FIGURE 3-67

4 Copy and paste the hyperlink to create back hyperlinks for each of the remaining sections containing bookmarks. Do not create a back hyperlink in the cell containing the Summary bookmark at the top of the page. Insert or delete blank lines to adjust heights as needed. To properly space after the line, Research and Practicum, position the insertion point before the paragraph that begins, This summer, press the BACKSPACE key and then press SHIFT+ENTER. Save and close the Resume page.

Because the back hyperlinks all reference the same location, the top of the page, the first back hyperlink was copied and pasted into multiple locations in the page. This saves time, rather than inserting the text and creating a hyperlink for each one separately.

More About

The Pictures Toolbar

The Pictures toolbar provides a number of useful tools for images. Similar to the Photo Gallery component, you can click the Auto Thumbnail button to create a thumbnail of a large image. The Auto Thumbnail button automatically inserts a hyperlink to the original, larger image.

Modifying an Image on a Web Page

Often, you want to use images that need some modification to be useable on a Web page. Typically, this has to do with the displayed size of the image, but also may include other properties, such as the image background or the size of the image file. FrontPage provides tools to modify these properties, thus making the images more useful.

Many images used on a Web page may appear to be irregular in shape when in fact they are rectangular. When the background color of the image is not the same as that of the Web page, the rectangular shape of the image becomes very obvious. To hide this rectangular shape, you can use images that have the same background color as the Web page, or you can use images that have a transparent background. Using images with a transparent background allows the color or graphic used in a Web page background to show through the background of the image, thus hiding the rectangular shape of the image.

Displaying the Pictures Toolbar

FrontPage has features for manipulating images within a Web page. The **Pictures toolbar** contains a set of buttons that perform actions such as rotating the image and changing the brightness and contrast. The buttons on the Pictures toolbar may be active or inactive, depending on the type of image and its context. The Pictures toolbar can be hidden or displayed, depending on the setting on the View menu.

Perform the following steps to insert an image and display the Pictures toolbar.

Steps To Insert an Image and Display the Pictures Toolbar

1 **Double-click the file, index.htm, in the Folder List pane. Position the insertion point before the Home hyperlink on the bottom line. Press the ENTER key twice.**

The Home page is opened in Page view and two additional blank lines are inserted (Figure 3-68).

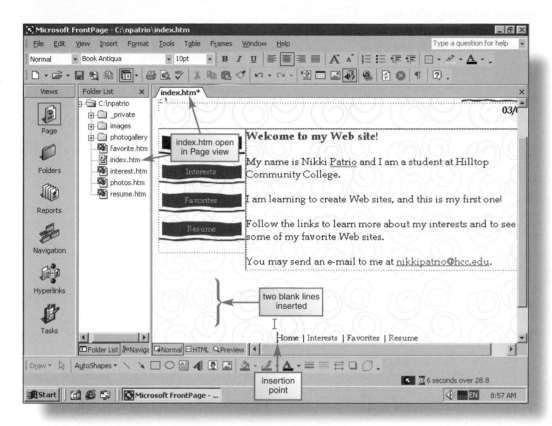

FIGURE 3-68

2 **Click Insert on the menu bar and then point to Picture on the Insert menu. Click From File on the Picture submenu. When the Picture dialog box displays, select the camera03.gif file from the Project3 folder on the Data Disk. Point to the Insert button.**

The Picture dialog box displays with the file, camera03.gif, selected (Figure 3-69).

FIGURE 3-69

3 **Click the Insert button. When the image is inserted, click the image to select it. If the Pictures toolbar does not display, point to Toolbars on the View menu and then point to Pictures on the Toolbars submenu.**

The Pictures command is selected on the Toolbars submenu (Figure 3-70). The selected check marks indicate the toolbars that currently are visible.

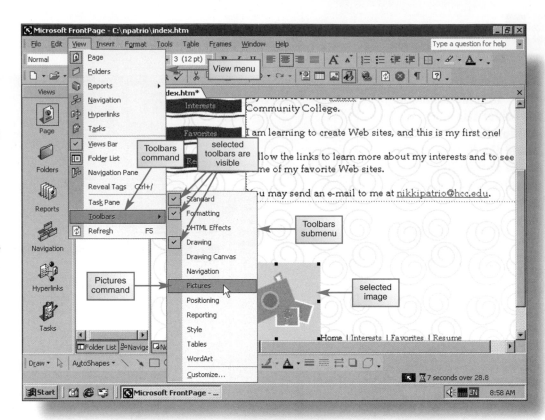

FIGURE 3-70

4 **Click Pictures. Point to the Set Transparent Color button on the Pictures toolbar.**

The Pictures toolbar displays (Figure 3-71).

FIGURE 3-71

1. Press ALT+V, T, click Pictures
2. In Voice Command mode, say "View, Toolbars, Pictures"

By selecting an image and then selecting the Pictures toolbar on the Toolbars submenu, the Pictures toolbar only will display when an image currently is selected.

If the image is deselected, the Pictures toolbar will not display. In order for the Pictures toolbar always to be visible on the screen, however, no image currently should be selected when the Pictures toolbar on the Toolbars submenu is chosen. In this case, the Pictures toolbar will always display, whether or not an image currently is selected. All buttons will be inactive, except the first, the Insert Picture From File button, until an image is selected.

Creating a Transparent Image

A **transparent image** sometimes is referred to as a **floating image** because it appears to float on the Web page. To make an image transparent, you select one of the colors in the image to be the **transparent color**. The transparent color is replaced by the background color or image of the page.

An image can have only one transparent color. If you select another transparent color, the first transparent color reverts to its original color. Use the **Set Transparent Color button** on the Pictures toolbar to make a selected color transparent. When you click the Set Transparent Color button, the mouse pointer changes to the **Set Transparent Color pointer** when it is positioned over the image. You then click a color on the image to make it transparent.

To make an image transparent, it must be in the GIF file format. FrontPage will ask you if you want to convert a JPEG image to GIF format if you try to make a JPEG image transparent. Because GIF supports a maximum of only 256 colors, you may lose some image quality by converting from JPEG to GIF.

The procedure for making a transparent image is to select the image and then choose the transparent color using the Set Transparent Color pointer.

Perform the following steps to set the color blue around the sides of the camera image as the transparent color.

More About

GIF Files and Transparency

An animated GIF image consists of several images that display in rapid succession. GIF images that are animated will not allow you to select a transparent color.

Steps **To Create a Transparent Image**

 If necessary, click the image to select it. Click the Set Transparent Color button on the Pictures toolbar. Position the mouse pointer over the image.

Sizing handles display around the image to indicate that it is selected (Figure 3-72). The mouse pointer changes to the Set Transparent Color pointer when it is moved over the image.

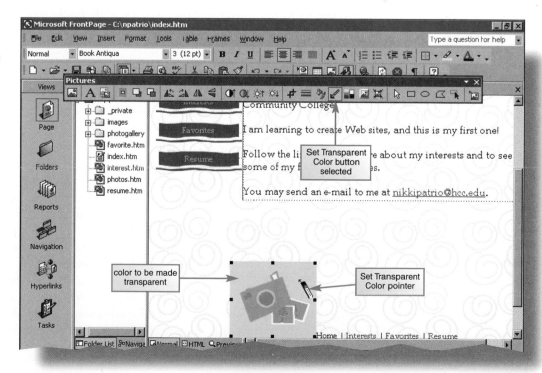

FIGURE 3-72

2 **Click the light blue color surrounding the image.**

The light blue color becomes transparent and is replaced by the background (Figure 3-73). The mouse pointer is restored to the normal block arrow pointer and the Set Transparent Color button no longer is selected.

FIGURE 3-73

Other Ways

1. Click image, in Voice Command mode, say "Set Transparent Color"

You must take care when selecting a color to be transparent. If the color appears in other sections of the image, it will become transparent in the other sections as well, and this might have an unexpected or undesirable effect. You could run into problems if, for example, you have a purple background and an image containing a face. If you make white the transparent color, it could result in a face with purple eyes and purple teeth.

Resizing and Resampling an Image

Sometimes an image you want to use is too small or too large to fit within the space you have set aside for it in your Web page design. You can resize an image, shrinking or stretching it, by selecting the image and dragging its handles until it becomes the desired size. This was done in Project 2 with the book image on the Photos page. You also may specify the width and height of the image directly.

Resizing an image does not automatically change the size of the image file. It changes only the HTML tags for the image, so the browser actually does the shrinking or stretching when the image is displayed. This is an advantage for small images that you have stretched to a larger size. The small image file takes less time to load than if the file contained the image at its larger size.

Conversely, for images you have made smaller, the file still contains the image at its original size, and it still must be loaded even though the browser displays a smaller version of the image. To take advantage of the download performance brought about by a smaller image, you must resample the image. **Resampling** an image stores the image in the file at its new size.

Once an image has been resampled as a smaller size it may appear better at the smaller size than before it was resampled. Once the resampled file is saved, trying to stretch it back to its original size will result typically in a poorer quality image. In both cases, this is due to the amount of information needed in the file to display the image at the given size. In the first case, too much information was provided for a smaller image. In the second, information was lost in the resampling that is needed for the larger displayed image. If you are going to resample an image but may need the larger version later, then make a backup copy.

Resampling an image becomes particularly important when inserting photographs, because the JPEG files usually are rather large. You did not have to resample the photos used in the Photos page, because FrontPage created the smaller thumbnail pictures for you.

Images can be resized and resampled as needed. The new images can be saved in the images folder of the project when the project is saved. If inserted images are not saved before resampling, the original images will remain unchanged and will not be included in the project. If the image was saved before resizing and resampling, then you may overwrite the saved version with the new one. Perform the following steps to resize and resample the camera image for this project.

More About

Resampling an Image

Because resampling overwrites the image file you may want to make a backup copy of the original image file. If you save an unwanted change accidentally, you can retrieve the backup copy of the file and continue with your development.

Steps **To Resize and Resample an Image**

1 **If necessary, click the image to select it. Use the sizing handles to resize the image to the approximate size illustrated in Figure 3-74. Point to the Resample button on the Pictures toolbar.**

The image is resized using the sizing handles (Figure 3-74).

FIGURE 3-74

2 **With the image still selected, click the Resample button on the Pictures toolbar. Point to the Position Absolutely button on the Pictures toolbar.**

The resized and resampled image displays (Figure 3-75).

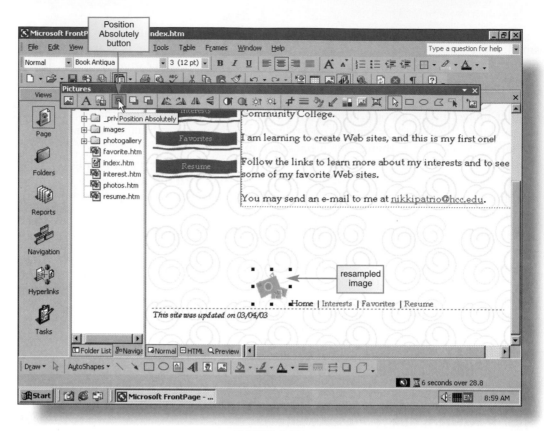

FIGURE 3-75

Other Ways

1. Click image, in Voice Command mode, say "Resample"

Once an image is resampled, it cannot be resampled again unless the size of the image is changed. The resample action can be undone, however, by clicking the Undo button.

Using Absolute Positioning with an Image

Although tables can be helpful in positioning elements on a Web page, at times even a table does not provide enough control over placement of an image. In other circumstances, using a table to position an image may prove to be difficult.

To provide more exact image placement, FrontPage supports absolute positioning for images. **Absolute positioning** refers to the ability to display page content at a specified distance from the upper left corner of its container, which by default is the space that the Web page occupies in the browser. Unfortunately, due to differences in browsers and monitors, the results are not always consistent. Also, when an image is positioned absolutely, text and other items do not flow around the image. If your Web page content changes, you may need to reposition the image. Internet Explorer 5.0 and Netscape Navigator 6.0 both support absolute positioning; however, you should always verify your page in any browser your visitors are likely to use.

To use absolute positioning with the camera image, perform the following steps.

To Use Absolute Positioning with an Image

1 **If necessary, click the image to select it. Click the Position Absolutely button on the Pictures toolbar. Position the mouse pointer over the image.**

The Position Absolutely button is selected and the pointer displays as a double two-headed arrow (Figure 3-76).

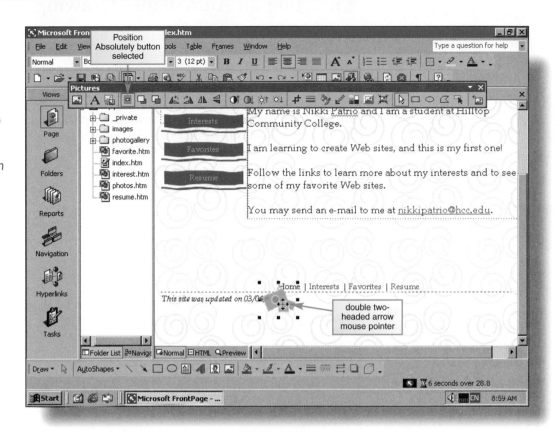

FIGURE 3-76

2 **Drag the image to the approximate location illustrated in Figure 3-77. Click the page off of the image to deselect the image.**

The image is repositioned (Figure 3-77). The Pictures toolbar no longer displays because no image is selected.

Other Ways

1. Click image, in Voice Command mode, say "Position Absolutely"

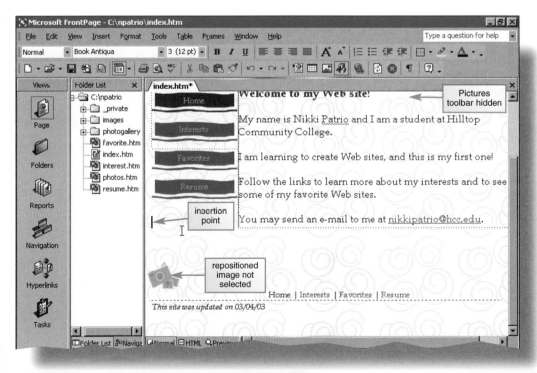

FIGURE 3-77

Inserting an AutoShapes Drawing Object

At times, finding just the right image can be time-consuming, even if it is rather simple. Users of other Office products, such as Word and PowerPoint, are accustomed to adding drawings, as well as richly formatted text, directly to their documents. FrontPage now supports drawing line graphics and rich text formatting within Web pages. The **Drawing toolbar** provide the ability to draw arrows, rectangles, lines, and other shapes. **AutoShapes** adds geometric shapes, block arrows, flowchart symbols, stars, banners and other predrawn shapes. **WordArt** provides rich text formatting capabilities, such as shadowing and curving text.

Perform the following steps to add an AutoShapes object to a Web page.

 Steps **To Add an AutoShapes Object**

1 **If necessary, click View on the menu bar, point to Toolbars, and then click Drawing. Click the AutoShapes button on the Drawing toolbar. Point to Stars and Banners, and then point to Explosion 1.**

The shape, Explosion 1, is highlighted and a ScreenTip displays (Figure 3-78).

FIGURE 3-78

2 **Click Explosion 1. Position the mouse pointer below the Links bar.**

The mouse pointer changes to a crosshair (Figure 3-79).

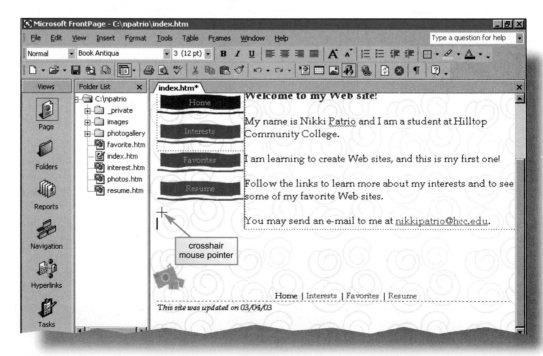

FIGURE 3-79

3 Drag the mouse pointer to the opposite corner to create a shape that is approximately the same width as the Links bar. Release the mouse button. Right-click the shape and then click Add text on the shortcut menu.

The shape is drawn and a text box displays on the shape (Figure 3-80).

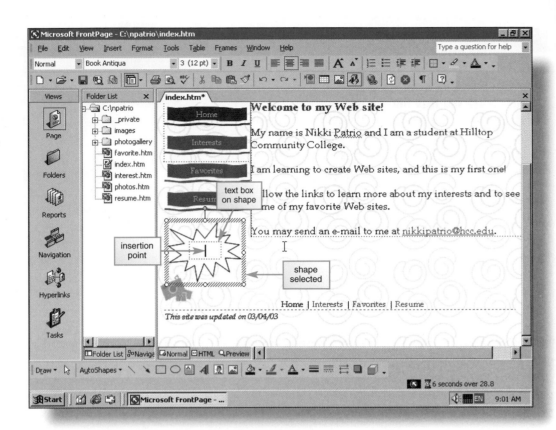

FIGURE 3-80

4 Click the Font Size button arrow on the Formatting toolbar and then select 2 (10 pt). Type See my photos in the text box on the shape. Drag through the text and then point to the Font Color button arrow on the Drawing toolbar.

The extered text displays on the shape (Figure 3-81).

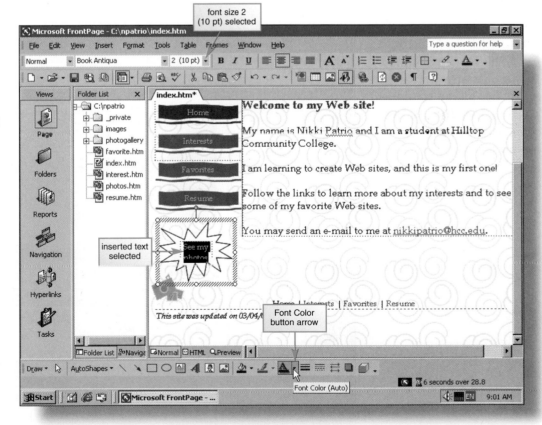

FIGURE 3-81

5 **Click the Font Color button arrow. Click More Colors. When the More Colors dialog box displays, click the title bar and drag the dialog box so it does not hide the text on the Link bar buttons. Point to the Select button.**

The More Colors dialog box displays and is repositioned (Figure 3-82).

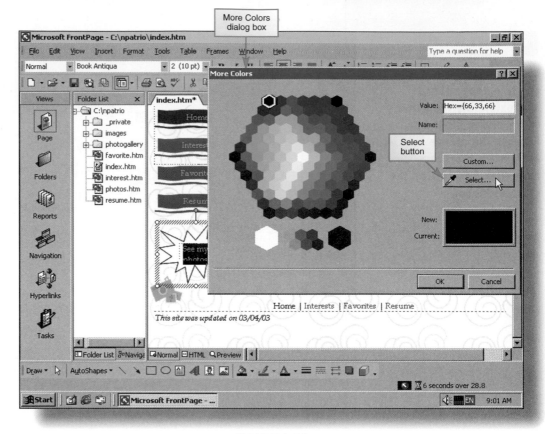

FIGURE 3-82

6 **Click the Select button. Position the mouse pointer over text on a Link bar button so that the New area displays the same color as the Link bar button text.**

The mouse pointer changes to a dropper and the New area displays the color under the mouse pointer (Figure 3-83).

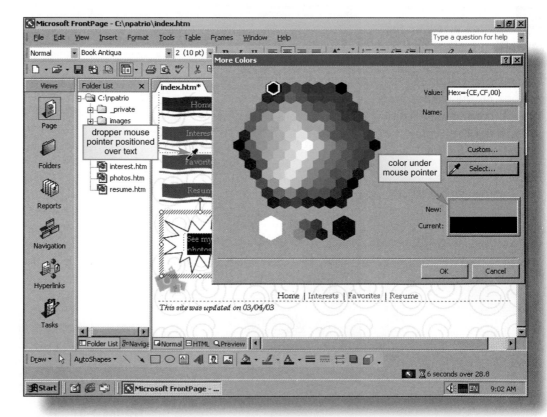

FIGURE 3-83

7 Click the mouse button. Click the OK button. Click the shape outside of the text box to deselect the text. Point to the Fill Color button arrow on the Drawing toolbar.

The text in the shape displays using the new color (Figure 3-84).

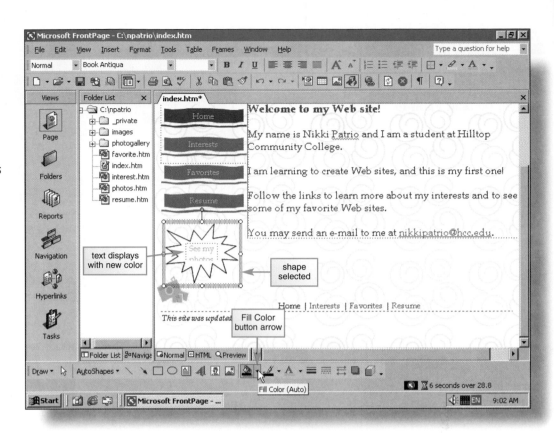

FIGURE 3-84

8 Click the Fill Color button arrow. Click More Fill Colors. When the More Colors dialog box displays, drag the dialog box so that the Link bar buttons are visible. Click the Select button and then position the mouse pointer over a Link bar button.

The mouse pointer changes to a dropper and the New area displays the color under the mouse pointer (Figure 3-85).

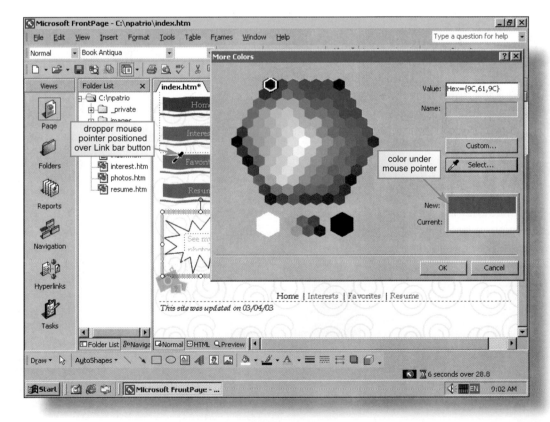

FIGURE 3-85

9 Click the mouse button. Click the OK button. Click the Line Color button arrow on the Drawing toolbar. Point to No Line.

The shape displays using the selected color (Figure 3-86).

FIGURE 3-86

10 Click No Line. If necessary, resize the shape so that the text in the text box is fully visible. Position the pointer over the shape and then drag the shape to reposition it.

The line around the shape is removed (Figure 3-87). When the mouse pointer is positioned over the shape, it becomes a double two-headed arrow, while if over the text, it becomes an I-beam.

Other Ways

1. Press ALT+U, S, click shape
2. In Voice Command mode, say "AutoShapes, Stars and Banners, TAB, ENTER"

FIGURE 3-87

Besides simply creating line drawings and shapes, the Drawing toolbar has tools to change drawing colors, add three-dimensional style effects, and to add drop shadows.

These line drawing graphics use a technology called Vector Markup Language, or VML. VML is a way to describe images using curves, lines, and coordinates so that the instructions to draw the picture can be downloaded rather than the entire picture. A line drawing expressed in VML is usually much smaller than the same drawing stored as a GIF or JPEG file, and therefore can download more quickly.

Assigning a Hyperlink to an Image

Previous projects used text as hyperlinks, whether typed or created on a Link bar. This project also will use images as hyperlinks. Now that the two images have the desired appearance, it is time to make them function as hyperlinks.

Adding a hyperlink to the Explosion 1 shape can be accomplished in several ways. The text on the shape could be selected and assigned a hyperlink; however, this would require users to click the text, not just the shape, to activate the hyperlink.

As mentioned earlier, many images used on a Web page may appear to be irregular in shape when in fact they are rectangular. When the Explosion 1 shape is selected, a rectangular box with sizing handles displays. You might think that clicking any area within the rectangle would activate a hyperlink added to a shape. By adding a hyperlink to the shape itself, however, any location on the shape activates the hyperlink, while locations not on the shape but within the rectangular area do not. This is true even for irregular shapes, such as the Explosion 1 shape.

Perform the following steps to add a hyperlink to the Explosion 1 AutoShape object.

More About

Displaying Images

Current computers allow you to specify the bit resolution your computer monitor will display. If the resolution is smaller than the bit resolution of an image, the image will not display properly. Right-click the desktop and then click Properties. When the Display Properties dialog box displays, click the Settings tab to see the current setting for your computer monitor.

Steps **To Add a Hyperlink to an AutoShapes Object**

1 **Right-click the Explosion 1 object. Point to Hyperlink on the shortcut menu.**

A submenu displays and Hyperlink is highlighted (Figure 3-88). Be sure to select the shape and not the text on the shape. If the Set AutoShape Defaults command does not appear on the shortcut menu, then you did not select the shape.

FIGURE 3-88

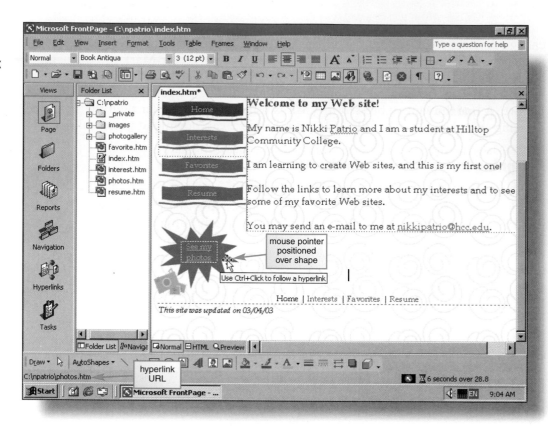

2 **Click Hyperlink. If necessary, when the Insert Hyperlink dialog box displays, click the Existing File or Web Page button in the Links to bar. Select the file, photos.htm, in the Web folder location (c:\npatrio). Click the OK button. Click off of the shape to deselect it. Position the mouse pointer over the shape.**

The new URL for the image hyperlink displays on the status bar (Figure 3-89). If the mouse pointer is positioned off of the shape, the URL does not display.

FIGURE 3-89

Adding a hyperlink to the camera image can be as simple as adding one to text. In such a case, any location within the rectangle encompassing the image would activate the hyperlink. To activate a hyperlink only from within the contours of the image, as was done with the AutoShape object, a hotspot must be defined first.

Image Maps

Rather than assign a hyperlink to an entire graphic, an image map may be used. **Image maps** are graphic images containing special areas called hotspots. A **hotspot** is a specially designated portion of the image that is set up as a hyperlink. Clicking a hotspot is the same as clicking a regular text hyperlink. The hotspot lets you jump to the URL that is defined for that region of the image.

Image maps provide new ways to create interactive Web pages. They provide an alternative to plain text hyperlinks. They also allow you to economize on images, because a single image can contain multiple hotspots and, thus, multiple hyperlinks. A well-designed image map gives the viewer clues about the destination of each hyperlink. For example, an art gallery might have an image containing a diagram of the various rooms in which different types of art are exhibited. Clicking a room displays another Web page containing images of related works of art. A college or university could have an image containing a map of the campus with hotspots defined for each building. Clicking a building would display another Web page describing the building.

When creating an image map, you want to use a motif, or metaphor, for your images. For example, a campus map of different buildings might be used for obtaining navigation assistance. A bookshelf with books listing different topics might be used in a help desk application.

Defining Hotspots

To create an image map, you first decide on an image to use and then you define hotspots on the image. Finally, you assign URLs to each hotspot.

Hotspots can be circles, rectangles, or irregularly shaped areas called polygons. You designate hotspots using the hotspot buttons on the Pictures toolbar. For example, when you click the Rectangle button, the mouse pointer changes to a pencil pointer. To draw a rectangular hotspot, click and hold one corner of the desired rectangle, drag to the opposite corner, and then release the mouse button. The Insert Hyperlink dialog box automatically opens so that you can enter the target URL that will be assigned to the hotspot. You also can add text to an image and then create hyperlinks for the text making it, in effect, a labeled rectangular hotspot. When adding hotspots other than as text, the Insert Hyperlink dialog box automatically is invoked. This is not done for text, because text may be added to an image without making it a hotspot.

The camera image only needs a single hotspot because it links only to the Photos page. Using an appropriate image, however, hotspots could be created to link to each page of interest in the Web site. Perform the following steps to add a hotspot to the camera image.

More About

Image Map Hotspots

You can set a default hyperlink for any area on the image map that does not have a hotspot defined. Click the General tab in the Picture Properties dialog box.

Steps **To Add a Hotspot to an Image**

1 **If necessary, click the camera image to select it and then point to the Polygonal Hotspot button on the Pictures toolbar.**

The Pictures toolbar displays with the polygonal hotspot button selected (Figure 3-90).

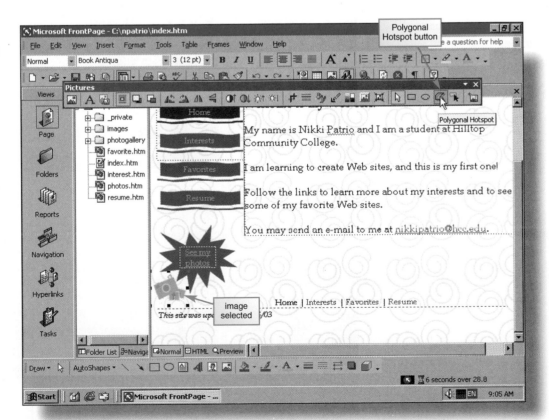

FIGURE 3-90

2 Click the Polygonal Hotspot button. Carefully draw around the perimeter of the camera image, using a single click to create a new edit point with each change of direction. When you have completed tracing around the perimeter, click the starting point to complete the hotspot. When the Insert Hyperlink dialog box displays, click the file name, photos.htm, and then point to the OK button.

The Insert Hyperlink dialog box displays with the photos.htm file selected (Figure 3-91).

FIGURE 3-91

3 Click the OK button. Position the mouse pointer on the camera image.

The file name, photos.htm, displays on the status bar (Figure 3-92).

FIGURE 3-92

1. Click image, in Voice Command mode, say "Polygonal Hotspot"

You successfully have created a hotspot on an image map. Although this image contains only a single hotspot, it is an image map because the entire rectangular image was not used for the hyperlink. Image maps are an excellent way to present links visually in an intuitive and user-friendly fashion. Creating your own image maps is not hard to do, but requires some careful preparation.

Highlighting Image Map Hotspots

The hotspot on the camera image map is easy to find because there is only one and it has well-defined and intuitive boundaries. Some image maps will not have any text or image features associated with hotspots. Lines surrounding the hotspots display when the image is selected. When multiple hotspots are used, or an image already has similar lines, the boundaries around each hotspot may be difficult to locate.

The Pictures toolbar includes the **Highlight Hotspots button** that toggles between displaying hotspots only and displaying the image and the hotspot. Perform the following steps to highlight the hotspot on the camera image map.

More *About*

Highlighting Hotsports

When you highlight hotspots on an image, any hotspot currently not selected displays with a black outline. If a hotspot is selected, it displays as solid black.

Steps **To Highlight Hotspots on an Image Map**

1 **If necessary, click the camera image used as an image map. Click the Highlight Hotspots button on the Pictures toolbar.**

The image becomes white, and the selected hotspot is revealed as solid black (Figure 3-93). In this view, you easily can see hotspots.

2 **Click the Highlight Hotspots button again to remove the highlight.**

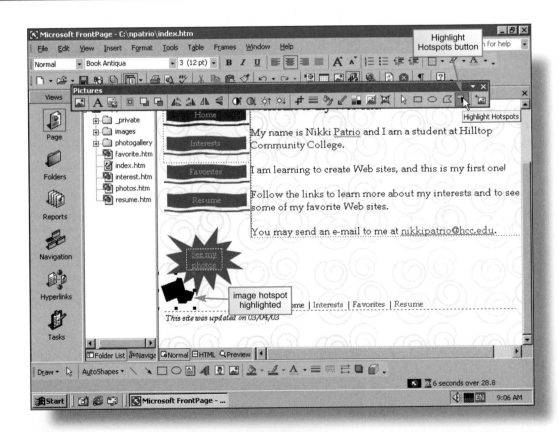

FIGURE 3-93

The Highlight Hotspots button is useful when image features make it difficult to see the hotspot outlines that are superimposed on the image.

Other Ways

1. Click image, in Voice Command mode, say "Highlight Hotspots"

Displaying the Hyperlinks in a FrontPage Web

More About

Hyperlinks View

If Hyperlinks view reveals a misspelled hyperlink in one of your Web pages, you can load the page in FrontPage by double-clicking the page icon in Hyperlinks view and then quickly correcting the hyperlink.

In this and previous projects, you have created links to other pages in your web, to Web sites not within your web, and to an e-mail address. You want to avoid having any of these hyperlinks point to nonexistent files. Hyperlinks that point to nonexistent files are referred to as **broken hyperlinks**.

Several reasons exist for encountering broken hyperlinks. The file that is the target of the hyperlink could have been deleted, renamed, moved to another folder, or moved to another Web server. The Web server on which the file resides could have its Internet address changed, could be out of service for some period of time, or could be permanently out of service.

Keeping track of broken hyperlinks in a small web like Nikki's is simple because it contains only a few hyperlinks. When developing very large webs, with many files and hyperlinks, however, it would be very difficult to try to remember the pages that have hyperlinks, the targets where they link, and which hyperlinks are broken.

The **Hyperlinks view** in FrontPage alleviates this problem. For a given Web page, it displays in a graphical format the hyperlinks and their URLs, and indicates which hyperlinks are broken. Perform the following step to display the Hyperlinks view and determine whether Nikki's web has any broken hyperlinks.

Steps To Display the Hyperlinks in a FrontPage Web

1 **Make sure that you have saved all changes, saving the camera03.gif file in the images folder when prompted to save the embedded image. If necessary, open the file index.htm in the Folder List pane. Click the Hyperlinks button on the Views bar. If necessary, click the plus sign on the interest.htm icon to display its links.**

FrontPage displays the web in Hyperlinks view (Figure 3-94). The plus sign on the interest.htm icon turns to a minus sign.

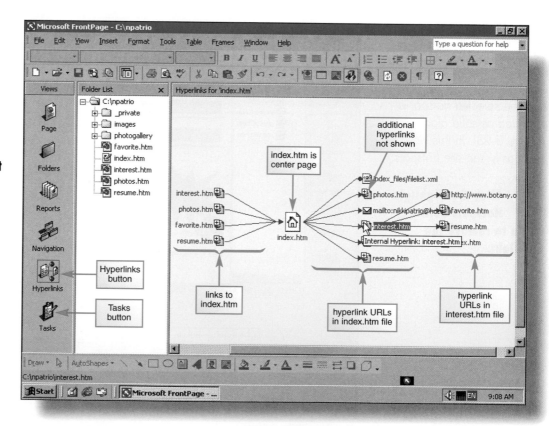

FIGURE 3-94

The Hyperlinks view displays a graphical diagram of the hyperlinks in a center page. The **center page** is the page for which you want to see all hyperlinks, both to and from it, in the current FrontPage web. In this case it is the Home page, index.htm, which displays the hyperlinks shown in Figure 3-102 on page FP 3.68. Hyperlinks exist from the Home page to the Photos page, the Interests page, the Favorites page, and the Resume page, as well as a mailto: link. You also may see links to embedded script files or style sheets created by FrontPage. None of the hyperlinks is known to be broken. A broken hyperlink displays like any other hyperlink, except that it shows as a broken line. A plus sign indicates additional hyperlinks that are not shown. You can view links on these pages by clicking the plus sign, as was done for the interest.htm file.

You can use the Hyperlinks view to verify quickly which links, if any, are broken in the current FrontPage web.

Managing Tasks with FrontPage

Web pages for large sites typically are maintained either on a Web server or on a file server, where several people can access the pages at the same time. Tracking and coordinating tasks assigned to multiple developers can be a tedious and complex job. FrontPage has several management tools that ease this process, including tools that manage task assignment and tracking. Even in the case of a smaller web, with a single developer, some of these tools are helpful for tracking work progress and recording pending development work.

Nikki indicated that she has some ideas for new pages, but is not ready to begin working on them. She would like to establish a free personal ads page so students could post ads to buy or sell items, find roommates, share rides for holiday trips home, and so forth. This would require a page to collect the data, one to request a view of the ads by category and one to display the results. To save these ideas for a later time, ensuring that they are not forgotten, you decide to add them as FrontPage tasks for later completion.

Perform the following steps to assign new tasks for the web.

Steps To Assign Tasks for a Web

1 **Click the Tasks button on the Views bar. Click File on the menu bar and then point to New on the File menu. When the New submenu displays, point to Task on the New submenu.**

The web displays in Tasks view. The New submenu displays with the Task command selected (Figure 3-95).

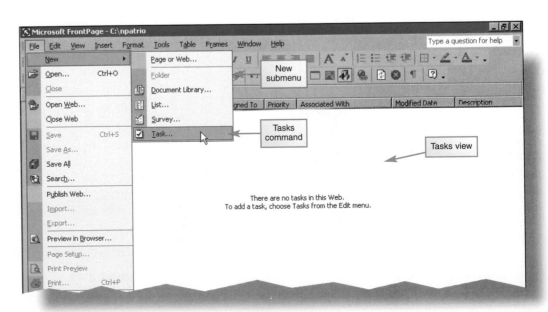

FIGURE 3-95

2 **Click Task. When the New Task dialog box displays, type** Create form for data collection **in the Task name text box. In the Assigned to list box, type** Nikki **(you may substitute your own name). In the Description text box, type** Create a form to collect data for personal ads **and then point to the OK button.**

The New Task dialog box displays (Figure 3-96). This task is not associated with any file because it will be a new page. To associate a task with a particular file, add the task while that file is open in Page view.

FIGURE 3-96

3 **Click the OK button.**

The new task displays in Tasks view (Figure 3-97). New tasks are marked with a status of Not Started.

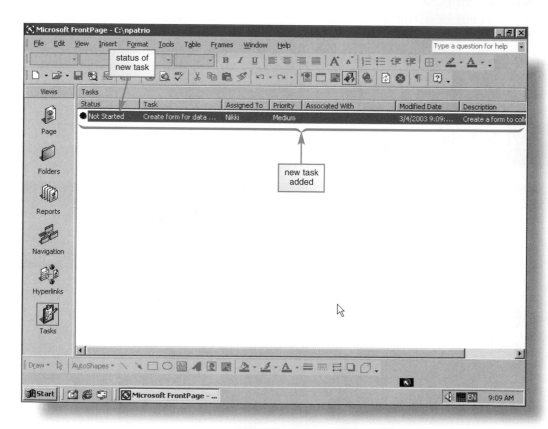

FIGURE 3-97

| 4 | **Repeat Steps 2 and 3 to add the remaining two tasks, as listed in Table 3-5.** |

The added tasks display in Tasks view (Figure 3-98).

FIGURE 3-98

Table 3-5 New Task Assignments

TASK NAME	ASSIGNED TO	DESCRIPTION
Create form for data collection	Nikki	Create a form to collect data for personal ads
Request to view or place ads	Nikki	Create a page where users can request to view or place an ad
Display results of ad query	Nikki	Create a page to display the results of a request to view ads

Other Ways

1. On Edit menu point to Tasks, click Add Task
2. Right-click Tasks Pane, click Add Task on shortcut menu
3. Press ALT+F, N, T
4. Press ALT+E, K, A
5. In Voice Command mode, say "Tasks, File, New, Task"

Reporting on the Web Site

Even a relatively small Web site consists of many files and hyperlinks to possibly many more files, even on destinations outside of the Web site itself. Managing all of the pieces of a Web site can be a daunting task. FrontPage provides various reports to illustrate the status of the FrontPage web. FrontPage tracks many items in the Web such as the number of picture files, broken hyperlinks, slow pages, recently added files, and so forth.

Viewing Reports on the Web Site

FrontPage provides a summary report on a variety of items such as uncompleted tasks and broken hyperlinks. FrontPage can generate many reports for a web, even if the web is not yet published to a server. The web must be opened on an appropriate server, however, to generate usage summary reports. Also, if you have made any changes to your Web pages, they should be saved before viewing reports or verifying hyperlinks.

Clicking through each file in Hyperlinks view to find broken hyperlinks would display only verified hyperlinks that are known to be broken. This could be a daunting and time-consuming task. Finding unverified hyperlinks could be more difficult because they do not show as broken in Hyperlinks view. Another difficult task, if performed manually, would be finding pages that no longer are linked and cannot be reached by starting from the Home page. The Site Summary report summarizes various statistics for the current web. From this report, you also can access reports for hyperlinks and files, such as the Unlinked Files report and the Broken Hyperlinks report. The Broken Hyperlinks report has multiple views available from the Site Summary, including all hyperlinks in the Web site, broken hyperlinks, and unverified hyperlinks. Perform the following steps to view the FrontPage Site Summary report.

Steps **To View the Site Summary Report**

1 **Click View on the menu bar and then point to Reports. Point to Site Summary on the Reports submenu.**

The View menu and Reports submenu display (Figure 3-99). The selected check mark to the left of the Site Summary command on the Reports submenu indicates the report that currently is visible when in Reports view.

FIGURE 3-99

2 **Click Site Summary. Point to the Verifies hyperlinks in the current web button on the Reporting toolbar.**

The FrontPage window switches to Reports view and the Site Summary report displays (Figure 3-100).

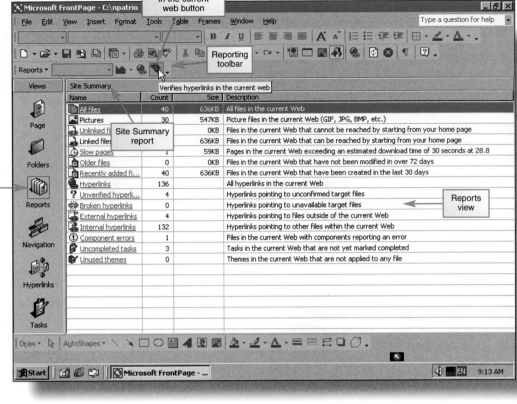

FIGURE 3-100

Verifying Hyperlinks

Just verifying that all hyperlinks in a Web site are correct is a critical and possibly time-consuming task. FrontPage provides a means of verifying that the hyperlinks to external destinations (destinations that are outside of the web) are valid.

Hyperlinks can be verified by using the Reporting toolbar. You need to be connected to the World Wide Web to verify external hyperlinks. Perform the following steps on the next page to use the Reporting toolbar to verify hyperlinks in the web.

Other Ways

1. Click Reports on Reporting toolbar, click Site Summary
2. Press ALT+V, R, M
3. In Voice Command mode, say "View, Reports, Site Summary"

More About

Verifying Hyperlinks

Be aware that if you choose to verify the status of all the hyperlinks in the current web, it could take a significant length of time. FrontPage not only will verify hyperlinks to Web pages in the current web, but also will search the World Wide Web to make sure the other hyperlink targets specified in your current web exist.

Steps **To Use the Reporting Toolbar to Verify Hyperlinks in the Web**

1 If necessary, point to Toolbars on the View menu and then click Reporting to display the Reporting toolbar. Click the Verifies hyperlinks in the current web button on the Reporting toolbar. If necessary, when the Verify Hyperlinks dialog box displays, click Verify all hyperlinks. Point to the Start button.

The Verify Hyperlinks dialog box displays and the report displayed changes to the Broken Hyperlinks report (Figure 3-101).

FIGURE 3-101

2 Click the Start button.

FrontPage verifies the hyperlinks and displays individual hyperlink results in the Broken Hyperlinks report (Figure 3-102). A count of broken internal and external hyperlinks is displayed on the status bar.

3 Click the Page icon on the Views bar. If you have any unsaved changes, click the Save button on the Standard toolbar.

FIGURE 3-102

Other Ways

1. Press ALT+V, T, click Reporting
2. In Voice Command mode, say "View, Toolbars, Reporting"

The Reporting toolbar also may be displayed in any of the other views as well as Reports view.

After completing these modifications to the web, you should publish your changes. Remember, changes made locally do not appear to visitors to the Web site until those changes have been published.

TO PUBLISH CHANGES TO AN EXISTING FRONTPAGE WEB

1 Click the Publish Web button on the Standard toolbar. Because this web was previously published, FrontPage does not display the Publish Destination dialog box, but assumes that you will publish to the same location.

2 Type your user name and password. Click the OK button.

3 Click the Done button.

You now can view the changes by entering http://www.hcc.edu/~npatrio/index.htm (use your own URL) in any browser and pressing the ENTER key. Be sure to test the hyperlinks to the Photos and Resume pages and from those pages to the Home page.

Quitting Microsoft FrontPage

When you have published Nikki's web, you can quit Microsoft FrontPage. Perform the following step to quit FrontPage.

TO QUIT MICROSOFT FRONTPAGE

1 If necessary, click the Done button. Click the Close button on the FrontPage title bar.

The FrontPage window closes and the Windows desktop displays.

CASE PERSPECTIVE SUMMARY

Nikki agreed that customizing her web site was surprisingly easy. Learning how easily she could make custom themes for use in other Web pages also was a pleasant surprise. She commented that the ability to incorporate and manipulate images would help her experiment with future theme customizations. She is anxious to see the hit counter accumulate as visitors view her site. Although her web is small, she was grateful for the reporting and task management features, knowing that they will help her stay organized with her work. She is certain that once the tasks entered in her web are complete, they will attract additional visitors, so she is ready to get started on the next phase of development.

Project Summary

Previously, you learned about essential Web page development. In Project 3, you learned how to customize your Web pages. You customized a theme, saved it for later reuse, and applied it to a single Web page. You learned about image file formats and customized images by creating a transparent image and resampling an image to change its file size. You created an image map and assigned a target URL to the hotspot. You copied text from a Word document and pasted it into a Web page. You inserted bookmarks in a Web page for easier navigation. You learned how to display the status of the hyperlinks used in the Web pages of the current FrontPage web. Finally, you learned how to use FrontPage reporting features and how to verify hyperlinks.

What You Should Know

Having completed this project, you now should be able to perform the following tasks:

▶ Add a Hit Counter *(FP 3.14)*

▶ Add a Hotspot to an Image *(FP 3.59)*

▶ Add a Hyperlink to an AutoShapes Object *(FP 3.57)*

▶ Add a Link Bar Component *(FP 3.23)*

▶ Add a New Page in Page View *(FP 3.22)*

▶ Add a Row to a Table *(FP 3.13)*

▶ Add a Shared Border *(FP 3.17)*

▶ Add an AutoShapes Object *(FP 3.52)*

▶ Assign Tasks for a Web *(FP 3.63)*

▶ Bookmark a Location in a Web Page *(FP 3.37)*

▶ Bookmark Text in a Web Page *(FP 3.38)*

▶ Copy and Paste from a Word Document *(FP 3.34)*

▶ Create a Hyperlink to a Bookmark *(FP 3.40)*

▶ Create a Transparent Image *(FP 3.47)*

▶ Create and Apply a Customized Theme *(FP 3.09)*

▶ Create Back Hyperlinks *(FP 3.43)*

▶ Display the Hyperlinks in a FrontPage Web *(FP 3.62)*

▶ Highlight Hotspots on an Image Map *(FP 3.61)*

▶ Insert an Image and Display the Pictures Toolbar *(FP 3.45)*

▶ Modify the Navigation Structure *(FP 3.24)*

▶ Open an Existing Page in FrontPage Web *(FP 3.07)*

▶ Publish Changes to an Existing FrontPage Web *(FP 3.69)*

▶ Quit Microsoft FrontPage *(FP 3.69)*

▶ Resize and Resample an Image *(FP 3.49)*

▶ Use a Custom Background Color for a Table *(FP 3.28)*

▶ Use Absolute Positioning with an Image *(FP 3.51)*

▶ Use the Reporting Toolbar to Verify Hyperlinks in the Web *(FP 3.68)*

▶ View the Site Summary Report *(FP 3.66)*

Learn It Online

Instructions: To complete the Learn It Online exercises, start your browser, click the Address bar, and then enter scsite.com/offxp/exs.htm. When the Office XP Learn It Online page displays, follow the instructions in the exercises below.

1 Project Reinforcement TF, MC, and SA

Below FrontPage Project 3, click the Project Reinforcement link. Print the quiz by clicking Print on the File menu. Answer each question. Write your first and last name at the top of each page, and then hand in the printout to your instructor.

2 Flash Cards

Below FrontPage Project 3, click the Flash Cards link. When Flash Cards displays, read the instructions. Type 20 (or a number specified by your instructor) in the Number of Playing Cards text box, type your name in the Name text box, and then click the Flip Card button. When the flash card displays, read the question and then click the Answer box arrow to select an answer. Flip through Flash Cards. Click Print on the File menu to print the last flash card if your score is 15 (75%) correct or greater and then hand it in to your instructor. If your score is less than 15 (75%) correct, then redo this exercise by clicking the Replay button.

3 Practice Test

Below FrontPage Project 3, click the Practice Test link. Answer each question, enter your first and last name at the bottom of the page, and then click the Grade Test button. When the graded practice test displays on your screen, click Print on the File menu to print a hard copy. Continue to take practice tests until you score 80% or better. Hand in a printout of the final practice test to your instructor.

4 Who Wants to Be a Computer Genius?

Below FrontPage Project 3, click the Computer Genius link. Read the instructions, enter your first and last name at the bottom of the page, and then click the Play button. Hand in your score to your instructor.

5 Wheel of Terms

Below FrontPage Project 3, click the Wheel of Terms link. Read the instructions, and then enter your first and last name and your school name. Click the Play button. Hand in your score to your instructor.

6 Crossword Puzzle Challenge

Below FrontPage Project 3, click the Crossword Puzzle Challenge link. Read the instructions, and then enter your first and last name. Click the Play button. Work the crossword puzzle. When you are finished, click the Submit button. When the crossword puzzle redisplays, click the Print button. Hand in the printout.

7 Tips and Tricks

Below FrontPage Project 3, click the Tips and Tricks link. Click a topic that pertains to Project 3. Right-click the information and then click Print on the shortcut menu. Construct a brief example of what the information relates to in FrontPage to confirm you understand how to use the tip or trick. Hand in the example and printed information.

online

8 Newsgroups

Below FrontPage Project 3, click the Newsgroups link. Click a topic that pertains to Project 3. Print three comments. Hand in the comments to your instructor.

9 Expanding Your Horizons

Below FrontPage Project 3, click the Articles for Microsoft FrontPage link. Click a topic that pertains to Project 3. Print the information. Construct a brief example of what the information relates to in FrontPage to confirm you understand the contents of the article. Hand in the example and printed information to your instructor.

10 Search Sleuth

Below FrontPage Project 3, click the Search Sleuth link. To search for a term that pertains to this project, select a term below the Project 3 title and then use the Google search engine at google.com (or any major search engine) to display and print two Web pages that present information on the term. Hand in the printouts to your instructor.

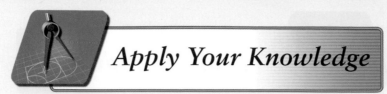

Microsoft **FrontPage 2002**

Apply Your Knowledge

1 Customizing a Web Page Using AutoShapes and Color

Instructions: Start FrontPage. Open the web, Starting, that you modified in Project 2. If you did not complete this exercise for Project 2, see your instructor for a copy of the required files.

1. If necessary, double-click the file, index.htm, in the Folder List pane to display The Starting Block home page in Page view.

2. On the Format menu, click Themes. When the Themes dialog box displays, click the Modify button. When the What would you like to modify? area displays, click the Colors button.

3. If necessary, when the Modify Theme dialog box displays, click the Color Schemes tab and, if necessary, scroll down and click the color scheme for Construction Zone. Verify that Vivid colors is selected. Click the OK button.

4. Verify that Vivid colors and Active graphics are selected in the Themes dialog box. If necessary, click Background picture so that it does not contain a check mark. Apply the theme to all pages in the web. Click Save As and save the new theme as In Motion Zone, or a name of your choice.

5. Click the AutoShapes button on the Drawing toolbar. Point to Stars and Banners, and then click 5-Point Star. Position the mouse pointer centered under the Links bar. Drag the mouse pointer to the opposite corner to create a small star shape. Release the mouse button. Click the Fill Color button arrow on the Drawing toolbar. Click Yellow on the color palette. Copy the shape and paste copies to the left and to the right of the original, positioned a little lower than the original star image.

6. Click the AutoShapes button on the Drawing toolbar, point to Stars and Banners, and then click Curved Down Ribbon. Position the mouse pointer under the star images. Drag the mouse pointer to the opposite corner to create a ribbon banner shape. Release the mouse button.

7. Right-click the ribbon shape. Click Add Text on the shortcut menu. Click the Font Size button arrow on the Formatting toolbar and then select 2 (10 pt). Type SGRA in the text box on the shape. Drag through the text and then click the Font Color button arrow on the Drawing toolbar. Click White on the color palette. Click the Fill Color button arrow on the Drawing toolbar and then click Navy.

8. Click the Text Box button on the Drawing toolbar. Position the mouse pointer under the ribbon image. Drag the mouse pointer to the opposite corner to create a text box and then release the mouse button. Using font 2 (10 pt), type For the fifth consecutive year, named as a 3-Star Blue Ribbon Dealer - the highest award of the Sporting Goods Retailers Association. in the text box. If necessary, drag the sizing handles so all of the text is visible. Drag through the text and then click the Font Color button arrow on the Drawing toolbar. Click Maroon on the color palette. Click the text box to select it. Click the Fill Color button arrow. Click No Fill.

9. In the upper left corner of the Web page, click the runner image to select it. If the Pictures toolbar does not display, point to Toolbars on the View menu and then click Pictures on the submenu. When the Pictures toolbar displays, click the Set Transparent Color button. Click the white area on the image to make it transparent.

10. Click the Preview tab to preview the Web page. When you have finished, click the Normal tab.

11. Print and save the Web page. When prompted to save the modified image, save it in the images folder, overwriting the previous version. Close FrontPage and hand in the printout to your instructor.

Apply Your Knowledge

FIGURE 3-103

In the Lab

1 Adding Link Bars and Creating Bookmarks in a Table Copied from Word

Problem: The owner of The Sweet Tooth wants to add a price list for various candy items. The list currently exists in a Word document. Because the list is rather long, you want to create hyperlinks that direct the visitor to the various sections of interest.

Instructions: Perform the following tasks.

1. Open the Sweet Tooth web that you modified in Project 2. If you did not complete that exercise for Project 2, see your instructor for a copy of the required files.
2. In Navigation view, add a new page under the Products page and then drag the new page icon to the left of the Prepackaged page icon. Right-click the New Page 1 icon and then click Rename on the shortcut menu. Type Price Sheet as the new page title. Double-click the Price Sheet icon to open the page in Page view. Rename the page as prices.htm in the Folder List pane.
3. Click the Center button on the Formatting toolbar. Insert a Link bar based on navigation structure. Use the page's theme as the Link bar style and select a horizontal orientation for the bar. In the Link Bar Properties dialog box, select Back and next for hyperlinks. Select Home page and Parent page as additional pages. Click the OK button. If necessary, press the right-arrow key to deselect the Link bar. Press the ENTER key.
4. Create a 2 × 4 table and, beginning with the leftmost top cell, enter the hyperlink text from the first column in Table 3-6 into all the cells across the first row, and then the first three columns of the second row. In the Table Properties dialog box, set the Alignment to Center, the border size to 0, and if necessary, click Specify width so that it does not contain a check mark. Drag the table borders to prevent the text from wrapping. Position the insertion point after the table. On the Insert menu, click Horizontal Line.
5. Using Microsoft Word, open the file, prices.doc, on the Data Disk. See the inside back cover of this book for instructions for downloading the Data Disk or see your instructor for information on accessing the files required in this book. Click in the table and then click Table on the menu bar. Point to Select and then click Table on the Select submenu. Press CTRL+C to copy the table. Switch back to FrontPage. Position the insertion point under the horizontal line and then press CTRL+V to paste the copied table.
6. Click the Page Banner at the top of the page and then click the Center button on the Formatting toolbar.
7. Position the insertion point to the left of the horizontal Link bar at the top of the page. Insert a bookmark. When the Bookmark dialog box displays, type Top in the Bookmark name text box. Click the OK button.
8. Select the section heading, FUDGES, in the pasted table and insert a bookmark using the default name for the bookmark name. Select the text, Fudges, in the leftmost top cell in the table above the horizontal line. Create a hyperlink to the FUDGES bookmark. Repeat this process for each of the remaining section headings and the corresponding text in each cell of the top table as listed in Table 3-6.
9. Beginning with the second section heading, SUGAR FREE ITEMS, position the insertion point to the right of the bookmarked section heading. Insert a space, type back to top and then insert spaces before this text to align it to the right side of the column. Select the text

Table 3-6 Hyperlink Text for Section Headings	
HYPERLINK TEXT	*SECTION HEADING*
Fudges	FUDGES
Sugar-Free	SUGAR FREE ITEMS
Bulk Wrapped	BULK WRAPPED CANDY
Bulk Unwrapped	BULK UNWRAPPED CANDY
Jelly Beans	JELLY BEANS
Product Gifts	PRODUCT GIFT ITEMS
Novelty Candy	NOVELTY CANDY ITEMS

In the Lab

just inserted and insert a hyperlink to the Top bookmark. Copy and paste this hyperlink after each subsequent section heading, inserting spaces as needed to align the hyperlink to the right of the column.

10. Save the changes to this page. Preview the changes in your browser. Print the Web page, and then close FrontPage. Write your name on the printout and hand it to your instructor.

FIGURE 3-104

In the Lab

2 Expanding an Existing Table

Problem: Earlier, you added a Web page about summer fun to your Personal web; however, that page had none of the items common on the other pages, such as navigation links or the date last updated. You decide to add these items to your summer fun Web page.

Instructions: Perform the following tasks.

1. Open the web, funsites, that you modified in Project 2. If you did not complete that exercise for Project 2, see your instructor for a copy of the required files.
2. Click the table used to position elements on the page. Add a new row at the top and a new column at the left of the table. Merge the three rightmost cells in the top row just added. Merge the cells in rows two through five in the left column just added.
3. Click the page banner at the top of the page and drag it into the merged cells in the top row of the table. Delete the blank line remaining above the table.
4. In the merged cells of the leftmost column, insert a vertical navigation bar with links to the Home page and children under Home. Adjust table cell widths as necessary (see Figure 3-105).
5. Add a shared border for all pages at the bottom of the page. Type This site was last updated in place of the comment component text and insert a Date and Time component for the date last updated. Edit the other pages in the web to remove similar information not in the shared border.
6. Save the changes to the Web pages. Print the Summer Fun Web page, write your name on the page and submit it to your instructor.

In the Lab

FIGURE 3-105

In the Lab

3 Creating an Image Map

Problem: Your one-page vacation web includes links to pages for several of the Hawaiian Islands. These links are only text, and visitors may not know the islands by name. You decide to add an image map so visitors can click on a map of the islands in addition to the text links.

Instructions: Using the vacation web you modified in Project 2, perform the following tasks. If you did not complete this exercise in Project 2, see your instructor for a copy of the required files.

1. Open the web and position the insertion point after the link that reads, The State of Hawaii. Press SHIFT+ENTER.
2. Insert an image of the Hawaiian Islands using the file, Hawaii map02.gif, from the Data Disk, or another image as directed by your instructor. See the inside back cover of this book for instructions for downloading the Data Disk or see your instructor for information on accessing the files required in this book.
3. Right-click the text hyperlink for Oahu near the bottom of the page. Click Hyperlink Properties on the shortcut menu. When the Edit Hyperlink dialog box displays, drag through the hyperlink in the Address text box to select it. Press CTRL+C to copy the hyperlink. Click the Cancel button.
4. Click the map image and draw a Polygonal Hotspot around the island Oahu and the text name next to the image. When the Insert Hyperlink dialog box displays, if necessary, click in the Address text box to position the insertion point. Press CTRL+V to paste the copied hyperlink. Click the OK button.
5. Repeat Step 3 and Step 4 for each of the island hyperlinks, Maui, Hawaii, Lanai, Molokai, and Kauai. Click the Highlight Hotspots button on the Pictures toolbar to see the hotspot outlines. Click the Highlight Hotspots button again to remove the highlighting.
6. If necessary, click the map image to select it. Set the background color as the transparent color for the image.
7. Add a shared border at the bottom of the page and apply it to all pages. Remove the comment component from the shared border. Move the name and e-mail information at the bottom of the page into the shared border.
8. Save the Web page and then verify all hyperlinks in the web.
9. Preview the pages in your browser and then print the Web pages, write your name on the pages, and give them to your instructor.
10. Close your browser and quit FrontPage.

In the Lab

FIGURE 3-106

Cases and Places

The difficulty of these case studies varies:
▶ are the least difficult; ▶▶ are more difficult; and ▶▶▶ are the most difficult.

1 ▶ You want to make it easy for visitors to navigate to the different sections of the resume Web page that you created in Project 2. Create bookmarks for each section heading. Add a column to the left side of the table that contains the resume and then place hyperlinks in that column to each of the various bookmarked sections.

2 ▶ Open the web that you created for your course in Classical Literature, and that you modified in Project 2. Add a shared bottom border for all pages and place in it your name, your e-mail address, and a date component for when the web was updated.

3 ▶▶ Add a new page to the Personal web that you created for your grandparents' 50th wedding anniversary. On the new page, draw a family tree using AutoShapes, such as a rectangle, for each family member, beginning with grandparents. Use lines to connect each rectangle and use text and fill colors appropriately. Add a hyperlink from the rectangle for the grandparents to the home page and make links for any other family members that have their own Web sites.

4 ▶▶ Modify the theme for the intramural basketball Web page that you updated in Project 2. Search the Web for replacement graphics and modify the theme, replacing buttons, background picture, and bullets as needed. Add a marquee web component to display announcements about upcoming games.

5 ▶▶▶ Go to your department at your school and offer to develop a Web page. Include a page listing all courses in the department and include course descriptions for each course. Add bookmarks for each course and at the top of the page, create links to each of the bookmarks. Add a horizontal or vertical Link bar to each page, as appropriate. Check with the department for other enhancements, such as personal pages for each professor or pages for different plans of study. The department should be able to supply you with any needed faculty photos and appropriate graphics.

Microsoft FrontPage 2002

Creating and Using Interactive Forms on the Web

You will have mastered the material in this project when you can:

OBJECTIVES

- Describe forms and types of form fields
- Describe available form handlers
- Describe the methods and format used to send form data
- Manage files in Folders view
- Modify a page title in Folders view
- Copy and paste a page banner and a Link bar
- Hide the Folder List pane
- Insert a form in a Web page and a table
- Insert a table in a form
- Insert a text box in a form
- Insert a check box in a form
- Assign text as a label for a check box
- Insert a Line Drawing AutoShape in a table
- Create a nested table
- Insert a drop-down list box in a form
- Insert a group box in a form
- Insert an option button in a form
- Assign text as a label for an option button
- Insert a text area in a form
- Modify form button properties
- Choose a form handler
- Modify HTML code directly in FrontPage

Online Link to the Past

Reconnect with Old Friends

Flipping through the pages of your high school yearbook brings to mind old friends, favorite teachers, a sweetheart or two, and memories of treasured experiences. Do you wonder what happened to your senior class president, the homecoming queen, or class clown? When summer rolls around, and you hear about reunions, are you curious to know if your class is planning one?

Now you may be able to find former school chums and information about class reunions with the help of Classmates, an Internet service reuniting classmates, military friends, and teachers. The Web site is the brainchild of Randy Conrads, who devised the concept while perusing the list of America Online and Prodigy subscribers in search of former classmates. He found the name of a friend he had not seen in many years, and the two subsequently met. Then, in Conrads's words, he became "the first spammer" in 1995 by contacting every AOL and Prodigy subscriber and asking for participants in his alumni matching project.

The response was overwhelming, and Conrads found himself trying to manage the thousands of people expressing an interest. As a nonprogrammer setting up a computer business on a UNIX server, his early efforts in database design and report generation soon became inadequate and outdated. Conrads's son convinced him to buy an IBM-compatible computer and use FrontPage to design the effective Classmates.com web site.

http://www.classmates.com

Today, Classmates serves more than 19 million members, adding 80,000 to 100,000 members each day. Basic registration is free and allows members a way to contact registrants and a way for registrants to search the database for familiar names from a specific high school in a particular graduating class. Gold members pay a small fee to participate in activities such as acquiring reunion information, sharing photographs with friends, and other services.

When registering, users enter data in interactive forms like the form you will create in Project 4. The Classmates.com Web page forms include text boxes, check boxes, and command buttons that capture name, high school, year of graduation, and personal biography. The form you will create in Project 4 also contains form fields that provide a means for interested users to supply information for classified ads and items for sale. Interactive forms are relatively easy to create and make it simple to collect the desired information and to direct the data appropriately for response or other uses.

Conrads is very concerned about attempts to exploit members and to invade their privacy. He does not allow advertisers to sell products to members, nor does he allow the members to distribute the data for any commercial purpose, except for planning a class reunion.

While a traditional class reunion involves face-to-face contact, Classmates.com provides online class reunions for alumni scattered throughout the world. For example, one such reunion for a Miami high school included participants dialing in from a New Jersey hotel, a military base in Australia, and Singapore.

The site includes message boards that allow former schoolmates to reminisce about high school experiences, friends, teachers, and hangouts and view photos and celebrity yearbooks. These features are popular for graduates who have moved to different parts of the country or world.

Conrads calls business on the Web, "a tremendous opportunity field," even for computer users with little Web page authoring experience. He adds, "FrontPage allows people like me to put a site together."

Classmates consistently is ranked among the top 50 more highly trafficked Web properties on the Internet according to Nielsen/Net Ratings. Everyday, Conrads receives hundreds of e-mail messages and letters from satisfied members. Friends and classmates are rediscovering their past using this successful online service.

Microsoft FrontPage 2002

Creating and Using Interactive Forms on the Web

PROJECT
4

CASE PERSPECTIVE

Nikki Patrio's Web site offers visitors several interesting Web pages, including a photo gallery and her resume. She now is ready to begin some of the planned enhancements to her site; specifically, she wants to add a page that allows visitors to place free classified advertisements. Nikki is unclear about how she is to implement this task and the impact on future tasks of organizing and displaying the results. She wants to collect the information in a format more structured than an e-mail message, and she does not want to receive large amounts of data via e-mail and then have to sort and post it manually. Using a form would provide consistency and completeness in data collection. She has seen other Web sites that accept information by having visitors complete a form and she would like to do the same. She also wants to know how she can increase awareness of this service to potential users.

You assure Nikki that by using features of FrontPage, the information visitors enter into a form can be added automatically to a database. Later, she can use the database to sort, select, and post the advertisements. Finally, you suggest some ideas for promoting her free classified ads service by using the Web site itself.

Introduction

You have created Web pages that go in one direction: from you to your reader. Most of the flow of information over the Web uses this technique. A Web server sends the majority of Web pages to your computer for viewing without any way for you to send information or data back to the Web server.

Methods do exist, however, for providing feedback and interaction with Web pages. Special HTML objects, called forms, provide two-way communication between you and a Web server. Using forms, you can order products, do banking, engage in live conversations, leave comments or suggestions, and use Web search engines. Forms make a Web page interactive. Users can respond to a Web site by filling in forms and submitting them.

Project Four — Creating and Using an Interactive Form

In this project, you will learn how to use forms and form fields by creating the Classified Ads Request page shown in Figure 4-1b. The Classified Ads Request page will be used to collect information from individuals wanting to post advertisements. When the visitor clicks the Send button in the form, that information is sent to a database, as illustrated by the receipt of a Confirmation page in Figure 4-1c. A hyperlink to the Classified Ads Request page from the Home page also will be added (Figure 4-1a). Before you begin creating the Classified Ads Request page, you should familiarize yourself with some important concepts and definitions about forms.

(a) Home Page

(b) Classified Ads Request Page

(c) Confirmation Page

FIGURE 4-1

HTML Forms

Two components are required to send data using forms: (1) a Web page containing the form and (2) a form handler. A **form** is a collection of input fields in a Web page that enables a user to enter data and send it to be processed on the Web server by a form handler. The **form fields** can be text boxes, check boxes, option buttons, drop-down list boxes, or buttons. Table 4-1 lists commonly used form fields and briefly describes each field type.

A typical form, such as the one created in this project, is composed of one or more form fields, along with a Submit button and a Reset button. The **Submit button** sends the completed form to the Web server for processing. The **Reset button** clears the fields and sets them back to their original default condition. The user simply fills in the form and then clicks the Submit button to send the data to be processed.

Because you can have more than one form in a Web page, you could have more than one Submit button in a Web page. You must use caution when using multiple forms in a Web page. When you click the Submit button for one of the forms, only the form fields in that form are sent to the Web server. Form fields that are not part of that form are ignored. You would have to click every Submit button in every form to send each separate collection of data entered in each form back to the Web server.

Table 4-1 Common FrontPage Form Fields	
FORM FIELD	**DESCRIPTION**
Option button	A form field used in groups of two or more to present a set of one or more mutually exclusive options, one of which typically is set by default. Selecting a new option button in the form deselects the currently selected option button. For multiple sets on a single form, all sets except one must be in a group box.
Checkbox	A form field you can select by clicking a box. Unlike option buttons, check boxes are not mutually exclusive, so you can choose none, one, or more.
Textbox	A form field that allows you to enter alphanumeric text. You can type a maximum of 500 characters. If you type nothing in the text box, only the text box name is sent to the server.
Group box	A form field that provides a border to surround a group of related fields. The border may include a title.
Drop-down box	A form field that presents a list of selections in a drop-down list box style. You can use it to present a wide variety of choices — more than option buttons can handle effectively. You can configure a drop-down box to allow single or multiple selections.
Text area	A form field in which users can type multiple lines of free-form text. You can set the properties of the scrolling text box to consist of 999 columns and 999 rows.
Push Button	A form field that typically invokes an action. Each form has two default buttons: a Submit button, which sends a form to the Web server, and a Reset button, which sets each form field back to its default setting. Additional buttons can be used to submit or reset the form or invoke scripts. An advanced button also can display HTML content on its face.

Some applications might require several forms in a Web page. This allows you to have the same Web page return one of several potential sets of data and process the data differently depending on which Submit button the user clicks. Whenever a user clicks the Submit button, the server processes the data in the form using a form handler.

Form Handlers

A form handler provides a means of collecting information entered on a form. A **form handler** is a program that resides on the server and is executed when a user submits a form using the Submit button. A form handler normally is not visible to a user viewing a Web page.

Form handler programs are highly dependent on the computer operating system and Web server software. Because of this, writing form handler programs can be a complex process and requires advanced programming skills.

You can use one of several available techniques when deciding how to handle the form data. Several standard techniques are available on the Web. In addition, FrontPage has several form handlers included in the **FrontPage Server Extensions**, a set of programs and scripts that support authoring in FrontPage and extend the functionality of a Web server. Table 4-2 describes the standard Web techniques as well as the Server Extensions available with FrontPage. The most popular way of handling forms is the **Common Gateway Interface**, or **CGI**. In addition to the standard techniques, you can have the data e-mailed to an e-mail address or placed into a file or database.

More About

CGI Scripts

You do not need a form to use a CGI script. You can use a hyperlink that points to a CGI script to generate dynamic Web pages based on real-time data.

Table 4-2 Standard and FrontPage Form Handlers

FORM HANDLER	DESCRIPTION
CGI	Common Gateway Interface - A standard method of extending Web server functionality by executing programs or scripts on a Web server in response to Web browser requests.
ISAPI	Internet Server Application Program Interface - A Web server application development interface developed by Process Software and Microsoft Corporation that can be used in place of CGI.
NSAPI	Netscape Server Application Program Interface - A Web server application development interface developed by Netscape Communications Corporation.
ASP	Active Server Page - A method of creating programs that execute on a Web server, first available on the Microsoft Internet Information Server 3.0.
Discussion Form Handler	A FrontPage form handler that allows users to participate in an online discussion. The Discussion Form Handler collects information from a form, formats it into an HTML page, and adds the page to a table of contents and text index.
Registration Form Handler	A FrontPage form handler that allows users to register themselves automatically for access to a service implemented as a World Wide Web site. The Registration Form Handler adds the user to the service's authentication database, then gathers optional information from the form and stores it in one of many supported formats.
Save Results Form Handler	A FrontPage form handler that gathers information from a form and stores it in one of a selection of formats or sends the information to an e-mail address.

More About

CGI Script Languages

On UNIX systems, most CGI scripts are written in C or Perl. On Windows systems, most CGI scripts are written in Visual Basic or Visual C++. To locate free CGI scripts, visit the FrontPage 2002 More About Web page (scsite.com/fp2002/more.htm) and then click CGI Scripts.

CGI Scripts

CGI is a universal way to execute programs on the Web. CGI programs can be written in one of several available programming languages such as Perl, Java, or Visual Basic. These programs frequently are called **CGI scripts**.

CGI scripts begin executing after the user supplies data by filling in form fields and then clicking the Submit button. The browser sends the data fields from the form to the Web server. The name of the CGI script is stored in the form. The CGI script processes the data and sends back a confirmation Web page.

The CGI script can perform many different functions with the data, including retrieving or updating data from a database, storing data in a series of data files, or executing other programs. When finished, the CGI script usually returns information to the browser in the form of a new HTML document indicating the status of the form processing.

You can choose a form handler that will append the data to a data file, send the data to an e-mail address, or immediately process the data with a user-supplied CGI program. If you use the FrontPage handlers rather than a custom form handler, such as a CGI script, a server that has the FrontPage Server Extensions installed is required. Regardless of the technique you choose to process the data, two basic formats, or methods, are used to send data for processing: Get and Post.

Get and Post Methods

The creator of the Web page form assigns names to the form fields (for example, Full Name or City). When the user enters values or selects form fields, and then clicks the Submit button, the data is sent in plain ASCII text in a name=value format, with the name of the field first, followed by an equal sign, and then followed by the data the user entered in the field. Values that have embedded spaces have those spaces replaced with plus (+) signs, to indicate that this text is concatenated together to form a single value. Names cannot have spaces in them, so when assigning a name to a field, uppercase and lowercase letters, along with underscores, are used to make the names more readable. Figure 4-2 shows the format of the collection of name=value pairs from a sample form. Each name=value pair is separated by an ampersand (&).

```
FullName=Ima+Student&Address=45+Elm+Street&City=Washington&State=DC&PostalCode=20010
&FTStudent=YES&Contact=Ima&Phone=&EmailAddress=mymail@home.net&Category=Buy&Payment
=Cash&Description=Good+used+DVD+player+wanted&SendButton=Send
```

FIGURE 4-2

The way in which the form handler reads the information depends on which one of the two methods is used to send the form. The **Get method** stores the name=value pairs in an environment variable called QUERY_STRING. The form handler program must contain instructions to access the QUERY_STRING environment variable in order to read the name=value pairs.

The **Post method** reads the name=value pairs as input directly to the form handler from a standard input stream. A **stream** is similar to a data file. Most programs have a standard input and a standard output stream automatically defined when they are compiled.

Post is the preferred method, as most programs can be written to read from the standard input stream with little effort and remain portable across different computer platforms. Reading environment variables can require sets of instructions that are unique to each computer platform, requiring more programming effort to migrate the programs from one computer system to another.

Regardless of the method you choose to handle the form, the steps to use the form remain the same: you fill in the form by typing data in the text boxes, clicking option buttons and check boxes, and selecting items from lists. You then send the data in the form by clicking the Submit button. A default Web page normally is returned, confirming the reception of the data by the form handler. You can supply a customized Web page containing the confirmation information.

Get and Post

Other related information about forms data, such as the length of the data string and the Internet address of the computer sending the data, are available in environment variables. To understand more about Get and Post methods, visit the FrontPage 2002 More About Web page (scsite.com/ fp2002/more.htm) and then click Get and Post.

Designing a Form

In this project, you will design and create a form in a Web page to obtain useful information from potential advertisers, such as their name and address, their status with the school, and information about the classified advertisement they want to place. Figure 4-3 illustrates the design for the Classified Ads Request Web page. The form data will be sent to an Access database on the server by a FrontPage form handler, so a server with the FrontPage Server Extensions installed is required for this project.

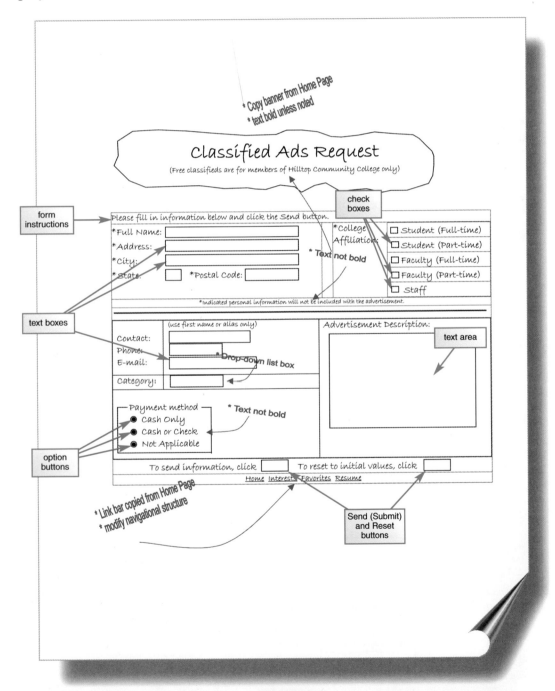

FIGURE 4-3

The form shown in Figure 4-3 on the previous page consists of two logical sections. The purpose of each section is to obtain a certain type of information. The number and purpose of the sections in your form design will depend on the types of information you are requesting and any design concerns and issues for the Web page.

When designing a form for a Web page, typically you will lay out the input fields in the order you would read a book — from left to right and top to bottom. You can use tables to organize and control the spacing of the form fields in the Web page.

Adding Web Pages

Before beginning any work on a form, you first must add a new page to the Nikki Patrio FrontPage web. Additionally, you will need to add a hyperlink from an existing page to the new page. Often, the hyperlink is from the Home page, as it is in this project.

To add a new Web page, you will need to start FrontPage and then open the original FrontPage web. Perform the following steps to start FrontPage and open Nikki's FrontPage web created in Project 3. If you did not complete Project 3, see your instructor for a copy.

TO START FRONTPAGE AND OPEN AN EXISTING WEB

1 Click the Start button on the taskbar. Point to Programs on the Start menu.

2 Click Microsoft FrontPage on the Programs submenu.

3 Click the Open button arrow on the Standard toolbar.

4 Click Open Web on the Open menu. When the Open Web dialog box displays, if necessary, click the Look in box arrow and select the folder location where you stored the web for Project 3 (e.g., C:\npatrio).

5 Click the Open button. If necessary, display the Folder List and then double-click index.htm in the Folder List pane. Point to the Folders icon on the Views bar.

The previously created FrontPage web is loaded, and the file, index.htm, displays in Page view (Figure 4-4).

More About

The FrontPage Help System

Need Help? It is no further than the Ask a Question box in the upper-right corner of the window. Click the box that contains the text, Type a question for help (Figure 4-4), type help, and then press the ENTER key. FrontPage will respond with a list of items you can click to learn about obtaining help on any FrontPage-related topic. To find out what is new in FrontPage 2002, type what's new in FrontPage in the Ask a Question box.

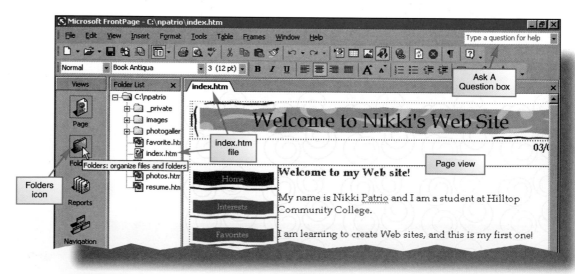

FIGURE 4-4

Managing Files in Folders View

FrontPage has several ways you can manage the files in your FrontPage web. The Folder List pane displays the files included in the current web. Operations on these files, such as renaming or deleting files, can be performed in the Folder List pane, as previously demonstrated. Another view, Folders view, allows for similar file management and displays additional information about files in the current web, such as file size, title, when the file was last modified, and who last modified it.

Use the following step to display the FrontPage web in Folders view.

 To Display Files in Folders View

 Click the Folders icon on the Views bar.

The pages in the FrontPage web display in Folders view (Figure 4-5).

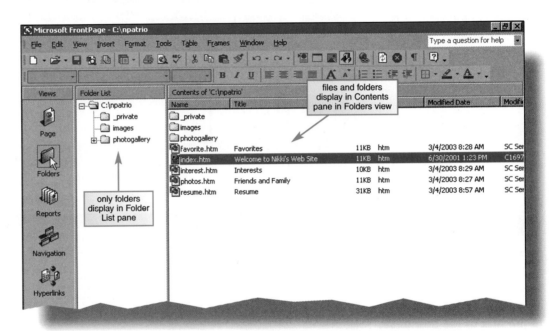

FIGURE 4-5

Notice that the individual files in the web display in detail in the Contents pane in Folders view; therefore, the Folder List pane does not show the individual files, only folders. The Folder List pane is a subset of the more expanded Folders view.

Other **Ways**

1. On View menu click Folders
2. Press ALT+V, F
3. In Voice Command mode, say "View, Folders"

Adding and Renaming a Web Page in Folders View

While viewing the web in Folders view, you can add a new page to a FrontPage web. Adding a page in this view causes the page to be saved and added to the list of files in the web as soon as you rename the new page or change views. When you add a new page in Folders view, FrontPage supplies a default name and title for the page and allows you to change the name of the new page immediately. You also can change the name later. The New Page button is accessible in all views allowing you to add a new page at anytime. Adding a new page in any view other than Navigation or Folders view automatically changes the view to Page view. For a new page created in another view to display in Folders view, you must save it before switching to Folders view.

Use the steps on the next page to add and rename a new Web page in Folders view.

Steps | To Add and Rename a Web Page in Folders View

1 **Click the Create a new normal page button on the Standard toolbar in Folders view.**

A new file is added to the Web and displays in the file list in the Contents pane. The name of the new file is highlighted (Figure 4-6).

FIGURE 4-6

2 **Type** classified .asp **as the new file name and then press the ENTER key. Click the Yes button in the Microsoft FrontPage dialog box. Point to the title of the new page.**

The file name and the title both change to classified.asp (Figure 4-7). This page later will have code added by FrontPage that requires the .asp extension.

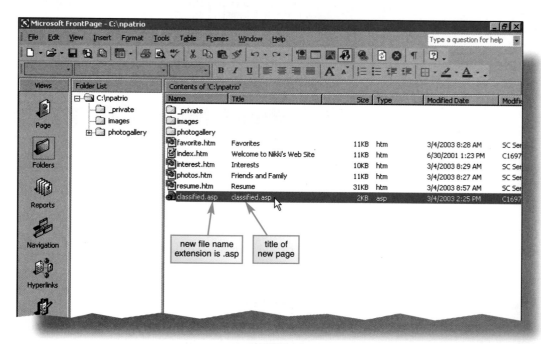

FIGURE 4-7

Other Ways

1. Click file name in Contents pane to select it, click file name, type new file name
2. Right-click file name in Contents pane, click Rename on shortcut menu, type new file name

Adding a new page in this manner causes FrontPage to use the supplied file name as the default title for the new Web page. You likely will want to change the title, as the title displays on the title bar of the Web browser when the page is viewed.

To modify the title of a Web page in Folders view, perform the following steps.

Steps To Modify a Page Title in Folders View

1 **Click the title of the page, classified.asp, to select it.**

The page title, classified.asp, is highlighted and an edit text box displays around the page title (Figure 4-8).

FIGURE 4-8

2 **Type** Classified Ads Request **as the new page title. Press the ENTER key.**

The Contents pane displays the new title for the page (Figure 4-9).

FIGURE 4-9

If you did not rename the file when it was created, you can change the file name using the same steps as changing the title. After selecting the line containing the file you want to rename, simply click the file name to select it, type a new name, and then press the ENTER key. When renaming a file, FrontPage determines if other pages reference the current file name and, if they do, FrontPage prompts for permission to update any such links accordingly.

Other Ways

1. Right-click title, click Properties on shortcut menu, click General tab
2. In Voice Command mode, say "File, Properties"

Editing a New Web Page

When creating a new Web page, you likely will want some similarity between the new page and existing pages in the FrontPage web. Using a theme allows certain aspects, such as the color scheme, to be carried over to new pages. You also may want to have similar page banners and hyperlinks on each page. FrontPage provides Navigation bars that automatically provide continuity in hyperlinks, as was done in Project 1. Even without using Navigation bars, you can copy elements, such as hyperlinks and page banners, from one Web page to another. To maintain continuity among pages, you can copy the page banner from Nikki's Home page using Windows copy and paste features; however, for the banner to display, the page must be added to the web navigation structure.

Copying and Pasting Objects from Another Web Page

In FrontPage, the procedure to copy objects from one Web page to another is very similar to that used earlier to copy text from a Word document to a Web page. First, open the source Web page, select the object to be copied, place it on the Clipboard, open the target Web page, and then paste the copied object into the target Web page.

The following steps summarize how to add the Classified Ads Request Web page to the navigation structure of the web, and then copy the Home page banner, paste it into the Classified Ads Request Web page, and modify the page banner text.

TO COPY AND PASTE A PAGE BANNER

1 Click the Navigation icon on the Views bar. Drag and drop the file, classified.asp, below the Resume page icon.

2 Double-click the Home page icon to display the Home page in Page view.

3 When the Home page displays, click the page banner to select it. Press CTRL+C to copy the page banner.

4 Double-click the file classified.asp in the Folder List. Click the Center button on the Formatting toolbar. Press CTRL+V to paste the copied page banner.

5 Hold down the SHIFT key and then press the ENTER key.

6 Select a font size of 2 (10 pt). Type (Free classifieds are for members of Hilltop Community College only) as text centered below the page banner. Press the ENTER key.

Figure 4-10 shows the page, classified.asp, with the pasted page banner and new text.

FIGURE 4-10

This project uses tables to control spacing of objects in the Web page. In this case, one table contains the form and a Link bar with hyperlinks to other pages, while additional tables are used within the form to position form fields and text. Although no name is associated with a given table in FrontPage, it can be helpful for discussion to reference them by the order in which they are created. The banner and text inserted earlier are not in a table, so the next table to add is the first table for this page, or table-T1. The following steps summarize how to add a table, table-T1, to the Classified Ads Request page.

TO ADD A TABLE TO A WEB PAGE

1 If necessary, position the insertion point below the text below the page banner. Click the Insert Table button on the Standard toolbar and then drag to select two rows and one column (2 by 1 Table). Click the mouse button.

2 Right-click the table and then click Table Properties on the shortcut menu. When the Table Properties dialog box displays, type 0 in the Size box in the Borders area and then click the OK button.

Figure 4-11 shows the FrontPage window after the insert table operation is completed. The table displays on the Web page with two rows and one column.

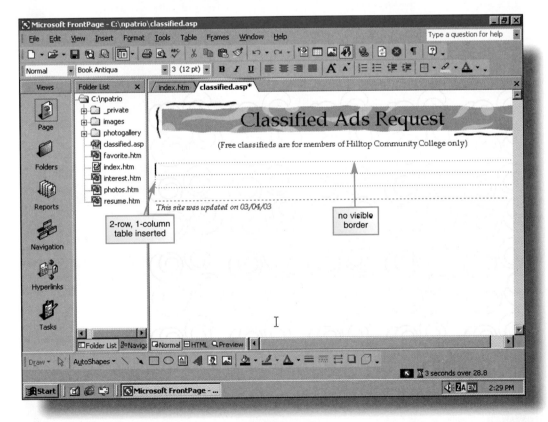

FIGURE 4-11

The table just inserted, table-T1, will contain the interactive form in the top row and the Link bar hyperlinks to other pages in this web in the bottom row. Copying and pasting the Link bar from the Home page to the Classified Ads Request page is done in a similar manner as copying and pasting the page banner.

Perform the steps on the next page to copy and paste the Link bar from the Home page to the Classified Ads Request page.

Steps To Copy and Paste a Link Bar from a Web Page

1 **Click the tab index.htm at the top of the Page pane. If necessary, scroll down and then select the Link bar at the bottom of the page.**

The Home page displays and the Link bar is selected (Figure 4-12).

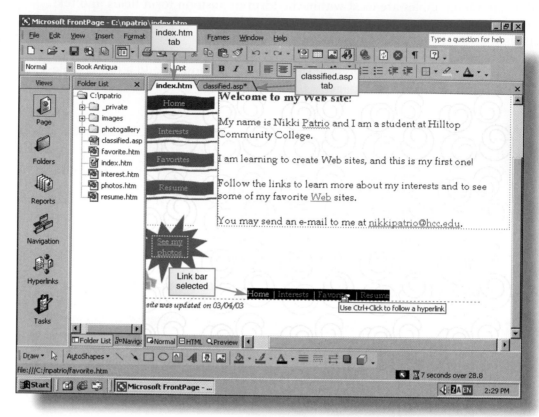

FIGURE 4-12

2 **Press CTRL+C to copy the selected component. Click the classified.asp tab to display the Classified Ads Request page. Click in the bottom row of table-T1 to position the insertion point.**

The Link bar component is copied and the insertion point is positioned in the bottom row of table-T1 on the Classified Ads Request page (Figure 4-13).

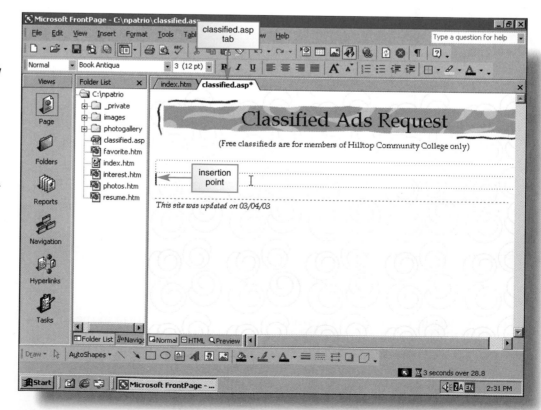

FIGURE 4-13

3 Press CTRL+V to paste the copied Link bar. If necessary, click the Center button on the Formatting toolbar.

The copied Link bar with the Home link displays centered on the page (Figure 4-14).

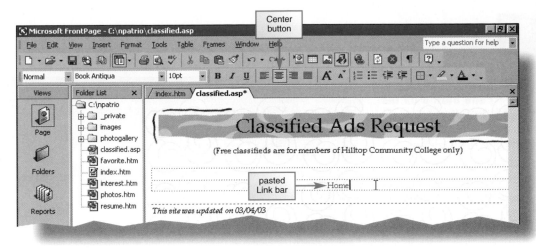

FIGURE 4-14

4 If necessary, press the BACKSPACE key to remove any extra line. Double-click the Link bar. When the Link Bar Properties dialog box displays, click Parent level in the Hyperlinks to add to page area. Verify that Home page is selected in the Additional pages area. Click the OK button. Deselect the Link bar component. Point to the Toggle Pane button on the Standard toolbar.

The Classified Ads Request page displays the Link bar with the required hyperlinks (Figure 4-15).

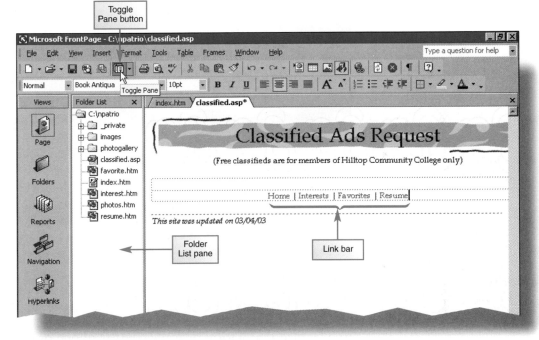

FIGURE 4-15

A copy of the Link bar from the Home page is pasted into the Classified Ads Request page. The Link bar component displays hyperlinks based on the position of the page in the Web navigation structure and the selection of hyperlinks to relative pages. Because the Home page Link bar was set to display hyperlinks to the Home page and Child level pages (Interests, Favorites, Resume), the Link bar retained those properties when pasted into the Classified Ads Request page. However, no Child level pages exist for the Classified Ads Request page. The Child level pages for the Home page are at the Parent level for the Classified Ads Request page. Consequently, you modified the Link bar properties accordingly so the links display to the same pages as the links on the Home page.

Recall that the Toggle Pane button can be used to display or hide the Folder List pane. Hiding the Folder List pane provides additional space for editing the page. When the form fields and text are added later, having a larger area for editing the page will make positioning such elements easier. Perform the step on the next page to hide the Folder List pane.

To Hide the Folder List Pane

1 **Click the Toggle Pane button on the Standard toolbar.**

FrontPage displays the current page in Page view with the Folder List pane hidden (Figure 4-16). This button is a **toggle**, *so repeating the same steps will redisplay the Folder List pane.*

FIGURE 4-16

Other Ways

1. Click Toggle Pane button arrow on Standard toolbar, click Folder List
2. On View menu click Folder List
3. Press ALT+V, E
4. In Voice Command mode, say "View, Folder List"

With the page banner, table-T1, and the Link bar added, this page now is ready to have the form and form fields added to it, which will provide the mechanism for feedback from the user.

Inserting a Form in a Web Page

You learned that a form typically consists of one or more form fields along with Submit and Reset buttons. FrontPage automatically creates the Submit and Reset buttons when you insert a form in the Web page. You also can create a new form by inserting any of the form fields outside of an existing form. Within any one form in a Web page, you may have many form fields, but you will have only one Submit button and only one Reset button.

Inserting a Form in a Table

Although FrontPage will automatically create a form when you insert the first form field in the Web page, you also can insert a form before inserting any form fields. In both cases, FrontPage inserts a form HTML tag in the Web page, along with the HTML tags describing the form field you inserted, if any. Additional form fields subsequently can be added to the existing form. A form can be added to a Web page without using a table. Using a table, however, allows you to control the positioning of text, relative to a form, whether the text is external to the form or within the form. Perform the following steps to insert a form in table-T1 on the Classified Ads Request page.

To Insert a Form in a Table

1 **Position the insertion point in the first row of table-T1 in the form.**

The insertion point displays in the first row of the table on the Classified Ads Request page (Figure 4-17).

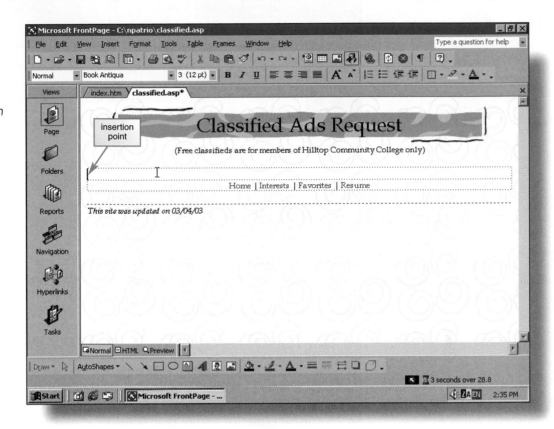

FIGURE 4-17

2 **Click Insert on the menu bar and then point to Form. Point to Form on the Form submenu.**

The Form submenu displays the form fields that you can add to a page (Figure 4-18).

FIGURE 4-18

3 **Click Form on the Form submenu.**

A form is inserted in the first row of table-T1 (Figure 4-19). FrontPage adds the Submit and Reset buttons automatically.

FIGURE 4-19

Other **Ways**

1. Press ALT+I, R, F
2. In Voice Command mode, say "Insert, Form", click Form

Inserting a Table in a Form

The use of a table to contain the form allows better positioning of the form with respect to text outside the form. Within the form, a table also is useful to position text and form fields. A table allows a physical grouping of related fields and text, although it does not affect the function of the form in the collection of data. In each cell of this second table, table-T2, you will place several form fields and in one case, an additional table. To ensure that table-T2 is part of the form, you must insert the form in the Web page before inserting the table.

If you insert the table first, followed by the form, the form location is inside one of the table cells, as was done with table-T1. Inserting form fields in another table cell (table-T1) would insert another form, complete with its own Submit and Reset buttons. In this form, you want the user to be able to send all the information he or she enters by clicking only one Submit button. Remember that each Submit button controls only those fields within the same form. The following steps summarize how to insert a table, table-T2, in the form just created.

TO INSERT A TABLE IN A FORM

1 If necessary, position the insertion point before the Submit button in the form.

2 Click the Insert Table button on the Standard toolbar and then drag to select five rows and four columns (5 by 4 table). Release the mouse button.

3 Right-click the table and then click Table Properties on the shortcut menu. When the Table Properties dialog box displays, type 99 in the Specify width text box in the Layout area. Verify In percent is selected. Type 0 in the Size text box in the Borders area and then click the OK button.

4 Select all columns of the top row, right-click, and then click Merge Cells on the shortcut menu. Follow the same steps to merge the columns of each of the bottom three rows into single columns. Adjust column widths in the second row as shown in Figure 4-20.

5 Position the insertion point in the row below the Submit button and then press the BACKSPACE key to delete the extra line. Click the Save button on the Standard toolbar to save the changes.

Figure 4-20 shows the form with the table, table-T2, added and with the indicated adjustments made.

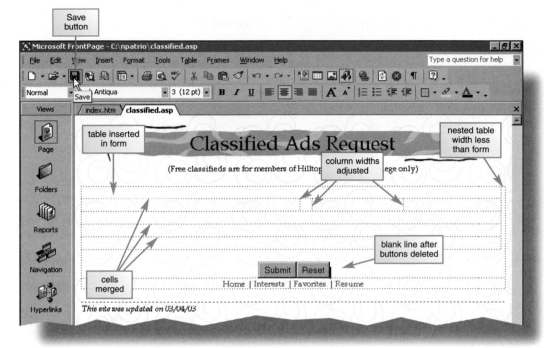

FIGURE 4-20

Inserting Text in a Form

Forms often include text for descriptive reasons, such as giving a user instructions on the actions they should take. Inserting text in a form is as simple as positioning the insertion point and then typing. Using tables, as in this project, is helpful for controlling the position of the text. The following steps summarize how to insert descriptive text in the form just created.

TO INSERT TEXT IN A FORM

1 Position the insertion point in row 1 of table-T2. Click the Underline button and then the Bold button on the Formatting toolbar. Type To place an ad, please fill in information below and click the Send button in the first row.

2 Position the insertion point in row 2 and column 3 of table-T2. Click the Bold button. Type *College Affiliation: and then drag the right cell border to the left, if necessary, to wrap the text onto two lines. Right-click the cell and then click Cell Properties on the shortcut menu. In the Cell Properties dialog box, set the Horizontal alignment to Left and the Vertical alignment to Top for the cell. Click the OK button.

3 Position the insertion point in row 3 of table-T2. Click the Bold button. Select a font size of 1 (8 pt) in the Font Size list. Type *Indicated personal information will not be included with the advertisement in row 3. Select the word, not, in the sentence just entered and then click the Underline button. Click the Center button on the Formatting toolbar to center the text.

4 Position the insertion point before the Submit button. Click the Bold button. Type To send information, click and then press the SPACEBAR to include a space between the last word and the button.

5 Position the insertion point between the Submit button and the Reset button. Press the SPACEBAR four times to insert four spaces. Click the Bold button. Type To reset to initial values, click and then press the SPACEBAR to include a space between the last word and the Reset button. If necessary, click the Center button on the Standard toolbar to center the line.

Figure 4-21 shows the form with the added text and with the last line centered.

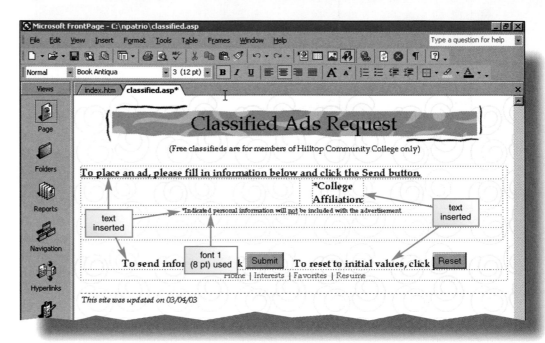

FIGURE 4-21

Inserting Form Fields in a Form

Although a form is created with Submit and Reset buttons, the buttons have little value until the form includes form fields to collect data from the user. This is done by means of form fields. Form fields allow the user to enter text, initiate actions by clicking buttons, and make choices by means of drop-down list boxes, option buttons, and check boxes.

The two steps used to insert a form field in a Web page are (1) adding the form field and any accompanying descriptive text, and (2) modifying the properties of the form field. When adding form fields, be sure to place all form fields for the same form within the dashed lines that indicate the boundaries of the form. Inserting a form field outside of the form causes the insertion of a new form with its own Submit and Reset buttons.

You will notice that as you insert form fields, they typically contain no text label. Inserting a form field inserts only the form field object, such as an option button or text box. You must add the specific label for the form field. As you do, you can assign the text as the label for a particular field, so when the user clicks the label text, the form field is selected. This makes it easier for users to select small items such as option buttons and check boxes.

Form Fields

Inserting a field outside a form causes a new form to be created by default, with its own submit and reset buttons. The new field is inserted inside the form. You can disable this feature, however, if you want to use fields with scripts rather than inside forms. Click Page Options on the Tools menu, click the General tab sheet, and then click the Automatically enclose form fields within a form check box so that it is not selected.

Because form fields of the same type have the same set of properties, when multiple instances are needed, it often is easier to create one instance, set the property values, copy the form field, and then paste the needed copies. This particularly is true when you need to modify a number of the properties from their default values. Although you may need to change some properties, such as the field name, for each instance, the number of changes needed for each form field will be decreased.

Inserting Text Box Form Fields in a Form

As listed in Table 4-1 on page FP 4.06, FrontPage provides two types of text form fields: a text area and a text box. A **text area** is used when the user may enter multiple lines of text. A text area includes a vertical scroll bar. A **text box** is used when the user may enter only a single line of text. Although it does not have a scroll bar, a text box can accommodate entered text that is longer than the width of the box displayed in the form. The width of the box and the length of text it will accept are independent property values that can be set for each text box.

Perform the following steps to insert text box form fields in a form.

Text Boxes

A text box can be configured as a password field. When a user enters data in the field, the field will display a series of asterisks rather than the text actually entered as data.

Steps ## To Insert Text Box Form Fields in a Form

---

1 **Position the insertion point in the second row and first column of table-T2. Right-click the cell and then click Cell Properties on the shortcut menu. In the Cell Properties dialog box, set the Horizontal alignment to Left and the Vertical alignment to Top for the cell. Click the OK button. Click the Bold button. Type** *Full Name: **and then press the SPACEBAR one time.**

The inserted text displays in the second row and first column of the table in the form on the Web page (Figure 4-22).

FIGURE 4-22

2 **Click Insert on the menu bar and then point to Form. Point to Textbox on the Form submenu.**

The Form submenu displays (Figure 4-23).

FIGURE 4-23

3 **Click Textbox.**

A text box form field is inserted in the form with a default length (Figure 4-24).

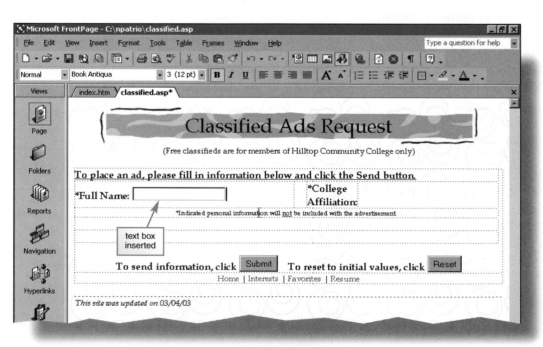

FIGURE 4-24

Other Ways

1. Press ALT+I, R, T
2. In Voice Command mode, say "Insert, Form", click Textbox

You have inserted a text box field in a form successfully. The text box form field has a default set of properties, several of which must be modified. The following steps describe how to modify the properties of a text box form field.

Steps **To Modify the Properties of a Text Box Form Field**

---

1 **Right-click the text box. Point to Form Field Properties on the shortcut menu.**

The text box form field is selected and a shortcut menu displays (Figure 4-25).

FIGURE 4-25

---

2 **Click Form Field Properties. When the Text Box Properties dialog box displays, type** FullName **in the Name text box, type** 50 **in the Width in characters text box, and then type** 1 **in the Tab order text box. Point to the Validate button.**

The Text Box Properties dialog box displays as shown in Figure 4-26. Because the Name property cannot contain spaces, it is a common practice to use a combination of uppercase and lowercase letters to distinguish each word in a field name.

FIGURE 4-26

3 **Click the Validate button. When the Text Box Validation dialog box displays, click Required in the Data length area and then type** Full Name **in the Display name text box. Point to the OK button.**

The Text Box Validation dialog box displays with the changes indicated (Figure 4-27). With Required selected, an error will display, using the Display name, if the user enters no data in this form field.

FIGURE 4-27

4 **Click the OK button in the Text Box Validation dialog box. Click the OK button in the Text Box Properties dialog box. If necessary, click the text box to select it. Press CTRL+C to copy the text box and its properties and validations.**

The Full Name text box displays in the form, with a width of 50 characters (Figure 4-28).

FIGURE 4-28

1. On Format menu click Properties
2. Press ALT+O, T
3. Press ALT+ENTER
4. In Voice Command mode, say "Format, Properties"

You have modified the properties of a text box form field successfully. The form requires several other similar text box form fields to collect the information needed about potential advertisers. The following steps describe how to insert additional text box form fields in the Classified Ads Request Web page.

TO INSERT ADDITIONAL TEXT BOX FORM FIELDS

1 Press the RIGHT ARROW key to position the insertion point after the Full Name text box. Hold down the SHIFT key and then press the ENTER key. Type *Address: and then press the SPACEBAR five times. Press CTRL+V to paste the Full Name text box. Right-click the text box. Click Form Field Properties on the shortcut menu. When the Text Box Properties dialog box displays, type Address in the Name text box. Verify that 50 is in the Width in characters text box. Press the TAB key three times and then type 2 in the Tab order text box. Click the Validate button. When the Text Box Validation dialog box displays, verify that the Required check box in the Data length area is selected. Type Address in the Display name text box. Click the OK button in each dialog box.

2 Press the RIGHT ARROW key to position the insertion point after the Address text box. Hold down the SHIFT key and then press the ENTER key. Type *City: and then press the SPACEBAR twelve times. Press CTRL+V to paste a copy of the Full Name text box. Right-click the text box. Click Form Field Properties on the shortcut menu. When the Text Box Properties dialog box displays, type City in the Name text box. Press the TAB key and then type Washington in the Initial value text box. Verify that 50 is in the Width in characters text box. Press the TAB key twice then type 3 in the Tab order text box. Click the Validate button. When the Text Box Validation dialog box displays, verify that the Required check box in the Data length area is selected. Type City in the Display name text box. Click the OK button in each dialog box.

3 Press the RIGHT ARROW key to position the insertion point after the City text box. Hold down the SHIFT key and then press the ENTER key. Type *State: and then press the SPACEBAR eleven times. Press CTRL+V to paste the Full Name text box. Right-click the text box. Click Form Field Properties on the shortcut menu. When the Text Box Properties dialog box displays, type State in the Name text box. Press the TAB key and then type DC in the Initial value text box. Press the TAB key and then type 3 in the Width in characters text box. Press the TAB key and then type 4 in the Tab order text box. Click the Validate button. When the Text Box Validation dialog box displays, verify that the Required check box in the Data length area is selected. Type State in the Display name text box. Select Text in the Data type drop-down list. Click Letters in the Text format area. In the Data length area, type 2 in the Min length text box and then type 2 in the Max length text box. In the Data value area, click Field must be, select Greater than or equal to in the drop-down list, and type AA in the Value text box. Click And must be, select Less than or equal to in the drop-down list, and type ZZ in the Value text box. Click the OK button in each dialog box.

4 Press the RIGHT ARROW key to position the insertion point after the State text box. Press the SPACEBAR two times. Type *Postal Code: and press the SPACEBAR one time. Press CTRL+V to paste a copy of the Full Name text box. Right-click the text box. Click Form Field Properties on the shortcut menu. When the Text Box Properties dialog box displays, type PostalCode in the Name text box. Press the TAB key and then type 20010 in the Initial value text box. Press the TAB key and then type 10 in the Width in characters text box. Press the TAB key and then type 5 in the Tab order text box. Click the Validate button. When the Text Box Validation dialog box displays, verify that the Required check box in the Data length area is selected. Type Postal Code in the Display name text box. Select Text in the Data type drop-down list. In the Text format area, click Letters, click Digits, click Other and type a hyphen (-) in the Other text box. In the Data length area, type 5 in the Min length text box and type 10 in the Max length text box. Click the OK button in each dialog box.

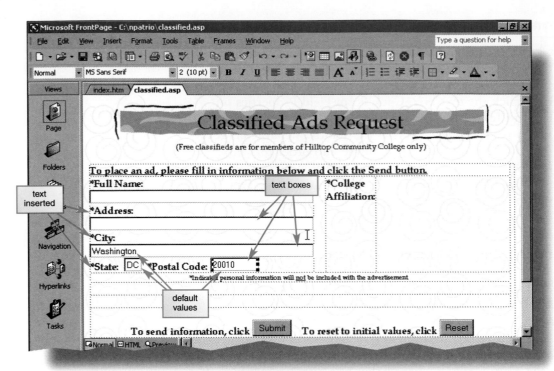

5 If necessary, drag the cell borders to widen the current cell. Click the Save button on the Standard toolbar to save your changes.

The Web page displays as shown in Figure 4-29. The labels, properties, and validations for the form fields in this table are listed in Table 4-3.

FIGURE 4-29

Table 4-3	Labels, Properties, and Validations for Text Box Form Fields in Table-T1	
LABEL	**PROPERTY VALUES TO SET**	**VALIDATIONS TO SET**
*Full Name:	Name=FullName Width=50 Tab order=1	Display name=Full Name In Data length area, click Required
*Address:	Name=Address Width=50 Tab order=2	Display name=Address In Data length area, click Required
*City:	Name=City Initial value=Washington Width=50 Tab order=3	Display name=City In Data length area, click Required
*State:	Name=State Initial value=DC Width=3 Tab order=4	Display name=State Data type=Text In Text format area, click Letters In Data length area, click Required, Min length=2, Max length=2 In Data value area, click Field must be, select Greater than or equal to, set Value to AA; check And must be, select Less than or equal to, set Value to ZZ
*Postal Code:	Name=PostalCode Initial value=20010 Width=10 Tab order=5	Display name=Postal Code Data type=Text In Text format area, click Digits, click Letters, click Other; in Other text box, type a hyphen (–) In Data length area, click Required, Min length=5, Max length=10

You have entered several text boxes in the Web page. The values you typed in the Name text box in the Form Field Properties dialog box will be the name portion of the name=value pair that is sent to the Web server to be processed. Even if a user types nothing in the text box, the name is returned to the server when the user submits the form. You should keep track of the names you use, so you do not duplicate any of the names in later form field properties.

You can toggle between Normal and Preview modes to see how the fields are aligned. Use the SPACEBAR and the table cell borders to adjust the text boxes to display as desired in the Web page. You also may preview the page in your browser as you adjust page elements, if you save the page between changes.

Inserting Check Boxes in a Form

As listed in Table 4-1 on page FP 4.06, inserting a check box in a form allows a user to choose zero, one, or more choices from a set of options. Unlike option buttons, check boxes are not mutually exclusive; that is, selecting one check box does not deselect another check box. When the user submits the form, the name=value pair for each selected check box is sent to the server. If a check box is not selected, nothing will be returned for that check box. Perform the following steps to insert a check box form field in the form.

To Insert a Check Box Form Field in a Form

1 **Position the insertion point in the fourth column of the second row of table-T2. Right-click the cell and then click Cell Properties on the shortcut menu. When the Cell Properties dialog box displays, in the Layout area, select Left for the Horizontal alignment and Top for the Vertical alignment for the cell. Point to the OK button.**

The Cell Properties dialog box displays (Figure 4-30). The layout for the cell is set to align to the top and left.

FIGURE 4-30

2 Click the OK button. Click Insert on the menu bar and then point to Form. Point to Checkbox on the Form submenu.

The Form submenu displays (Figure 4-31).

FIGURE 4-31

3 Click Checkbox.

The inserted check box displays in the form (Figure 4-32).

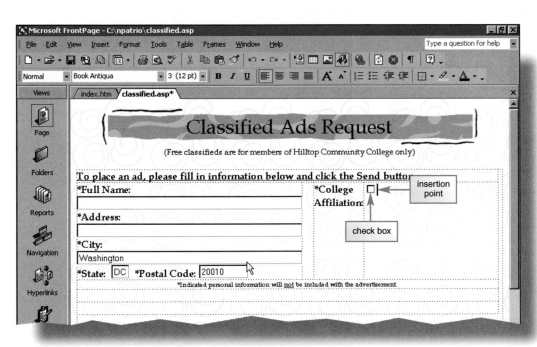

FIGURE 4-32

Other Ways

1. Press ALT+I, R, C
2. In Voice Command mode, say "Insert, Form", click Checkbox

You have added a check box to the form; next, you will add a label to inform the user what he or she is checking. Perform the following steps to add text to the form and assign the text as a label for the check box.

Steps | **To Assign Text as a Label for a Check Box**

1 **Type** Student (Full-time) **to the right of the check box. Hold down the SHIFT key and then press the ENTER key.**

The inserted check box and its label text display in the form (Figure 4-33).

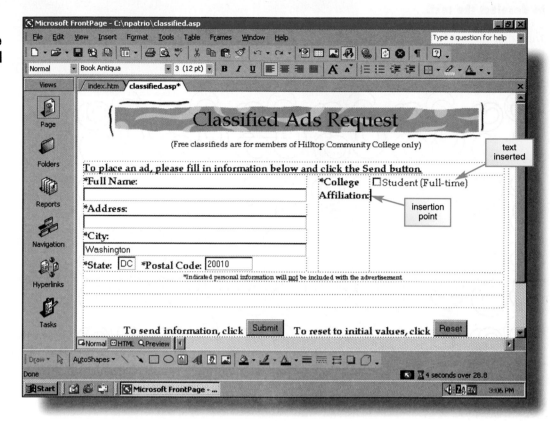

FIGURE 4-33

2 **Drag through both the check box and the text to select them together. Click Insert on the menu bar and then point to Form. Point to Label on the Form submenu.**

The Form submenu displays (Figure 4-34).

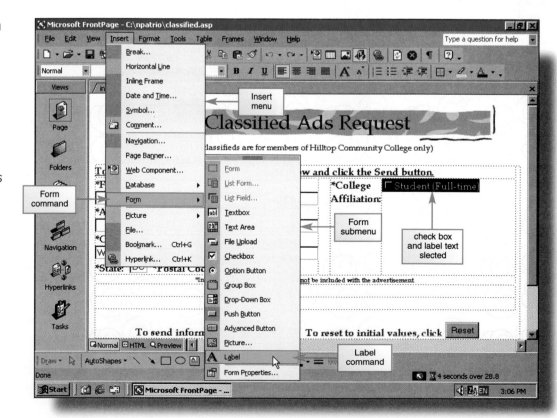

FIGURE 4-34

3 **Click Label. Press the RIGHT ARROW key to deselect the text.**

The selected text now has a box around it, indicating that it is a label for the corresponding check box form field (Figure 4-35).

FIGURE 4-35

Other Ways

1. Press ALT+I, R, A
2. In Voice Command mode, say "Insert, Form", click Label

The check box now has an assigned label to describe the option and to make it easier for the user to select the check box. Next, you will give the check box a particular data name and value by modifying its properties. Perform the following steps to modify the check box properties.

Steps **To Modify the Properties of a Check Box Form Field**

1 **Right-click the check box and then point to Form Field Properties on the shortcut menu.**

The check box form field is selected and a shortcut menu displays (Figure 4-36).

FIGURE 4-36

2 **Click Form Field Properties. When the Check Box Properties dialog box displays, type** FTStudent **in the Name text box and then type** YES **in the Value text box. If necessary, click Checked in the Initial state area to select it. Type** 6 **in the Tab order text box. Point to the OK button.**

The Check Box Properties dialog box displays as shown in Figure 4-37.

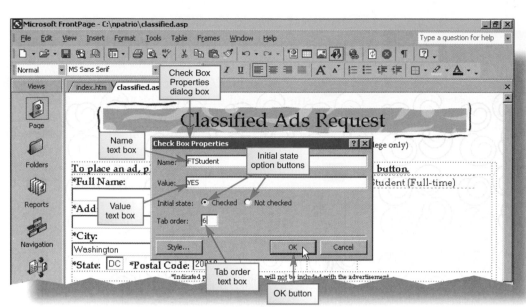

FIGURE 4-37

3 **Click the OK button.**

The dialog boxes close and the check box and its label display in the form (Figure 4-38). The check box is initially selected.

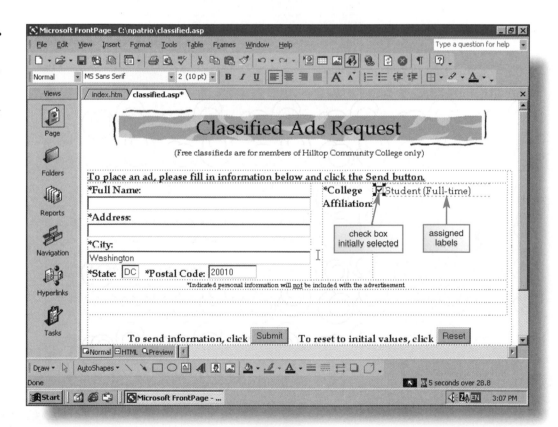

FIGURE 4-38

Four other check boxes must be inserted to complete this area of the form. Perform the steps on the next page to insert the additional check boxes.

Other Ways

1. On Format menu click Properties
2. Press ALT+O, T
3. Press ALT+ENTER
4. In Voice Command mode, say "Format, Properties"

TO INSERT ADDITIONAL CHECK BOX FORM FIELDS

Check Boxes

You can assign the same name to a group of related check boxes and then differentiate them by their values. This method of naming them causes them to function similarly to option buttons. The check boxes, however, will not be mutually exclusive.

1 Click below the check box to position the insertion point. Click Insert on the menu bar, point to Form, and then click Checkbox on the Form submenu.

2 Type Student (Part-time) to the right of the check box. Hold down the SHIFT key and then press the ENTER key. Drag through both the check box and the text to select them. Be sure to select only the check box and text, not the previous label. Click Insert on the menu bar, point to Form, and then click Label on the Form submenu.

3 Right-click the check box and then click Form Field Properties on the shortcut menu. When the Check Box Properties dialog box displays, type PTStudent in the Name text box and then type YES in the Value text box. Verify that the Initial state Not checked option button is selected. Type 7 in the Tab order text box. Click the OK button.

4 Repeat Steps 1 through 3 for each of the remaining check boxes using the labels and properties listed in Table 4-4. Do not press the ENTER key after typing the last label text. If necessary, drag table borders and columns to adjust the form the way you want it to display in the Web page. Click the Save button on the Standard toolbar to save your changes.

The Web page displays with the additional check boxes and labels as shown in Figure 4-39.

FIGURE 4-39

Table 4-4 Labels and Properties for Check Boxes				
LABEL	*NAME*	*VALUE*	*INITIAL STATE*	*TAB ORDER*
Student (Full-time)	FTStudent	YES	Checked	6
Student (Part-time)	PTStudent	YES	Not checked	7
Faculty (Full-time)	FTFaculty	YES	Not checked	8
Faculty (Part-time)	PTFaculty	YES	Not checked	9
Staff	Staff	YES	Not checked	10

You have inserted check boxes in a form, assigned labels to the check boxes, and modified properties successfully. Notice the Check Box Properties dialog box shown in Figure 4-37 on page FP 4.33 contains no Validate button. Check boxes only can be checked or unchecked, and cannot be required, so there is no data that needs validation.

Inserting a Line Drawing AutoShape in a Table

Depending on your Web page design, you may want more than just text to direct the user's attention. In addition to text, you can insert other objects in a form, such as pictures or line art, in the same manner as you would with any other Web page. Being in a form has no particular effect on these objects.

For this Web page, a line is used to separate the personal information that will not be published from the contact and descriptive information that will be published in the classified advertisement.

Perform the following steps to insert a line drawing AutoShape object in a table.

More About

AutoShape Drawings

To draw an AutoShape while keeping its default proportions, press and hold the SHIFT key while you draw the object. To resize an AutoShape while keeping its default proportions, press and hold the CTRL key while you resize the object.

Steps **To Insert a Line Drawing AutoShape in a Table**

1 **Position the insertion point in the fourth row of table-T2. Click the Center button on the Formatting toolbar.**

The insertion point is centered in the fourth row of table-T2 (Figure 4-40).

FIGURE 4-40

2 If necessary, click View on the menu bar, click Toolbars, and then click Drawing on the Toolbars submenu to display the Drawing toolbar. Click the Line button on the Drawing toolbar. Position the mouse pointer at the left side of the fourth row of table-T2. Hold down the SHIFT key. Click the mouse button and then drag a horizontal line drawing across the width of the fourth row. Release the mouse button and the SHIFT key.

A straight line is drawn in the fourth row of the table (Figure 4-41). Holding down the SHIFT key ensures that the line is straight.

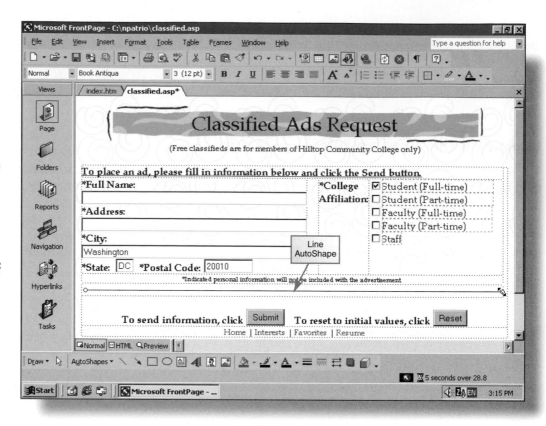

FIGURE 4-41

3 Right-click the line drawing and then click AutoShape on the shortcut menu. When the Format AutoShape dialog box displays, if necessary, click the Layout tab. Click None in the Positioning style area. Point to the OK button.

A positioning style of None is selected for the line AutoShape (Figure 4-42).

FIGURE 4-42

4 Click the OK button. Click the Line Style button on the Drawing toolbar and then point to 2¼ pt.

A new line style of 2¼ pt is selected (Figure 4-43).

FIGURE 4-43

5 Click 2¼ pt. Click the Line Color button arrow on the Drawing toolbar and then point to the fifth color box in the Theme's Colors area (Hex={66,00,66}).

The colors for the current theme display below the standard colors (Figure 4-44).

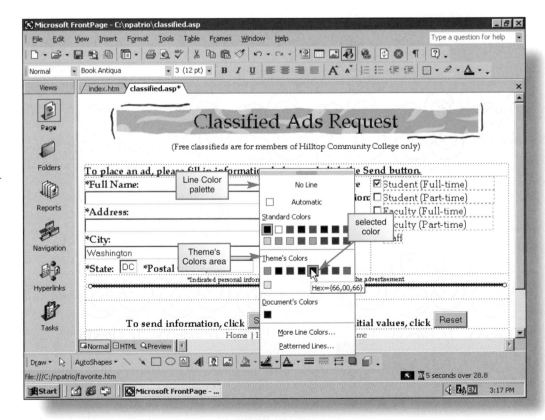

FIGURE 4-44

6 Click the color box (Hex={66,00,66}). If necessary, drag the ends of the line drawing to adjust the width to just less than the width of the table. Click the Save button to save the changes.

The line AutoShape is centered in the fourth row of the table and displays in the new color (Figure 4-45).

FIGURE 4-45

Because the line drawing has a positioning style of None, the table will widen if the line is drawn wider than the current table width.

Creating a Nested Table

The next step in the design of this Web page is to create a third table, table-T3, to help control positioning of additional elements in the form. You will insert the table within a cell of table-T2 to create a **nested table**. You saw an example of a nested table in Project 3, where a table was imported into the project as part of a Word document. In this case, you will create the nested table by inserting a table in an existing table. The following steps summarize how to create a nested table.

TO CREATE A NESTED TABLE

1 Click in the fifth row of table-T2 (the row below the line) to position the insertion point. Click the Insert Table button on the Standard toolbar and then drag to select three rows and four columns (3 by 4 table). Click the mouse button.

2 Select the first two columns in the bottom row of the table and merge the cells. Select all three rows in the third column and merge the cells. Select all three rows in the fourth column and merge the cells. Select all four columns in the first row. Right-click the selected cells and then click Cell Properties on the shortcut menu. In the Layout area of the Cell Properties dialog box, select Left for the Horizontal alignment and select Top for the vertical alignment. Click the OK button.

3 Right-click the table and then click Table Properties on the shortcut menu. When the Table Properties dialog box displays, type 0 in the Size box in the Borders area. Click the OK button.

Figure 4-46 shows the FrontPage window after the nested table is inserted.

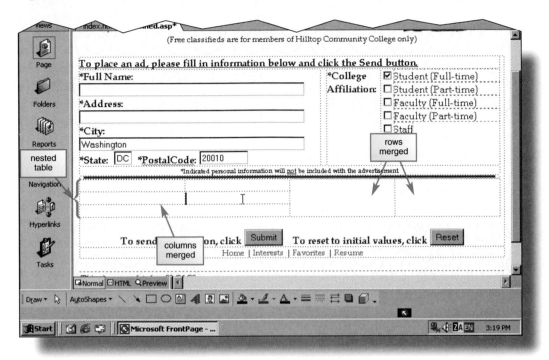

FIGURE 4-46

As you can see, creating a nested table is no different from making any other table, except that the entire new table is located within a cell of an existing table.

As Figure 4-1b on page FP 4.05 illustrates, three additional text boxes are yet to be added to the form. As discussed earlier, tables often are used to align elements in a Web page. The previous text boxes were aligned by pressing the SPACEBAR after the accompanying label text. The new text boxes will not require additional spaces for alignment. Instead, these text boxes are aligned by placing the labels in one cell of the table and then placing the text boxes in an adjacent cell. By adjusting the position of the cell borders, you can obtain the required alignment.

Perform the following steps to insert and align the label text and text box elements in a nested table.

TO INSERT AND ALIGN ELEMENTS IN A NESTED TABLE

1 Position the insertion point in the first row and the first column of table-T3. Click the Bold button on the Formatting toolbar. Hold down the SHIFT key and then press the ENTER key.

2 Type Contact: and then hold down the SHIFT key and press the ENTER key. Type Phone: and then hold down the SHIFT key and press the ENTER key. Type E-mail: as the last label.

3 Position the insertion point in the first row and the second column of table-T3. Click the Bold button on the Formatting toolbar. Click the Font Size box arrow and then click 2 (10 pt). Type (use first name or alias only) and then hold down the SHIFT key and press the ENTER key.

4 Insert a text box form field. Right-click the text box. Click Form Field Properties on the shortcut menu. When the Text Box Properties dialog box displays, type Contact in the Name text box, type 29 in the Width in characters text box, and then type 11 in the Tab order text box.

5 Click the Validate button. When the Text Box Validation dialog box displays, click Required in the Data length area and then type Contact Name in the Display name text box. Click the OK button in the Text Box Validation dialog box. Click the OK button in the Text Box Properties dialog box. Press CTRL+C to copy the text box. Press the RIGHT ARROW key.

6 Hold down the SHIFT key and then press the ENTER key. Press CTRL+V to insert the copied text box. Right-click the text box. Click Form Field Properties on the shortcut menu. When the Text Box Properties dialog box displays, type Phone in the Name text box, type 20 in the Width in characters text box, and then type 12 in the Tab order text box.

7 Click the Validate button. When the Text Box Validation dialog box displays, type Phone Number in the Display name text box and then select Text in the Data type list. Click Digits, click Whitespace, and click Other in the Text format area; then type (-) (left parenthesis, hyphen, right parenthesis) in the Other text box. In the Data length area, verify that the Required check box is not selected. Click the OK button in the Text Box Validation dialog box and then click the OK button in the Text Box Properties dialog box. Press the RIGHT ARROW key.

8 Hold down the SHIFT key and then press the ENTER key. Press CTRL+V to insert the copied text box. Right-click the text box. Click Form Field Properties on the shortcut menu. When the Text Box Properties dialog box displays, type EmailAddress in the Name text box, type 33 in the Width in characters text box, and then type 13 in the Tab order text box. Click the OK button.

9 Drag the right border of the cell in the first column to align the text and form fields. Click the Save button on the Standard toolbar.

The Web page displays as shown in Figure 4-47. The properties and validations for the text boxes in this table are listed in Table 4-5.

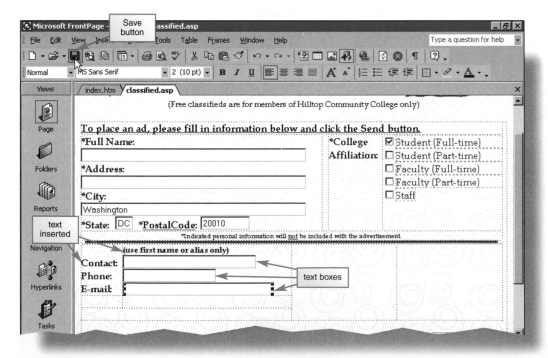

FIGURE 4-47

The next section of the form contains a drop-down list box so a potential advertiser can indicate the category of advertisement he or she wants to submit.

Inserting a Drop-Down List Box in a Form

As listed in Table 4-1 on page FP 4.06, a drop-down list box is useful when you have a variety of choices — more than option buttons can handle effectively.

With a drop-down list box, you give the drop-down list box a name and then add choices to the list. You can order the list choices from the most frequently occurring choice to the least frequently occurring choice, alphabetically, or in another sequence.

When the user makes a selection and clicks the Submit button, the list name and the value associated with the selected choice are sent. You can select a default choice that will be returned automatically if the user makes no selection. You also can make an item that is descriptive only and cannot be selected by the user, forcing him or her to make a selection. The following steps show how to insert a drop-down list box form field in a form.

Table 4-5 Properties and Validations for Text Box Form Fields in Table-T3		
TEXT BOX	**PROPERTY VALUES TO SET**	**VALIDATIONS TO SET**
Contact	Name=Contact Width=29 Tab order=11	Display name=Contact Name In Data length area, click Required
Phone	Name=Phone Width=20 Tab order=12	Display name=Phone Number Select Text in the Data type list In Text format area, select Digits, Whitespace, and Other In Other text box, type (-) (left parenthesis, hyphen, right parenthesis) In Data length area, deselect Required
E-mail Address	Name=EmailAddress Width=33 Tab order=13	

More About

Drop-Down Lists

Drop-down list boxes are useful for presenting a large number of choices in a small space. The choices do not display unless the user clicks the list box arrow. When a choice is selected, the list of choices is hidden once again. You can alter the properties of a list to allow the selection of more than one choice. This method is an alternative to using a group of check boxes.

Steps **To Insert a Drop-Down List Box Form Field in a Form**

1 Position the insertion point in the second row and first column of table-T3, the second table in the form. Click the Bold button on the Formatting toolbar. Type Category: and then position the insertion point in the second row and second column of table-T3.

The inserted text displays in the second row and first column of the third table in the form (Figure 4-48). The column will widen, if necessary, to accommodate the text.

FIGURE 4-48

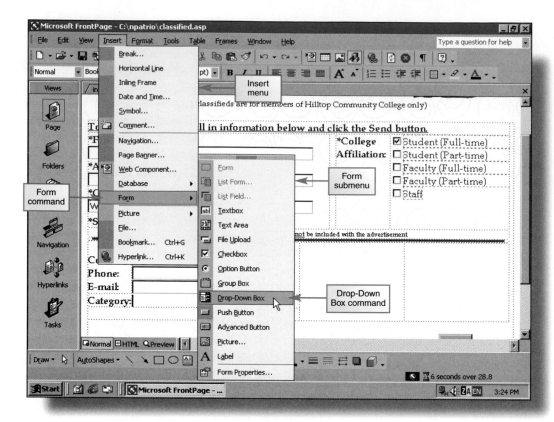
2 **Click Insert on the menu bar and then point to Form. Point to Drop-Down Box on the Form submenu.**

The Form submenu displays (Figure 4-49).

FIGURE 4-49

3 **Click Drop-Down Box.**

A drop-down list box is inserted in the form with a default size (Figure 4-50).

FIGURE 4-50

Other Ways

1. Press ALT+I, R, D
2. In Voice Command mode, say "Insert, Form", click Drop-Down Box

You have inserted a drop-down list box successfully. To be useful, however, the drop-down list box needs additional modification. Specifically, you need to set the choices that the user can select, along with their specific properties. Use the following steps to modify the properties of a drop-down list box form field.

Steps To Modify the Properties of a Drop-Down List Box Form Field

1 **Right-click the drop-down list box. Point to Form Field Properties on the shortcut menu.**

The drop-down list box form field is selected and a shortcut menu displays (Figure 4-51).

FIGURE 4-51

2 **Click Form Field Properties. When the Drop-Down Box Properties dialog box displays, drag through the text D1 and then type** `Category` **in the Name text box. Point to the Add button.**

The Drop-Down Box Properties dialog box displays (Figure 4-52).

FIGURE 4-52

3 Click the Add button. When the Add Choice dialog box displays, type `Select Ad Category` in the Choice text box. If necessary, click Not selected in the Initial state area. Point to the OK button in the Add Choice dialog box.

The Add Choice dialog box displays as shown in Figure 4-53.

FIGURE 4-53

4 Click the OK button. Click the Add button. When the Add Choice dialog box displays, type `For Sale` in the Choice text box. Click Specify Value. Drag through the text, For Sale, automatically inserted and then type `Sell` in the Specify Value text box. If necessary, click Not Selected in the Initial state area. Point to the OK button in the Add Choice dialog box.

The Add Choice dialog box displays with the second choice entered (Figure 4-54).

FIGURE 4-54

5 Click the OK button. Repeat Step 4 for the remaining choices listed in Table 4-6 on page FP 4.47. After adding the fifth choice, type 14 in the Tab order text box in the Drop-Down Box Properties dialog box. Point to the Validate button.

The Drop-Down Box Properties dialog box displays with all of the choices added (Figure 4-55). The value specified is the value sent to the server when the form is submitted. If no value is specified, the choice name is used as the value.

FIGURE 4-55

6 Click the Validate button. When the Drop-Down Box Validation dialog box displays, click Data required. Click Disallow first choice. Type Ad Category in the Display name text box. Point to the OK button in the Drop-Down Box Validation dialog box.

The Drop-Down Box Validation dialog box displays with the changes indicated (Figure 4-56). Selecting Disallow first choice sets the first choice, Ad Category, as a descriptive field that a user cannot select.

FIGURE 4-56

7 **Click the OK button. Verify that the Allow multiple selections No option button is selected. Point to the OK button in the Drop-Down Box Properties dialog box.**

The Drop-Down Box Validation dialog box closes, and the choices display in the Choice list box in the Drop-Down Box Properties dialog box (Figure 4-57).

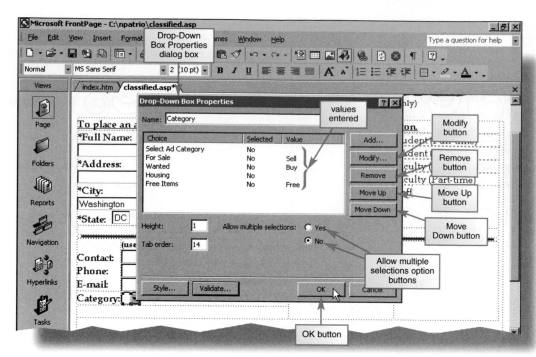

FIGURE 4-57

8 **Click the OK button. Click the Save button to save your changes.**

The first choice displays in the drop-down list box in the form (Figure 4-58). Periodically saving changes as you proceed through the project is recommended.

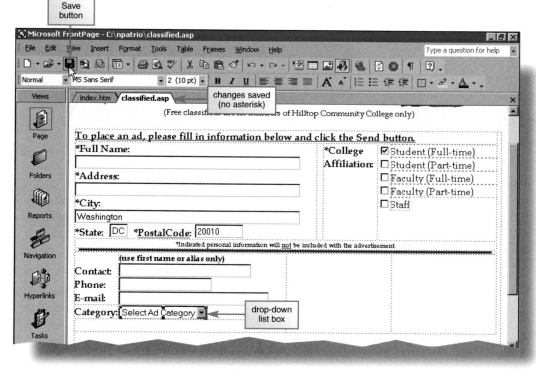

FIGURE 4-58

When the user clicks the drop-down list box arrow, the choices just entered will display in the order you entered them. You can modify the choices in the Drop-Down Box Properties dialog box (Figure 4-51 on page FP 4.43) by using the **Move Up button** and the **Move Down button** to move a given choice higher or lower in the list, the **Remove button** to delete a choice altogether, and the **Modify button** to modify a choice previously entered by changing its name, value, or initial state.

Inserting a Group Box and Option Buttons in a Form

As listed in Table 4-1 on page FP 4.06, an **option button** is useful when you must choose one option from among a small set of mutually exclusive options. Each option button in a form consists of an option button and a corresponding label. As indicated earlier, text can be assigned as the label for a form field so that clicking the text is like clicking the form field.

Related option buttons are defined in a group. A **group box** is a titled border that surrounds a group of related fields. Option buttons not contained within a group box are considered the default group in a form; that is, they are mutually exclusive. Therefore, to have more than a single group of option buttons, a form must have at least one group box.

The process of inserting option buttons begins with the insertion of the group box, if one is needed. Even if only one group of option buttons is used, a group box can provide a visual clue that the option buttons are related.

Perform the following steps to insert a group box form field in a form.

Table 4-6 Choices for Category Drop-Down Box Form Field

CHOICE TEXT BOX	SPECIFY VALUE	INITIAL STATE
Select Ad Category	not checked	Not selected
For Sale	checked, value=Sell	Not selected
Wanted	checked, value=Buy	Not selected
Housing	not checked	Not selected
Free Items	checked, value=Free	Not selected

 Steps **To Insert a Group Box Form Field in a Form**

1 **Position the insertion point in the third row and first column of table-T3, the nested table you just created. Click Insert on the menu bar, point to Form, and then point to Group Box on the Form submenu.**

The Form submenu displays (Figure 4-59).

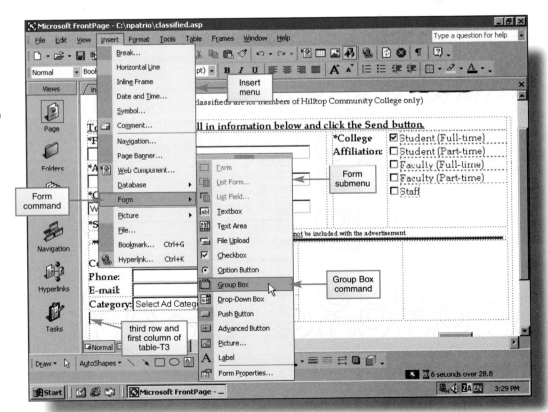

FIGURE 4-59

2   Click Group Box.

The group box displays in the form (Figure 4-60).

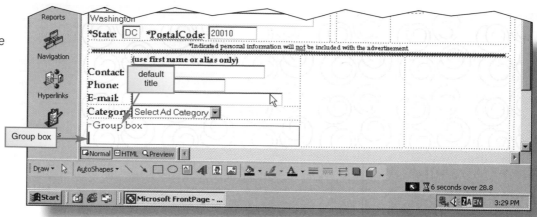

FIGURE 4-60

You should change the default title for the group box to reflect the purpose of the option button choices. Perform the following step to modify the title of a group box form field.

Steps   To Modify the Title of a Group Box Form Field

1   Drag through the title text to select it. Click the Bold button on the Formatting toolbar and then type Payment method as the new title.

The new title for the group box displays (Figure 4-61).

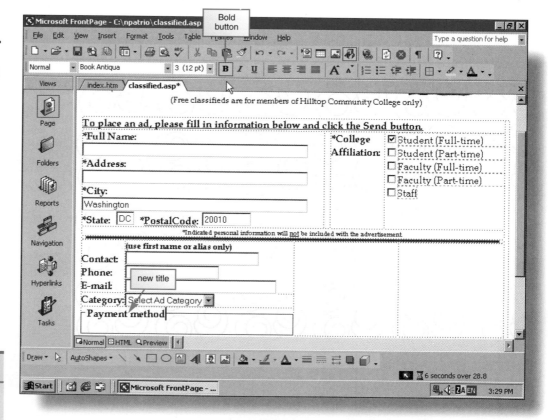

FIGURE 4-61

After adding a group box, the next step is to add option buttons. You should add labels to each option button for the same reasons that you added a label with a check box: to make the choice easier for the user to select and to indicate which of the mutually exclusive options that option button represents. You then adjust the properties of the option button and identify the value that will be sent to the Web server when a user clicks the Submit button.

Perform the following steps to insert an option button form field in a group box.

Steps To Insert Option Button Form Fields in a Group Box

1 Position the insertion point in the group box. Click Insert on the menu bar, point to Form, and then point to Option Button on the Form submenu.

The Form submenu displays (Figure 4-62).

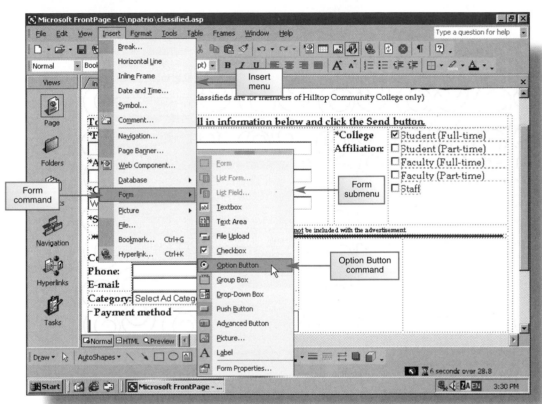

FIGURE 4-62

2 Click Option Button.

The inserted option button displays in the form (Figure 4-63).

FIGURE 4-63

Other Ways

1. Press ALT+I, R, O
2. In Voice Command mode, say "Insert, Form", click Option Button

Recall that inserting a form field inserts only the form field object, as with this option button. You must provide a label for each form field you insert. Furthermore, just typing text next to the form field does not assign the text as a label for the field. You explicitly have to assign the text entered as the label for the field. Perform the following steps to assign a label to the option button.

Steps **To Assign a Label to an Option Button Form Field**

1 **Type** Cash Only **to the right of the option button. Hold down the SHIFT key and then press the ENTER key. Drag through both the option button and the text to select them together. Click Insert on the menu bar, point to Form, and then point to Label on the Form submenu.**

The Form submenu displays (Figure 4-64).

FIGURE 4-64

2 **Click Label. Click to the right of the label text to deselect it.**

The text displays with a box around it, indicating that it is the assigned label for the corresponding option button form field (Figure 4-65).

FIGURE 4-65

Other **Ways**

1. Press ALT+I, R, A
2. In Voice Command mode, say "Insert, Form", click Label

Finally, you need to modify some properties of the option button, such as the value that will be returned when the option button is selected, whether the option button is selected by default (initial state), and the group name with which the option button will be associated. Remember that option buttons are mutually exclusive; that is, selecting any option button in a given group will deselect all of the others in that same group. Perform the following steps to modify the properties of an option button form field.

Steps | **To Modify the Properties of an Option Button Form Field**

1 **Right-click the option button. Point to Form Field Properties on the shortcut menu.**

The option button form field is selected and a shortcut menu displays (Figure 4-66).

FIGURE 4-66

2 **Click Form Field Properties. When the Option Button Properties dialog box displays, type** Payment **in the Group name text box, press the TAB key and then type** Cash **in the Value text box. If necessary, click Not selected in the Initial state area to select it. Type** 15 **in the Tab order text box. Point to the Validate button.**

The Option Button Properties dialog box displays (Figure 4-67). The Group name, Payment, will be used automatically for all option buttons in the same group.

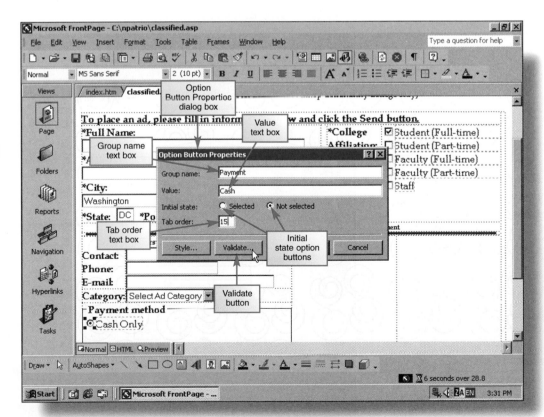

FIGURE 4-67

3 **Click the Validate button. When the Option Button Validation dialog box displays, click Data required and then type** Payment method **in the Display name text box. Point to the OK button in the Option Button Validation dialog box.**

The Option Button Validation dialog box displays with the indicated changes (Figure 4-68).

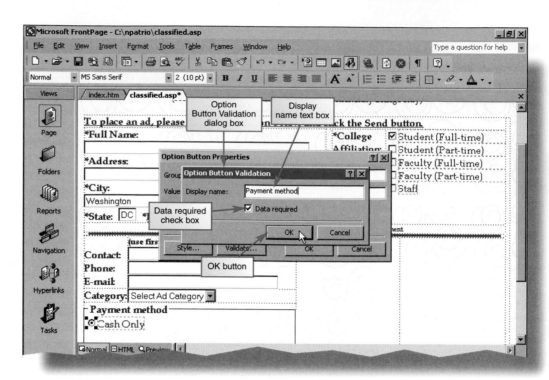

FIGURE 4-68

4 **Click the OK button. Click the OK button in the Option Button Properties dialog box.**

The option button and its label display (Figure 4-69).

FIGURE 4-69

5 **For each of the option button fields listed in Table 4-7, insert the option button, assign its label, and modify its properties accordingly. Click the OK button.**

The dialog boxes close and all of the Payment group option buttons and their assigned labels display in the form (Figure 4-70).

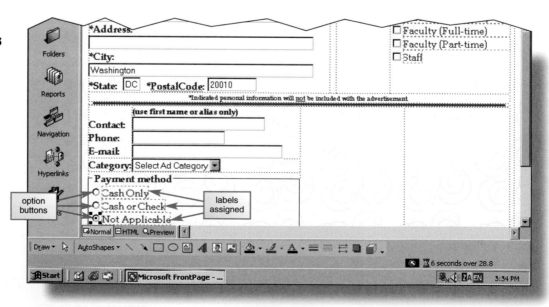

FIGURE 4-70

6 Click the border of the group box and then use the sizing handles to drag the right border to the left. Click the Save button to save your changes.

The group box is sized proportionately to the contents (Figure 4-71).

FIGURE 4-71

Table 4-7	Option Button Fields for Payment Group		
LABEL	*VALUE*	*INITIAL STATE*	*TAB ORDER*
Cash Only	Cash	Not selected	15
Cash or Check	Cash/Check	Not selected	16
Not Applicable	N/A	Selected	17

Other Ways

1. On Format menu click Properties
2. Press ALT+O, T
3. Press ALT+ENTER
4. In Voice Command mode, say "Format, Properties"

You have inserted option buttons successfully in a form in a Web page. The values for each option button — as entered in the Value text box — will be sent to the form handler when the user clicks the Submit button. In this form, the values of the option buttons are the same as the button labels. Codes could have been used (eliminating any space characters) to reduce the amount of data sent back to the form handler for processing, but creating reports with this data would require subsequent interpretation of the codes.

Because the text for each of the option buttons was assigned as a label, the user can click the text and the option button will be selected. This makes selection a little easier for users and can reduce data entry time.

Because these option buttons all are in the same group (in this case, the Payment group), a user can select only one option button at a time, and only one value is sent to the server when a user clicks the Submit button. For example, if a user clicks the option button, Cash Only, the name=value pair sent for processing is Payment=Cash, because Payment is the name of the group of option buttons and Cash is the value associated with the Cash Only option button.

More About

Option Buttons

You always should choose one option button in a group to be initially selected, even though FrontPage does not force you to do so. Because option buttons in a group are mutually exclusive, pre-selecting one button reduces confusion for your users and may reduce their data entry time.

In Figure 4-67 on page FP 4.51, notice the two options in the Initial state area of the Option Button Properties dialog box. The **Initial state option** indicates the state of the option button when the user first views the Web page. **Selected** means the option button displays initially in the form as active. **Not selected** means the option button displays initially in the form as inactive.

You should choose an option button as the default value, typically the one chosen most frequently, and then set its initial state to Selected. This saves the user some time when filling out the form because the option button most frequently chosen already is active, the user can move on to other fields.

Inserting a Text Area Form Field in a Form

The text boxes inserted earlier only allow the user to enter a single line of text. If you are collecting a textual description, such as a classified advertisement, then you want to offer the user a means of entering multiple lines of text. A text area is a single form field that allows entry of multiple lines of text. A text area not only accommodates a larger amount of text, but also allows for easier reading and reviewing of the text entered by the user.

Perform the following steps to insert a text area form field in the form.

 To Insert a Text Area Form Field in a Form

1 **Position the insertion point in the first row and the fourth column of table-T3, the nested table. Click the Bold button on the Formatting toolbar.** **Type** Advertisement Description: **and then hold the SHIFT key and then press the ENTER key. Point to Insert on the menu bar.**

The entered text displays aligned to the top and left in the cell (Figure 4-72).

FIGURE 4-72

2 **Click Insert on the menu bar and then point to Form. Point to Text Area on the Form submenu.**

The Form submenu displays (Figure 4-73).

FIGURE 4-73

3 **Click Text Area.**

A text area form field displays in the form with a default size and a vertical scroll bar (Figure 4-74).

FIGURE 4-74

As with previous form fields entered, the text area has a default set of properties that must be modified for this project. Perform the steps on the next page to modify the properties of a text area form field.

Other Ways

1. Press ALT+I, R, E
2. In Voice Command mode, say "Insert, Form", click Text Area

Steps To Modify the Properties of a Text Area Form Field

1 **Right-click the text area and then click Form Field Properties on the shortcut menu. When the TextArea Box Properties dialog box displays, type** Description **in the Name text box. Press the TAB key twice and then type** 37 **in the Width in characters text box. Press the TAB key and then type** 18 **in the Tab order text box. Press the TAB key and then type** 15 **in the Number of lines text box. Point to the Validate button.**

The TextArea Box Properties dialog box displays (Figure 4-75).

FIGURE 4-75

2 **Click the Validate button. When the Text Box Validation dialog box displays, click Required in the Data length area, and then type** Advertisement Description **in the Display name text box. Point to the OK button.**

The Text Box Validation dialog box displays (Figure 4-76).

FIGURE 4-76

3 Click the OK button in the Text Box Validation dialog box. Click the OK button in the TextArea Box Properties dialog box. Drag cell borders to adjust widths, if necessary.

The text area form field displays with the new size (Figure 4-77).

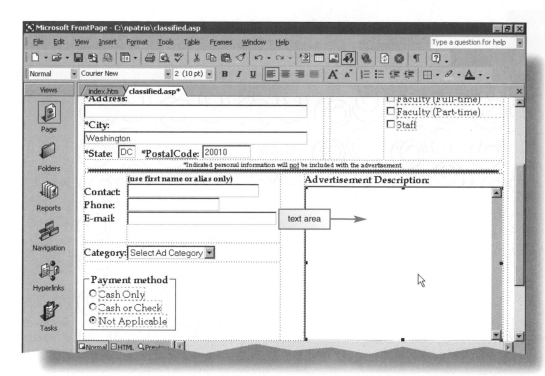

FIGURE 4-77

You can change the size of a text area by modifying its properties, as done here, or by selecting the text area and dragging the sizing handles to the required size.

The form almost is complete. The last two steps are to adjust the properties of the Submit and Reset buttons as needed and to adjust the properties of the form itself.

Modifying the Properties of a Push Button Form Field

As previously described, two buttons usually display in every form — Submit and Reset. The purpose of the Submit button is to send the data entered in the form to the Web server. Recall that the data will be in the form of name=value pairs separated by ampersands (&).

The purpose of the Reset button is to clear any data typed in text boxes, clear any check boxes, and change any option buttons and selected items back to the default choices. This allows an individual to clear his or her changes and start over. Both the Submit and Reset buttons are considered Push Buttons.

In addition to these push buttons, you can add other buttons to the form and assign actions to be performed when a user clicks those buttons. The **Push Button command** on the Forms submenu allows you to add other regular buttons to the form. The default label for a new push button is Button. The **Advanced Button command** allows you to add buttons with HTML as the button label. The default label for an Advanced Button displays, Type Here, and initially is selected. You can insert HTML, including a picture, as the button label just as you would insert it in a Web page.

You can adjust the properties of form buttons, such as the data value they return or the text label that displays on the button. In some cases, the default label on a button will be sufficient and not require changes. Perform the steps on the next page to modify form button properties and change the text labels of the buttons.

Steps **To Modify the Properties of a Push Button Form Field**

1 **If necessary, scroll down to display the Submit and Reset buttons. Right-click the Submit button and then click Form Field Properties on the shortcut menu.**

The Submit button is selected and the shortcut menu displays (Figure 4-78).

FIGURE 4-78

2 **Click Form Field Properties. When the Push Button Properties dialog box displays, type** SendButton **in the Name text box. Drag through the text, Submit, in the Value/label text box and then type** Send **in the text box. Type** 19 **in the Tab order text box. Point to the OK button.**

The Push Button Properties dialog box displays. The new name and label text display and the tab order is set to 19 (Figure 4-79).

FIGURE 4-79

3 Click the OK button.

The new text label displays in the button (Figure 4-80).

FIGURE 4-80

4 Right-click the Reset button. Click Form Field Properties on the shortcut menu. Type ResetButton in the Name text box. Type 20 in the Tab order text box. Point to the OK button.

The button is assigned a new name and the tab order is set to 20 (Figure 4-81). The value/label for the button remains unchanged.

FIGURE 4-81

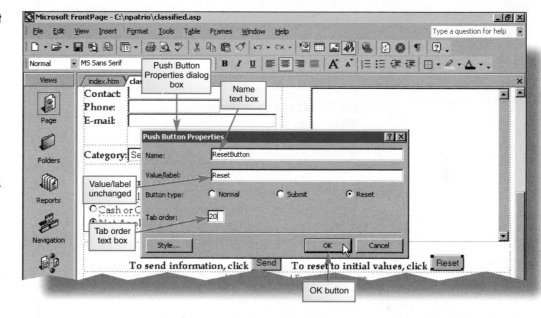

5 Click the OK button.

The completed form displays (Figure 4-82).

Other Ways

1. On Format menu click Properties
2. Press ALT+O, T
3. Press ALT+ENTER
4. In Voice Command mode, say "Format, Properties"

FIGURE 4-82

In the Push Button Properties dialog box shown in Figure 4-81 on page FP 4.59, you can set a button type to be Normal, Submit, or Reset. You can use the **Normal** type to add other buttons to the form and then assign a script to be run if a user clicks the Normal button. Be sure to give the button a name and label that correctly indicate its purpose.

When a user clicks the Submit button, it sends the form and initiates the form handler. When the form has been completely designed, you must decide how the form will be handled when a user clicks the Submit button.

Choosing the Form Handler for the Form

After a user fills out the form and clicks the Submit button, the form data is sent back to the Web server where an appropriate form handler will be invoked to process the form data. Table 4-2 on page FP 4.07 lists several types of form handlers you can use to process form data.

Recall that the form data for the Classified Ads Request page is to be sent to a database. You can let FrontPage create the database or you can provide the name of an existing database. FrontPage will insert ASP (Active Server Page) scripts to enable the Web page to access the database. **Scripts** are program statements inserted in the Web page, typically intended for execution on the Web server. To use Active Server Pages, the page must have a file extension of .asp and the server also must support Active Server Pages.

Setting the Form Properties and Form Handler

FrontPage provides several ways to store form data entered by users. By default, form information is saved to a text file. With FrontPage, you also can create a form that saves form results in a different file format, sends form results in an e-mail message, submits information to a database, or saves form results using a custom or FrontPage form handler, as listed in Table 4-2 on page FP 4.07.

In this project, the form will submit information to an Access database. A database organizes data into tables. A **table** is a means of organizing data into columns and rows within a database.

To submit information to a database, FrontPage must establish a connection to an existing database or to a newly created database. A **connection** is an object that provides a path to a database. FrontPage then must use a valid table name from the database and insert the information into that table.

Perform the following steps to modify the form properties and choose a form handler.

More *About*

Active Server Pages

Using Active Server Pages (ASP) has become a popular way to process information from Web pages and to make Web pages dynamic. To learn more about Active Server Pages, visit the FrontPage 2002 More About Web page (scsite.com/fp2002/more.htm) and then click Active Server Pages.

More *About*

Database Terminology

Database terminology may seem confusing at first, but it does not have to be. To learn more about database terminology, visit the FrontPage 2002 More About Web page (scsite.com/fp2002/more.htm) and then click Database Terminology.

Steps: To Modify Form Properties and Set a Form Handler

1 **Right-click the form. Point to Form Properties on the shortcut menu.**

A shortcut menu displays (Figure 4-83). The Form Properties command allows you to change the form handler, as well as set other form properties.

FIGURE 4-83

2 **Click Form Properties. When the Form Properties dialog box displays, point to the Send to database option button.**

The Form Properties dialog box displays (Figure 4-84). The Form Properties dialog box contains text boxes and option buttons that control what type of form handler you want to use to store form data.

FIGURE 4-84

3 **Click Send to database. Point to the Options button.**

The Form Properties dialog box displays with the above changes (Figure 4-85). The default file name in the File name text box is removed.

FIGURE 4-85

4 **Click the Options button. When the Options for Saving Results to Database dialog box displays, if necessary, click the Database Results tab. Point to the Create Database button.**

The Options for Saving Results to Database dialog box displays with the Database Results sheet (Figure 4-86).

FIGURE 4-86

5 Click the Create Database button. When the Microsoft FrontPage dialog box displays, point to the OK button.

A Microsoft FrontPage dialog box displays indicating FrontPage created a database for you using the page name as the name for the database connection (Figure 4-87).

FIGURE 4-87

6 Click the OK button in the Microsoft FrontPage dialog box. Point to the OK button in the Options for Saving Results to Database dialog box.

The Microsoft FrontPage dialog box closes. FrontPage created a table in the new database with a default name of Results (Figure 4-88). A corresponding entry exists in the new database for each form field.

FIGURE 4-88

7 **Click the OK button in the Options for Saving Results to Database dialog box. Click the OK button in the Form Properties dialog box. Point to the HTML tab at the bottom of the FrontPage window.**

The dialog boxes close and FrontPage displays the completed page in Page view (Figure 4-89).

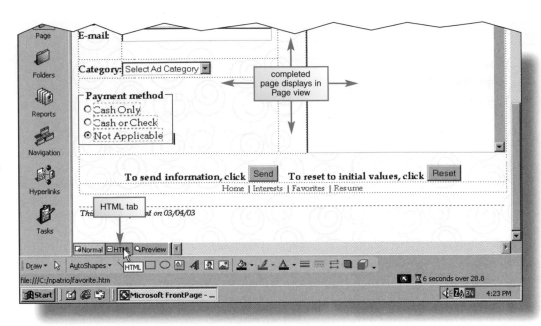

FIGURE 4-89

The Options for Saving Results to Database dialog box shown in Figure 4-86 on page FP 4.62 contains several tabbed sheets. In addition to specifying the database connection and table to use, the Database Results sheet allows you to specify a customized confirmation page be returned to the user after he or she submits the form and a failure page if an error occurs. Because FrontPage provides default pages, both are optional. The **Saved Fields sheet** allows you to choose which form fields actually are saved and to change the field column name in the database. The **Additional Fields sheet** provides similar capabilities for additional information, such as the date and time the form was submitted, the browser type, remote computer name, and user name.

Modifying HTML Code Directly

The World Wide Web is a vast resource of information that is largely unstructured. To find information of interest, a Web user typically performs a search using a search engine. A **search engine** is software that indexes, or organizes, a portion of the information available on the Web. That organization of information focuses on text supplied within the indexed Web pages themselves. Some search engines use whatever text they find near the top of your Web page. Others utilize special HTML tags to define keywords and a description for the page. Meta tags are one category of these special HTML tags.

A **meta tag** can contain keywords or a description of the content of the page. Recall that HTML tags have the form <tag-name> and that some HTML tags can contain keyword-value pairs in the form keyword=value. Meta tags are of this variety. Most meta tags have the format

<META name="name of meta tag" content= "descriptive content for meta tag">

and are not case-sensitive with respect to the tag name or keywords. By appropriately organizing the content of your Web page and inserting some of these tags, you increase the likelihood that users of search engines will more readily locate your site.

Modifying HTML Code on the HTML Sheet

Not all search engines use the same information from your Web pages for indexing. Most search engines will retrieve the text contained in the Web page title. Some search engines use information within meta tags and some only use text near the top of your page. You may use meta tags for the search engines that support their use and insert a comment for those that do not.

A comment in HTML code has the format

<!-- comment text goes here --> with all text between the <!-- and the --> ignored by the browser.

Perform the following steps to modify the HTML code directly in FrontPage to insert meta tags and comments in the Classified Ads Request Web page.

 To Modify HTML Code and Insert Meta Tags

1 **Click the HTML tab. If necessary, scroll toward the top of the Web page until the form <head> tag displays. Position the insertion point at the beginning of the line below the <title> tag.**

The HTML source for the Classified Ads Request Web page displays (Figure 4-90). Notice that FrontPage automatically includes some meta tags in each Web page it creates. Your tags and HTML code may appear somewhat different.

FIGURE 4-90

2 **Type** `<META name="description" content="Members of Hilltop Community College may place Free Classified Ads at the Web site of Nikki Patrio.">` **and then press the ENTER key.**

The entered meta tag displays (Figure 4-91). The entire meta tag does not display as it extends beyond the right edge of the screen.

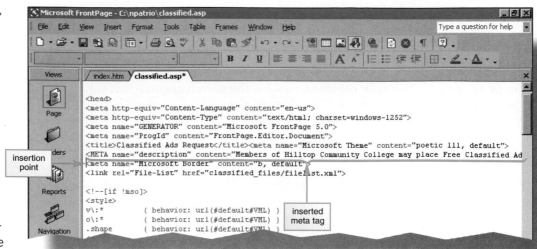

FIGURE 4-91

3 **Type** `<META name="keywords" content="Free Classified Ads, Hilltop Community College, Nikki Patrio">` **and then press the ENTER key.**

The meta tag for keywords for this Web page displays (Figure 4-92). When using meta tags, use distinctive keywords for each Web page and limit the number to approximately ten keywords.

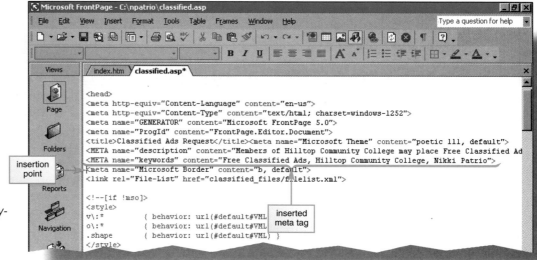

FIGURE 4-92

4 **Type** `<!-- Members of Hilltop Community College may place Free Classified Ads at the Web site of Nikki Patrio.-->` **and then press the ENTER key.**

The entered comment displays (Figure 4-93). Comments are for information only and do not represent executable code statements.

FIGURE 4-93

5 **Click the Save button on the Standard toolbar and then click the Normal tab.**

The HTML view closes and the Web page displays in Normal view (Figure 4-94).

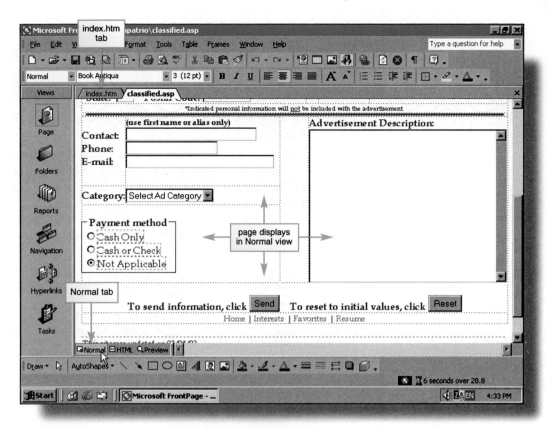

FIGURE 4-94

You have modified the Web page so that it may be indexed by search engines more effectively. Given that the title already in place is Classified Ads Request, a search using an engine that supports meta tags would return a search result such as:

> **Classified Ads Request**
> Members of Hilltop Community College may place Free Classified Ads at the Web site of Nikki Patrio.
> http://www.hcc.edu/~npatrio/classified.asp

You have provided descriptive text and keywords for search engines that may index the Web site. The Web site is not indexed, however, and will not display on any search until you manually submit the page to a search engine, requesting that the page be indexed, or until a search engine that looks for Web sites (usually called a **spider** or **crawler**) finds the site and indexes it automatically.

Another simple and obvious means to publicize the existence of the new Classified Ads Request page is to provide a link from the Web site Home page. Visitors to the Web site, whether new or returning, will be more aware of the new page if the hyperlink for it is obvious. Perform the steps on the next page to add a link for the new page to the Home page.

HTML Code

For resources to help you better understand HTML, visit the FrontPage 2000 More About Web page (scsite.com/fp2002/more.htm) and then click HTML.

Quick Reference

For a table that lists how to complete tasks covered in this book using the mouse, menu, shortcut menu, and keyboard, see the Quick Reference Summary at the back of this book or visit the Shelly Cashman Series Office XP Web page (scsite.com/offxp/qr.htm) and then click Microsoft FrontPage 2002.

TO ADD A HYPERLINK TO A PAGE

1 Click the tab, index.htm, at the top of the Page pane to display the Home page.

2 Position the insertion point below the last line of text that begins, You may send. If necessary, click the Center button on the Formatting toolbar.

3 Click the Bold button on the Formatting toolbar and then type Try my free Classified Ads!

4 Drag through the words Classified Ads. Click the Insert Hyperlink button on the Standard toolbar. When the Insert Hyperlink dialog box displays, click the file classified.asp (open) and then click the OK button. Click the page to dese-lect the hyperlink. Click the Save button on the Standard toolbar.

The Home page displays a hyperlink to the Classified Ads Request page (Figure 4-95).

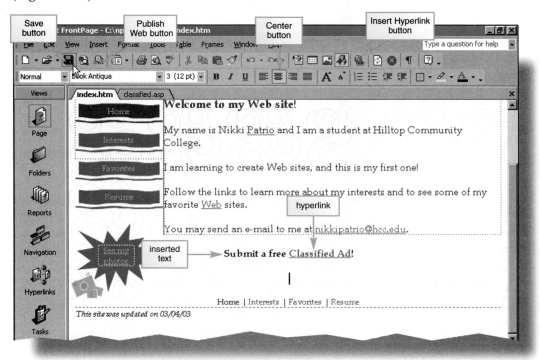

FIGURE 4-95

After saving the Web page on disk, you should publish the changes to the web.

Publishing Changes to a FrontPage Web

In Project 3, changes to Nikki's Web site were published on the World Wide Web. Because you have made additional changes to the FrontPage web, you must publish the FrontPage web again.

When you publish a FrontPage web that has been published before, FrontPage will add and update only those parts of the web that are new or have changed since the last time the web was published. This reduces the amount of data transfer that takes place and speeds the publishing of a web with many folders, Web pages, and files.

Perform the following steps to publish changes to a FrontPage web. Be sure to use your own URL or an error will occur. If you do not know what URL to use, ask your instructor.

TO PUBLISH CHANGES TO A FRONTPAGE WEB

1 Click the Publish Web button on the Standard toolbar.

2 When the Publish Web dialog box displays, verify that the Publish to location is correct.

3 Click the Publish button.

4 Click the Done button.

To view the Classified Ads Request page, type `http://www.hcc.edu/~npatrio/classified.asp` (or use your own URL) in any browser and then press the ENTER key. Be sure to test the hyperlinks to the other pages in the web and from the Home page to the Classified Ads Request page.

Quitting FrontPage

When you have published the changes to Nikki's web, you can quit Microsoft FrontPage. Perform the following step to quit FrontPage.

TO QUIT FRONTPAGE

1 Click the Close button on the FrontPage title bar.

The FrontPage window closes and the Windows desktop displays.

More About

Microsoft Certification

The Microsoft Office User Specialist (MOUS) Certification program provides an opportunity for you to obtain a valuable industry credential — proof that you have the FrontPage 2002 skills required by employers. For more information, see Appendix E or visit the Shelly Cashman Series MOUS Web page at scsite.com/offxp/cert.htm.

CASE PERSPECTIVE SUMMARY

Nikki was impressed to find that creating an interactive form was so easy with FrontPage. Although she liked the various options for form handlers, she was particularly pleased with the simplicity of adding the responses to a database. She thinks that the capability of influencing search engines by viewing and entering HTML code directly in FrontPage is fascinating. Now that data can flow into her Web site, she is eager to learn how to extract and use that information.

Project Summary

Having completed Project 4, you now are ready to create interactive forms and use them to obtain information from the users of your Web pages. In this project, you learned about forms and form handlers, including different types of form handlers. You learned about the Get and Post methods of sending form data and the format in which form data is sent to a server for processing. You learned how to create nested tables to help position form elements. You learned how to insert form fields such as option buttons, text boxes, text areas, drop-down list boxes, and check boxes in a form. You learned how to adjust the properties of the different types of form fields. You learned how to adjust the properties of the form and specify the form handler to be used to process the data from the form. Finally, you learned how to insert meta tags to help identify the page to Web search engines.

What You Should Know

Having completed this project, you now should be able to perform the following tasks:

▸ Add a Hyperlink to a Page *(FP 4.68)*

▸ Add a Table to a Web Page *(FP 4.15)*

▸ Add and Rename a Web Page in Folders View *(FP 4.12)*

▸ Assign a Label to an Option Button Form Field *(FP 4.50)*

▸ Assign Text as a Label for a Check Box *(FP 4.31)*

▸ Copy and Paste a Link Bar from a Web Page *(FP 4.16)*

▸ Copy and Paste a Page Banner *(FP 4.14)*

▸ Create a Nested Table *(FP 4.38)*

▸ Display Files in Folders View *(FP 4.11)*

▸ Hide the Folder List Pane *(FP 4.18)*

▸ Insert a Check Box Form Field in a Form *(FP 4.29)*

▸ Insert a Drop-Down List Box Form Field in a Form *(FP 4.41)*

▸ Insert a Form in a Table *(FP 4.19)*

▸ Insert a Group Box Form Field in a Form *(FP 4.47)*

▸ Insert a Line Drawing AutoShape in a Table *(FP 4.35)*

▸ Insert a Table in a Form *(FP 4.20)*

▸ Insert a Text Area Form Field in a Form *(FP 4.54)*

▸ Insert Additional Check Box Form Fields *(FP 4.34)*

▸ Insert Additional Text Box Form Fields *(FP 4.27)*

▸ Insert and Align Elements in a Nested Table *(FP 4.39)*

▸ Insert Option Button Form Fields in a Group Box *(FP 4.49)*

▸ Insert Text Box Form Fields in a Form *(FP 4.23)*

▸ Insert Text in a Form *(FP 4.21)*

▸ Modify a Page Title in Folders View *(FP 4.13)*

▸ Modify Form Properties and Set a Form Handler *(FP 4.61)*

▸ Modify HTML Code and Insert Meta Tags *(FP 4.65)*

▸ Modify the Properties of a Check Box Form Field *(FP 4.32)*

▸ Modify the Properties of a Push Button Form Field *(FP 4.58)*

▸ Modify the Properties of a Text Area Form Field *(FP 4.56)*

▸ Modify the Properties of a Text Box Form Field *(FP 4.25)*

▸ Modify the Properties of an Option Button Form Field *(FP 4.51)*

▸ Modify the Title of a Drop-Down List Box Form Field *(FP 4.43)*

▸ Modify the Title of a Group Box Form Field *(FP 4.48)*

▸ Publish Changes to a FrontPage Web *(FP 4.69)*

▸ Quit FrontPage *(FP 4.69)*

▸ Start FrontPage and Open an Existing Web *(FP 4.10)*

Learn It Online

Instructions: To complete the Learn It Online exercises, start your browser, click the Address bar, and then enter scsite.com/offxp/exs.htm. When the Office XP Learn It Online page displays, follow the instructions in the exercises below.

1 Project Reinforcement TF, MC, and SA

Below FrontPage Project 4, click the Project Reinforcement link. Print the quiz by clicking Print on the File menu. Answer each question. Write your first and last name at the top of each page, and then hand in the printout to your instructor.

2 Flash Cards

Below FrontPage Project 4, click the Flash Cards link. When Flash Cards displays, read the instructions. Type 20 (or a number specified by your instructor) in the Number of Playing Cards text box, type your name in the Name text box, and then click the Flip Card button. When the flash card displays, read the question and then click the Answer box arrow to select an answer. Flip through Flash Cards. Click Print on the File menu to print the last flash card if your score is 15 (75%) correct or greater and then hand it in to your instructor. If your score is less than 15 (75%) correct, then redo this exercise by clicking the Replay button.

3 Practice Test

Below FrontPage Project 4, click the Practice Test link. Answer each question, enter your first and last name at the bottom of the page, and then click the Grade Test button. When the graded practice test displays on your screen, click Print on the File menu to print a hard copy. Continue to take practice tests until you score 80% or better. Hand in a printout of the final practice test to your instructor.

4 Who Wants to Be a Computer Genius?

Below FrontPage Project 4, click the Computer Genius link. Read the instructions, enter your first and last name at the bottom of the page, and then click the Play button. Hand in your score to your instructor.

5 Wheel of Terms

Below FrontPage Project 4, click the Wheel of Terms link. Read the instructions, and then enter your first and last name and your school name. Click the Play button. Hand in your score to your instructor.

6 Crossword Puzzle Challenge

Below FrontPage Project 4, click the Crossword Puzzle Challenge link. Read the instructions, and then enter your first and last name. Click the Play button. Work the crossword puzzle. When you are finished, click the Submit button. When the crossword puzzle redisplays, click the Print button. Hand in the printout.

7 Tips and Tricks

Below FrontPage Project 4, click the Tips and Tricks link. Click a topic that pertains to Project 4. Right-click the information and then click Print on the shortcut menu. Construct a brief example of what the information relates to in FrontPage to confirm you understand how to use the tip or trick. Hand in the example and printed information.

8 Newsgroups

Below FrontPage Project 4, click the Newsgroups link. Click a topic that pertains to Project 4. Print three comments. Hand in the comments to your instructor.

9 Expanding Your Horizons

Below FrontPage Project 4, click the Articles for Microsoft FrontPage link. Click a topic that pertains to Project 4. Print the information. Construct a brief example of what the information relates to in FrontPage to confirm you understand the contents of the article. Hand in the example and printed information to your instructor.

10 Search Sleuth

Below FrontPage Project 4, click the Search Sleuth link. To search for a term that pertains to this project, select a term below the Project 4 title and then use the Google search engine at google.com (or any major search engine) to display and print two Web pages that present information on the term. Hand in the printouts to your instructor.

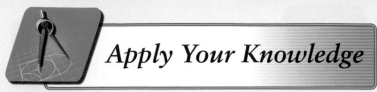

Apply Your Knowledge

1 Sending Form Results with E-mail

Instructions: Start FrontPage. Open the web, Starting, that you modified in Project 3. If you did not complete this exercise for Project 3, see your instructor for a copy of the required files.

1. If necessary, double-click the file, serv01.htm, in the Folder List pane to display The Starting Block Service 1 page in Page view.

2. Select the text that begins, This is a brief description, through the text that ends, Description of capability 3, and then press the DELETE key. Click Insert on the menu bar, point to Form, and then click Form on the Form submenu. When the Form displays, type To receive a copy of our weekly e-mail sports newsletter, please provide the following information. and then press the ENTER key.

3. Type Name: followed by a space. Click Insert on the menu bar, point to Form, and then click Textbox on the Form submenu. Right-click the text box and then click Form Field Properties on the shortcut menu. When the Text Box Properties dialog box displays, type Name in the Name text box, type 40 in the Width in characters text box, and then type 1 in the Tab order text box. Click the Validate button. When the Text Box Validation dialog box displays, click Required in the Data length area and then type Name in the Display name area. Click the OK button in the Text Box Validation dialog box. Click the OK button in the Text Box Properties dialog box.

4. Press the RIGHT ARROW key to deselect the text box and to position the insertion point after the text box. Hold down the SHIFT key and then press the ENTER key. Type E-mail: and then click Insert on the menu bar. Point to Form and then click Textbox on the Form submenu. Right-click the text box and then click Form Field Properties on the shortcut menu. When the Text Box Properties dialog box displays, type Email in the Name text box, type 40 in the Width in characters text box, and then type 2 in the Tab order text box. Click the Validate button. When the Text Box Validation dialog box displays, click Required in the Data length area and then type E-mail address in the Display name area. Click the OK button in both dialog boxes.

5. Press the RIGHT ARROW key to deselect the text box and to position the insertion point after the text box. Press the ENTER key. Click the Center button on the Formatting toolbar. Position the insertion point between the Submit and Reset buttons. Press the SPACEBAR five times.

6. Right-click the form and then click Form Properties on the shortcut menu. When the Form Properties dialog box displays, drag through the default file name in the File name text box in the Where to store results area and then press the DELETE key. Type newsletter@startingblock.com in the E-mail address text box (you may substitute your own e-mail address). Click the Options button. When the Saving Results dialog box displays, type Subscribe to newsletter in the Subject line text box. Verify that the Form field name check box is not selected for this text box. Type Email in the Reply-to-line text box. Verify that the Form field name check box is selected for this text box. Click the OK button in the Saving Results dialog box. Click the OK button in the Form Properties dialog box. If a Microsoft FrontPage dialog box displays, click the No button.

7. Double-click the page banner. When the Page Banner Properties dialog box displays, drag through the text in the Page banner text box. Type Get Newsletter in the text box. Click the OK button. Click the Save button on the Standard toolbar to save your changes. If a Confirm Save dialog box displays, click the Yes button.

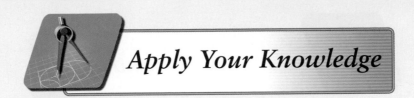

Apply Your Knowledge

8. Double-click the file, services.htm, in the Folder List pane to display The Starting Block Services page in Page view. Select the text that begins, Comment: Write a, through the text that ends, description pages., and then press the DELETE key twice. Drag to select the hyperlink, Name of service 1 and then type Subscribe to Newsletter. Drag to select the text, Description of service 1 ..., and then type Get our weekly sports newsletter to keep up to date on sporting events and our sporting goods sales. Click the Save button on the Standard toolbar to save your changes.

9. Click the Preview tab to preview the Web page. When you have finished, click the Normal tab.

10. Print the Web pages. Quit FrontPage and hand in the printouts to your instructor.

FIGURE 4-96

In the Lab

1 Adding a Frequently Asked Questions (FAQ) Page to a Web Site

Problem: The Sweet Tooth often gets e-mail messages asking questions about its products and services. To reduce the number of e-mails asking common questions, the owner wants to add a Frequently Asked Questions (FAQ) page to the site.

Instructions: Perform the following tasks.

1. Open The Sweet Tooth web that you modified in Project 3. If you did not complete that exercise for Project 3, see your instructor for a copy of the required files.
2. If necessary, double-click the file, index.htm, to display the Home page in Page view. Scroll down and then select the line that reads, Contact Information. Click Bookmark on the Insert menu. When the Bookmark dialog box displays, click the OK button.
3. Position the insertion point after the word, Sales: and then type sales@sweettooth.com. Select the text and insert an e-mail hyperlink. Save the changes to the Home page.
4. Click the Create a new normal page button arrow on the Standard toolbar and then click Page.
5. When the Page Templates dialog box displays, scroll down, if necessary, and then click the Frequently Asked Questions icon. Click the OK button.
6. Select the bookmarked text, Table of Contents, and then type Frequently Asked Questions as the new text.
7. Select the text for bullet number 1, How do I ...? and then type How do I place an order? as the new hyperlink text. Repeat this process for each of the remaining hyperlinks as listed in Table 4-8.
8. If necessary, scroll down to the bookmark that reads, How do I ... ?, select the text and then type How do I place an order? as the replacement text. Select the text below the bookmark, [This is the answer to the question.] and then type Orders may be placed by mail, phone, fax, or e-mail. See the addresses and phone numbers listed on our Home page. Select the text, Home page, and create a hyperlink to the Home page, index.htm. Repeat this process for each of the remaining bookmarks as listed in Table 4-9.
9. Delete the three lines of text at the bottom of the page that begin, Author information.
10. Save the page as FAQ.htm and add it to the navigation structure below the Home page and to the right of the Products page. Double-click the FAQ page and then double-click the page banner. Type FAQ in the page banner text box and then click OK. Double-click the Link bar on the left side of the page and add a hyperlink to the parent page (Figure 4-97 on page FP 4.76).
11. Preview the changes in your browser. Print the Web page, and then close FrontPage. Write your name on the printout and hand it in to your instructor.

Optional: Perform the following tasks as an additional exercise.

1. In Tasks view, right-click the task, Customize Home Page and then click Mark Complete.
2. Point to New on the File menu and then click Task. Type Add Order Page in the Task name text box. Type your name in the Assigned to list box. Type Create a Web page for online orders. in the Description text box. Click the OK button.
3. Point to Reports on the View menu and then point to Workflow. Click Publish Status to display the Publish Status report. Right-click the report and then click copy Report on the shortcut menu. Start Word and paste the copied report into a new document. Print the document and hand it in to your instructor.

In the Lab

Table 4-8   Replacement Hyperlink Text

BULLET NUMBER	HYPERLINK TEXT	NEW HYPERLINK TEXT
1	How do I ...?	How do I place an order?
2	Where can I find ...?	Where can I find sugar-free items?
3	Why doesn't ... ?	Why can't I place an order online?
4	Who is ... ?	Who created the Sweet Tooth?
5	What is ... ?	What is The Sweet Tooth Candy Festival?
6	When is ... ?	When is The Sweet Tooth Candy Festival?

Table 4-9   Replacement Bookmarks and Text

OLD BOOKMARK TEXT	NEW BOOKMARK TEXT	TEXT BELOW BOOKMARK	HYPERLINKED TEXT
How do I ...?	How do I place an order?	Orders may be placed by mail, phone, fax, or e-mail. See the addresses and phone numbers listed on our Home page.	Home page Hyperlinked to index.htm
Where can I find ...?	Where can I find sugar-free items?	See Sugar-Free Items on our Price Sheet.	Sugar-Free Items Hyperlinked to bookmark prices.htm#SUGAR FREE ITEMS
Why doesn't ... ?	Why can't I place an order online?	We're working on it! Our Web pages are new, but we hope to have online order processing soon.	
Who is ... ?	Who created The Sweet Tooth?	Ruth and Marge Smith! As sisters, they shared a common sweet tooth while growing up and decided to continue it as a business!	
What is ... ?	What is The Sweet Tooth Candy Festival?	A yearly opportunity for candy inventors to display their delights to the public. Winners of the new candy contest have the opportunity to have their creation produced and marketed by The Sweet Tooth.	
When is ... ?	When is The Sweet Tooth Candy Festival?	Sponsored by The Sweet Tooth, the festival is held annually over the Labor Day weekend in September.	

(continued)

In the Lab

Adding a Frequently Asked Questions (FAQ) Page to a Web Site *(continued)*

FIGURE 4-97

In the Lab

2 Adding a Feedback Form to a Web

Problem: You would like to know something about visitors to your summer fun Personal web and receive their comments about your site, but you do not want the comments to be public. You decide to incorporate a Feedback page, in which visitors can make private comments.

Instructions: Perform the following tasks.

1. Open the web, funsites, that you modified in Project 3. If you did not complete that exercise for Project 3, see your instructor for a copy of the required files.
2. Create a new normal page using the Feedback Form page template.
3. Select the text above the form and then type `Tell me about your favorite Web sites and summer fun activities. See if your favorites can make the Top Ten list! Also, you can comment on the links you see on this Web site.`
4. In the line of text that begins, What about us do you, select the word, us, and then type `my Web page` as the replacement text.
5. Right-click the drop-down list box. Select the choice, Company, click the Modify button, and then type `Activity` as the new name. Delete all other choices except Web Site and (Other).
6. In the line of text that begins, Tell us how, select the word, us, and then type me as the replacement text.
7. Delete the three lines of text at the bottom of the page that begin, Author information.
8. Save the Web page as feedback.htm. In Navigation view, add the page below the Home page.
9. Delete the comment component at the top of the page and insert a page banner component. Type `Feedback` as the page banner text (Figure 4-98 on the next page). Save your changes.
10. Print the Feedback and Home Web pages, write your name on the pages and submit them to your instructor.

(continued)

In the Lab

Adding a Feedback Form to a Web *(continued)*

FIGURE 4-98

In the Lab

3 Adding a Guest Book to a Web

Problem: Your vacation web provides information about your vacation to visitors, but does not provide a means of response from them. You would like visitors to be able to discuss their favorite vacation spots. You decide to add a public guest book to your web where visitors can make comments and read comments made by others.

Instructions: Using the vacation web you modified in Project 3, perform the following tasks. If you did not complete this exercise in Project 3, see your instructor for a copy of the required files.

1. Open the Home page for the web and position the insertion point after the graphic hyperlink that reads, Vacation Pictures. Press the ENTER key.
2. Type Please visit my Guest Book page and share your comments and favorite vacation spots.
3. Create a new normal page using the Guest Book page template.
4. On the new page, delete the text, We'd like to know what you think about our web site. Select the word, we, in the text that begins, Please leave your. Type I and then position the insertion point to the right of the text area. Press the ENTER key.
5. Type URL of your favorite vacation spot: followed by a space. Insert a text box and modify the form field properties. Type URL in the Name text box and 40 in the Width in characters text box.
6. Delete the three lines of text at the bottom of the page that begin, Author information. Save the page as guestbook.htm. Click the Navigation icon. In Navigation view, add the page below the Vacation Pictures page.
7. Double-click the Guest book page icon to display the Guest book page in Page view. Delete the comment component at the top of the page and insert a page banner component. Type Guest Book as the page banner text (see Figure 4-99).
8. After the text that ends, with other visitors., press the ENTER key and then type Back to followed by a space. Copy and paste the Link bar component from the Home page. Modify the Link bar to link to the Home page. Save your changes.
9. Open the Home page in Page view. Select the text, Guest Book, and make a hyperlink to the Guest Book page.
10. Save the Web pages and then preview the pages in your browser. Print the Web pages, write your name on the pages, and hand them in to your instructor.
11. Close your browser and quit FrontPage.

Optional: Perform the following tasks as an additional exercise.

1. Open the Guest Book page, if necessary. Modify the theme to use a different background. You may use the file, travntbk.jpg, from the Data Disk. See the inside back cover of this book for instrucions for downloading the Data Disk or see your instructor for information on accessing the files required in this book. Save the new theme as Travel Notebook.
2. Insert a 6 by 3 Table before the page banner. Drag and drop the items on the page (page banner, horizontal rule, etc.) into respective rows in the table, only in the second column. Leave the first column empty. Adjust the width of the first column to position the elements away from the left edge of the page.
3. Print the completed page and hand it in to your instructor.

In the Lab

Adding a Guest Book to a Web *(continued)*

FIGURE 4-99

Cases and Places

The difficulty of these case studies varies:
▶ are the least difficult; ▶▶ are more difficult; and ▶▶▶ are the most difficult.

1 ▶ In the previous project, you modified your resume on the Web. Now, you would like to receive suggestions for improvement as well as responses from potential employers. Add a new page with a feedback form and a hyperlink from the resume to the new page. Verify all hyperlinks in the web and repair any broken hyperlinks that appear on the Broken hyperlinks report. Have the results sent to your e-mail address.

2 ▶ The web for the classical literature course you modified in Project 3 has your reviews for the books in the course. Allow class members or other visitors to post their reviews by adding a discussion forum to your web.

3 ▶▶ Add a new page to the web you created for your grandparents' 50th wedding anniversary. Use a form to collect family memories and save the results to a database. On the new page, collect the visitor's name, relationship (family or friend) to your grandparents, and have a text area for their comments. Allow them to enter contact information, such as a mailing address, telephone number, or e-mail address.

4 ▶▶ Modify the intramural basketball Web page you updated in Project 3. Add a discussion forum for fans to comment on the latest game. Add a form to collect names and e-mail addresses for addition to a notification list for upcoming games. Store the collected information in a database. Verify the external hyperlinks added earlier and replace any hyperlinks that appear on the Broken hyperlinks report.

5 ▶▶▶ Modify the departmental Web page you created for your school in the previous project to include a course evaluation page using a form. Use drop-down list boxes to allow students to select the course, section, and term. Use option buttons for class standing, expected grade, whether the course was required, and whether the department is their major area. Present a list of evaluation questions or statements and option buttons to determine the student's response. Provide a text area for general comments and record the results to a database. Use nested tables to help control positioning of elements in the form.

Microsoft FrontPage 2002

Using Frames to Display Database Results in Web Pages

You will have mastered the material in this project when you can:

O B J E C T I V E S

- Describe frames pages and explain how they work
- Import files into an existing FrontPage web
- Use the Database Results Wizard
- Use a custom SQL query
- Use a frames page template
- Save a frames page
- Set an existing Web page as the initial page in a frame
- Modify the size of a frame
- Create a new Web page for the initial page in a frame
- Modify the properties of a frame
- Modify the properties of a frames page
- Create hyperlinks to pages in a frame
- Create a hyperlink to a whole page
- Display the No Frames view
- Print framed Web pages

Winning Web Page Design

Imaginative and Impressive

Working at Ericsson's Research Triangle Park (RTP), a challenging initial assignment for a new media architect was to assist more than one thousand Ericsson employees share information within the company and with the rest of the world as quickly as possible. Such an undertaking would have been overwhelming to most individuals. Without missing a beat, however, this architect seized the challenge, utilizing FrontPage Web development skills to complete the task.

Swedish-based Ericsson is a world-leading supplier of telecommunications and data communications equipment, offering advanced communications solutions for mobile and fixed networks, as well as consumer products. Ericsson has more than 100,000 employees, representation in 140 countries, and the world's largest customer base in the telecommunications field. Ericsson connects nearly 40 percent of the world's mobile callers.

Its largest single market is the United States, where demand for its mobile telephones and cellular systems has driven the company's profits skyward. European countries account for 50 percent of the company's net sales.

The RTP site supports Ericsson's worldwide workforce in various business units, including research and development, quality assurance, sales, marketing, and human resources. Employees use Microsoft Office applications and access the intranet to collaborate on projects, obtain benefits information, manage deadlines, project sales, and develop marketing strategies.

The original intranet lacked organization and had limited capabilities. Employees could not perform a global search and replace or a global spell check, so verifying information or correcting data, such as an employee's new telephone number, had to be done manually, page by page. Navigational links were difficult to verify and individual pages were unstructured.

FrontPage was the obvious software to resolve these difficulties, particularly because the employees were familiar with Microsoft Office applications. A new FrontPage web was created, followed by moving the root directory for the existing site into FrontPage.

Using FrontPage to create the intranet made it possible for a single architect to produce the initial custom theme in four hours, using unique background, graphics, and templates that reflected Ericsson's image and mission.

The new intranet with 2,000 pages resulted in less than half the number of pages of the original intranet. Part of this reduction occurred because employees used FrontPage to sort files and eliminate duplicate pages. It contains tables and frames resembling those you will create in Project 5.

Each RTP business unit posted its respective information. Training was minimal if the Web administrators already were familiar with Microsoft Office applications. These employees claim they now can create Web content up to 50 percent more quickly using FrontPage instead of the former system.

Utilizing this project's focus of creating frames, in addition to the skills you have mastered in the previous assignments, will enable you to develop impressive and professional looking Web sites quickly and precisely.

Microsoft FrontPage 2002

Using Frames to Display Database Results in Web Pages

PROJECT
5

CASE PERSPECTIVE

Students at Hilltop Community College can visit Nikki Patrio's Web site and place free classified advertisements, which are stored in a database. With her Web site almost complete, the only remaining item on her task list is to create pages that display results from the database to the user. Nikki plans to have a separate page for each of the categories of advertisements (For Sale, Housing, Wanted, and Free). She wants to be sure she does not include too many hyperlinks on her Home page and does not want to confuse her users by directing them to many different pages.

You explain that creating pages to retrieve information and display portions of that information to her users will be easy using FrontPage. You also assure Nikki that a simple solution to including too many links on her home page is to use the single hyperlink for classified ads on her Home page. From the Home page, she can direct users to a frames page that will allow them to place and view advertisements. When viewing a frames page, users will have the feeling of viewing only a single page with an area that changes depending on the action desired.

Introduction

As you learned in Project 4, Web pages increasingly use forms and other methods to allow users to interact with the Web pages and provide data that can be collected and stored for future use. A major reason to collect data from users is to organize the data and then allow other users to view it. In creating the Classified Ads Request page, for example, you allowed users to enter classified advertisements in a form that submitted that data to an Access database. In Project 5, you will create Web pages that can retrieve and display the data to users who want to browse through the classified advertisements.

Typically, a Web page will display a particular view of stored data to a user, not all of the data stored in the database. A **view** is a subset of data presented in a specific context. A view arranges the data in some order and can make only certain fields visible; however, the physical organization of the database is not affected. Each particular view of data often is presented on a single Web page. A user might request to see only those classified ads with free items. The view of the data would define which ads are appropriate to display on the page.

Up to this point, you have created single Web pages with links to other single Web pages. When a user views a single Web page, the page display fills the entire browser window. Clicking a link to a different Web page replaces the previous Web page in the browser window.

Using frames gives you the ability to divide the browser window into multiple regions, or panes. A **frame** is an independent region within a browser window that can act independently of other regions in the window. Each frame can be given a unique URL, so it can load information independently of the other frames, and a unique name, so it can be targeted by other URLs. Each frame also can be set to resize dynamically if the user changes the window's size, or can have its sizing disabled, ensuring a constant frame size.

Frames provide greater flexibility in Web page design. With frames, you can display several Web pages in the same browser window, with each Web page displaying in its own frame. For example, if the pages in a Web site share many of the same links, creating and maintaining these links for each page involves a lot of duplication. With frames, you can create a Web page to display the common links in one frame and display the linked target Web pages in another frame. Some typical uses of frames include: displaying a table of contents consisting of hyperlinks in one frame and displaying the corresponding Web pages in another; placing a list of products for sale in one frame and displaying the accompanying descriptions and details in another; and placing a list of vocabulary words in one frame and displaying their definitions in another.

With frames, a Web page author can place elements the user always should see, such as copyright notices and title graphics, in a static frame that does not change. As the user navigates through the site, the static frame's contents remain fixed, even as new pages display in adjoining frames. Placing frames side by side also allows a user to enter a query and view the answer in the same browser window, with one frame holding the query form and another displaying the results. You also can place hyperlinks for selecting different views of data in one frame, with the selected view of the data in another.

Although most Web browsers support frames, some users of your site may have browsers that do not support frames or may prefer a nonframe version. Developers of sites that use frames often create an alternative set of pages without frames to display to those users.

Project Five — Using Frames to Display Database Results

In this project, you will learn how to create a view of data from a database and then display that view in a framed Web page. Microsoft FrontPage provides a Database Results Wizard that simplifies the process of defining the view of the data and displaying those database results into a Web page. You will learn how to query the database using a custom SQL query. You then will learn how to create frames and display Web pages within a frame, including those providing a view of database results.

Creating and Using Frames

Creating framed Web pages is more complex than creating regular pages without frames. To create framed Web pages, you first create a frames page in HTML. A **frames page**, also called a *frame definition file* or a *frameset document*, contains the layout of the frames on the Web page and specifies an initial Web page to display in each frame. To create a frames page, you use a combination of three tags: <FRAMESET>, <FRAME>, and <NOFRAME>. A **frameset** is used to define the layout of the frames when displayed on the screen. A pair of <FRAMESET> tags contains the content and structure of each frame. Within each pair of <FRAMESET> tags, the <FRAME> tag defines what Web page content displays in each frameset. A pair of <NOFRAMES> tags is used to specify alternate text that displays on the page if a user's browser doesn't support frames.

To facilitate this process, Microsoft FrontPage includes several ready-to-use frame templates, each of which contains a variety of frames of various sizes. Recall from Project 1 that a template is one or more Web pages that have been organized and formatted with a basic framework of content on which new Web pages can be built. You can select from one of the templates and customize it to suit your needs — and even save the customized version as a new template. In addition, you can resize the existing frames in the template or add new frames using the mouse and/or special key combinations.

In this project, you will learn how to create a frames page to display the classified adverstisements results pages (Figures 5-1a through 5-1g). The pages use frames to display the Place New Ad request form, views of the classified advertisements retrieved from the database, as well as a common page banner and common hyperlinks. Before you begin creating the results pages, however, you should familiarize yourself with some important concepts and definitions relating to frames.

(a) Home Page

(b) Classified Ads Frames Web Page (initial display)

FIGURE 5-1

(c) Place New Ad Web Page

(d) For Sale Web Page

(e) Housing Web Page

(f) Wanted Web Page

(g) Free Web Page

FIGURE 5-1 (continued)

Using Frames Pages

As previously noted, a frames page contains the layout of the frames on the Web page and specifies an initial Web page to display in each frame. The frames page itself contains little or no visible content; instead, it serves as a container that holds two or more frames and specifies which pages to display and how to display them. For example, in a frame page with two frames, a table of contents page may be set as the initial page for the left frame, while another initial page displays in the right frame. When the user clicks a hyperlink in the left frame, the selected Web page displays in the right frame, replacing the initial page in that frame. The table of contents displayed in the left frame remains the same. The user can select another hyperlink from the table of contents and the corresponding Web page replaces the page currently in the right frame.

Designing the Frames Page

In this project, the frames page allows users to navigate easily between the form page used to place a new ad and the four database results pages that display views of the classified ads by category. The frames page — which is named the Classified Ads main page — includes three frames, shown in Figures 5-2a and 5-2b.

(a)

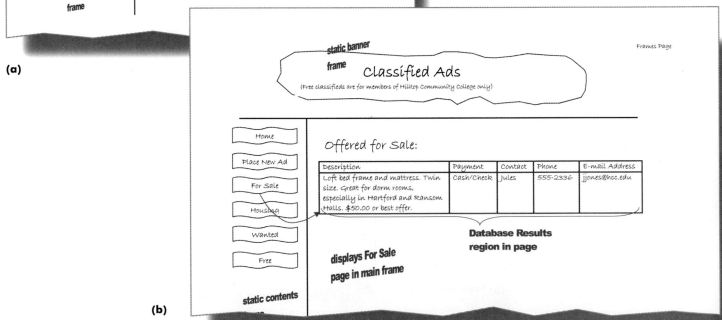

(b)

FIGURE 5-2

The top frame contains a common banner heading similar to the one used with other pages in the web. The contents of the top banner frame will remain the same, or static, while the frames page is displayed.

The left frame contains a table of contents type list of hyperlinks to the Place a New Ad form page form and the various database results Web pages. The contents of the left frame will remain static while the frames page is displayed. At the top of the left contents frame is a hyperlink to the Home page. Clicking this hyperlink will display the Home page, replacing the entire frames Web page.

The right, or main, frame initially will contain a welcome page with instructions for the user. The contents of this frame will change depending on which hyperlink a user clicks in the left frame.

The Web page design in Figure 5-2b illustrates the general design used for each database results Web page. Altogether, nine Web pages will be used to implement this design: the frames page, the three initial Web pages, shown in Figure 5-2a, four pages for views of the database results, and one form page for collection of data. With the design of the page completed, you now can implement the design using Microsoft FrontPage.

Using Frames in a FrontPage Web

Implementing frames in a FrontPage Web requires the creation and coordination of links between multiple Web pages. As previously noted, you must first create a frames page. The frames page contains the HTML tags describing the number, sizes, and properties of the frames and defining the initial page to display in each frame. The frames page itself usually has little other HTML content; instead, it serves as a container that defines how the frames and the initial pages display in the browser window.

Next, you must create or add one complete HTML document for each frame in the frames page. The Web page for each frame is the initial page that users first see in each frame when they display the frames page.

Finally, you must create hyperlinks to each target Web page that can display in a frame. Typically, you would include these hyperlinks within one of the initial pages, so that users can click a hyperlink to view the target page. Each hyperlink contains tags that define the URL of the target Web page and, if needed, tags that define the frame in which the page should display, referred to as a **target frame**. If desired, you can opt to specify a default target frame for all links within a particular frame by including a special base target tag in the header section of the frames page.

When deciding how to target Web pages when using frames, you have several choices. You can have the Web page replace the currently displayed Web page in the same frame or you can target the page to display in a different frame. You also can have the Web page use the entire browser window. Finally, you can have the Web page display in a new browser window, keeping the original browser window's contents intact.

You can create the initial pages and target pages before or during the creation of the frames page. With FrontPage, the frames page template has buttons that allow you to select an existing page or create a new page as the initial page to display in a frame.

Importing Files into an Existing FrontPage Web

Using frames in a Web site can involve a great amount of effort. Because the content of each frame is a complete Web page, if you are the only person performing the development work, you will have to create the frames page, the initial page for each frame, and possibly any target pages for which you have hyperlinks in the initial pages.

Importing Files

You can import an image simply by dragging the image from another Windows application to the Navigation or Folders view. You also may copy a file in Windows Explorer and paste it into the Folder List or the Contents pane while in Folders view.

The Classified Ads section of the Web site in this project uses nine different Web pages within frames. In order for you to complete the project within a reasonable amount of time, four of the nine Web pages are available on the Data Disk. See the inside back cover of this book for instructions for downloading the Data Disk or see your instructor for information on accessing the files required in this book.

You first will import the four files from the Data Disk into the FrontPage web. You then will create a new page for one of the database results views. Finally, you will create a frames page with three frames, define the initial pages for the frames in the frames page, and modify an existing page for use in a frame.

Perform the following steps to start FrontPage and then open the FrontPage web from Project 4. If you did not complete Project 4, see your instructor for a copy.

TO START FRONTPAGE AND OPEN AN EXISTING WEB

1 Click the Start button on the taskbar. Point to Programs on the Start menu.

2 Click Microsoft FrontPage on the Programs submenu.

3 Click the Open button arrow on the Standard toolbar.

4 Click Open Web on the Open menu. When the Open Web dialog box displays, if necessary, click the Look in box arrow and select the folder location where you saved the web for Project 4 (e.g., C:\npatrio).

5 Click the Open button. If necessary, display the Folder List and then double-click index.htm in the Folder List pane.

The existing web is opened, and the file, index.htm, displays in Page view (Figure 5-3).

The FrontPage Help System

Need help? It is no further than the Ask a Question box in the upper-right corner of the window. Click the box that contains the text, Type a question for help (Figure 5-3), type help and then press the ENTER key. FrontPage will respond with a list of items you can click to learn about obtaining help on any FrontPage-related topic. To find out what is new in FrontPage 2002, type what's new in FrontPage in the Ask a Question box.

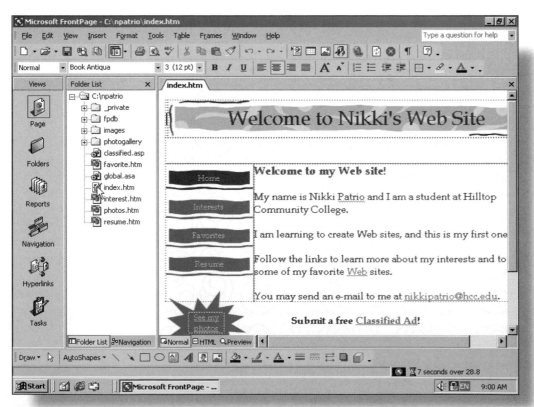

FIGURE 5-3

As you begin developing the Classified Ads section of the Web site, you need to import the four Web pages from the Data Disk into the current FrontPage web. You cannot just copy the files into the web folder, as FrontPage may not recognize and include the pages automatically. You will use the Import command to import existing Web pages into a current web.

Perform the following steps to import existing Web pages into the current FrontPage web.

Steps **To Import Files into an Existing FrontPage Web**

1 **Insert the Data Disk in drive A. Click File on the menu bar and then point to Import.**

The File menu displays with the Import command selected (Figure 5-4).

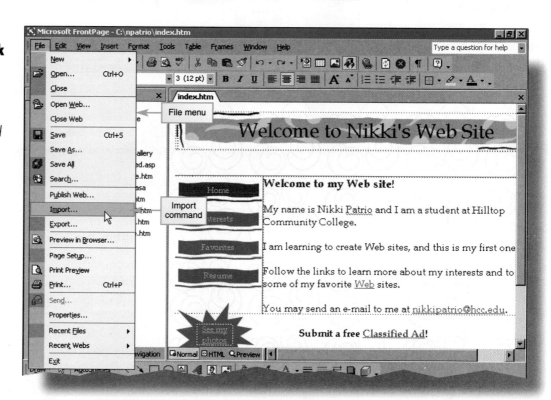

FIGURE 5-4

2 **Click Import. When the Import dialog box displays, point to the Add File button.**

The Import dialog box displays (Figure 5-5). Buttons are available for importing files or entire folders from your local machine or for importing pages from the Web.

FIGURE 5-5

3 **Click the Add File button. When the Add File to Import List dialog box displays, if necessary, click the Look in box arrow and then click 3½ Floppy (A:). If necessary, double-click the Project5 folder. Hold down the CTRL key and select the files ClassAdsBanner.htm, Free.asp, Housing.asp and Wanted.asp. Point to the Open button.**

The Add File to Import List dialog box displays (Figure 5-6). The four selected files in the Project5 folder are highlighted.

FIGURE 5-6

4 **Click the Open button. When the Import dialog box displays, point to the OK button.**

The files to be imported into the web display in the Import dialog box (Figure 5-7).

FIGURE 5-7

5 **Click the OK button. Point to the Create a new normal page button.**

The Import dialog box closes, and the imported files display in the Folder List pane (Figure 5-8).

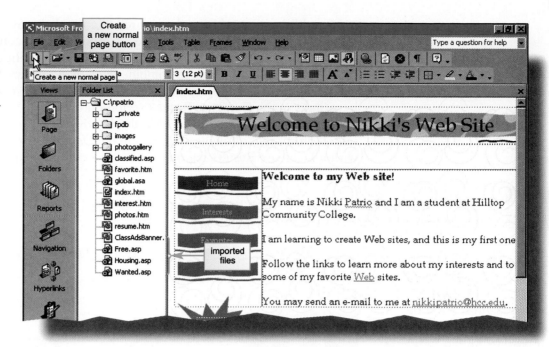

FIGURE 5-8

Figure 5-8 shows the Folder List pane after the existing files have been imported into the current web. Using the Import command, you not only can import Web page files, but also images and other files. By default, all files are imported into the same directory as the Web pages. Once you import the files, you can move files, such as images, to other folders, such as the images folder.

Using the Database Results Wizard

Three of the pages you imported include a Database Results region that was created using the Database Results Wizard. A **Database Results region** is an area on a Web page where data retrieved from a database will display. In this project, the results pages will retrieve and display a subset of data from the advertisements placed in the database by category: for sale, housing, wanted for purchase, or free items. The pages select the appropriate advertisements to display by querying the database with a statement written in SQL.

SQL (pronounced as separate letters, es-que-el), is an abbreviation for Structured Query Language, and is the most widely used language for communicating with a relational database management system. A **relational database management system** (**RDBMS**), such as Microsoft Access, helps users manage data by modelling the data as tables. Each data field is represented by a column and each entry, or record, is represented by a row, in a manner similar to a spreadsheet. Special keywords in the SQL query statement instruct the RDBMS to select the desired columns (fields) of data to display and then display only those rows (records) where a specified field or fields contain specific values.

A SELECT statement defines which columns of data are selected for display. For example, if you wanted to select the Description and Payment columns, you would write the SELECT statement, SELECT Description, Payment. To select all columns in the database, you can use an asterisk in the SELECT statement, SELECT *. Additionally, the WHERE clause is used to limit rows selected to only those containing specific data values. For example, the clause, WHERE (Category='Sell'), limits the selected records to those where the category field contains the value 'Sell'.

In addition to retrieving data stored in a database, SQL can perform other functions. One capability is to create a temporary field constructed from one or more fields from the database and other constant data. In this project, you will create a custom SQL query to combine the e-mail address field and the appropriate HTML code in a temporary field called email, so that e-mail addresses display as hyperlinks in the Database Results region on the page.

An additional page is needed to display the classified advertisements of items for sale. Perform the following steps to use the Database Results Wizard to create a page with a Database Results region containing a custom SQL query.

Steps To Create a Database Results Region and Custom SQL Query

1 **Click the Create a new normal page button. Click Insert on the menu bar, point to Database, and then point to Results on the Database submenu.**

A new normal page is created (Figure 5-9). The Insert menu and the Database submenu display.

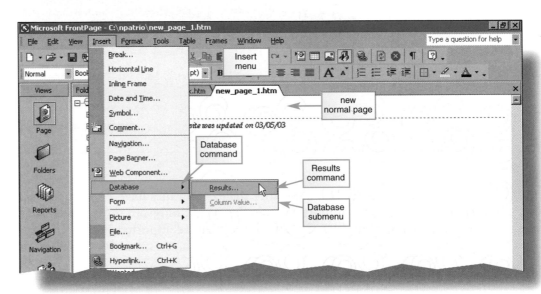

FIGURE 5-9

2 **Click Results. When the Database Results Wizard - Step 1 of 5 dialog box displays, verify that Use an existing database connection is selected and that classified displays in the list box. Point to the Next button.**

The Database Results Wizard - Step 1 of 5 dialog box displays (Figure 5-10). The database connection, classified, represents the database used for data collection in the previous project.

FIGURE 5-10

3 Click the Next button. When the Database Results Wizard - Step 2 of 5 dialog box displays, click Custom query and then point to the Edit button.

The Database Results Wizard - Step 2 of 5 dialog box displays (Figure 5-11). Selecting Custom query allows you to create a custom query using an SQL statement.

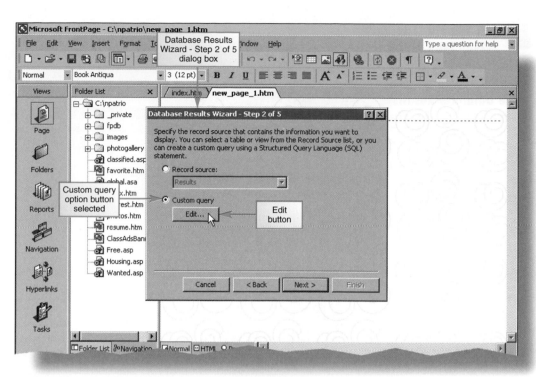

FIGURE 5-11

4 Click the Edit button. When the Custom Query dialog box displays, if necessary, select all of the text in the SQL Statement text area. Type SELECT Description, Payment, Contact, Phone, ('<a href=' & Chr$(34) & 'mailto:' & EMailAddress & Chr$(34) & '>' & EMailAddress & '</a>') as email FROM Results WHERE (Category = 'Sell') **and then point to the OK button.**

The Custom Query dialog box displays with the custom SQL statement entered (Figure 5-12). You can click the Verify Query button to verify that the query references valid fields within the selected database.

FIGURE 5-12

5 **Click the OK button. When the Custom Query dialog box closes, point to the Next button in the Database Results Wizard - Step 2 of 5 dialog box.**

The Custom Query dialog box closes and the Database Results Wizard - Step 2 of 5 dialog box displays (Figure 5-13).

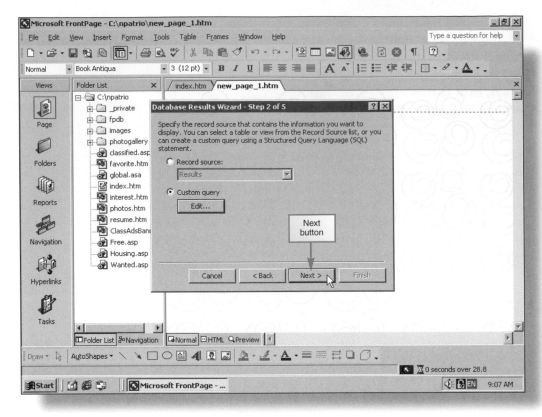

FIGURE 5-13

6 **Click the Next button. When the Database Results Wizard - Step 3 of 5 dialog box displays, point to the Next button.**

The Database Results Wizard - Step 3 of 5 dialog box displays (Figure 5-14). The fields to display in the database results are listed in order. If necessary, use the scroll bar to view the fields.

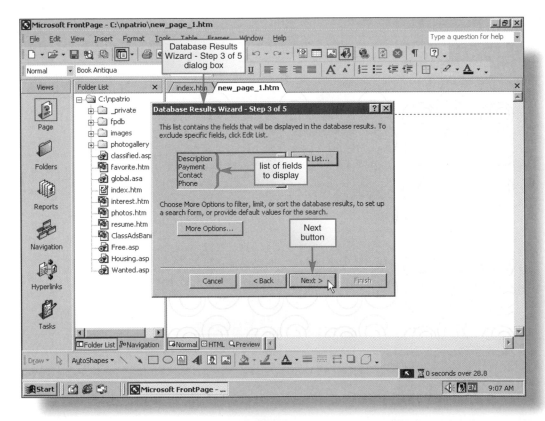

FIGURE 5-14

7 Click the Next button. When the Database Results Wizard - Step 4 of 5 dialog box displays, point to the Next button.

The Database Results Wizard - Step 4 of 5 dialog box displays (Figure 5-15). By default, FrontPage selects formatting options to display table borders, expand the table to page width, and include a header row with column labels. A preview graphic of the resulting table displays.

FIGURE 5-15

8 Click the Next button. When the Database Results Wizard - Step 5 of 5 dialog box displays, select Display all records together. Point to the Finish button.

The Database Results Wizard - Step 5 of 5 dialog box displays (Figure 5-16). If you expect a large number of records to satisfy the selection criteria in the custom SQL query, you can opt to return the records in smaller groups.

FIGURE 5-16

9 **Click the Finish button. Select the text in the column heading, email, and then type** E-mail Address **as the new column heading. Point to the database column value component,** <<email>>.

A Database Results region displays as a table with default column headings derived from the field names (Figure 5-17). The last column heading is changed from the default. FrontPage automatically inserts Database Column Value components as placeholders for displayed records.

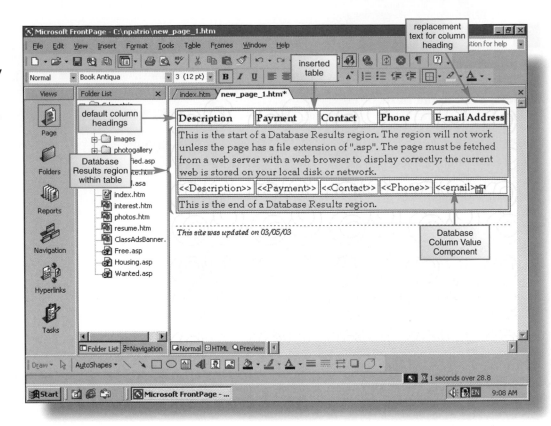

FIGURE 5-17

10 **Right-click the Database Column Value component,** <<email>>, **and point to Database Column Value Properties on the shortcut menu.**

The Database Column Value component, <<email>>, *is selected (Figure 5-18).*

FIGURE 5-18

11 **Click Database Column Value Properties. When the Database Column Value dialog box displays, click Column value contains HTML and then point to the OK button.**

The Database Column Value dialog box displays (Figure 5-19). The Database Column Value, <<email>>, is set to display formatted HTML when the page is viewed in a browser.

FIGURE 5-19

12 **Click the OK button. Click the Save button on the Standard toolbar. When the Save As dialog box displays, type** ForSale.asp **in the File name text box. Point to the Change title button.**

The Save As dialog box displays (Figure 5-20). Note that FrontPage defaults to save the page as an Active Server Page, which is why the file extension is .asp.

FIGURE 5-20

13 **Click the Change title button. When the Set Page Title dialog box displays, type** For Sale **in the Page title text box. Point to the OK button.**

The Set Page Title dialog box displays the new page title that will display when the page is viewed in a browser (Figure 5-21).

FIGURE 5-21

14 **Click the OK button. Point to the Save button in the Save As dialog box.**

The file name and title are changed (Figure 5-22).

FIGURE 5-22

15 **Click the Save button. Point to the Close button on the page pane window.**

The page is saved in the FrontPage web as ForSale.asp (Figure 5-23).

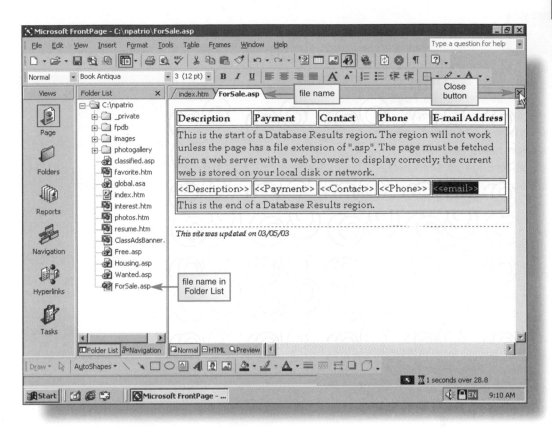

FIGURE 5-23

The four database results pages used to retrieve data from the database now are complete. Next, you will use a frames template to create a frames page that displays database results pages within the frames.

Using Frames Page Templates

FrontPage comes with 10 frames page templates with each varying in the number, orientation, and size of the contained frames. The layouts provided in the frames page templates include a simple table of contents, a small header at the top, a small footer at the bottom, and a window split into any number of horizontal or vertical frames.

Creating a Frames Page Using a Frames Page Template

When using a frames page template, you should choose a template that best satisfies your design requirements. You then can alter the size and number of frames within the template until you have the exact size and number of frames you need.

When you select a frames page template, FrontPage opens a new document and places the template within the new document. Perform the steps on the next page to create a frames page using a frames page template.

Steps | To Create a Frames Page Using a Frames Page Template

1 **Click the Close button on the Page pane window. Click the Create a new normal page button arrow and then point to Page on the Create a new normal page menu.**

The Create a new normal page menu displays with the Page command selected (Figure 5-24).

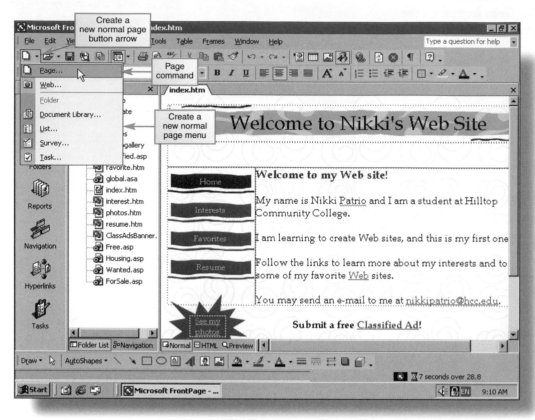

FIGURE 5-24

2 **Click Page. When the Page Templates dialog box displays, point to the Frames Pages tab.**

The Page Templates dialog box displays (Figure 5-25).

FIGURE 5-25

3 Click the Frames Pages tab. If necessary, click the Banner and Contents icon. Point to the OK button.

The Frames Pages sheet displays (Figure 5-26). Each frames page template displays as an icon with a descriptive name below. A description of the selected frames template displays in the Description area and a preview of the frames page displays in the Preview area.

FIGURE 5-26

4 Click the OK button. Point to the border between any of the frames.

A new frames page displays with three frames: a banner frame, a contents frame, and a main frame (Figure 5-27).

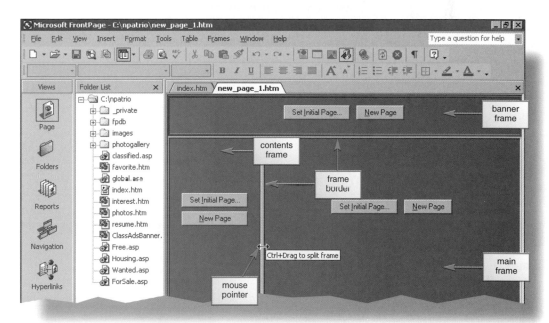

FIGURE 5-27

Figure 5-27 shows the new frames page. As you have learned, each frame within the frames page will display a separate Web page. Within each frame are two buttons you use to define what page initially displays in each frame. The Set Initial Page button allows you to select a preexisting Web page as the initial Web page for that frame. The page can be from the current FrontPage web, another Web page on the

Other Ways

1. On File menu point to New, click Page or Web, on New Page or Web task pane click Page Templates
2. Press ALT+F, N, P
3. In Voice Command mode, say "File, New, Page or Web, Page Templates, Frames Pages"

Web server where the frames page will be published, or any page on the World Wide Web. The New Page button allows you to create a new Web page, directly in the frame, to display as the initial Web page for that frame.

Notice the blue highlighted border surrounding the top frame shown in Figure 5-27 on the previous page. The blue highlighted border indicates the current active frame. Any steps you perform — such as defining special formats, inserting objects, or saving a file — will be performed on the Web page in the active frame. You can change the active frame simply by clicking the desired frame. The highlighted border will surround the frame you clicked to indicate that it is the current active frame.

As shown in Figure 5-27, two additional tabs display at the bottom of the window. The No Frames tab displays the Web page that the user will see if the browser does not support frames. The Frames Page HTML tab displays the HTML source code for the frames page. To view the HTML source code for the Web page in the current active frame, you click the HTML tab, which also displays in other views.

Frames Template Description

The description for the selected frames template usually will indicate when hyperlinks in one frame affect the contents of another frame. Typically, the frame or frames to contain the hyperlinks as well as the target frame all are identified in the frames page description.

Saving the Frames Web Page

You now are ready to create the initial Web pages that will display in each frame. Before you begin, however, you should save the frames page.

As you work on pages in a Web, FrontPage keeps track of whether or not you saved a file. If you create an initial Web page and then try to save it, you will be prompted twice — once to save the initial Web page and once to save the frames page. This happens every time you try to save, until you finally save the frames page. Saving the frames page first prevents the second prompt from displaying, saving you time and reducing confusion over which page you are saving.

Before you can save the frames Web page, you must select it to make it the active page. You can select the frames page to be the current active page by clicking any of the frames borders. The blue highlighted border will surround the entire window, indicating that the frames page is the current active page. Perform the following steps to save the frames page.

 To Save the Frames Web Page

1 Click the border between any of the frames to select the frames page as the current active page. Point to the Save button on the Standard toolbar.

The highlighted border surrounds the entire frames page (Figure 5-28).

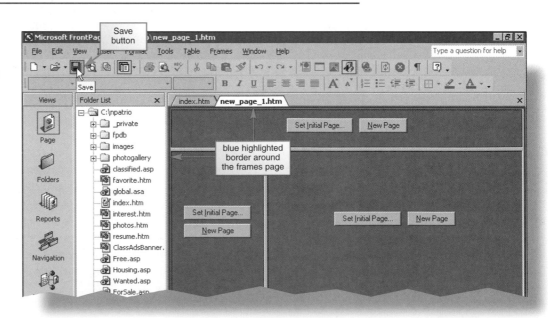

FIGURE 5-28

2 Click the Save button. When the Save As dialog box displays, point to the Change title button.

The Save As dialog box displays with a default file name and page title for the new frames page (Figure 5-29). A graphic map indicates the frames page as the frame to be saved.

FIGURE 5-29

3 Click the Change title button. When the Set Page Title dialog box displays, type Classified Ads main frames page in the Page title text box and then point to the OK button.

The Set Page Title dialog box displays with the new title for the frames page (Figure 5-30).

FIGURE 5-30

4 **Click the OK button. Drag through the file name in the File name text box, type** ClassAdsMain.htm **as the new file name, and then point to the Save button in the Save As dialog box.**

The Set Page Title dialog box closes. The Page title is set to Classified Ads main frames page and the file name is set to ClassAdsMain.htm (Figure 5-31).

FIGURE 5-31

5 **Click the Save button. Point to the Set Initial Page button in the banner frame.**

The frames Web page is saved using the file name, ClassAdsMain.htm (Figure 5-32).

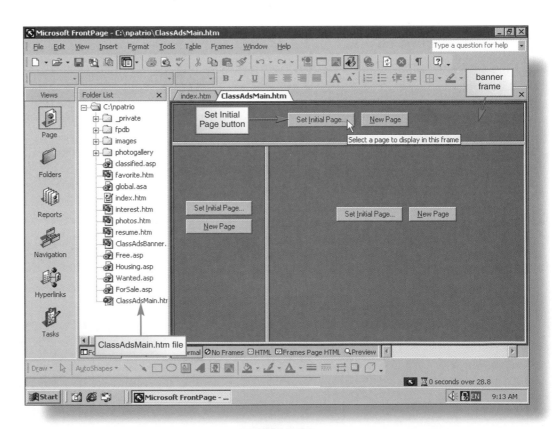

FIGURE 5-32

With the frames page saved, FrontPage will not prompt you to save it every time you save one of the other Web pages you will develop in this project. The next step is to set the initial Web page to display in the banner frame.

Setting an Initial Page to Display in a Frame

You can set an initial page to display in a frame by selecting an existing Web page or creating a new Web page within the frames page.

In this project, you will set an existing Web page as the initial page to display in the banner frame. You will then create two new Web pages to use as the initial pages for the contents frame and main frame.

Using an Existing Web Page as the Initial Page in a Frame

Using an existing Web page as the initial page on a frame provides flexibility in the design process. Using this technique, you can assign different individuals or work groups to develop the Web pages simultaneously, thus reducing the time it takes to implement complex frames pages.

Once all of the initial Web pages and target Web pages exist, creating the frames Web page is a short, simple process. Simply select a template, arrange the frame borders if necessary, identify the initial Web pages, and then save and test the frames page. Perform the following steps to set an existing Web page as the initial page in a frame.

Custom Frame Templates

You can make your own custom templates for frames pages. Open a current frames template, make your changes, and save the current frames page not as a Web page, but as a template file. Click Save As on the File menu, and then change the Save as type to FrontPage template before saving. To learn more about custom frame templates, visit the FrontPage 2002 More About Web page (scsite.com/fp2002/more.htm) and then click Frame Templates.

Steps **To Set an Existing Web Page as the Initial Page in a Frame**

1 **Click the Set Initial Page button in the top frame. When the Insert Hyperlink dialog box displays, if necessary, scroll through the Look in list until the file ClassAdsBanner.htm, displays. Click the file, ClassAdsBanner.htm and then point to the OK button.**

The Insert Hyperlink dialog box displays (Figure 5-33). The banner frame becomes the current active frame. The ClassAdsBanner.htm file name displays in the Address box.

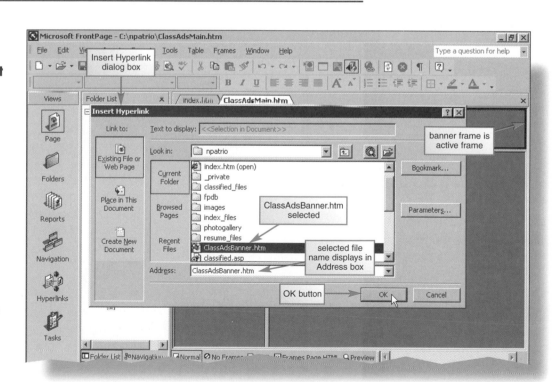

FIGURE 5-33

2 **Click the OK button. Point to the Navigation icon on the Views bar.**

The ClassAdsBanner.htm file displays in the banner frame (Figure 5-34). The banner image will not display until the page has been added to the Navigation view.

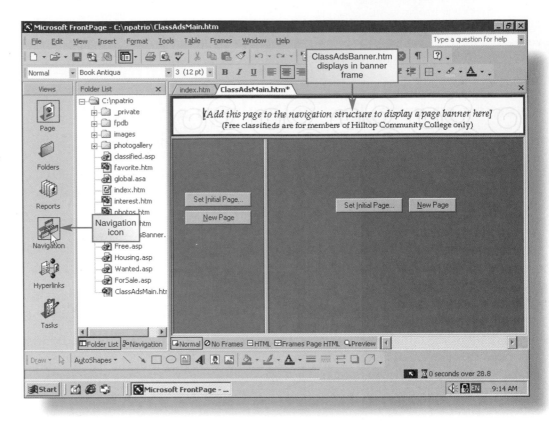

FIGURE 5-34

3 **Click the Navigation icon. Point to the ClassAdsBanner.htm file in the Folder List pane.**

The current web displays in Navigation view (Figure 5-35). The file, ClassAdsBanner.htm, is selected.

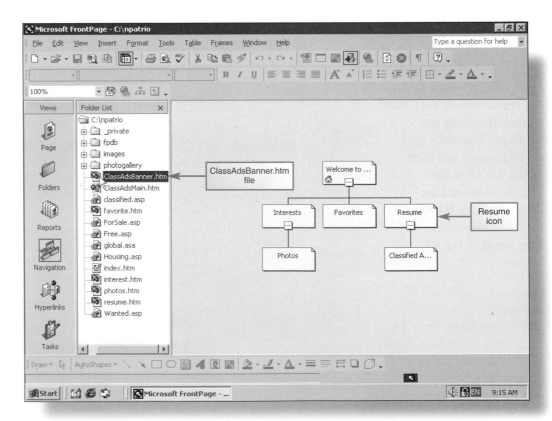

FIGURE 5-35

4 **Drag the ClassAdsBanner.htm file from the Folders List pane and drop it into the Navigation pane under the Resume page icon. Point to the Page icon on the Views bar.**

The Classified Ads icon for the ClassAdsBanner.htm file displays in the Navigation pane under the Resume icon (Figure 5-36).

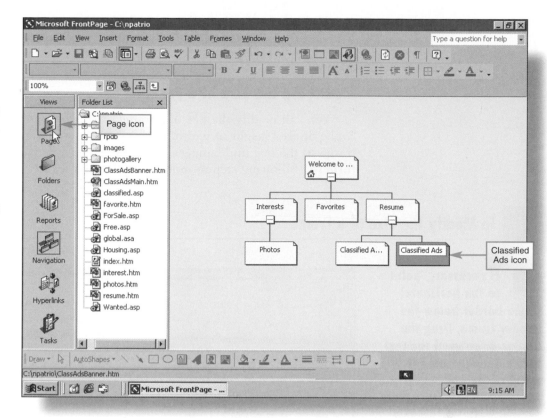

FIGURE 5-36

5 **Click the Page icon. Point to the horizontal frame border below the top frame.**

The frames page displays in Page view. The banner frame displays the file, ClassAdsBanner.htm, with a banner image (Figure 5-37). The mouse pointer changes to a double-headed arrow when placed over a frame border.

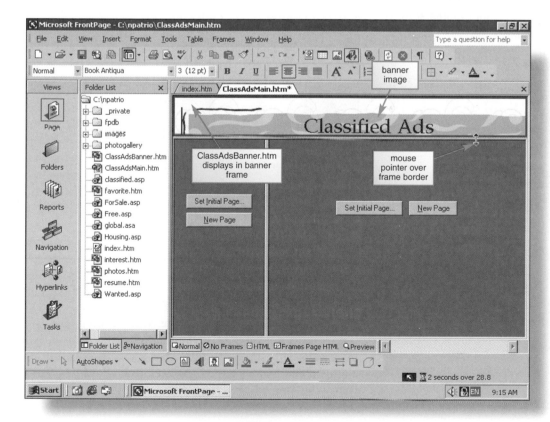

FIGURE 5-37

With the banner image now displaying, you cannot see the text below the banner. To accommodate both the banner and the text, you can modify the size of the banner frame.

Modifying the Size of a Frame

You can modify the size of a frame by dragging the frame border to set the frame to the desired height or width. In this project, you will increase the size of the banner frame so the text and banner image display without the need for a scroll bar. Perform the following step to modify the size of a frame.

Steps **To Modify the Size of a Frame**

1 **If necessary, point to the horizontal frame border below the banner frame. Drag the border down until the text in the banner frame is visible.**

The frame border has been dragged to modify the frame size (Figure 5-38). To determine the appropriate size, you should preview the Web page in a browser.

FIGURE 5-38

 Ways

1. On Frames menu click Frame Properties, type new size values
2. Right-click frame, click Frame Properties on shortcut menu, type new size values
3. Press ALT+R, P
4. In Voice command mode, say "Frames, Frame Properties"

You can decrease the size of a frame in the same fashion – simply by dragging the frame border until the frame is the desired size.

You do not have to save this Web page, ClassAdsBanner.htm, because you have not changed it since you imported it into the web in previous steps. You have changed the frames page, however, and should save these changes. Perform the following step to save the changes to the frames page.

TO SAVE CHANGES TO THE FRAMES PAGE

1 Click the Save button on the Standard toolbar.

Creating a New Web Page for the Initial Page in a Frame

Creating a new Web page to use as the initial page for a frame is just like creating any new Web page. With a frames page template, you indicate that you want to create a new Web page as the initial page for that frame by clicking the New Page button in the desired frame. You then create the Web page. All the objects and text inserted in the page will display in that frame only. Perform the following steps to create the initial Web page that will display in the main frame when the user first displays the frames page.

 To Create a New Web Page for the Initial Page in a Frame

1 **Point to the New Page button in the main frame.**

The initial page, ClassAdsBanner.htm, displays in the banner frame. The contents frame and the main frame still contain buttons, as the initial page has not been assigned for either frame (Figure 5-39).

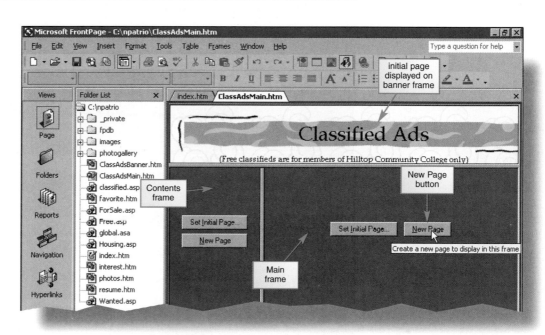

FIGURE 5-39

2 **Click the New Page button.**

A new Web page displays in the main frame with the current theme applied (Figure 5-40). The main frame is the current active frame and the insertion point is located in the new Web page.

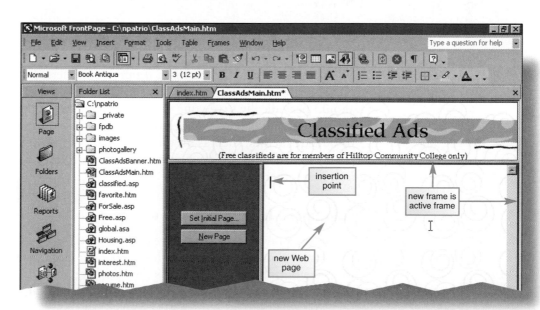

FIGURE 5-40

You now can modify this Web page just as you modified Web pages in previous projects. Perform the following steps to insert text in the initial page for the main frame.

TO INSERT TEXT IN THE INITIAL PAGE FOR THE MAIN FRAME

1 If necessary, click the Web page in the main frame to position the insertion point.

2 Type Welcome to my Free Classified Ads Page for Hilltop Community College. and then press the ENTER key.

3 Type To place a new advertisement or to view advertisements by category, click the corresponding link in the frame to the left. to enter the remaining text. Point to the Save button on the Standard toolbar.

The main page displays in the frames page with the added text (Figure 5-41).

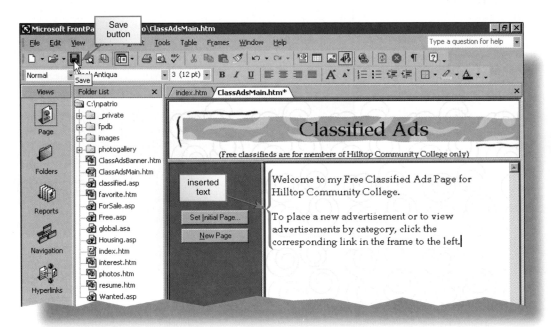

FIGURE 5-41

The initial page for the main frame is complete. Because the Web page was created rather than imported, you should save it before continuing. In general, you should periodically save your work. Although FrontPage will prompt you to save changes when you close a page or quit FrontPage, any unsaved pages can be lost due to outside factors, such as an unexpected loss of power. Another reason for saving a frame page is that you must save it first before you can use it as a target for a hyperlink in another frame.

Saving the Initial Page for a Frame

In the previous steps, you created the initial page for the main frame directly in the frame. You now must save this Web page in the FrontPage web. When you click the Save button, FrontPage saves the Web page in the current active frame by default. Perform the following steps to save the initial page for a frame.

Steps **To Save the Initial Page for the Main Frame**

1 **Click the Save button on the Standard toolbar.**

The Save As dialog box displays (Figure 5-42). A graphic map displays with the current active frame highlighted to indicate which Web page will be saved. You should save the page with a file name that represents the function of the initial page.

FIGURE 5-42

2 **Type**

ClassAdsWelcome.htm **in the File name text box. Point to the Change title button.**

The new file name displays in the File name text box (Figure 5-43).

FIGURE 5-43

Microsoft **FrontPage** 2002

3 Click the Change title button. When the Set Page Title dialog box displays, type Welcome to my Free Classified Ads Page in the Page title text box and then point to the OK button.

The new title displays in the Page title text box (Figure 5-44).

FIGURE 5-44

4 Click the OK button. Point to the Save button in the Save As dialog box.

The Page title in the Save As dialog box is set to Welcome to my Free Classified Ads page (Figure 5-45).

FIGURE 5-45

5 **Click the Save button.**

The initial page for the main frame is saved as ClassAdsWelcome.htm (Figure 5-46).

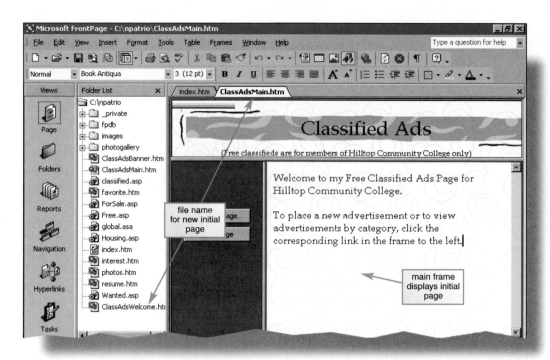

FIGURE 5-46

You now have created one of the initial pages for a frame, directly within the frame itself. To create the other initial Web pages, you will follow steps similar to the preceding steps. The next page you will create is the contents page, which will display as the initial page for the contents frame. According to the design, this page will contain a table of contents with hyperlinks to the other target pages. Perform the steps below to create the initial page for the contents frame.

TO CREATE THE INITIAL PAGE FOR THE CONTENTS FRAME

1 Click the New Page button in the contents frame. Right-click the page and then click Page Properties on the shortcut menu. Type Contents Page in the Title text box. Click the OK button.

2 Click the Save button on the Standard toolbar. When the Save As dialog box displays, type ClassAdsTOC.htm in the File name text box. Click the Save button in the Save As dialog box.

The initial page for the contents frame is saved (Figure 5-47).

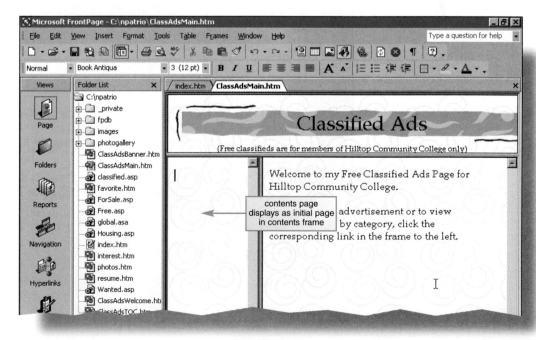

FIGURE 5-47

Modifying Properties of Frames and Frames Pages

In previous steps, you modified the size of a frame by dragging its border. While this sets the initial size of the frame, you also can set other properties such as whether a frame is resizeable or has a scroll bar.

Modifying the Properties of a Frame

The appearance of a frame within a frames page is defined by both properties of the frame itself and properties of the frames page. When modifying frame properties, you should make decisions about frame properties carefully because they can affect the ability of the user to see all of the frame content.

Some decisions, such as whether the frame should display with scroll bars, are made on a frame-by-frame basis. Some frames will not need scroll bars while other frames, even in the same frames page, may need them. A frame can be set to always show scroll bars, never show scroll bars, or show them only if needed.

Other decisions, such as allowing the user to resize the frame in a browser, are made for multiple frames together, even though the property value is set for an individual frame. For example, if one frame is set to be resizable and the frames around it are not resizable, then the setting for that one frame has no effect.

Perform the following steps to modify the properties of a frame.

Steps **To Modify the Properties of a Frame**

1 **Right-click the contents frame. Point to Frame Properties on the shortcut menu.**

The shortcut menu displays (Figure 5-48).

FIGURE 5-48

2 **Click Frame Properties. When the Frame Properties dialog box displays, click the Show scrollbars box arrow in the Options area and then click Never. If necessary, click Resizable in browser to select the check box. Point to the OK button.**

The Frames Properties dialog box displays with the changes (Figure 5-49). Selecting Never on the Show scrollbars list indicates that scroll bars will never display in the contents frame.

FIGURE 5-49

3 **Click the OK button.**

The contents frame displays without scroll bars (Figure 5-50).

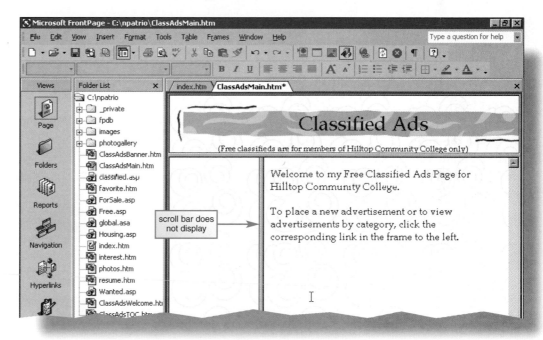

FIGURE 5-50

Modifying the Properties of the Frames Page

Certain properties of the frames page itself also affect the appearance of each individual frame. For example, the amount of spacing between frames is a property of the frames page, not the individual frames. Whether or not borders display between frames also is a frames page property. To modify the properties of the frames page, perform the steps on the next page.

Steps **To Modify the Properties of the Frames Page**

1 **Click the border between any of the frames to select the frames page. Click File on the menu bar and then point to Properties.**

The blue highlighted border indicates that the frames page is the current active page (Figure 5-51).

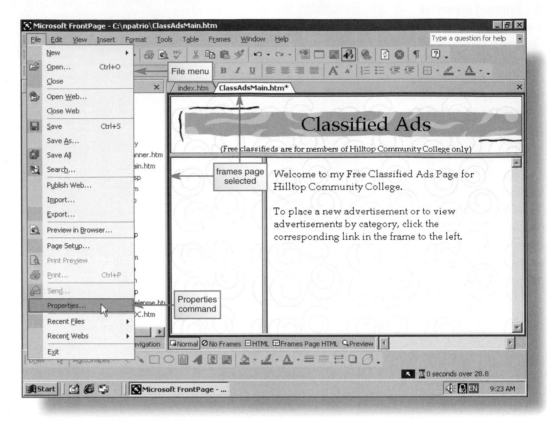

FIGURE 5-51

2 **Click Properties. When the Page Properties dialog box displays, point to the Frames tab.**

The Page Properties dialog box displays (Figure 5-52).

FIGURE 5-52

3 Click the Frames tab. If necessary, type 1 in the Frame Spacing box. Point to the OK button.

The Frames sheet displays (Figure 5-53). The spacing between frames is set to 1 and borders are set to display.

FIGURE 5-53

4 Click the OK button. Click the Save button on the Standard toolbar.

The modified frames page displays (Figure 5-54).

1. On Frames menu click Frame Properties, click Frames Page button
2. Right-click frame, click Frame Properties on shortcut menu, click Frames Page button
3. Press ALT+F, I
4. In Voice Command mode, say "File, Properties, Frames"

FIGURE 5-54

In the previous steps, you created the initial page for the contents frame and set the frame and frames page properties to affect how it displays. Next, you will add hyperlinks to the initial page to allow users to navigate to new pages. Before creating these hyperlinks, it is useful to have some background regarding the choices for a target frame for a hyperlink.

Setting Targets for Hyperlinks in Frames

You can create a hyperlink in a frame page just as you would any other page. Clicking a hyperlink in a regular page causes the current page to be replaced with a new page. Hyperlinks in frames usually display the new pages in another frame, leaving the original page with the hyperlink unaffected. In this project, for instance, most of the hyperlinks in the contents page in the contents frame will cause target Web pages to display in the main frame. In this example, the main frame is considered the default or base target for hyperlinks in the contents frame.

The frame target for a hyperlink also can be set to display a page in frames or windows other than the default target. As shown in Table 5-1, you also can set a frame to display a Web page in the same frame; in a different frame; in the entire browser window, thus replacing the frames page; or in a new browser window. The available choices for a target frame are predefined frame settings that are understood by all Web browsers that support frames.

Table 5-1	Common Settings for Frame Targets
FRAME TARGET	**DESCRIPTION**
Page Default	Specifies that the linked page should be displayed in the default target frame for the active page. This is the recommended method of specifying target frames for hyperlinks.
Same Frame	Sets the target frame of the hyperlink to the same frame that contains the hyperlink. This setting overrides the page's default target frame.
Whole Page	Sets the target frame of the hyperlink to the entire Web browser window.
New Window	Specifies that a new Web browser window should be launched on the user's desktop, and the target page should be displayed in the new Web browser window.
Parent Frame	Specifies that the linked page should be displayed in the frame that contains the current frameset tag. This is an advanced feature.

Creating Hyperlinks to Pages in Frames

The purpose of the contents page in the contents frame is to present the user with a list of hyperlinks to different Web pages in the classified ads section of the Web site. As noted earlier, these hyperlinks can link to Web pages in the same FrontPage web, to other Web pages on the same Web server, or to any Web page on the World Wide Web. For these hyperlinks, the target Web pages will display in the main frame.

The frames page template you selected sets the main frame as the base target for hyperlinks in the contents frame. Figure 5-55 shows the HTML code in the header section of the contents frame. The **base target** tag in each frame sets the default target for hyperlinks in this frame. Because the main frame is set as the default or base target for the contents frame, you do not need to set the main frame as the target for each link within the frame. Therefore, you can use a Link bar component to create hyperlinks that use the default target frame. Perform the following steps to create a Link bar component in the contents page that targets the default frame.

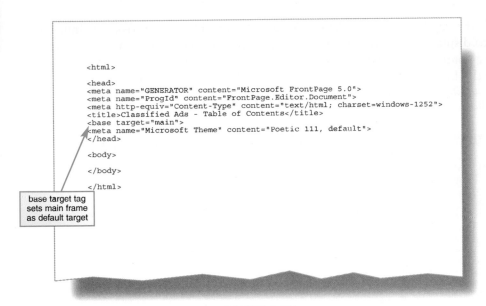

```
<html>

<head>
<meta name="GENERATOR" content="Microsoft FrontPage 5.0">
<meta name="ProgId" content="FrontPage.Editor.Document">
<meta http-equiv="Content-Type" content="text/html; charset=windows-1252">
<title>Classified Ads - Table of Contents</title>
<base target="main">
<meta name="Microsoft Theme" content="Poetic 111, default">
</head>

<body>

</body>

</html>
```

base target tag
sets main frame
as default target

FIGURE 5-55

TO CREATE A LINK BAR TARGETING THE DEFAULT FRAME

1 If necessary, click the contents frame to position the insertion point. Click Insert on the menu bar and then click Navigation. When the Insert Web Component dialog box displays, click Bar based on navigation structure in the Choose a bar type list. Click the Next button. When the Choose a bar style list displays in the Insert Web Component dialog box, verify that the Use Page's Theme icon is selected and then click the Next button. When the Choose an orientation list displays in the Insert Web Component dialog box, click the second icon to insert the Link bar with the links arranged vertically. Click the Finish button.

2 When the Link Bar Properties dialog box displays, if necessary click the General tab. Verify that Child level is selected in the Hyperlinks to add to page area and that no pages are selected in the Additional pages area. Click the OK button. Click the Save button on the Standard toolbar.

3 Double-click the file, classified.asp, in the Folder List to open the Classified Ads Request page in Page view. Delete the page banner and all text above the form. Click the Save button on the Standard toolbar. Close the Classified Ads Request page.

4 Click the Navigation icon on the Views bar. Right-click the Classified Ads Request icon. Click Rename on the shortcut menu. Type Place New Ad as the new page label and then press the ENTER key. Drag and drop the file ClassAdsTOC.htm below the Classified Ads icon. Drag and drop the Place New Ad icon below the Contents Page icon.

5 Drag the file, ForSale.asp, from the Folder List and drop it below the Contents Page to the right of the Place New Ad icon. Drag the file, Housing.asp, from the Folder List and drop it below the Contents Page to the right of the For Sale icon. Drag the file, Wanted.asp, from the Folder List and drop it below the Contents Page to the right of the Housing icon. Drag the file, Free.asp, from the Folder List and drop it below the Contents Page to the right of the Wanted icon.

6 Click the Page icon on the Views bar. If necessary, click the ClassAdsMain.htm tab to display the ClassAdsMain.htm page in Page view. Drag the right border of the contents frame, if necessary, to adjust the size of the frame to accommodate the Link bar. Click the Save button on the Standard toolbar.

The Link bar displays in the contents frame (Figure 5-56).

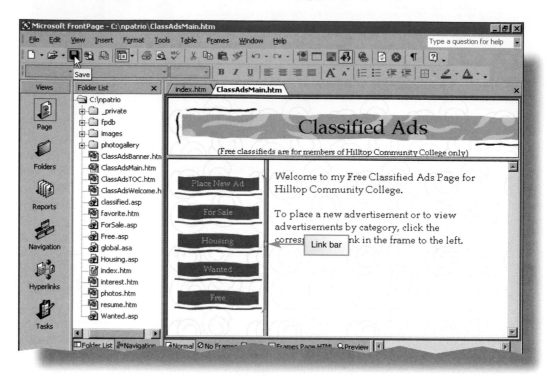

FIGURE 5-56

The contents page now contains a Link bar with hyperlinks to all of the pages that the user can choose to display in the main frame. To complete the contents page, you will create one more hyperlink to the Home page.

Creating a Hyperlink to a Whole Page

As listed in Table 5-1, a hyperlink in a frame can be used to display a Web page in an entire browser window, instead of a frame. This is the purpose of the hyperlink for the Home Page. Because the Link bar hyperlinks use the default main frame as the target, you cannot use the link bar to link to the Home page and display it in the entire browser window. If you did, the Home Page would display in the main frame, instead of replacing the frames page, causing a cascading effect that is not desired. To avoid displaying its target Web page in the frame, the Home page hyperlink must indicate a target of a whole page.

Because you will not use the Link bar to link to the Home Page, you first must insert an image identical to those used in the Link bar. Because the Poetic theme is used for this page, the images used in the Link bar are available in the poetic folder within the _themes folder in this web. Perform the following steps to insert an image from the current theme used in this web.

TO INSERT AN IMAGE FROM THE CURRENT THEME

1 Click the contents frame to position the insertion point at the top and left of the frame.

2   Click Insert on the menu bar, point to Picture, and then click From File on the Picture submenu. When the Picture dialog box displays, double-click the _themes folder and then double-click the poetic folder. Click the file, poehbuda.gif, and then click the Insert button. The _themes folder typically is hidden. If you cannot access hidden folders, obtain the file from the Project5 folder on the Data Disk.

3   When the Picture dialog box closes, hold down the SHIFT key and press the ENTER key. Click the newly inserted image and then click the Text button on the Pictures toolbar. Type Home as the label text. Drag through the text to select it.

4   Click the Font Color button arrow on the Standard toolbar and then click More Colors. When the More Colors dialog box displays, position the dialog box so text on the Link bar is visible. Click the Select button. When the mouse pointer changes to an eye dropper, position the mouse pointer over some text on the Link bar and then click the text to select its color. Click the OK button. If necessary, click the Font Size button arrow on the Standard toolbar and then click 3 (12 pt). If necessary, click the Bold button on the Formatting toolbar to remove bold formatting.

5   Click in the contents frame, left of the Home image, to deselect the image.

The inserted image displays in the contents frame (Figure 5-57).

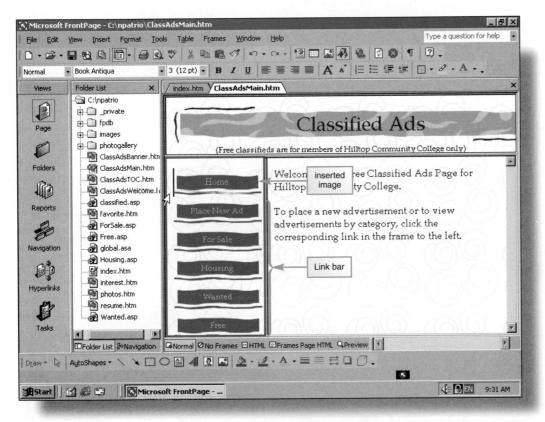

FIGURE 5-57

Now that you have placed the image in the page, you can insert a hyperlink that will link to the Home page and will target the whole frames page, not just a single frame. Perform the steps on the next page to create a hyperlink with the target frame set as a Whole Page.

Steps **To Create a Hyperlink to a Whole Page**

1 **Right-click the Home image, not the text, and then click Hyperlink on the shortcut menu. When the Insert Hyperlink dialog box displays, click index.htm (open) and then point to the Target Frame button.**

The Insert Hyperlink dialog box displays (Figure 5-58). The file, index.htm, is selected as the linked page.

FIGURE 5-58

2 **Click the Target Frame button. When the Target Frame dialog box displays, click Whole Page in the Common targets area. Point to the OK button in the Target Frame dialog box.**

The Target Frame dialog box displays (Figure 5-59). When Whole Page is selected, FrontPage automatically enters _top in the Target setting text box.

FIGURE 5-59

3 **Click the OK button. When the Target Frame dialog box closes, point to the OK button in the Insert Hyperlink dialog box.**

The Target Frame dialog box closes. The selected target frame displays in the Insert Hyperlink dialog box (Figure 5-60).

FIGURE 5-60

4 **Click the OK button. When the Insert Hyperlink dialog box closes, click in the Contents frame, left of the Link bar component, to deselect the image. Click the Save button on the Standard toolbar. Position the mouse pointer over the image hyperlink.**

The URL for the hyperlink displays on the status bar (Figure 5-61).

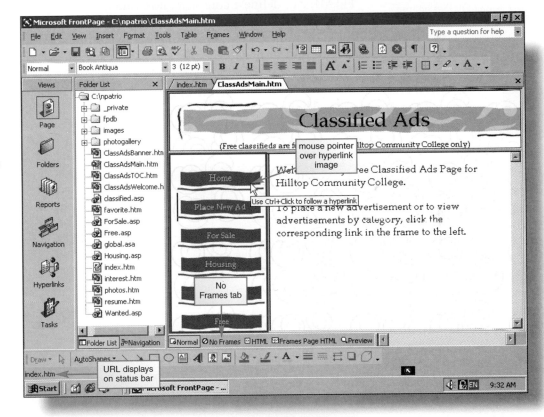

FIGURE 5-61

With Whole Page selected, the Home hyperlink now will display the Home page in the entire browser window when clicked. The Current frames page area, shown in the Target Frame dialog box in Figure 5-59, displays a map of the frames page. When specifying a target frame using the Target Frame dialog box, you can click the target frame in this map or type the name of the target frame in the target settings text box. The name of that frame then displays in the Target setting field.

The Set as page default check box at the bottom of the Target Frame dialog box in Figure 5-59 is used to make the selected target frame the default for all hyperlinks on the current active Web page.

You have created all of the initial pages and hyperlinks to pages in the frames page. The frames page almost is complete. Next, you will view the HTML code in the No Frames view, to view what displays to users when using browsers that do not support frames.

More About

No Frames View

HTML code inserted into the No Frames View is displayed only for browsers that do not accommodate frames pages. Browsers that are frames-compatible do not display this view. To allow your users to select whether to view frames, include a hyperlink on the frames page to a version of your page that does not use frames.

Displaying the No Frames View

Initially, only the Netscape Navigator 2.0 browser supported frames. Since then, support for frames has been added to virtually all modern browsers. It is possible, however, that some users still use older versions of browsers that do not support frames.

If a user displays a frames page in a browser that does not support frames, special no frames HTML code is displayed instead.

The **No Frames HTML code** is contained inside the frames Web page and usually advises a user that his or her browser does not support frames. The No Frames HTML can define a complete, nonframes Web page and supply hyperlinks to other nonframes versions of the Web pages used in your frames page. You can customize the No Frames HTML code by displaying the No Frames view. Perform the following steps to display the No Frames view.

Steps | **To Display the No Frames View**

1 **Click the No Frames tab at the bottom of the FrontPage window. Point to the Normal tab.**

The Web page displays in No Frames view (Figure 5-62). A message displays to the user, stating that the page uses frames, which the user's browser does not support.

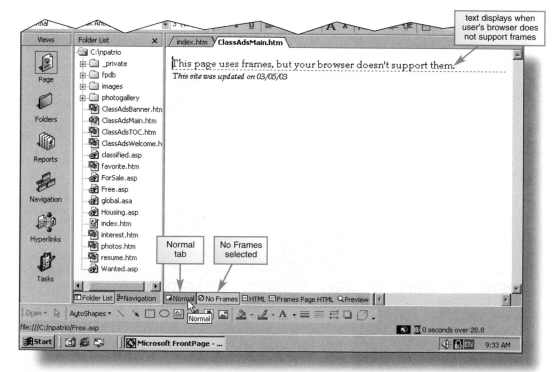

FIGURE 5-62

2 **Click the Normal tab.**

The Web page redisplays in Normal view (Figure 5-63).

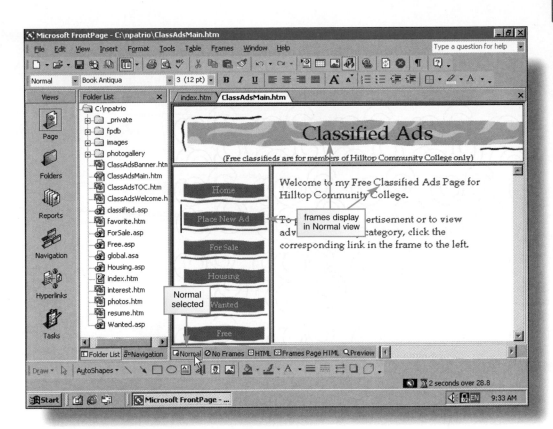

FIGURE 5-63

You can edit the No Frames HTML code as you would any other Web page. This feature is becoming less important as the use of the older browsers diminishes.

Now that you have a completed frames page, you must modify the hyperlink on the Home page. Recall that you modified the original Classified Ads Request page, classified.asp, to incorporate it into a frame. The hyperlink on the Home Page links to the page classified.asp, not to the frames page, ClassifiedAdsMain.htm. Perform the following steps to modify the hyperlink on the Home Page to link to the frames page.

TO MODIFY A HYPERLINK TO LINK TO A FRAMES PAGE

1 Click the index.htm tab to display the Home page in Page view.

2 Scroll down, if necessary, and drag through the text, Submit a, and then type Visit my as the replacement text.

3 Drag through the text, Ad, in the hyperlink and then type Ads as the replacement text.

4 Right-click the hyperlink and then click Hyperlink Properties on the shortcut menu. When the Edit Hyperlink dialog box displays, click the file ClassAdsMain.htm (open) and then click the OK button. Click the Save button on the Standard toolbar. Click the hyperlink to remove the selection.

The URL for the hyperlink displays on the status bar (Figure 5-64 on the next page).

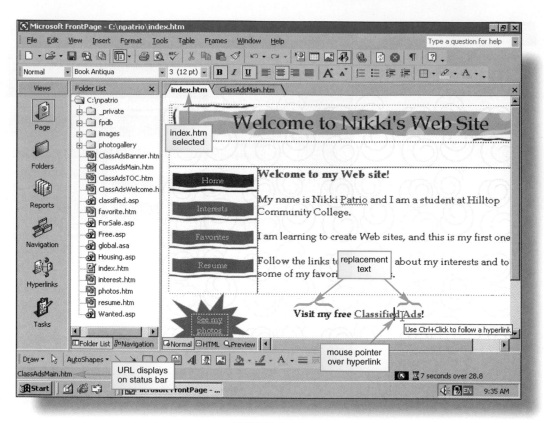

FIGURE 5-64

Printing Web Pages in Frames

Once all of the pages in the frames have been saved, you can print them. You cannot print the entire frames page at one time, however. Instead, you must print each individual Web page in a frame. You do this by clicking the frame containing the desired Web page to make it the active frame, and then by printing that individual Web page.

To display the different Web pages in the main frame so you can print them, you need to click the hyperlinks in the contents frame. Perform the following steps to print all the separate pages that display in the Classified Ads frames page.

To Print the Web Pages in Frames

1 **Ready the printer.
Click the
ClassAdsMain.htm tab.
Click the banner frame.
Click File on the menu bar
and then click Print. When
the Print dialog box
displays, point to the OK
button.**

*The banner frame becomes
the active frame and the Print
dialog box displays
(Figure 5-65).*

FIGURE 5-65

2 **Click the OK button.
Click the contents
frame to make it the
current active frame. Point
to the Print button on the
Standard toolbar.**

*The Web page in the top
frame prints and the contents
frame becomes the active
frame (Figure 5-66).*

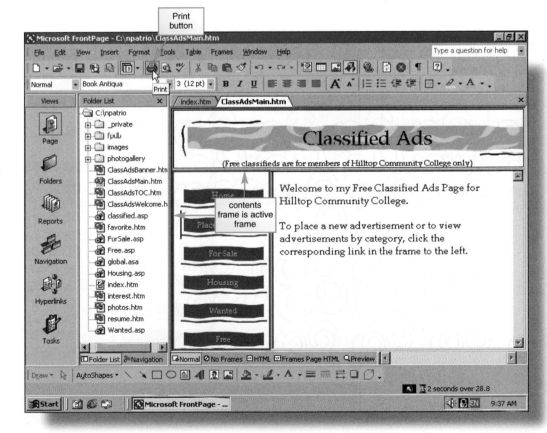

FIGURE 5-66

3 **Click the Print button. Click the main frame to make it the current active frame. Point to the Print button on the Standard toolbar.**

The Web page in the contents frame prints and the main frame becomes the active frame (Figure 5-67). The Classified Ads Welcome page displays in the main frame.

FIGURE 5-67

4 **Click the Print button. While holding down the CTRL key, click the Place New Ad image hyperlink in the contents frame. Release the CTRL key. If necessary, click the right frame to make it the active frame. Point to the Print button on the Standard toolbar.**

The Classified Ads Welcome page prints and the modified Classified Ads Request Web page displays in the main frame (Figure 5-68). Earlier, you removed the page banner from this page because it would be redundant with the banner frame contents.

FIGURE 5-68

5 Click the Print button. While holding down the CTRL key, click the For Sale image hyperlink in the contents frame. Release the CTRL key. If necessary, click the right frame to make it the active frame. Point to the Print button on the Standard toolbar.

The Classified Ads request page prints and the For Sale Web page displays in the main frame (Figure 5-69). Pages displaying database results must be retrieved from a Web server to display actual data. Until the web is published, the Database Column Value placeholders display instead of data.

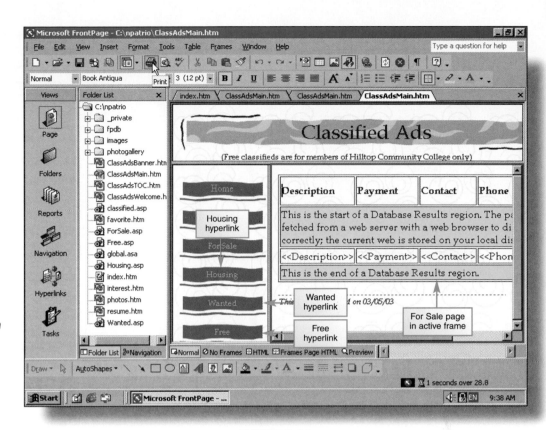

FIGURE 5-69

6 Click the Print button. Repeat Step 5 to print the remaining pages, Housing, Wanted, and Free. Close all of the pages.

When the printer stops, retrieve the printouts (Figure 5-70 on this and the next page).

(a)

(b)

(c)

FIGURE 5-70

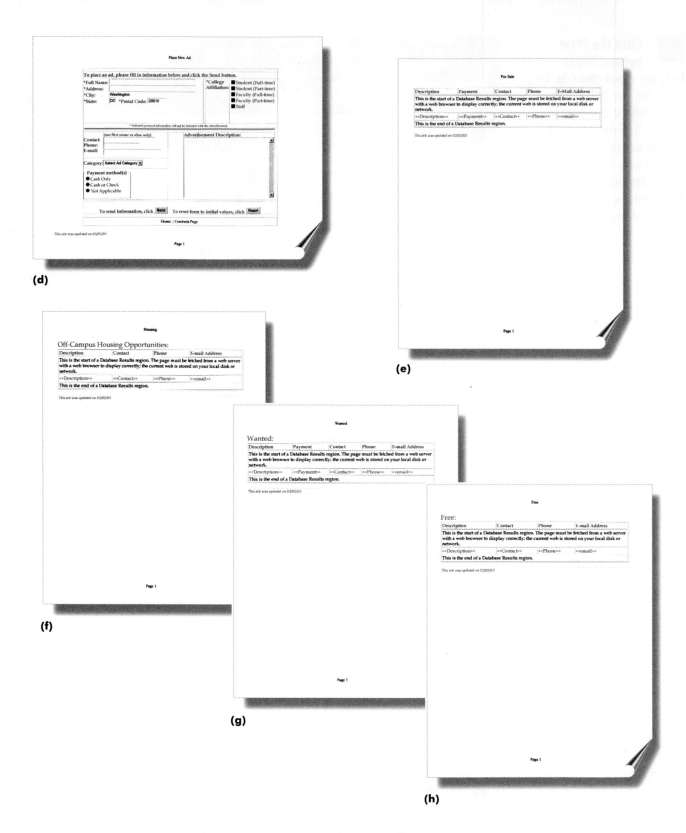

FIGURE 5-70 *(continued)*

In this project, you have imported Web pages to the FrontPage web, added a frames page, set or created three initial Web pages, and created the For Sale Database Results page. You also modified the Classified Ads Request page and the Home page. For these Web pages to be available on the World Wide Web, you must publish the FrontPage web again, as shown in the following steps.

TO PUBLISH CHANGES TO AN EXISTING FRONTPAGE WEB

1 Click the Publish Web button on the Standard toolbar. Because this web was published previously, FrontPage does not display the Publish Destination dialog box, but assumes that you will publish to the same location.

2 Type your user name and password. Click the OK button.

3 Click the Done button.

You now can view the changes by entering http://www.hcc.edu/~npatrio/ index.htm in any browser and pressing the ENTER key. Be sure to test the hyperlink to the Classified Ads page and each of the hyperlinks on that page.

Quitting Microsoft FrontPage

When you have published Nikki's web, you can quit Microsoft FrontPage. Perform the following step to quit FrontPage.

TO QUIT MICROSOFT FRONTPAGE

1 If necessary, click the Done button. Click the Close button on the FrontPage title bar.

The FrontPage window closes and the Windows desktop displays.

More About

Quick Reference

For a table that lists how to complete tasks covered in this book using the mouse, menu, shortcut menu, and keyboard, see the Quick Reference Summary at the back of this book or visit the Shelly Cashman Series Office XP Web page (scsite.com/ offxp/qr.htm) and then click Microsoft FrontPage 2002.

More About

Microsoft Certification

The Microsoft Office User Specialist (MOUS) Certification program provides an opportunity for you to obtain a valuable industry credential — proof that you have the FrontPage 2002 skills required by employers. For more information, see Appendix E or visit the Shelly Cashman Series MOUS Web page at scsite.com/ offxp/cert.htm.

CASE PERSPECTIVE SUMMARY

Nikki's Web site is essentially complete and she is very satisfied with the result and with what she has learned. She is pleased to have a site that allows a user to interact by placing and retrieving classified advertisements. She continues to be impressed with the capabilities of FrontPage and wants to gain more experience with it. Realizing that more needs to be done to allow her to manage her site, such as the ability to delete outdated classified advertisements, she looks forward to future development with you as her experience with her site grows.

Project Summary

Having completed Project 5, you now are ready to incorporate frames and database results in your own Web pages. In this project, you learned about frames and how you can use them. You imported Web pages into a FrontPage web. You learned how to use the Database Results Wizard and to create a custom SQL query to retrieve information from a relational database. The project demonstrated how to use a frames page template. You learned how to set an existing Web page as the initial Web page in a frame and how to modify the size of a frame. You created a new initial Web page for a frame, and then you created hyperlinks to Web pages in frames and a hyperlink to a whole page. You learned how to modify properties of a frame and of a frames page. You learned how to display and edit the No Frames HTML code. Finally, you learned how to print pages within frames in FrontPage.

What You Should Know

Having completed this project, you now should be able to perform the following tasks:

- Create a Database Results Region and Custom SQL Query (FP 5.14)
- Create a Frames Page Using a Frames Page Template (FP 5.22)
- Create a Hyperlink to a Whole Page (FP 5.44)
- Create a Link Bar Targeting the Default Frame (FP 5.41)
- Create a New Web Page for the Initial Page in a Frame (FP 5.31)
- Create the Initial Page for the Contents Frame (FP 5.35)
- Display the No Frames View (FP 5.46)
- Import Files into an Existing FrontPage Web (FP 5.11)
- Insert an Image from the Current Theme (FP 5.42)
- Insert Text in the Initial Page for the Main Frame (FP 5.32)
- Modify a Hyperlink to Link to a Frames Page (FP 5.47)
- Modify the Properties of a Frame (FP 5.36)
- Modify the Properties of the Frames Page (FP 5.38)
- Modify the Size of a Frame (FP 5.30)
- Print the Web Pages in Frames (FP 5.49)
- Publish Changes to an Existing FrontPage Web (FP 5.53)
- Quit Microsoft FrontPage (FP 5.53)
- Save Changes to the Frames Page (FP 5.30)
- Save the Frames Web Page (FP 5.24)
- Save the Initial Page for the Main Frame (FP 5.33)
- Set an Existing Web Page as the Initial Page in a Frame (FP 5.27)
- Start FrontPage and Open an Existing Web (FP 5.10)

Learn It Online

Instructions: To complete the Learn It Online exercises, start your browser, click the Address bar, and then enter scsite.com/offxp/exs.htm. When the Office XP Learn It Online page displays, follow the instructions in the exercises below.

1 Project Reinforcement TF, MC, and SA

Below FrontPage Project 5, click the Project Reinforcement link. Print the quiz by clicking Print on the File menu. Answer each question. Write your first and last name at the top of each page, and then hand in the printout to your instructor.

2 Flash Cards

Below FrontPage Project 5, click the Flash Cards link. When Flash Cards displays, read the instructions. Type 20 (or a number specified by your instructor) in the Number of Playing Cards text box, type your name in the Name text box, and then click the Flip Card button. When the flash card displays, read the question and then click the Answer box arrow to select an answer. Flip through Flash Cards. Click Print on the File menu to print the last flash card if your score is 15 (75%) correct or greater and then hand it in to your instructor. If your score is less than 15 (75%) correct, then redo this exercise by clicking the Replay button.

3 Practice Test

Below FrontPage Project 5, click the Practice Test link. Answer each question, enter your first and last name at the bottom of the page, and then click the Grade Test button. When the graded practice test displays on your screen, click Print on the File menu to print a hard copy. Continue to take practice tests until you score 80% or better. Hand in a printout of the final practice test to your instructor.

4 Who Wants to Be a Computer Genius?

Below FrontPage Project 5, click the Computer Genius link. Read the instructions, enter your first and last name at the bottom of the page, and then click the Play button. Hand in your score to your instructor.

5 Wheel of Terms

Below FrontPage Project 5, click the Wheel of Terms link. Read the instructions, and then enter your first and last name and your school name. Click the Play button. Hand in your score to your instructor.

6 Crossword Puzzle Challenge

Below FrontPage Project 5, click the Crossword Puzzle Challenge link. Read the instructions, and then enter your first and last name. Click the Play button. Work the crossword puzzle. When you are finished, click the Submit button. When the crossword puzzle redisplays, click the Print button. Hand in the printout.

7 Tips and Tricks

Below FrontPage Project 5, click the Tips and Tricks link. Click a topic that pertains to Project 5. Right-click the information and then click Print on the shortcut menu. Construct a brief example of what the information relates to in FrontPage to confirm you understand how to use the tip or trick. Hand in the example and printed information.

8 Newsgroups

Below FrontPage Project 5, click the Newsgroups link. Click a topic that pertains to Project 5. Print three comments. Hand in the comments to your instructor.

9 Expanding Your Horizons

Below FrontPage Project 5, click the Articles for Microsoft FrontPage link. Click a topic that pertains to Project 5. Print the information. Construct a brief example of what the information relates to in FrontPage to confirm you understand the contents of the article. Hand in the example and printed information to your instructor.

10 Search Sleuth

Below FrontPage Project 5, click the Search Sleuth link. To search for a term that pertains to this project, select a term below the Project 5 title and then use the Google search engine at google.com (or any major search engine) to display and print two Web pages that present information on the term. Hand in the printouts to your instructor.

online

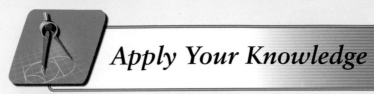

Apply Your Knowledge

1 Creating a New Frames Page Template

Instructions: Perform the following tasks.

1. Start FrontPage 2002. Click the Create a new normal page button arrow and then click Page on the Create a new normal page menu. When the Page Templates dialog box displays, click the Frames Pages tab. Click the Header, Footer, and Contents icon. Click the OK button.

2. A new frames page displays with four frames. If the top frame is not the currently selected frame, click in that frame to select it.

3. Click Frames on the menu bar and then click Delete Frame. The top frame is deleted and the outline is around the entire outer frame.

4. Click File on the menu bar and then click Save As. When the Save As dialog box displays, click the Save as type box arrow. Click FrontPage Template in the list. Type footTOC.tem in the File name text box. If necessary, change the directory. Click the Save button in the Save As dialog box.

5. When the Save As Template dialog box displays, type Footer and Contents in the Title text box. This title will display when accessing the template to create a new page.

6. In the Description text box, drag through the text, Type your description here. to select it. Type Creates a Contents frame on the left which directs hyperlinks to change the main page on the right by default. Hyperlinks in the Footer change the Contents frame by default. to enter a short description of what this frames page template does. Click the OK button. Close the Web page.

7. Create a new Web page using the template you have just created. The new frames page template should display as the Footer and Contents template in the Frames Pages sheet, as shown in Figure 5-71. The title you entered should show with a new frames page icon and the description you typed should show in the Description area. A preview of the frames page should display.

8. Test the new page to verify that hyperlinks in the contents frame target the contents of the main frame, and that links in the footer frame target the contents frame.

9. Save the Web page. Print the Web page, write your name on it, and hand it in to your instructor.

FIGURE 5-71

In the Lab

1 Modify an Existing Web to Use Frames

Problem: The price list created earlier for The Sweet Tooth has all items on one Web page. Different people are responsible for price updates in different categories, so you decide to use frames with separate pages for each product category.

Instructions: Perform the following tasks.

1. Open The Sweet Tooth web that you modified in Project 4. If you did not complete that exercise for Project 4, see your instructor for a copy of the required files.

2. If necessary, double-click the file, prices.htm, to open the Price Sheet page. Click Page on the Create a new normal page menu. When the Page Templates dialog box displays, click the Frames Pages tab and then click the Banner and Contents icon. Click the OK button. Save the frames page and type pricesFrames.htm as the file name. Click the Change title button. When the Set Page Title dialog box displays, type Price Sheet frames page as the new title text. Click the OK button in the Set Page Title dialog box. Click the Save button in the Save As dialog box.

3. Click the New Page button in the top (banner) frame. Insert a Page Banner component. Save the banner page and type pricesBanner.htm as the file name. Change the Page title and type Price Sheet Banner as the new title text. In Navigation view, drag and drop the file, pricesFrames.htm, to the left and below the Products icon.

4. In Page view, click the Create a new normal page button. Because this web applies shared borders to new pages by default, the shared borders must be removed from the page before using the page in a frame. Right-click the page and then click Page Properties on the shortcut menu. Click the Custom tab in the Page Properties dialog box. In the User variables area, select the Name, Microsoft Border. Click the Remove button and then click the OK button. Save the page and type fudges.htm as the file name. Click the Change title button and then type Fudges Price Sheet as the page title. Click the OK button in the Set Page Title dialog box. Click the Save button in the Save As dialog box.

5. Click the prices.htm tab to display the Price Sheet page. Select the table cells for the FUDGES section, including all columns and rows in that section. Click the Copy button on the Standard toolbar to copy the selected cells. If necessary, set the Font Size for all text except the section title to 2 (10 pt). If necessary, adjust the borders to align the table contents properly. Click fudges.htm to display the Fudges Price Sheet page and then paste the copied table cells into the page. Right-click the bookmarked text, FUDGES. Click Bookmark Properties and then click the Clear button in the Bookmark dialog box. Save your changes and then close the Fudges Price sheet page.

6. Repeat steps 4 and 5 for each of the remaining sections as listed in Table 5-2 on page FP 5.59. Be sure to remove the hyperlinked text, back to top, from each pasted section of cells.

7. Click the New Page button in the left (contents) frame. Insert a Navigation component based on the navigation structure. Create links to pages at the Child level. Save the page and type pricesTOC.htm as the file name and type Price Sheet Contents as the page title. In Navigation view, drag and drop the file, pricesTOC.htm, below the Price Sheet frames page icon. Drag and drop each of the files listed in Table 5-2 below the Price Sheet Contents icon. Modify the page labels as listed in Table 5-3 on page FP 5.59. Drag and drop the file, pricesBanner.htm, to the left and below the Novelty icon. In Page view, modify the frame size on the frames page to display the page banner.

(continued)

In the Lab

Modify an Existing Web to Use Frames *(continued)*

8. Close the prices.htm page and delete the file, prices.htm, from the web. Position the insertion point at the top and left of the Link bar and then insert the image, swhbh.gif, from the sweets folder within the _themes folder. Hold down the CTRL key and press the ENTER key. Using the image, insert a hyperlink to the Home page, using Whole Page as the target. If you cannot access hidden folders, obtain the file from the Project5 folder on the Data Disk. Adjust the width of the contents frame of the frames page, if necessary.

9. Click the New Page button in the right (main) frame. Type `Select a category in the leftmost frame to view the corresponding price sheet.` and then save the page. Type `pricesMain.htm` as the file name and type `Price Sheets main page` as the page title.

10. Save all changes, if necessary. Print the contents, banner, and initial main frame pages as well as each of the pages linked by the Link bar (Figure 5-72). Write your name on the pages, and hand them in to your instructor.

FIGURE 5-72

In the Lab

Table 5-2 Price Sheet File Sections and Titles		
SECTION TO COPY	*FILE NAME*	*PAGE TITLE*
FUDGES	fudges.htm	Fudges Price Sheet
SUGAR-FREE ITEMS	sugarFree.htm	Sugar-Free Price Sheet
BULK WRAPPED CANDY	bulkWrapped.htm	Bulk Wrapped Price Sheet
BULK UNWRAPPED CANDY	bulkUnwrapped.htm	Bulk Unwrapped Price Sheet
JELLY BEANS	jellyBeans.htm	Jelly Beans Price Sheet
PRODUCT GIFT ITEMS	productGifts.htm	Product Gifts Price Sheet
NOVELTY CANDY ITEMS	novelty.htm	Novelty Candy Price Sheet

Table 5-3 Price Sheet Page Labels	
FILE NAME	*PAGE LABEL*
fudges.htm	Fudges
sugarFree.htm	Sugar-Free
bulkWrapped.htm	Wrapped
bulkUnwrapped.htm	Unwrapped
jellyBeans.htm	Jelly Beans
productGifts.htm	Product Gifts
novelty.htm	Novelty
priceFrames.htm	Price Sheet

2 Adding a Database Results Page to a Web

Problem: You have an inventory database created by another process and would like to display results from the database to visitors of your Web. You decide to incorporate a Database Results page and test it with a smaller sample database of the same format.

Instructions: Perform the following tasks.

1. Open the web, Starting, that you modified in Project 4. If you did not complete that exercise for Project 4, see your instructor for a copy of the required files.
2. Create a new normal page. On the File menu, click Import. When the Import dialog box displays, add the sample database file, inventory.mdb, to the web.
3. When the Add Database Connection dialog box displays, type Inventory in the Name text box and then click the Yes button. Import the resulting database file into the fpdb folder.
4. Using the Database Results Wizard, insert a Database Results region using the existing database connection of Inventory. Select Products in the Record source list.
5. Edit the list of database fields to exclude specific fields. Select and remove all fields except Category, ProductDescription, BarCodeNumber, UnitsInStock, and UnitPrice.
6. Click the More Options button. When the More Options dialog box displays, click the Criteria button. When the Criteria dialog box displays, click the Add button to display the Add Criteria dialog box. Click the Field Name box arrow and then click the field name, Category. Select a comparison of Equals. Type Football in the Value text box. Click the Use this search form field to remove the selection. Click the OK button and then click the OK button in the Criteria dialog box.
7. When the More Options dialog box again is visible, click the Ordering button. Select Supplier for the Sort order. Display all records together in the results. Edit the column headings from the defaults, if necessary. Save the page and type football.asp as the file name and type Football as the page title.
8. Edit the page, prod02.htm, and select the text, image caption goes here. Type Football products as the replacement text. Select the text and insert a hyperlink to the football.asp page. Save all changes, publish your page, and test it.

(continued)

In the Lab

Adding a Database Results Page to a Web *(continued)*

9. Print the results displayed on the Football products page (Figure 5-73). Write your name on the page and hand it in to your instructor.

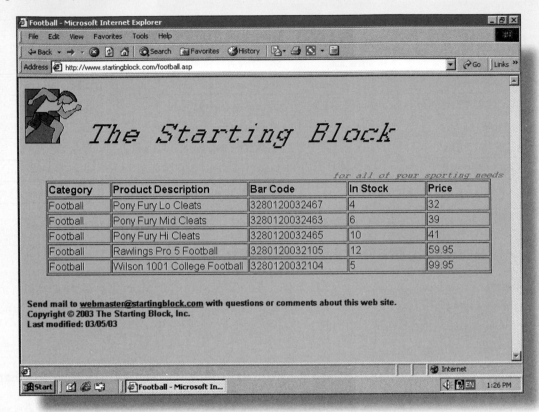

FIGURE 5-73

3 Creating a No Frames Page

Problem: You like the frames used in Project 5, but believe that users should have a choice to not use frames, regardless of the capabilities of their browser. You want to add a No Frames version to Nikki's Web site.

Instructions: Using Nikki's Web from Project 5, perform the following tasks. If you did not complete this exercise in Project 5, see your instructor for a copy of the required files.

1. Open the Contents page, ClassAdsTOC.htm. Insert a 1 by 3 table at the top of the page. Drag the image hyperlink and Link bar and drop them into the left cell. Position the insertion point in the center cell. Hold down the CTRL key and the SHIFT key and then press the SPACEBAR three times to insert three non-breaking spaces. Position the insertion point in the right cell and then type To place a new advertisement or to view advertisements by category, click the corresponding link in the list to the left. to enter the cell text. Drag the cell borders to adjust cell widths as needed. Modify the table properties and set the border size to zero. Save the changes.

2. Open the Class Ads main page, ClassAdsMain.htm. Right-click the left frame. Click Frame Properties on the shortcut menu. When the Frame Properties dialog box displays, click to deselect the Resizable in browser check box in the Options area. Click the OK button.

In the Lab

3. Click the No Frames tab. Position the insertion point after the line that begins, This page uses frames, press the ENTER key and then type Use the No Frames version to access the same content. Select the text, No Frames version, and then insert a hyperlink to ClassAdsTOC.htm.

4. Click the Normal tab. In the index.htm page, position the insertion point below the hyperlink to the Classified Ads page. Use a font size of 2 (10 pt) and then type (no frames version) to enter the text. Center the line, if necessary. Select the inserted text and create a hyperlink to ClassAdsTOC.htm. Save all changes and publish your changed pages.

5. Test the no frames version by viewing the frames page in a browser and clicking the (no frames version) hyperlink. Each of the hyperlinks should display the corresponding page in a new browser window, except for the Home page link, which returns you to the Home page. Your pages should resemble those shown in Figure 5-74.

6. Print the modified No Frames page, Home page, and the ClassAdsTOC.htm page. Write your name on them, and hand them in to your instructor.

FIGURE 5-74

Cases and Places

The difficulty of these case studies varies:
▶ are the least difficult; ▶▶ are more difficult; and ▶▶▶ are the most difficult.

1 ▶ Modify your resume page from Project 4 to use frames. Remove the leftmost column with the hyperlinks and place them into a contents frame. Include a hyperlink to the page for suggestions and responses created in the previous project.

2 ▶ Modify the web for your classical literature course from Project 4 to use frames for the book reviews and the discussion forum.

3 ▶▶ Modify the departmental Web page you created for your school in the previous project to provide results of the course evaluations page.

4 ▶▶ If necessary, create a new frames page template to display a frames page with a main frame, a contents frame, and a footer frame. Incorporate this frames page for your grandparents' 50th wedding anniversary Web site. Add a database results page for the data collected into the database. Include hyperlinks to the pages created in previous projects, as well as the new page.

5 ▶▶▶ Create both a frames and a no frames page to provide access to all forms and pages in the intramural basketball Web page that you updated in Project 4. Create new database results pages to display results previously stored in the database.

APPENDIX A
Microsoft FrontPage Help System

Using the FrontPage Help System

This appendix shows you how to use the FrontPage Help system. At anytime while you are using FrontPage, you can interact with its Help system and display information on any FrontPage topic. It is a complete reference manual at your fingertips.

As shown in Figure A-1, you can access FrontPage's Help system in four primary ways:

1. Ask a Question box on the menu bar
2. Function key F1 on the keyboard
3. Microsoft FrontPage Help command on the Help menu
4. Microsoft FrontPage Help button on the Standard toolbar

If you use the Ask a Question box on the menu bar, FrontPage responds by opening the Microsoft FrontPage Help window, which gives you direct access to its Help system. If you use one of the other three ways to access FrontPage's Help system, FrontPage responds in one of two ways:

1. If the Office Assistant is turned on, then the Office Assistant displays with a balloon (lower-right side in Figure A-1).
2. If the Office Assistant is turned off, then the Microsoft FrontPage Help window opens (lower-left side in Figure A-1).

FIGURE A-1

The best way to familiarize yourself with the FrontPage Help system is to use it. The next several pages show examples of how to use the Help system. Following the examples are a set of exercises titled Use Help that will sharpen your FrontPage Help system skills.

Ask a Question Box

The **Ask a Question box** on the right side of the menu bar lets you type questions in your own words, or you can type terms, such as chart, replace, or freeze panes. FrontPage responds by displaying a list of topics related to the term(s) you entered. The following steps show how to use the Ask a Question box to obtain information on chart types.

Steps To Obtain Help Using the Ask a Question Box

1 Click the Ask a Question box on the right side of the menu bar, type themes, and then press the ENTER key. When the Ask a Question list displays, point to the Change the color scheme of a theme link.

The Ask a Question list displays (Figure A-2). Clicking the See more link displays additional links.

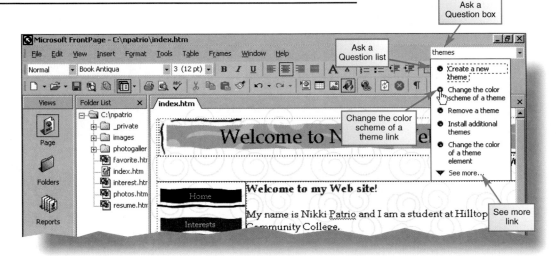

FIGURE A-2

2 Click Change the color scheme of a theme. Point to the Microsoft FrontPage Help window title bar.

The Microsoft FrontPage Help window displays information about changing the color scheme of a theme (Figure A-3).

FIGURE A-3

FIGURE A-4

3 **Double-click the Microsoft FrontPage Help window title bar. Click the Show All link in the upper-right corner of the window.**

The Microsoft FrontPage Help window displays across the entire screen (Figure A-4). Information about themes displays on the right side.

4 **Click the Close button on the Microsoft FrontPage Help window title bar.**

The Microsoft FrontPage Help window closes and the worksheet is active.

If the Contents sheet is active on the left side of the Microsoft FrontPage Help window, then FrontPage opens the book that pertains to the topic for which you are requesting help. In this case, FrontPage opens the Designing Web Pages book and the Themes book, which includes a list of topics related to themes. If the information on the right side is not satisfactory, you can click one of the topics in the Contents sheet to display alternative information related to the term, themes.

As you enter questions and terms in the Ask a Question box, FrontPage adds them to its list. Thus, if you click the Ask a Question box arrow, a list of previously asked questions and terms will display.

Use the six buttons in the upper-left corner of the Microsoft FrontPage Help window (Figure A-4) to navigate through the Help system, change the display, and print the contents of the window. Table A-1 lists the function of each of these buttons.

Table A-1	Microsoft FrontPage Help Toolbar Buttons	
BUTTON	**NAME**	**FUNCTION**
	Auto Tile	Tiles the Microsoft FrontPage Help window and Microsoft FrontPage window when the Microsoft FrontPage Help window is maximized
or	Show or Hide	Displays or hides the Contents, Answer Wizard, and Index tabs
	Back	Displays the previous Help topic
	Forward	Displays the next Help topic
	Print	Prints the current Help topic
	Options	Displays a list of commands

The Office Assistant

The **Office Assistant** is an icon (lower-right side of Figure A-1 on page E A.01) that displays in the FrontPage window when it is turned on and not hidden. It has dual functions. First, it will respond in the same way the Ask a Question box does with a list of topics that relate to the entry you make in the text box at the bottom of the balloon. The entry can be in the form of a word, phrase, or question written as if you were talking to a human being. For example, if you want to learn more about saving a file, in the balloon text box, you can type any of the following terms or phrases: save, save a file, how do I save a file, or anything similar. The Office Assistant responds by displaying a list of topics from which you can choose. Once you choose a topic, it displays the corresponding information.

Second, the Office Assistant monitors your work and accumulates tips during a session on how you might increase your productivity and efficiency. You can view the tips at anytime. The accumulated tips display when you activate the Office Assistant balloon. Also, if at anytime you see a lightbulb above the Office Assistant, click it to display the most recent tip.

You may or may not want the Office Assistant to display on the screen at all times. You can hide it and then show it at a later time. You may prefer not to use the Office Assistant at all. Thus, not only do you need to know how to show and hide the Office Assistant, but you also need to know how to turn the Office Assistant on and off.

Showing and Hiding the Office Assistant

When FrontPage initially is installed, the Office Assistant may be off. You turn it on by invoking the **Show the Office Assistant command** on the Help menu. If the Office Assistant is on the screen and you want to hide it, you click the **Hide the Office Assistant command** on the Help menu. You also can right-click the Office Assistant to display its shortcut menu and then click the **Hide command** to hide it. You can move it to any location on the screen. You can click it to display the Office Assistant balloon, which allows you to request Help.

Turning the Office Assistant On and Off

The fact that the Office Assistant is hidden does not mean it is turned off. To turn the Office Assistant off, it must be displaying in the FrontPage window. You right-click it to display its shortcut menu (right-side of Figure A-5). Next, click Options on the shortcut menu. Invoking the **Options command** causes the **Office Assistant dialog box** to display (left-side of Figure A-5).

FIGURE A-5

The top check box on the **Options sheet** determines whether the Office Assistant is on or off. To turn the Office Assistant off, remove the check mark from the **Use the Office Assistant check box** and then click the OK button. As shown in Figure A-1 on page FP A.01, if the Office Assistant is off when you invoke Help, then FrontPage opens the Microsoft FrontPage Help window instead of displaying the Office Assistant. To turn the Office Assistant on at a later date, click the Show the Office Assistant command on the Help menu.

Through the Options command on the Office Assistant shortcut menu, you can change the look and feel of the Office Assistant. For example, you can hide the Office Assistant, turn the Office Assistant off, change the way it works, choose a different Office Assistant icon, or view an animation of the current one. These options also are available by clicking the **Options button** that displays in the Office Assistant balloon (Figure A-6).

The **Gallery sheet** in the Office Assistant dialog box (Figure A-5) allows you to change the appearance of the Office Assistant. The default is the paper clip (Clippit). You can change it to a bouncing red happy face (The Dot), a robot (F1), the Microsoft Office logo (Office Logo), a wizard (Merlin), the earth (Mother Nature), a cat (Links), or a dog (Rocky).

Using the Office Assistant

As indicated earlier, the Office Assistant allows you to enter a word, phrase, or question and then responds by displaying a list of topics from which you can choose to display Help. The following steps show how to use the Office Assistant to obtain Help on summing a range.

 Steps **To Use the Office Assistant**

1 If the Office Assistant is not on the screen, click Help on the menu bar and then click Show the Office Assistant. Click the Office Assistant. When the Office Assistant balloon displays, **type** how do I publish a web **in the text box immediately above the Options button. Point to the Search button.**

The Office Assistant balloon displays as shown in Figure A-6.

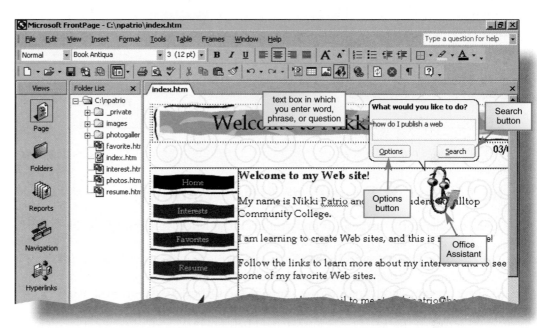

FIGURE A-6

2 Click the Search button. When the Office Assistant balloon redisplays, point to the topic, About publishing.

A new list of links display in the Office Assistant's balloon (Figure A-7).

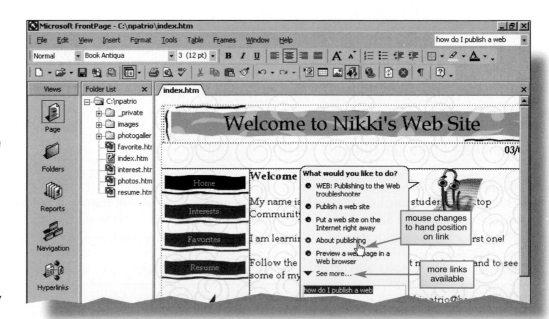

FIGURE A-7

3 **Click the topic About publishing.** If necessary, move or hide the Office Assistant so you can view all of the text in the Microsoft FrontPage Help window.

The Microsoft FrontPage Help window displays the information About publishing Web sites (Figure A-8).

4 **Click the Close button on the Microsoft FrontPage Help window title bar.**

FIGURE A-8

The Microsoft FrontPage Help Window

If the Office Assistant is turned off and you click the Microsoft FrontPage Help button on the Standard toolbar, the Microsoft FrontPage Help window opens (Figure A-9). The left side of this window contains three tabs: Contents, Answer Wizard, and Index. Each tab displays a sheet with powerful look-up capabilities.

Use the Contents sheet as you would a table of contents at the front of a book to look up Help. The Answer Wizard sheet answers your queries the same as the Office Assistant. You use the Index sheet in the same fashion as an index in a book to look up Help. Click the tabs to move from sheet to sheet.

Besides clicking the Microsoft FrontPage Help button on the Standard toolbar, you also can click the Microsoft FrontPage Help command on the Help menu, or press the F1 key to display the Microsoft FrontPage Help window to gain access to the three sheets.

Using the Contents Sheet

The **Contents sheet** is useful for displaying Help when you know the general category of the topic in question, but not the specifics. The following steps show how to use the Contents sheet to obtain information on how to create a hyperlink.

TO OBTAIN HELP USING THE CONTENTS SHEET

1 With the Office Assistant turned off, click the Microsoft FrontPage Help button on the Standard toolbar.

2 When the Microsoft FrontPage Help window opens, double-click the title bar to maximize the window. If necessary, click the Show button (see Table A-1 on page FP A.03) to display the tabs.

3 Click the Contents tab. Double-click the hyperlinks book on the left side of the window.

4 Click the topic Create a hyperlink below the hyperlinks book.

FrontPage displays Help on the subtopic Create a hyperlink (Figure A-9).

FIGURE A-9

Once the information on the subtopic displays, you can scroll through and read it or you can click the Print button to obtain a printed copy. If you decide to click another subtopic on the left or a link on the right, you can get back to the Help page shown in Figure A-9 by clicking the Back button.

Each topic in the Contents list is preceded by a book icon or question mark icon. A **book icon** indicates subtopics are available. A **question mark icon** means information on the topic will display if you double-click the title. The book icon opens when you double-click the book (or its title) or click the plus sign (+) to the left of the book icon.

Using the Answer Wizard Sheet

The **Answer Wizard sheet** works like the Office Assistant in that you enter a word, phrase, or question and it responds by listing topics from which you can choose to display Help. The following steps show how to use the Answer Wizard sheet to obtain Help on adding conditional formatting to a worksheet.

TO OBTAIN HELP USING THE ANSWER WIZARD SHEET

1 With the Office Assistant turned off, click the Microsoft FrontPage Help button on the Standard toolbar (see Figure A-6 on page FP A.05).

2 When the Microsoft FrontPage Help window opens, double-click the title bar to maximize the window. If necessary, click the Show button to display the tabs.

3 Click the Answer Wizard tab. Type formatting text in the What would you like to do? text box on the left side of the window. Click the Search button.

4 When a list of topics displays in the Select topic to display list, click Format text.

FrontPage displays Help on how to format text (Figure A-10 on the next page).

FIGURE A-10

If the topic, Format text, does not include the information you are seeking, click another topic in the list. Continue to click topics until you find the desired information.

Using the Index Sheet

The third sheet in the Microsoft FrontPage Help window is the Index sheet. Use the **Index sheet** to display Help when you know the keyword or the first few letters of the keyword you want to look up. The following steps show how to use the Index sheet to obtain Help on clip art.

TO OBTAIN HELP USING THE INDEX SHEET

1 With the Office Assistant turned off, click the Microsoft FrontPage Help button on the Standard toolbar.

2 When the Microsoft FrontPage Help window opens, double-click the title bar to maximize the window. If necessary, click the Show button to display the tabs.

3 Click the Index tab. Type clip art in the Type keywords text box on the left side of the window. Click the Search button.

4 When a list of topics displays in the Choose a topic list, click Find similar clips.

FrontPage displays Help on how to Find similar clips (Figure A-11). When you click the Search button, FrontPage automatically appends a semicolon to the keyword in the Type keywords text box.

What's This? Command and Question Mark Button • FP A.09

APPENDIX A

FIGURE A-11

An alternative to typing a keyword in the Type keywords text box is to scroll through the Or choose keywords list (the middle list on the left side of the window). When you locate the keyword you are searching for, double-click it to display Help on the topic. Also in the Or choose keywords list, the FrontPage Help system displays other topics that relate to the new keyword. As you begin typing a new keyword in the Type keywords text box, FrontPage jumps to that point in the middle list box. To begin a new search, click the Clear button.

What's This? Command and Question Mark Button

Use the What's This? command on the Help menu or the Question Mark button in a dialog box when you are not sure what an object on the screen is or what it does.

What's This? Command

You use the **What's This? command** on the Help menu to display a detailed ScreenTip. When you invoke this command, the mouse pointer changes to an arrow with a question mark. You then click any object on the screen, such as a button, to display the ScreenTip. For example, after you click the What's This? command on the Help menu and then click the Center button on the Formatting toolbar, a description of the Center button displays (Figure A-12 on the next page). You can print the ScreenTip by right-clicking it and then clicking Print Topic on the shortcut menu.

FIGURE A-12

Question Mark Button

In a fashion similar to the What's This? command, the **Question Mark button** displays a ScreenTip. You use the Question Mark button with dialog boxes. It is located in the upper-right corner on the title bar of dialog boxes, next to the Close button. For example, in Figure A-13, the AutoFormat dialog box displays on the screen. If you click the Question Mark button in the upper-right corner of the dialog box and then click one of the previewed formats in the AutoFormat dialog box, an explanation displays. You can print the ScreenTip by right-clicking it and then clicking Print Topic on the shortcut menu.

If a dialog box does not include a Question Mark button, press the SHIFT+F1 keys. This combination of keys displays an explanation or changes the mouse pointer to an arrow with a question mark. You then can click any object in the dialog box to display the ScreenTip.

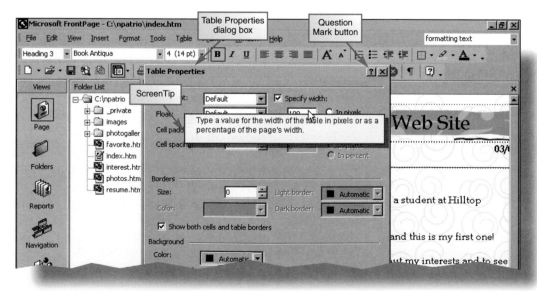

FIGURE A-13

Office on the Web Command

The **Office on the Web command** on the Help menu displays a Microsoft Web page containing up-to-date information on a variety of Office-related topics. To use this command, you must be connected to the Internet. When you invoke the Office on the Web command, the Assistance Center Home page displays. Read through the links that in general pertain to topics that relate to all Office XP topics. Scroll down and click the FrontPage link in the Help By Product area to display the Assistance Center FrontPage Help Articles Web page (Figure A-14). This Web page contains numerous helpful links related to FrontPage.

Other Help Commands

Four additional commands available on the Help menu are Activate Product, Detect and Repair, and About Microsoft FrontPage.

FIGURE A-14

Activate Product Command

The **Activate Product command** on the Help menu lets you activate FrontPage if it has not already been activated.

Detect and Repair Command

Use the **Detect and Repair command** on the Help menu if FrontPage is not running properly or if it is generating errors. When you invoke this command, the Detect and Repair dialog box displays. Click the Start button in the dialog box to initiate the detect and repair process.

About Microsoft FrontPage Command

The **About Microsoft FrontPage command** on the Help menu displays the About Microsoft FrontPage dialog box. The dialog box lists the owner of the software and the product identification. You need to know the product identification if you call Microsoft for assistance. The four buttons below the OK button are the System Info button, the Tech Support button, the Disabled Items button, and the Network Test button. The **System Info button** displays system information, including hardware resources, components, software environment, and applications. The **Tech Support button** displays technical assistance information. The **Disabled Items button** displays a list of Microsoft Office items disabled because they prevented FrontPage from functioning correctly. The **Network Test button** displays technical information about your network configuration.

Use Help

1 Using the Ask a Question Box

Instructions: Perform the following tasks using the FrontPage Help system.

1. Click the Ask a Question box on the menu bar, and then type how do I set table properties. Press the ENTER key.
2. Click Set the properties of a Table border in the Ask a Question list. Double-click the Microsoft FrontPage Help window title bar. Read and print the information. One at a time, click two of the links on the right side of the window to learn about table borders. Print the information. Hand in the printouts to your instructor. Use the Back and Forward buttons to return to the original page.
3. If necessary, click the Show button to display the tabs. Click the Contents tab to prepare for the next step. Click the Close button in the Microsoft FrontPage Help window.
4. Click the Contents tab. If necessary, click the plus sign (+) to the left of the Microsoft FrontPage Help book. Click the plus sign (+) to the left of the Hyperlinks book. One at a time, click the first three topics in the Hyperlinks book. Read and print each one. Close the Microsoft FrontPage Help window. Hand in the printouts to your instructor.

2 Expanding on the FrontPage Help System Basics

Instructions: Use the FrontPage Help system to understand the topics better and answer the questions listed below. Answer the questions on your own paper, or hand in the printed Help information to your instructor.

1. Right-click the Office Assistant. If it is not turned on, click Show the Office Assistant on the Help menu. When the shortcut menu displays, click Options. Click Use the Office Assistant to remove the check mark, and then click the OK button.
2. Click the Microsoft FrontPage Help button on the Standard toolbar. Maximize the Microsoft FrontPage Help window. If the tabs are hidden on the left side, click the Show button. Click the Index tab. Type undo in the Type keywords text box. Click the Search button. Click Restore original settings for buttons, commands, or toolbars. Print the information. Click the Hide and then Show buttons. Click the Show All link. Read and print the information. Close the Microsoft FrontPage Help window. Hand in the printouts to your instructor.
3. Press the F1 key. Click the Answer Wizard tab. Type help in the What would you like to do? text box, and then click the Search button. Click About getting help while you work. Read through the information that displays. Print the information. Click the first two links. Read and print the information for both.
4. Click the Contents tab. Click the plus sign (+) to the left of the Smart Tags book. One at a time, click the first three topics in the Hyperlinks book. Read and print each one. Close the Microsoft FrontPage Help window. Hand in the printouts to your instructor.
5. Click Help on the menu bar and then click What's This? Click the Format Painter button on the Standard toolbar. Right-click the ScreenTip and then click Print Topic on the shortcut menu. Click the Save As command on the File menu. When the Save As dialog box displays, click the Question Mark button on the title bar. Click the Save in box. Right-click the ScreenTip and then click Print Topic. Hand in the printouts to your instructor.

APPENDIX B
Speech and Handwriting Recognition

Introduction

This appendix discusses how you can create and modify worksheets using Office XP's new input technologies. Office XP provides a variety of **text services**, which enable you to speak commands and enter text in an application. The most common text service is the keyboard. Two new text services included with Office XP are speech recognition and handwriting recognition.

When Windows was installed on your computer, you specified a default language. For example, most users in the United States select English (United States) as the default language. Through text services, you can add more than 90 additional languages and varying dialects such as Basque, English (Zimbabwe), French (France), French (Canada), German (Germany), German (Austria), and Swahili. With multiple languages available, you can switch from one language to another while working in FrontPage. If you change the language or dialect, then text services may change the functions of the keys on the keyboard, adjust speech recognition, and alter handwriting recognition.

The Language Bar

You know that text services are installed properly when the Language Indicator button displays by the clock in the tray status area on the Windows taskbar (Figure B-1a) or the Language bar displays on the screen (Figure B-1b or B-1c). If the Language Indicator button displays in the tray status area, click it, and then click the **Show the Language bar command** (Figure B-1a). The Language bar displays on the screen in the same location it displayed last time.

You can drag the Language bar to any location in the window by pointing to its move handle, which is the vertical line on its left side (Figure B-1b). When the mouse pointer changes to a four-headed arrow, drag the Language bar to the desired location.

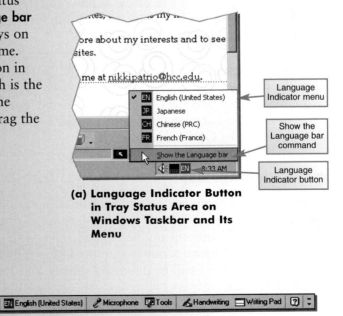

(a) Language Indicator Button in Tray Status Area on Windows Taskbar and Its Menu

(b) Language Bar with Text Labels Disabled

(c) Language Bar with Text Labels Enabled

FIGURE B-1

If you are sure that one of the services was installed and neither the Language Indicator button nor the Language bar displays, then do the following:

1. Click Start on the Windows taskbar, point to Settings, click Control Panel, and then double-click the Text Services icon in the Control Panel window.
2. When the Text Services dialog box displays, click the Language Bar button, click the Show the Language bar on the desktop check box to select it, and then click the OK button in the Language Bar Settings dialog box.
3. Click the OK button in the Text Services dialog box.
4. Close the Control Panel window.

You can perform tasks related to text services by using the **Language bar**. The Language bar may display with just the icon on each button (Figure B-1b) or it may display with text labels to the right of the icon on each button (Figure B-1c). Changing the appearance of the Language bar will be discussed shortly.

Buttons on the Language Bar

The Language bar shown in Figure B-2a contains eight buttons. The number of buttons on your Language bar may be different. These buttons are used to select the language, customize the Language bar, control the microphone, control handwriting, and obtain help.

When you click the **Language Indicator button** on the far left side of the Language bar, the Language Indicator menu displays a list of the active languages (Figure B-2b) from which you can choose. The **Microphone button**, the second button from the left, enables and disables the microphone. When the microphone is enabled, text services adds two buttons and a balloon to the Language toolbar (Figure B-2c). These additional buttons and the balloon will be discussed shortly.

The third button from the left on the Language bar is the Speech Tools button. The **Speech Tools button** displays a menu of commands (Figure B-2d) that allow you to hide or show the balloon on the Language bar; train the Speech Recognition service so that it can better interpret your voice; add and delete words from its dictionary, such as names and other words not understood easily; and change the user profile so more than one person can use the microphone on the same computer.

The fourth button from the left on the Language bar is the Handwriting button. The **Handwriting button** displays the **Handwriting menu** (Figure B-2e), which lets you choose the Writing Pad (Figure B-2f), Write Anywhere (Figure B-2g), or the on-screen keyboard (Figure B-2h). The **On-Screen Symbol Keyboard command** on the Handwriting menu displays an on-screen keyboard that allows you to enter special symbols that are not available on a standard keyboard. You can choose only one form of handwriting at a time.

The fifth button indicates which one of the handwriting forms is active. For example, in Figure B-1a on the previous page, the Writing Pad is active. The handwriting recognition capabilities of text services will be discussed shortly.

The sixth button from the left on the Language bar is the Help button. The **Help button** displays the Help menu. If you click the Language Bar Help command on the Help menu, the Language Bar Help window displays (Figure B-2i). On the far right of the Language bar are two buttons stacked above and below each other. The top button is the Minimize button and the bottom button is the Options button. The **Minimize button** minimizes (hides) the Language bar so that the Language Indicator button displays in the tray status area on the Windows taskbar. The next section discusses the Options button.

Customizing the Language Bar

The down arrow icon immediately below the Minimize button in Figure B-2a is called the Options button. The **Options button** displays a menu of text services options (Figure B-2j). You can use this menu to hide the Speech Tools, Handwriting, and Help buttons on the Language bar by clicking their names to remove the check mark to the left of each button. The Settings command on the Options menu displays a dialog box that lets you customize the Language bar. This command will be discussed shortly. The Restore Defaults command redisplays hidden buttons on the Language bar.

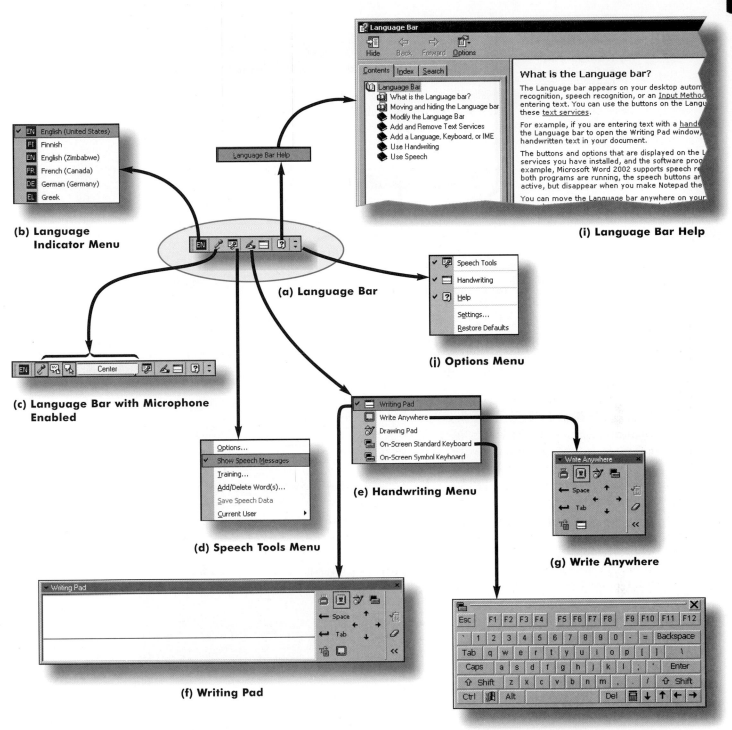

(b) Language Indicator Menu

(i) Language Bar Help

(a) Language Bar

(j) Options Menu

(c) Language Bar with Microphone Enabled

(e) Handwriting Menu

(d) Speech Tools Menu

(g) Write Anywhere

(f) Writing Pad

(h) On-Screen Standard Keyboard

FIGURE B-2

If you right-click the Language bar, a shortcut menu displays (Figure B-3a on the next page). This shortcut menu lets you further customize the Language bar. The **Minimize command** on the shortcut menu minimizes the Language bar the same as the Minimize button on the Language bar. The **Transparency command** toggles the Language bar between being solid and transparent. You can see through a transparent Language bar (Figure B-3b). The **Text Labels command** toggles text labels on the Language bar on (Figure B-3c) and off (Figure B-3a). The **Additional icons in taskbar command** toggles between only showing the Language Indicator button in the tray status area and showing icons that represent the text services that are active (Figure B-3d).

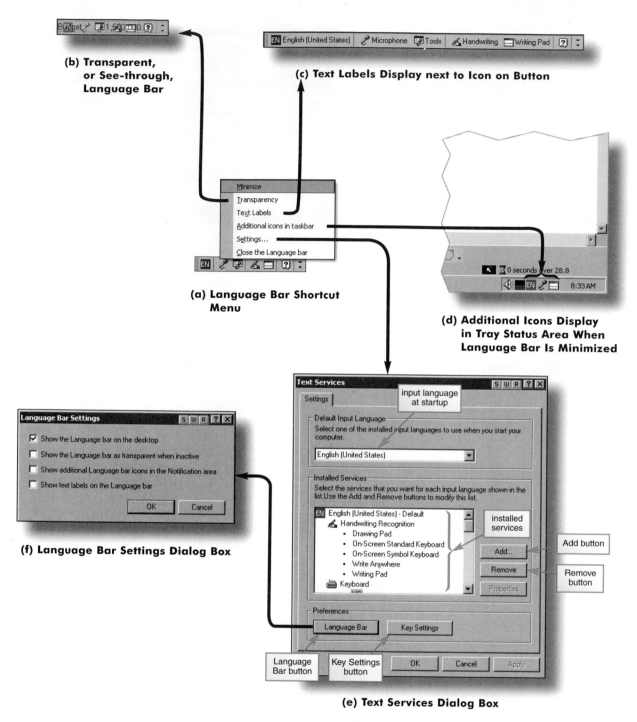

(b) Transparent, or See-through, Language Bar

(c) Text Labels Display next to Icon on Button

(a) Language Bar Shortcut Menu

(d) Additional Icons Display in Tray Status Area When Language Bar Is Minimized

(f) Language Bar Settings Dialog Box

(e) Text Services Dialog Box

FIGURE B-3

The **Settings command** displays the Text Services dialog box (Figure B-3e). The **Text Services dialog box** allows you to select the language at startup; add and remove text services; modify keys on the keyboard; and modify the Language bar. If you want to remove any one of the entries in the Installed Services list, select the entry, and then click the Remove button. If you want to add a service, click the Add button. The Key Settings button allows you to modify the keyboard. If you click the **Language Bar button** in the Text Services dialog box, the **Language Bar Settings dialog box** displays (Figure B-3f). This dialog box contains Language bar options, some of which are the same as the commands on the Language bar shortcut menu described earlier.

The **Close the Language bar command** on the shortcut menu shown in Figure B-3a closes the Language bar and hides the Language Indicator button in the tray status area on the Windows taskbar. If you close the Language bar and want to redisplay it, follow the instructions at the top of page E B.02.

Speech Recognition

The **Speech Recognition service** available with Office XP enables your computer to recognize human speech through a microphone. The microphone has two modes: dictation and voice command (Figure B-4). You switch between the two modes by clicking the Dictation button and the Voice Command button on the Language bar. These buttons display only when you turn on Speech Recognition by clicking the **Microphone button** on the Language bar (Figure B-5). If you are using the Microphone button for the very first time in FrontPage, it will require that you check your microphone settings and step through voice training before activating the Speech Recognition service.

The **Dictation button** places the microphone in Dictation mode. In **Dictation mode,** whatever you speak is entered as text in the active cell. The **Voice Command button** places the microphone in Voice Command mode. In **Voice Command mode,** whatever you speak is interpreted as a command. If you want to turn off the microphone, click the Microphone button on the Language bar or in Voice Command mode say, "Mic off" (pronounced mike off). It is important to remember that minimizing the Language bar does not turn off the microphone.

(a) Enter Text in the Active Page
(A1) in Dictation Mode

(b) Enter Commands in Voice
Command Mode

FIGURE B-4

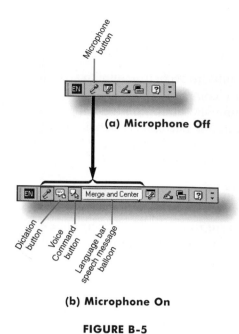

(a) Microphone Off

(b) Microphone On

FIGURE B-5

The **Language bar speech message balloon** shown in Figure B-5b displays messages that may offer help or hints. In Voice Command mode, the name of the last recognized command you said displays. If you use the mouse or keyboard instead of the microphone, a message will appear in the Language bar speech message balloon indicating the word you could say. In Dictation mode, the message, Dictating, usually displays. The Speech Recognition service, however, will display messages to inform you that you are talking too soft, too loud, too fast, or to ask you to repeat what you said by displaying, What was that?

Getting Started with Speech Recognition

For the microphone to function properly, you should follow these steps:

1. Make sure your computer meets the minimum requirements.
2. Install Speech Recognition.
3. Set up and position your microphone, preferably a close-talk headset with gain adjustment support.
4. Train Speech Recognition.

The following sections describe these steps in more detail.

SPEECH RECOGNITION SYSTEM REQUIREMENTS For Speech Recognition to work on your computer, it needs the following:

1. Microsoft Windows 98 or later or Microsoft Windows NT 4.0 or later
2. At least 128 MB RAM
3. 400 MHz or faster processor
4. Microphone and sound card

INSTALLING SPEECH RECOGNITION If Speech Recognition is not installed on your computer, start Microsoft Word and then click Speech on the Tools menu.

SETUP AND POSITION YOUR MICROPHONE Set up your microphone as follows:

1. Connect your microphone to the sound card in the back of the computer.
2. Position the microphone approximately one inch out from and to the side of your mouth. Position it so you are not breathing into it.
3. On the Language bar, click the Speech Tools button, and then click Options (Figure B-6a).
4. When the Speech Properties dialog box displays (Figure B-6b), if necessary, click the Speech Recognition tab.
5. Click the Configure Microphone button. Follow the Microphone Wizard directions as shown in Figures B-6c, B-6d, and B-6e. The Next button will remain dimmed in Figure B-6d until the volume meter consistently stays in the green area.
6. If someone else installed Speech Recognition, click the New button in the Speech Properties dialog box and enter your name. Click the Train Profile button and step through the Voice Training Wizard. The Voice Training Wizard will require that you enter your gender and age group. It then will step you through voice training.

You can adjust the microphone further by clicking the **Settings button** (Figure B-6b) in the Speech Properties dialog box. The Settings button displays the **Recognition Profile Settings dialog box** that allows you to adjust the pronunciation sensitivity and accuracy versus recognition response time.

(a) Speech Tools Menu

(b) Speech Properties Dialog Box

(c) Adjust Microphone

(d) Adjust Volume

(e) Test Microphone

FIGURE B-6

TRAIN THE SPEECH RECOGNITION SERVICE The Speech Recognition service will understand most commands and some dictation without any training at all. It will recognize much more of what you speak, however, if you take the time to train it. After one training session, it will recognize 85 to 90 percent of your words. As you do more training, accuracy will rise to 95 percent. If you feel that too many mistakes are being made, then continue to train the service. The more training you do, the more accurately it will work for you. Follow these steps to train the Speech Recognition service:

(a) Speech Tools Menu

(b) Voice Training Dialog Box

FIGURE B-7

1. Click the Speech Tools button on the Language bar and then click Training (Figure B-7a).
2. When the **Voice Training dialog box** displays (Figure B-7b), click one of the sessions and then click the Next button.
3. Complete the training session, which should take less than 15 minutes.

If you are serious about using a microphone to speak to your computer, you need to take the time to go through at least three of the eight training sessions listed in Figure B-7b.

Using Speech Recognition

Speech recognition lets you enter text into a page similarly to speaking into a tape recorder. Instead of typing, you can dictate text that you want to display in the page, and you can issue voice commands. In **Voice Command mode**, you can speak menu names, commands on menus, toolbar button names, and dialog box option buttons, check boxes, list boxes, and button names. Speech Recognition, however, is not a completely hands-free form of input. Speech recognition works best if you use a combination of your voice, the keyboard, and the mouse. You soon will discover that Dictation mode is far less accurate than Voice Command mode. Table B-1 lists some tips that will improve the Speech Recognition service's accuracy considerably.

Table B-1	Tips to Improve Speech Recognition
NUMBER	**TIP**
1	The microphone hears everything. Though the Speech Recognition service filters out background noise, it is recommended that you work in a quiet environment.
2	Try not to move the microphone around once it is adjusted.
3	Speak in a steady tone and speak clearly.
4	In Dictation mode, do not pause between words. A phrase is easier to interpret than a word. Sounding out syllables in a word will make it more difficult for the Speech Recognition service to interpret what you are saying.
5	If you speak too loudly or too softly, it makes it difficult for the Speech Recognition service to interpret what you said. Check the Language bar speech message balloon for an indication that you may be speaking too loudly or too softly.
6	If you experience problems after training, adjust the recognition options that control accuracy and rejection by clicking the Settings button shown in Figure B-6b on the previous page.
7	When you are finished using the microphone, turn it off by clicking the Microphone button on the Language bar or in Voice Command mode say, "Mic off." Leaving the microphone on is the same as leaning on the keyboard.
8	If the Speech Recognition service is having difficulty with unusual words, then add the words to its dictionary by using the Add/Delete Word(s) command on the Speech Tools menu (Figure B-8a). The last names of individuals and the names of companies are good examples of the types of words you should add to the dictionary.
9	Training will improve accuracy; practice will improve confidence.

The last command on the Speech Tools menu is the Current User command (Figure B-8a). The **Current User command** is useful for multiple users who share a computer. It allows them to configure their own individual profiles, and then switch between users as they use the computer.

For additional information on the Speech Recognition service, click the Help button on the Standard toolbar, click the Answer Wizard tab, and search for the phrase, Speech Recognition.

Handwriting Recognition

Using the Office XP handwriting recognition capabilities, you can enter text and numbers into FrontPage by writing instead of typing. You can write using a special handwriting device that connects to your computer or you can write on the screen using your mouse. Four basic methods of handwriting are available by clicking the **Handwriting button** on the Language bar: Writing Pad; Write Anywhere; Drawing Pad; and On-Screen Keyboard. The Drawing Pad button is dimmed, which means it is not available in FrontPage. Although the on-screen keyboard does not involve handwriting recognition, it is part of the Handwriting menu and, therefore, will be discussed in this section.

If your Language bar does not include the Handwriting button (Figures B-1b or B-1c on page E B.01), then for installation instructions click the Help button on the Standard toolbar, click the Answer Wizard tab, and search for the phrase Install Handwriting Recognition.

(a) Speech Tools Menu

(b) Add/Delete Word(s) Dialog Box

FIGURE B-8

Writing Pad

To display the Writing Pad, click the Handwriting button on the Language bar and then click Writing Pad (Figure B-9). The **Writing Pad** resembles a note pad with one or more lines on which you can use freehand to print or write in cursive. With the **Text button** enabled, you can form letters on the line by moving the mouse while holding down the mouse button. To the right of the note pad is a rectangular toolbar. Use the buttons on this toolbar to adjust the Writing Pad, select cells, and activate other handwriting applications.

FIGURE B-9

Consider the example in Figure B-9 on the previous page. With the page selected, the word, Computers, is written in cursive on the **Pen line** in the Writing Pad. As soon as the word is complete, the Handwriting Recognition service automatically assigns the word to the page.

You can customize the Writing Pad by clicking the **Options button** on the left side of the title bar and then clicking the Options command (Figure B-10a). Invoking the **Options command** causes the Handwriting Options dialog box to display. The **Handwriting Options dialog box** contains two sheets: Common and Writing Pad. The **Common sheet** lets you change the pen color and pen width, adjust recognition, and customize the toolbar area of the Writing Pad. The **Writing Pad sheet** allows you to change the background color and the number of lines that display in the Writing Pad. Both sheets contain a **Restore Default button** to restore the settings to what they were when the software was installed initially.

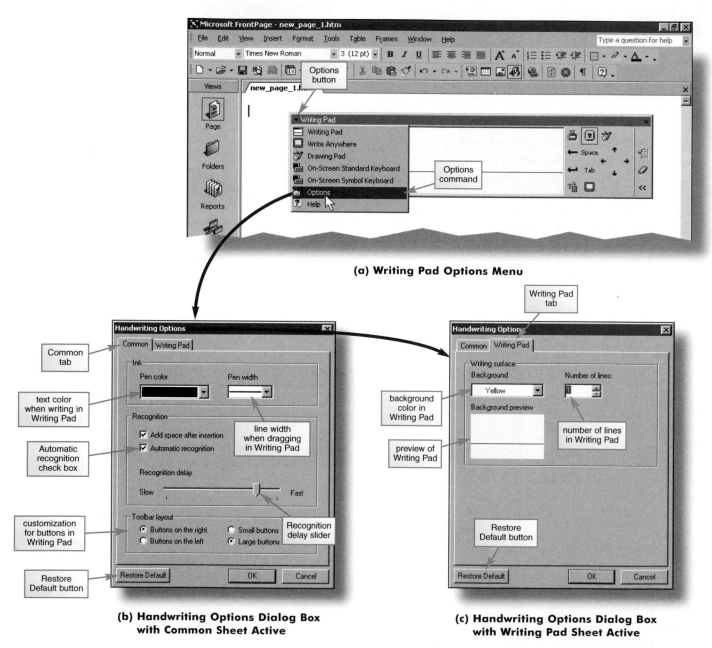

(a) Writing Pad Options Menu

**(b) Handwriting Options Dialog Box
with Common Sheet Active**

**(c) Handwriting Options Dialog Box
with Writing Pad Sheet Active**

FIGURE B-10

When you first start using the Writing Pad, you may want to remove the check mark from the **Automatic recognition check box** in the Common sheet in the Handwriting Options dialog box (Figure B-10b). With the check mark removed, the Handwriting Recognition service will not interpret what you write in the Writing Pad until you click the **Recognize Now button** on the toolbar (Figure B-9 on the previous page). This allows you to pause and adjust your writing.

The best way to learn how to use the Writing Pad is to practice with it. Also, for more information, click the Help button on the Standard toolbar, click the Answer Wizard tab, and search for the phrase, Handwriting Recognition.

Write Anywhere

Rather than use a Writing Pad, you can write anywhere on the screen by invoking the **Write Anywhere command** on the Handwriting menu (Figure B-11) that displays when you click the Handwriting button on the Language bar. In this case, the entire window is your writing pad.

In Figure B-11, the word, Chip, is written in cursive using the mouse button. Shortly after you finish writing the word, the Handwriting Recognition service interprets it, assigns it to the page, and erases what you wrote.

It is recommended that when you first start using the Writing Anywhere service that you remove the check mark from the Automatic recognition check box in the Common sheet in the Handwriting Options dialog box (Figure B-10b). With the check mark removed, the Handwriting Recognition service will not interpret what you write on the screen until you click the Recognize Now button on the toolbar (Figure B-11).

Write Anywhere is more difficult to use than the Writing Pad, because when you click the mouse button, FrontPage may interpret the action as selecting an item on the page rather than starting to write. For this reason, it is recommended that you use the Writing Pad.

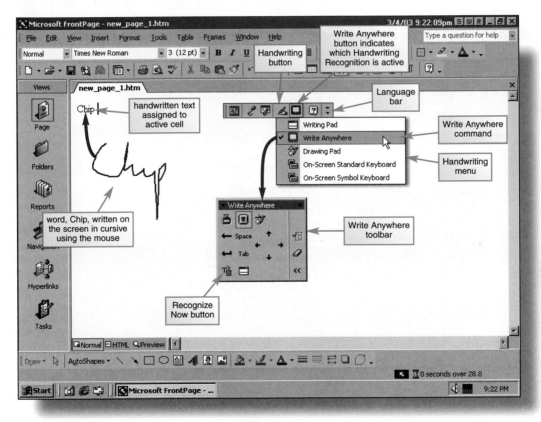

FIGURE B-11

On-Screen Keyboard

The **On-Screen Standard Keyboard command** on the Handwriting menu (Figure B-12) displays an on-screen keyboard. The **on-screen keyboard** lets you enter data onto a page by using your mouse to click the keys. The on-screen keyboard is similar to the type found on handheld computers.

The **On-Screen Symbol Keyboard command** on the Handwriting menu (Figure B-12) displays a special on-screen keyboard that allows you to enter symbols that are not on your keyboard, as well as Unicode characters. **Unicode characters** use a coding scheme capable of representing all the world's current languages.

FIGURE B-12

APPENDIX C
Publishing Office Web Pages to a Web Server

When you publish a FrontPage web, you can use one of two techniques: by using the Hypertext Transfer Protocol (HTTP), if the Microsoft FrontPage Server Extensions are installed, or by using File Transfer Protocol (FTP). In both cases, a Web folder for that location is created in My Network Places. A **Web folder** is an Office shortcut to a Web server. You may open and save your web directly on the server by accessing it via the Web folder, rather than editing your web locally and then using the publish procedure in FrontPage.

You should contact your network system administrator or technical support staff at your Internet Service Provider (ISP) to determine if their site supports the functionality that you need, and to obtain the necessary permissions to access the Web server. To use Web folders within Office products to publish to a server, you must have the Office Server Extensions (OSE) installed on your computer.

Using Web Folders to Edit Web Pages

Once your FrontPage web has been published, a Web folder is created on your machine. Office adds the name of the folder to the list of current Web folders. You can open the web just like you would open a local web. A **local web** is a web stored on your local machine. You may be asked to supply a user name and password when you access a Web folder. Table C-1 explains how to open a web using a Web folder.

Table C-1   Opening a Web with a Web Folder
1. Click File on the menu bar and then click Open Web.
2. When the Open Web dialog box displays, Click My Network Places on the Look in bar.
3. Click the Web folder name in the My Network Places list.
4. Click the Open button.
5. If the Enter Network Password dialog box displays, type the user name and password in the respective text boxes and then click the OK button.

You can use other Office programs to access this folder. For example, you can use Windows Explorer to view your Web folders and to open a given Web folder. By accessing your web on the server where it was published, you do not have to publish your changes, only save them as you would any other file. You should be aware that editing the web directly on the server has some risk: you might lose your changes if you lose your connection to the server, and you will not have a local copy of your web. Table C-2 on the next page explains how to save to a Web folder.

Table C-2 Saving to a Web Folder
1. Click File on the menu bar and then click Save As.
2. When the Save As dialog box displays, type the Web page file name in the File name text box. Do not press the ENTER key.
3. Click My Network Places on the Places Bar.
4. Double-click the Web folder name in the Save in list.
5. If the Enter Network Password dialog box displays, type the user name and password in the respective text boxes and then click the OK button.
6. Click the Save button in the Save As dialog box.

Using FTP to Publish Web Pages

In addition to using the FTP protocol when publishing a web (necessary when publishing to a server without the FrontPage Server Extensions), you also can create an FTP location and save your files to that location. An **FTP location**, also called an **FTP site**, is a collection of files that reside on an FTP server. Similar to the publishing procedure in FrontPage, when adding an FTP location you must obtain the name of the FTP site, typically a URL of the FTP server, a user name, and a password that allows you to access the FTP server. Table C-3 explains how to add an FTP location.

Table C-3   Adding an FTP Location
1. Click File on the menu bar and then click Save As (or Open).
2. In the Save As dialog box, click the Save in box arrow and then click Add/Modify FTP Locations in the Save in list; or in the Open dialog box, click the Look in box arrow and then click Add/Modify FTP Locations in the Look in list.
3. When the Add/Modify FTP Locations dialog box displays, type the name of the FTP site in the Name of FTP site text box. If the site allows anonymous logon, click Anonymous in the Log on as area; if you have a user name for the site, click User in the Log on as area and then enter the user name. Enter the password in the Password text box. Click the OK button.
4. Close the Save As or the Open dialog box.

Office adds the name of the FTP site to the FTP locations list. You can save files using this list. FrontPage does not support opening files from an FTP location. Table C-4 explains how to save to an FTP location.

Table C-4   Saving to an FTP Location
1. Click File on the menu bar and then click Save As.
2. When the Save As dialog box displays, type the Web page file name in the File name text box. Do not press the ENTER key.
3. Click the Save in box arrow and then click FTP Locations.
4. Double-click the name of the FTP site to which you wish to save.
5. When the FTP Log On dialog box displays, enter your user name and password and then click the OK button.
6. Click the Save button in the Save As dialog box.

APPENDIX D
Resetting the FrontPage Toolbars and Menus

FrontPage customization capabilities allow you to create custom toolbars by adding and deleting buttons and personalize menus based on their usage. Each time you start FrontPage, the toolbars and menus display using the same settings as the last time you used it. This appendix shows you how to reset the Standard and Formatting toolbars and menus to their installation settings.

 To Reset the Standard and Formatting Toolbars

1 **Click the Toolbar Options button on the Standard toolbar and then point to Add or Remove Buttons on the Toolbar Options menu.**

The Toolbar Options menu and Add or Remove Buttons submenu display (Figure D-1).

FIGURE D-1

2 **Point to Standard on the Add or Remove Buttons submenu. When the Standard submenu displays, scroll down and then point to Reset Toolbar.**

The Standard submenu displays indicating the buttons and boxes that display on the toolbar (Figure D-2). To remove any buttons, click a button name with a check mark to the left of the name to remove the check mark.

3 **Click Reset Toolbar.**

Excel resets the Standard toolbar to its installation settings.

4 **Reset the Formatting toolbar by following Steps 1 through 3 and replacing any reference to the Standard toolbar with the Formatting toolbar.**

 Ways

1. On View menu point to Toolbars, click Customize on Toolbars submenu, click Toolbars tab, click toolbar name, click Reset button, click OK button, click Close button

2. Right-click toolbar, click Customize on shortcut menu, click Toolbars tab, click toolbar name, click Reset button, click OK button, click Close button

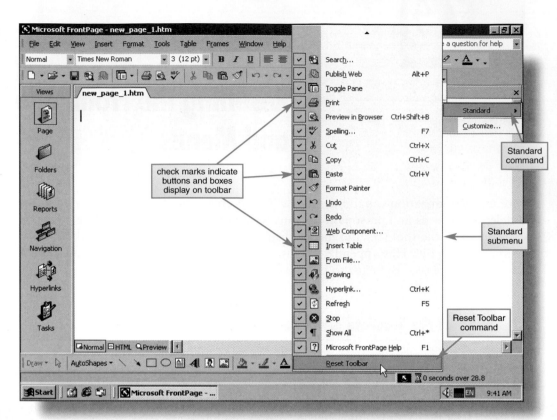

FIGURE D-2

Steps To Reset Menus

1 **Click the Toolbar Options button on the Standard toolbar and then point to Add or Remove Buttons on the Toolbar Options menu. Point to Customize on the Add or Remove Buttons submenu.**

The Toolbar Options menu and Add or Remove Buttons submenu display (Figure D-3).

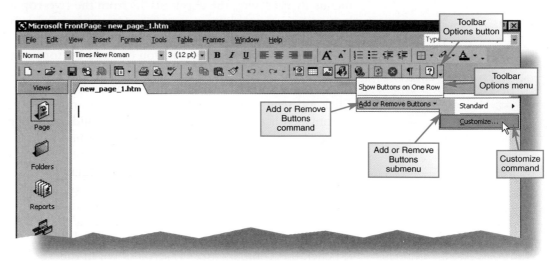

FIGURE D-3

2 **Click Customize. When the Customize dialog box displays, click the Options tab and then point to the Reset my usage data button.**

The Customize dialog box displays (Figure D-4). The **Customize dialog box** contains three tabbed sheets used for customizing the FrontPage toolbars and menus.

3 **Click the Reset my usage data button. When the Microsoft FrontPage dialog box displays, click the Yes button. Click the Close button in the Customize dialog box.**

FrontPage resets the menus to the installation settings.

FIGURE D-4

Other Ways

1. On View menu point to Toolbars, click Customize on Toolbars submenu, click Options tab, click Reset my usage data button, click Yes button, click Close button

In the **Options sheet** in the Customize dialog box shown in Figure D-4 on the previous page, you can turn off toolbars displaying on two rows and turn off short menus by removing the check marks from the two top check boxes. Click the **Help button** in the lower-left corner of the Customize dialog box to display Help topics that will assist you in customizing toolbars and menus.

Using the **Commands sheet**, you can add buttons to toolbars and commands to menus. Recall that the menu bar at the top of the FrontPage window is a special toolbar. To add buttons, click the Commands tab in the Customize dialog box. Click a category name in the Categories list and then drag the command name in the Commands list to a toolbar. To add commands to a menu, click a category name in the Categories list, drag the command name in the Commands list to the menu name on the menu bar, and then, when the menu displays, drag the command to the desired location in the menu list of commands.

In the **Toolbars sheet**, you can add new toolbars and reset existing toolbars. If you add commands to menus as described in the previous paragraph and want to reset the menus to their default settings, do the following: (1) Click View on the menu bar and then point to Toolbars; (2) click Customize on the Toolbars submenu; (3) click the Toolbars tab; (4) scroll down in the Toolbars list and then click Worksheet Menu Bar; (5) click the Reset button; (6) click the OK button; and then (7) click the Close button.

APPENDIX E
Microsoft Office User Specialist Certification Program

What Is MOUS Certification?

The Microsoft Office User Specialist (MOUS) Certification Program provides a framework for measuring your proficiency with the Microsoft Office XP applications, such as Word 2002, Excel 2002, Access 2002, PowerPoint 2002, Outlook 2002, and FrontPage 2002. The levels of certification are described in Table E-1.

Table E-1   Levels of MOUS Certification

LEVEL	DESCRIPTION	REQUIREMENTS	CREDENTIAL AWARDED
Expert	Indicates that you have a comprehensive understanding of the advanced features in a specific Microsoft Office XP application	Pass any ONE of the Expert exams: Microsoft Word 2002 Expert Microsoft Excel 2002 Expert Microsoft Access 2002 Expert Microsoft Outlook 2002 Expert Microsoft FrontPage 2002 Expert	Candidates will be awarded one certificate for each of the Expert exams they have passed: Microsoft Office User Specialist: Microsoft Word 2002 Expert Microsoft Office User Specialist: Microsoft Excel 2002 Expert Microsoft Office User Specialist: Microsoft Access 2002 Expert Microsoft Office User Specialist: Microsoft Outlook 2002 Expert Microsoft Office User Specialist: Microsoft FrontPage 2002 Expert
Core	Indicates that you have a comprehensive understanding of the core features in a specific Microsoft Office 2002 application	Pass any ONE of the Core exams: Microsoft Word 2002 Core Microsoft Excel 2002 Core Microsoft Access 2002 Core Microsoft Outlook 2002 Core Microsoft FrontPage 2002 Core	Candidates will be awarded one certificate for each of the Core exams they have passed: Microsoft Office User Specialist: Microsoft Word 2002 Microsoft Office User Specialist: Microsoft Excel 2002 Microsoft Office User Specialist: Microsoft Access 2002 Microsoft Office User Specialist: Microsoft Outlook 2002 Microsoft Office User Specialist: Microsoft FrontPage 2002
Comprehensive	Indicates that you have a comprehensive understanding of the features in Microsoft PowerPoint 2002	Pass the Microsoft PowerPoint 2002 Comprehensive Exam	Candidates will be awarded one certificate for the Microsoft PowerPoint 2002 Comprehensive exam passed.

Why Should You Get Certified?

Being a Microsoft Office User Specialist provides a valuable industry credential — proof that you have the Office XP applications skills required by employers. By passing one or more MOUS certification exams, you demonstrate your proficiency in a given Office XP application to employers. With over 100 million copies of Office in use around the world, Microsoft is targeting Office XP certification to a wide variety of companies. These companies include temporary employment agencies that want to prove the expertise of their workers, large corporations looking for a way to measure the skill set of employees, and training companies and educational institutions seeking Microsoft Office XP teachers with appropriate credentials.

The MOUS Exams

You pay $50 to $100 each time you take an exam, whether you pass or fail. The fee varies among testing centers. The Expert exams, which you can take up to 60 minutes to complete, consists of between 40 and 60 tasks that you perform online. The tasks require you to use the application just as you would in doing your job. The Core exams contain fewer tasks, and you will have slightly less time to complete them. The tasks you will perform differ on the two types of exams.

How Can You Prepare for the MOUS Exams?

The Shelly Cashman Series® offers several Microsoft-approved textbooks that cover the required objectives on the MOUS exams. For a listing of the textbooks, visit the Shelly Cashman Series MOUS site at scsite.com/offxp/cert.htm and click the link Shelly Cashman Series Office XP Microsoft-Approved MOUS Textbooks (Figure E-1). After using any of the books listed in an instructor-led course, you will be prepared to take the MOUS exam indicated.

How to Find an Authorized Testing Center

You can locate a testing center by calling 1-800-933-4493 in North America or visiting the Shelly Cashman Series MOUS site at scsite.com/offxp/cert.htm and then clicking the link Locate an Authorized Testing Center Near You (Figure E-1). At this Web site, you can look for testing centers around the world.

Shelly Cashman Series MOUS Web Page

The Shelly Cashman Series MOUS Web page (Figure E-1) has more than fifteen Web sites you can visit to obtain additional information on the MOUS Certification Program. The Web page (scsite.com/offxp/cert.htm) includes links to general information on certification, choosing an application for certification, preparing for the certification exam, and taking and passing the certification exam.

FIGURE E-1

Microsoft FrontPage 2002 User Specialist Certification Core and Expert Maps

This book has been approved by Microsoft as courseware for the Microsoft Office User Specialist (MOUS) program. After completing the projects and exercises in this book, students will be prepared to take the Core-level Microsoft Office User Specialist Exam for Microsoft FrontPage 2002. Table E-2 lists the Microsoft FrontPage 2002 Core Exam skill sets, activities, page numbers where the activities are demonstrated, and page numbers where the activities can be practiced.

Table E-3 lists the Microsoft FrontPage 2002 Expert Exam skill sets, activities, page numbers where the activities are demonstrated, and page numbers where the activities can be practiced. COMP in the rightmost two columns means that the activity is demonstrated in the companion textbook Microsoft FrontPage 2002: Comprehensive Concepts and Techniques (0-7895-6503-X).

Table E-2   Microsoft FrontPage 2002 MOUS Core Skill Sets, Activities, and Locations in Book

SKILL SET	ACTIVITY	ACTIVITY DEMONSTRATED IN BOOK	ACTIVITY EXERCISE IN BOOK
I. Creating and Modifying Web Sites	A. Create and manage a FrontPage web	FP 1.20-22	FP 1.71 (In the Lab 1 Step 1), FP 1.73 (In the Lab 2 Step 1), FP 1.75 (In the Lab 3 Steps 1-2)
	B. Create and preview web pages	FP 2.11-12, FP 3.22, FP 5.22, FP 5.35	FP 2.68 (In the Lab 2 Step 2), FP 2.70 (In the Lab 3 Step 1), FP 5.56 (Apply Your Knowledge Step 1), FP 5.57 (In the Lab 1 Step 3), FP 5.62 (Cases & Places 5)
	C. Open, view, and rename web pages	FP 1.24, FP 1.50, FP 2.09-10, FP 2.13-14, FP 2.18, FP 3.07-08, FP 3.25	FP 1.69 (Apply Your Knowledge Step 1), FP 1.71 (In the Lab 1 Step 2), FP 1.73 (In the Lab 2 Step 3), FP 1.75 (In the Lab 3 Step 3), FP 1.75 (In the Lab 3 Steps 11-12), FP 2.66 (Apply Your Knowledge Step 1), FP 2.67 (In the Lab 1 Steps 2-3, 8), FP 2.68 (In the Lab 2 Steps 1, 3), FP 2.70 (In the Lab 3 Steps 1, 3, and 5), FP 3.72 (Apply Your Knowledge Step 1), FP 3.74 (In the Lab 1 Step 2)
	D. Rename a web page	FP 2.13-14, FP 3.25	FP 2.68 (In the Lab 2 Step 3), FP 2.70 (In the Lab 3 Step 1)
	E. Change the title for a web page on banners and buttons	FP 1.44-46, FP 2.15-16, FP 2.16-17, FP 3.24	FP 1.69 (Apply Your Knowledge Step 12), FP 1.71 (In the Lab 1 Step 4), FP 1.73 (In the Lab 2 Step 6), FP 1.75 (In the Lab 3 Step 11), FP 2.67 (In The Lab 1 Step 6)
II. Importing Web Content	A. Insert text and images	FP 3.34-36	FP 3.74 (In the Lab 1), FP 3.78 (In the Lab 3 Step 2)
	B. Insert Office Drawings, AutoShapes, and WordArt	FP 2.28-30, FP 2.31-33, FP 2.34-35, FP 3.45-46, FP 3.52-56	FP 2.66 (Apply Your Knowledge Step 3), FP 2.68 (In the Lab 2 Steps 6-9), FP 3.80 (Cases & Places 3)
III. Formatting Web Pages	A. Apply text and paragraph formats	FP 1.40, FP 2.42-43, FP 2.45-48	FP 1.75 (In the Lab 3 Step 6), FP 2.66 (Apply Your Knowledge Steps 4-6), FP 2.68 (In the Lab 2 Steps 6-9), FP 3.80 (Cases & Places 3)
	B. Insert hyperlinks	FP 1.50-53, FP 1.54-56, FP 3.40-42, FP 3.43-.44, FP 3.57-58, FP 5.40-45	FP 1.69 (Apply Your Knowledge Step 6), FP 1.71 (In the Lab 1 Step 5), FP 1.71 (In the Lab 1 Step 8), FP 1.73 (In the Lab 2 Step 13), FP 2.70 (In the Lab 3 Step 5), FP 1.78 (Cases & Places 1), FP 1.78 (Cases & Places 2), FP 1.78 (Cases & Places 3), FP 1.78 (Cases & Places 4), FP 3.80 (Cases & Places 1), FP 3.80 (Cases & Places 3), FP 3.80 (Cases & Places 5)
	C. Insert a date using shared borders	FP 3.17-20	FP 3.76 (In the Lab 2 Step 5), FP 3.80 (Cases & Places 2)
	D. Create and edit tables	FP 1.33, FP 2.25-27, FP 3.13-14	FP 1.73 (In the Lab 2 Step 5), FP 2.68 (In the Lab 2 Steps 5, 10), FP 3.76 (In the Lab 2 Step 2), FP 3.80 (Cases & Places 1)
	E. Apply web themes	FP 1.26-27, FP 2.19-20, FP 3.09-12	FP 1.71 (In the Lab 1 Step 3), FP 1.73 (In the Lab 2 Step 4), FP 1.78 (Cases & Places 2), FP 2.66 (Apply Your Knowledge Step 2), FP 3.80 (Cases & Places 4)

Table E-2 Microsoft FrontPage 2002 MOUS Core Skill Sets, Activities, and Locations in Book *(continued)*

SKILL SET	ACTIVITY	ACTIVITY DEMONSTRATED IN BOOK	ACTIVITY EXERCISE IN BOOK
IV. Formatting Web Pages	A. Edit graphic elements	FP 3.47-48, FP 3.39-50, FP 3.51	FP 3.78 (In the Lab 3 Step 6)
	B. Create image maps	FP 3.58-61	FP 3.78 (In the Lab 3 Steps 3-5)
	C. Add a FrontPage Web component to a web page	FP 2.55-57, FP 3.15-16	FP 2.67 (In The Lab 1 Steps 5, 9), FP 2.68 (In the Lab 2 Step 4), FP 2.70 (In the Lab 3 Step 3), FP 3.76 (In the Lab 2 Step 4), FP 3.80 (Cases & Places 4)
	D. Add a Photo Gallery	FP 2.49-53	FP 2.70 (In the Lab 3 Step 4)
V. Organizing and Viewing FrontPage Web Sites	A. Use FrontPage views	FP 1.24, FP 1.50, FP 2.10, FP 2.11, FP 2.18, FP 3.25-26, FP 3.62, FP 3.63, FP 3.66, FP 5.46-47	FP 1.69 (Apply Your Knowledge Step 1), FP 1.71 (In the Lab 1 Step 2), FP 1.73 (In the Lab 2 Steps 2-3), FP 1.75 (In the Lab 3 Step 3), FP 1.75 (In the Lab 3 Steps 11-12), FP 2.66 (Apply Your Knowledge Step 1), FP 2.67 (In the Lab 1 Steps 2-3, 8), FP 2.68 (In the Lab 2 Steps 1, 3), FP 3.72 (Apply Your Knowledge Step 1), FP 3.74 (In the Lab 1 Step 2)
	B. Manage web structures	FP 1.47-49, FP 3.26-27, FP 3.62	FP 1.69 (Apply Your Knowledge Step 11), FP 1.73 (In the Lab 2 Step 7), FP 1.75 (In the Lab 3 Step 5)
	C. Organize web files	FP 1.47-48, FP 5.11-13	FP 1.73 (In the Lab 2 Step 2)
	D. Manage tasks	FP 3.63-65	FP 4.74 (In the Lab 1, Optional, Steps 1-2)
VI. Managing Web Sites	A. Publish a web page	FP 1.59-62, FP 2.63	FP 1.73 (In the Lab 2 Step 16)
	B. Create custom reports	FP 3.66-68	FP 4.74 (In the Lab 1, Optional, Step 3)

Table E-3 Microsoft FrontPage 2002 MOUS Expert Skill Sets, Activities, and Locations in Book

SKILL SET	ACTIVITY	ACTIVITY DEMONSTRATED IN BOOK	ACTIVITY EXERCISE IN BOOK
I. Creating and Customizing Web Sites	A. Modify web page layout	FP 1.28-41, FP 2.41-53, FP 2.44, FP 2.45-48	FP 1.69 (Apply Your Knowledge Step 2), FP 1.71 (In the Lab 1 Step 4), FP 1.75 (In the Lab 3 Step 4), FP 1.76 (In the Lab 3 Steps 6-8), FP 1.78 (Cases & Places 3), FP 2.66 (Apply Your Knowledge Steps 4-6), FP 2.67 (In the Lab 1 Step 5), FP 2.68 (In the Lab 2 Steps 4-6, 11)
	B. Create Sub webs	COMP	COMP
	C. Manage permissions for sub webs	COMP	COMP
	D. Create and apply custom themes	FP 3.08-12	FP 3.72 (Apply Your Knowledge Steps 2-4), FP 3.80 (Cases & Places 4)
	E. Customize shared borders	FP 3.16-21	FP 3.78 (In the Lab 3 Step 7), FP 3.80 (Cases & Places 2)
	F. Add and modify background images	FP 2.20-23, FP 3.28-30	FP 2.66 (Apply Your Knowledge Step 2), FP 3.72 (Apply Your Knowledge Step 4)
II. Using Navigational Features	A. Manage the structure of a web	FP 1.46-49; FP 3.23-27	FP 1.69 (Apply Your Knowledge Step 9), FP 1.73 (In the Lab 2 Step 7), FP 3.74 (In the Lab 1 Step 2), FP 1.76
	B. Add navigation bars to page banners	FP 5.40-45	FP 5.57 (In the Lab 1 Step 7), FP 5.62 (Cases & Places 1)
	C. Add link bars	FP 2.54-57	FP 2.67 (In the Lab 1 Step 5), FP 2.67 (In the Lab 1 Step 9), FP 2.70 (In the Lab 3 Step 3), FP 2.72 (Cases & Places 5)

Table E-3 Microsoft FrontPage 2002 MOUS Expert Skill Sets, Activities, and Locations in Book

SKILL SET	ACTIVITY	ACTIVITY DEMONSTRATED IN BOOK	ACTIVITY EXERCISE IN BOOK
III. Customizing Tables	A. Format Tables	FP 2.38-41, FP 3.28-29, COMP	FP 2.68 (In the Lab 2 Steps 6-11), FP 2.72 (Cases & Places 1-2), FP 3.74 (In the Lab 1 Step 4), COMP
	B. Split tables	COMP	COMP
	C. Apply table AutoFormats	COMP	COMP
	D. Nest tables	FP 4.38-39	FP 4.81 (Cases & Places 5)
IV. Inserting and Modifying FrontPage Components	A. Add FrontPage components to web pages	FP 2.49-53, FP 2.55-57, FP 3.14-16	FP 2.67 (In the Lab 1 Step 5), FP 2.68 (In the Lab 1 Step 6), FP 2.70 (In the Lab 3 Steps 3-4), FP 2.72 (Cases & Places 3, 5), FP 3.74 (In The Lab 1 Step 3), FP 3.76 (In The Lab 2 Steps 4-5), FP 3.78 (In The Lab 3 Step 7), FP 3.80 (Cases & Places 2, 5)
	B. Modify component properties	FP 1.44-46, FP 2.31-33, FP 3.28-30, FP 4.25-26, FP 4.32-33	FP 1.69 (Apply Your Knowledge Step 11), FP 1.73 (In the Lab 2 Step 7), FP 1.75 (In the Lab 3 Steps 5, 10-11), FP 1.78 (Cases & Places 3), FP 2.67 (In The Lab 1 Steps 4, 6, 9), FP 3.76 (In The Lab 2 Step 5)
V. Creating Customer and User Feedback Web pages	A. Create forms for user input	FP 4.18-20, FP 4.23-24, FP 4.29-30, FP 4.35-38, FP 4.41-42, FP 4.47-48, FP 4.49-50, FP 4.54-55	FP 4.72 (Apply Your Knowledge Step 2), FP 4.77 (In The Lab 2 Step 2), FP 4.79 (In The Lab 3 Step 3), FP 4.81 (Cases & Places 1, 3-5), FP 4.81 (Cases & Places 3, 5)
	B. Add search capabilities to web pages	COMP	COMP
VI. Integrating Databases	A. Connect a web site to a database	COMP	COMP
	B. Send form data to Access databases	FP 4.60-64	FP 4.81 (Cases & Places 3-5)
	C. Add query capabilities to web pages	FP 5.13-19	FP 5.59 (In The Lab 2 Step 4), FP 5.62 (Cases & Places 3-4)
VII. Using Collaboration Features	A. Check HTML files in and out	COMP	COMP
	B. Manage web folders	FP 1.47-49, FP 2.11-14, FP 2.60-62	FP 1.69 (Apply Your Knowledge Step 9), FP 1.73 (In The Lab 2 Step 2)
VIII. Inserting Frames	A. Create frames	FP 5.21-23	FP 5.57 (In The Lab 1 Step 2), FP 5.62 (Cases & Places 1, 2, 4-5)
	B. Specify target content in frames	FP 5.27-29, FP 5.31, FP 5.35, FP 5.40-45	FP 5.57 (In The Lab 1 Step 8)
	C. Create and customize banners	FP 1.44-46	FP 1.73 (In the Lab 2 Step 6), FP 2.70 (In the Lab 3 Step 2)
IX. Generating Reports	A. Find broken hyperlinks	COMP	COMP
	B. Locate most popular pages	COMP	COMP
	C. Locate problems	FP 3.66-68	FP 4.81 (Cases & Places 4)
X. Publishing Web Sites	A. Publish web sites from one server to another	COMP	COMP
	B. Use Personal Web Servers	COMP	COMP
	C. Publish a site from one location to another	COMP	COMP

Index

Microsoft
FRONTPAGE 2002
Quick Reference Summary

In Microsoft FrontPage 2002, you can accomplish a task in a number of ways. The following table provides a quick reference to each task presented in this textbook. The first column identifies the task. The second column indicates the page number on which the task is discussed in the book. The subsequent four columns list the different ways the task in column one can be carried out. You can invoke the commands listed in the MOUSE, MENU BAR and SHORTCUT MENU columns using Voice commands.

Microsoft FrontPage 2002 Quick Reference Summary

TASK	PAGE NUMBER	MOUSE	MENU BAR	SHORTCUT MENU	KEYBOARD SHORTCUT
Align Left	FP 2.36	Align Left button on Formatting toolbar	Format | Paragraph | Indents and Spacing tab	Paragraph | Indents and Spacing tab	CTRL+L
Align Right	FP 2.36	Align Right button on Formatting toolbar	Format | Paragraph | Indents and Spacing tab	Paragraph | Indents and Spacing tab	CTRL+R
AutoShape, Add	FP 3.52	AutoShapes button on Drawing toolbar	Insert | Picture | AutoShapes		ALT+U
AutoShape, Insert	FP 4.38	AutoShapes button on Drawing toolbar			ALT+U
Background Color, Modify	FP 2.20		Format | Background | Background tab	Page Properties | Background tab	ALT+O | K
Bold	FP 2.41	Bold button on Formatting toolbar	Format | Font | Font tab	Font | Font tab	CTRL+B or ALT+ENTER
Bookmark, Create	FP 3.36	Insert Hyperlink button on Standard toolbar	Insert | Bookmark	Hyperlink	CTRL+G
Center	FP 3.36	Center button on Formatting toolbar	Format | Paragraph | Indents and Spacing tab	Paragraph | Indents and Spacing tab	CTRL+F
Clip Art, Insert	FP 2.28	Insert Picture From File button on Standard toolbar	Insert | Picture | Clip Art; Insert | Picture | From File		
Clip Art, Replace	FP 2.31	Insert Picture From File button on Pictures toolbar	Insert | Picture | Clip Art; Insert | Picture | From File	Picture Properties | General tab | Browse	
Color Characters	FP 2.43	Font Color button arrow on Formatting toolbar	Format | Font | Font tab	Font | Font tab	ALT+ENTER
Copy	FP 2.34	Copy button on Standard toolbar	Edit | Copy	Copy	CTRL+C
Create Web, Template or Wizard	FP 1.20	New Page button arrow on Standard toolbar, Web	File | New | Page or Web		
Database Results, Insert	FP 5.14		Insert | Database | Results		ALT + I | D | R
Delete Page	FP 1.47		Edit | Delete	Right-click file name in Folder List pane, Delete	DELETE
Delete Text	FP 1.29	Cut button on Standard toolbar	Edit | Cut or Edit | Delete	Cut	DELETE or BACKSPACE
File, Import	FP 5.11		File | Import		
File, Rename	FP 2.13			Right-click file name in Folder List, click Rename	

Microsoft FrontPage 2002 Quick Reference Summary *(continued)*

TASK	PAGE NUMBER	MOUSE	MENU BAR	SHORTCUT MENU	KEYBOARD SHORTCUT
Folder List Pane, Hide or Display	FP 1.23	Folder List button on Standard toolbar	View | Folder List		ALT+E | E
Folders View	FP 4.11	Click Folders icon on Views bar	View | Folders		ALT+V | F
Font	FP 2.41	Font button on Formatting toolbar	Format | Font | Font tab	Font | Font tab	ALT+ENTER
Font Size	FP 2.47	Font Size box arrow on Formatting toolbar	Format | Font | Font tab	Font | Font tab	ALT+ENTER
Form, Insert	FP 4.20		Insert | Form | Form		ALT+I | R | F
Form, Modify Properties	FP 4.64		Insert | Form | Form Properties	Form Properties	ALT+I | R | R
Form Field, Assign Label	FP 4.31		Insert | Form | Label		ALT+I | R | A
Form Field, Insert Check Box	FP 4.30		Insert | Form | Checkbox		ALT+I | R | C
Form Field, Insert Drop-Down List Box	FP 4.42		Insert | Form | Drop-Down Box		ALT+I | R | D
Form Field, Insert Group Box	FP 4.48		Insert | Form | Group Box		ALT+I | R | G
Form Field, Insert Option Button	FP 4.49		Insert | Form | Option Button		ALT+I | R | O
Form Field, Insert Text Area	FP 4.55		Insert | Form | Text Area		ALT+I | R | E
Form Field, Insert Text Box	FP 4.24		Insert | Form | Textbox		ALT+I | R | T
Form Field, Modify Properties	FP 4.25		Format | Properties	Form Field Properties	ALT+ENTER
Form Handler	FP 4.64		Insert | Form | Form Properties	Form Properties	ALT+I | R | R
Full Menu	FP 1.15	Double-click menu name or click menu name, wait a few seconds	Tools | Customize | Options tab		
Frame, Modify Properties	FP 5.36		Frames | Frame Properties	Frame Properties	
Frame, Resize	FP 5.30	Drag frame border	Frames | Frame Properties	Frame Properties	ALT+R | P
Frames Page, Modify Properties	FP 5.38		Click frame border, then File | Properties | Frames tab	Frame Properties | Frames Page button	ALT+F | I
Help	FP 1.65 and Appendix A	Microsoft FrontPage Help button on Standard toolbar	Help | Microsoft FrontPage Help		F1
Horizontal Rule, Insert	FP 2.44		Insert | Horizontal Line		ALT+I | L
Hotspot, Add Polygonal	FP 3.59	Polygonal Hotspot button on Pictures toolbar			
Hotspots, Highlight	FP 3.60	Highlight Hotspots button on Pictures toolbar			
HTML, Modify or View	FP 4.65	HTML tab			
Hyperlink, Create	FP 1.54	Hyperlink button on Standard toolbar	Insert | Hyperlink	Hyperlink	CTRL+K
Hyperlink, Edit	FP 1.54	Hyperlink button on Standard toolbar		Hyperlink Properties	CTRL+K
Hyperlinks, Display	FP 3.61	Hyperlinks icon on Views bar	View | Hyperlinks		ALT+V | H
Hyperlinks, Verify	FP 3.66	Verify Hyperlinks button on Reporting toolbar	View | Toolbars | Reporting, Verify Hyperlinks button	Reporting	
Image, Insert from File	FP 2.28	Insert Picture From File button on Standard toolbar	Insert | Picture | From File		

Microsoft FrontPage 2002 Quick Reference Summary

TASK	PAGE NUMBER	MOUSE	MENU BAR	SHORTCUT MENU	KEYBOARD SHORTCUT
Image, Resample	FP 3.48	Resample button on Pictures toolbar			
Image, Resize	FP 3.48	Drag sizing handles	Format | Properties	Picture Properties | Appearance	
Image, Select	FP 2.34	Click graphic			Position insertion point before image, CTRL+SHIFT+ RIGHT ARROW
Image, Transparent	FP 3.47	Set Transparent Color button on Pictures toolbar			
Italicize	FP 2.41	Italic button on Formatting toolbar	Format | Font | Font tab	Font | Font tab	CTRL+I or ALT+ENTER
Language Bar	FP 1.19 and Appendix B	Language indicator button in tray	Tools | Speech		ALT+T | H
Line Break, Enter	FP 2.60				SHIFT+ENTER
Modify Component	FP 1.37	Double-click component		<component name> Properties	
Navigation View	FP 1.47	Navigation icon on Views bar	View | Navigation		
No Frames View, Display	FP 5.46	No Frames tab			
Page, Edit	FP 2.18	Double-click page icon in Navigation pane			
Page, New	FP 2.11	Create a new normal page button on Standard toolbar	File | New | Page or Web		CTRL+N
Page, View	FP 2.18	Page icon on Views bar	View | Page		
Page in Web, Open	FP 1.24	Double-click file name in Folder List pane	File | Open	Right-click Folder List pane, Open	CTRL+O
Page Label, Change	FP 2.17	Click page icon in Navigation view, click text box		Right-click page icon in Navigation view, click Rename	
Page Title, Change	FP 2.15		File | Properties	Right-click page icon in Navigation view, click Properties, click General tab; Right-click file name, click Properties, click General tab; right-click Page, click Page Properties, click General tab	
Paste	FP 2.34	Paste button on Standard toolbar	Edit | Paste	Paste	CTRL+V
Preview Page	FP 1.43	Preview tab			CTRL+PAGE UP, CTRL+PAGE DOWN
Preview Page in Browser	FP 1.43	Preview in Browser button on Standard toolbar	File | Preview in Browser		
Print Page	FP 1.57	Print button on Standard toolbar	File | Print		CTRL+P
Print Preview	FP 2.58		File | Print Preview		ALT+F | V
Publish Web	FP 1.59	Publish Web button on Standard toolbar	File | Publish Web		
Quit FrontPage	FP 1.66	Close button on title bar	File | Exit		ALT+F4
Redo	FP 2.27	Redo button on Standard toolbar	Edit | Redo		CTRL+Y
Reports, View Site Summary Report	FP 3.65	Report box arrow on Reporting toolbar, Site Summary	View | Reports | Site Summary		ALT+V | R | M
Save Page - Same Name	FP 1.42	Save button on Standard toolbar	File | Save		CTRL+S
Save Web - Embedded Files	FP 2.60	Save button on Standard toolbar	File | Save		CTRL+S
Shared Border, Add	FP 3.16		Format | Shared Borders		ALT+O | D
Shortcut menu	FP 1.17	Right-click object			SHIFT+F10

Microsoft FrontPage 2002 Quick Reference Summary *(continued)*

TASK	PAGE NUMBER	MOUSE	MENU BAR	SHORTCUT MENU	KEYBOARD SHORTCUT
Start FrontPage	FP 1.13	Start button on taskbar, Programs, Microsoft FrontPage			
Style, Modify Paragraph	FP 2.42	Style box arrow			
Table, Adjust Cell Borders	FP 2.37	Drag cell border	Table | Table Properties | Cell	Cell Properties	ALT+A | R | E
Table, Create	FP 2.24	Insert Table button on Standard toolbar	Table | Insert | Table		ALT+A | I | T
Table, Insert Column	FP 3.12		Table | Insert | Rows or Columns	Insert Columns	ALT+A | I | N
Table, Insert Row	FP 3.12		Table | Insert | Rows or Columns	Insert Rows	ALT+A | I | N
Table, Hide Borders	FP 2.40		Table | Table Properties | Table	Table Properties	
Table, Modify Properties	FP 2.38		Table | Table Properties | Table	Table Properties	
Table, Select	FP 1.32	Drag through table	Table | Select | Table		
Table Cells, Align	FP 2.46		Table | Table Properties | Cell	Cell Properties	ALT+A | R | E
Table Cells, Delete	FP 1.33		Table | Delete Cells	Delete Cells	ALT+A | D
Table Cells, Merge	FP 2.26		Table | Merge Cells	Merge Cells	
Table Cells, Select	FP 1.32	Click first cell, hold SHIFT key, click last cell	Table | Select | Cell		ALT+A | C | E
Task Pane	FP 1.15		View | Task Pane		ALT+V | K
Tasks, View	FP 3.63	Tasks icon on Views bar	View | Tasks		ALT+V | A
Template, Frames	FP 5.22		File | New | Page or Web | Page Templates | Frames Pages tab		ALT+F | N | P
Text, Add to Image	FP 3.53	Text button on Pictures toolbar		Add text	
Text, Select	FP 1.29	Drag through text			
Theme, Apply	FP 1.27		Format | Theme		ALT+O | H
Toolbar, Customize	FP 1.18	Toolbar Options button on toolbar, Add or Remove buttons, click Customize		Customize	
Toolbar, Dock	FP 1.17	Drag toolbar to dock			
Toolbar, Reset	FP 1.18 and Appendix D	Toolbar Options, Add or Remove Buttons, Customize, Toolbars tab		Customize | Toolbars tab	ALT+V | T | C | T
Underline	FP 2.41	Underline button on Formatting toolbar	Format | Font | Font tab	Font | Font tab	CTRL+U or ALT+ENTER
Undo	FP 2.27	Undo button on Standard toolbar	Edit | Undo		CTRL+Z
Web, Open	FP 2.09	Open Web button arrow on Standard toolbar, Open Web	File | Open Web		ALT+F | W
Web Component, Insert Hit Counter	FP 3.14	Web component button arrow on Standard toolbar, Hit Counter	Insert | Web Component | Hit Counter		ALT+I | W
Web Component, Insert Link bar	FP 2.54	Web component button arrow on Standard toolbar, Link Bars	Insert | Web Component | Link Bars		ALT+I | W
Web Component, Insert Photo Gallery	FP 2.49	Web component button arrow on Standard toolbar, Photo Gallery	Insert | Web Component | Photo Gallery		ALT+I | W